الجزء الأول

Part One

الكتاب

في تعلّم العربية

Al-Kitaab

Textbook for Beginning Arabic with Website

Kristen Brustad,

Mahmoud Al-Batal, and

Abbas Al-Tonsi

Georgetown University Press

Washington, DC

THIRD EDITION

AL-KITAAB FII TAᶜALLUM AL-ᶜARABIYYA PART ONE:
A TEXTBOOK FOR BEGINNING ARABIC, THIRD EDITION
WITH WEBSITE

ISBN 978-1-64712-186-0 (hardcover with website)
ISBN 978-1-64712-187-7 (paperback with website)
ISBN 978-1-64712-190-7 (ebook with website)

Library of Congress Control Number: 2021937615

∞ This paper meets the requirements of ANSI/NISO Z39.48-1992 (Permanence of Paper).

Printed in the United States of America

10 9 8 7 6 5 4 3 2   First printing

Contents

درس Lesson 1

أنا ساكنة في مدينة نيويورك

درس Lesson 2

أنا فعلاً وحيدة!

درس Lesson 3

عائلة والدي كبيرة

درس Lesson 4

كيف أحفظ كل الأسماء؟!

درس Lesson 5

الطقس حار جداً في الصيف

درس Lesson 6

معيد بكلّية التجارة

درس Lesson 7

اللّه يرحمها

درس Lesson 8

درس Lesson 9

درس Lesson 10

بيت العائلة

درس Lesson 11

أشعر بالخجل أحياناً

درس Lesson 12

أصعب قرار في حياتي

درس Lesson 13

لماذا قررت البقاء في أمريكا؟

About This Book

This third edition of *Al-Kitaab Part One* and its corresponding multimedia consists of:
- the thirteen chapters in this book and
- a companion website available at **www.alkitaabtextbook.com** with interactive, self-correcting exercises, all corresponding streaming audio and video, and course management features for teachers that can be accessed by following the instructions at the above URL.

The companion website includes all of the audio and video referenced in the book along with exercises. It should be used alongside the book and will enhance learning by providing learners with immediate feedback on many of the mechanical drills. Learners, your teacher may guide you to enroll in the class through the website, or you may use it independently.

The website is designed to be used alongside the book, which allows learners to complete and receive feedback on the mechanical drills in the book, freeing up class time for active participation in class. **Everything you need is on the website**. The autocorrected, online exercises play an important role in developing both language skills and language learning strategies, so it is very important not to take shortcuts and to seek help from an instructor or from peers if you are frustrated.

The audio and video materials that accompany this textbook are also central to its use, because the lessons were built around the story that is told in the videos. Each chapter revolves around the basic story line of Maha and Khalid Abu El-ᶜIla and their extended family, which is presented in two video versions, formal and spoken Egyptian; and on the story line of Nisreen and Tariq al-Nuuri and their extended family, which is presented in Damascene Arabic (called Levantine throughout the book). You can watch all of these videos on the website as often as you like.

Introduction to the Third Edition for Teachers

We are delighted to present this third edition of the textbook *Al-Kitaab fii Taʿallum al-ʿArabiyya Part One* and its companion website (**www.alkitaabtextbook.com**). This edition represents a new phase in the evolution of these materials both technologically and pedagogically. Like previous editions, the materials revolve around a story about a set of characters and focus on vocabulary activation and developing speaking, listening and reading comprehension, and writing and cultural skills. With this edition we add a companion website with interactive, autocorrecting exercises, and we place greater emphasis on the comprehension and production of spoken Arabic, offering a choice between Egyptian and Levantine dialect components.[1] Adding other dialects to the materials as options to the original Egyptian was part of our original vision, and we are very pleased to be able to realize this goal in part with the addition of the Damascene (as representative of Levantine) material here.

The increased presence and integration of spoken Arabic in this edition represents a natural evolution of these materials within the philosophy outlined in the first edition: Our goal is to present and teach language forms that reflect the linguistic behavior of educated native speakers. Increasingly, in written as well as formal spoken contexts, Arabic speakers produce and consume mixes of registers that include both formal and spoken elements. We believe it is important to introduce learners to this reality from the beginning. Our experience in the classroom with these materials and the approach outlined here is that learners' skills in all areas develop faster when basic spoken forms and expressions are taught early in the students' experience, and that these forms do not "fossilize" but rather continue to evolve. In other words, teaching spoken forms early results in an enhanced fluency that transfers to formal Arabic as well. In this introduction we will talk about our materials and our teaching philosophy. There is a separate introduction for students that we urge you to read and discuss with your students.

Learning Outcome Goals

In our experience teaching with this approach and these materials, students reach solid intermediate proficiency in all skills by the end of one year (two semesters). This means that your students should have, ان شاء الله, by the time you finish working through this book acquired the following skills:

---

[1] As in *Alif Baa*, we use the terms "formal" and "spoken" Arabic to refer to different registers that are not mutually exclusive. These registers are also known as Modern Standard, Standard, or Classical Arabic (الفصحى) on the one hand, and colloquial (العامية) on the other. We avoid the use of term "colloquial" because it has derogatory connotations. "Formal" Arabic refers to a standardized register that is mainly but not exclusively used in writing and reading (including reading aloud, as in news broadcasts); "spoken" refers to the wide range of registers and forms–including many words and forms it shares with formal Arabic–that are used in spoken and informal contexts, including written ones.

- The ability to speak about herself, her life, and her environment, to initiate and sustain conversations on daily-life topics with educated native speakers who are accustomed to conversing with learners of Arabic as a foreign language, and to paraphrase as necessary to make herself understood.
- The ability to read simple, authentic texts on familiar topics and understand the main ideas without using the dictionary, and have confidence to guess the meaning of new words from context and other clues.
- The ability to write informal notes and essays on familiar topics connected to daily life.
- The ability to comprehend and produce accurately the basic sentence structures of Arabic.
- Familiarity with the differences in sounds and basic structures between formal and spoken Arabic.
- A general understanding of aspects of Arab culture connected to everyday life, including culturally important expressions commonly used among friends and acquaintances.

In this third edition, *Part One* consists of thirteen chapters, which represent the amount of material that can reasonably be activated in a year of college-level Arabic with an average of five contact hours per week. We use the word "activated" rather than "covered" pointedly: Although it is possible to introduce vocabulary and structures at a faster pace, activating them so that students can produce them fluently in context and without prompting takes much more time. These materials are designed so that students can activate vocabulary and structures; in our experience, teaching the lessons included in this volume with full activation takes approximately 125 classroom hours plus 200–250 hours of preparation outside class.

Structure of the Chapters

The chapters in this book are structured according to a philosophy and methodology of teaching that has evolved with each subsequent edition of the *Al-Kitaab* language program. Each chapter is structured as closely as possible to the syllabus we use when we teach, with exercises to be done before class and activities to be done in class. Each chapter, thus, consists of cycles of exercises, usually one for each section—vocabulary, texts, grammar, and so forth—starting with one to three exercises labeled في البيت followed by one or two labeled في الصف. Each one or two cycles in a chapter represent one contact hour of class time. The exact number of cycles per class depends on the length of your class sessions as well as the length of the exercises. Some of the grammar exercises, in particular, are short, and multiple grammar points can sometimes be activated on the same day.

Each chapter begins with extensive work on vocabulary acquisition and activation because we believe that building vocabulary—with attention to its accurate use in context—is the core activity of building proficiency in Arabic. After vocabulary has been activated, learners are prepared for the story, which is followed by focused grammar work. The progression from learning new vocabulary to the story to grammar is important to maintain: Without activating the vocabulary, the story will be hard to understand, and grammar should emerge from a context—here, the context of the story. Culture, reading, and listening sections and their activities, along with additional speaking and writing activities, normally appear later in the chapter because they are designed to push students to expand their skills and use their vocabulary in new contexts. Each chapter ends with a new dialogue in the dialogue section, which presents the greatest challenge linguistically but is also meant to be fun. A section containing two or three review drills comes at the end of each chapter. The placement of the drills here is designed to give the instructor maximum flexibility. Most of these drills are autocorrected online exercises, which means that the student can do them at his or her leisure, perhaps as a review for a quiz.

Those of you who are familiar with the second edition will notice that the order of presentation of the formal and spoken versions of the story within each lesson has changed. Introducing the story in dialect before working with it in formal Arabic is a keystone of the integrated approach. This approach has the advantage of helping students develop listening and speaking skills in real-life Arabic and comprehension skills in formal Arabic, which follows the usage patterns of native speakers, for whom formal Arabic is a receptive language for the most part.

As in the third edition of *Alif Baa*, vocabulary is introduced in *Al-Kitaab Part One* in three varieties: Formal, Egyptian, and Levantine (Syrian). Also new here is that all active vocabulary words are presented at the beginning of the chapter, including words that do not occur in the story but do appear in the reading texts or the new dialogue. We hope this will make it easier to activate these words more fully and help learners keep track of the vocabulary for which they are responsible. The presentation of grammar has also undergone some revision, most notably an increased emphasis on morphology, especially noun and verb patterns. The sequencing of structures has not changed, but the introduction of plurals and verb patterns has been spread out across several lessons, allowing time for learners to recognize and activate these patterns.

The mechanical work necessary to activate vocabulary and grammar inevitably means long hours of homework for learners and equally long hours of correcting for instructors and assistants. New in the third edition, however, are mechanical exercises with a closed set of answers that are all provided online as autocorrecting drills, which provides students with instant feedback. It is our hope that autocorrection will allow both students and teachers to work more effectively and that by giving instant feedback, it will help them focus their efforts and build their confidence.

Finally, this edition of *Part One* contains new reading and listening comprehension texts. And the few remaining old texts are paired with new ones. We are happy to have succeeded in placing most of the structurally simple texts, such as lists within the first few chapters, so that beginning in chapter 5 the reading texts are in prose. We think you will find that the reading exercises are more challenging and more rewarding than those in the previous editions. In the new dialogue section at the end of each chapter you will find a linguistically challenging and culturally rich video dialogue in spoken Arabic. Each dialogue includes many of the vocabulary items that the chapter has aimed to activate and presents them in different kinds of scenes from everyday life. This dialogue can be used either as a comprehension exercise or as a second "basic text" of the chapter, depending on how much time and attention you decide to give it and how it fits in with your overall goals for the course.

Language Production in Speaking and Writing

Al-Kitaab Part One gives you two options for the spoken component of your class in addition to the formal register. The goal here is **not** for all three varieties to be learned. Rather, the goal is for the class to choose one variety of spoken Arabic and learn it along with the formal Arabic. You will notice that, aside from a few regular differences in some sounds (such as the pronunciation of ق and hamza, and the tendency of Syrian speakers to elide some short vowels and turn others into kasra), the overwhelming majority of words are shared among all three varieties of Arabic.

We have tried to be as accurate as possible to represent the way words are pronounced in the Cairene and Damascene dialects in particular, but we do not believe it is necessary or helpful to demand all the nuances of local dialect from beginning learners. Those of us who teach and learn outside the Arab world are usually in contact with speakers of multiple dialects and we often communicate in a type of panregional Arabic. Subconsciously, at least, we seek out shared forms and use them. Our students need to function in this environment, too, and they will be well served by an inclusive view of what spoken Arabic is.

It is up to you to decide which varieties the class will use and how they will be mixed, but remember that you do not have to be a native speaker of a dialect to allow it to be a presence in the classroom. If you speak a different variety of Arabic and want to teach it, we encourage you to introduce forms from your own dialect and adapt the story, too, if you like. Proficiency guidelines for intermediate-level language specify the achievement of language production in informal situations and contexts. Arabic speakers use spoken registers exclusively in these circumstances, even when interacting with speakers of dialects other than their own. In our view, the ability to produce formal language in speech and writing is a skill that takes even native speakers (who have a big head start) years to develop. To expect it exclusively from beginning learners, we believe, is counterproductive. Therefore, our expectation at this level is that learners will produce mixed forms, some formal and some informal, according to the tools they have available to express themselves. For example, it is not reasonable to expect ليس to be used in writing before students have learned it. However, they have acquired the spoken forms of negation ما and مش that are used by native speakers in informal contexts. This mixing will not always be natural, just as the grammatical forms themselves will not always be accurate. Structural accuracy emerges **gradually**, including accuracy in language register.

Teaching Vocabulary

Because Arabic has a long history and is spoken across a large geographical area, it has an expansive vocabulary. This will be learners' biggest challenge in reaching fluency in Arabic, and you should encourage them to devote as much effort as they can to actively acquire the vocabulary in each chapter. "Actively acquiring" means developing the ability to produce the word accurately in the appropriate context without being prompted—that is, without seeing the word in a list or word bank. Put another way, activated vocabulary is vocabulary that the learner owns, that he or she uses in the context of his or her life. It is crucial that students prepare vocabulary before class by listening to the audio and doing the drills designated as homework drills.

Each vocabulary item is contextualized in a sentence recorded in formal Arabic as well. These sentences are meant to serve two purposes: (1) to contextualize the new vocabulary, and (2) to give students practice in close listening skills. Ask the students to write out the vocabulary sentences in each chapter so that they can develop their recognition of sounds and word boundaries and their ability to use grammatical and background information to construct meaning. This exercise will help them prepare to interact with authentic listening texts and to comprehend language just beyond their current level.

As in *Alif Baa,* vocabulary in *Part One* is introduced in three color-coded varieties: المصري, الشامئ, الفصحى. Words shared by more than one variety are in **black**. It is important to remember that the vocabulary list is not a glossary and that the words given for each variety do not constitute an exhaustive list of equivalents. The vocabulary words presented also have not been chosen randomly, rather they are included because they occur in one of the video segments or reading texts in the chapter. Since most of these texts were originally composed in formal Arabic, the vocabulary lists originated in the formal register. Not all spoken words that are in use are given in these lists. Only those words the actors use in telling the Cairene and Levantine versions of the story are included. The words are listed separately when the word or its pronunciation, as it occurs in the story, differs from the formal word. You will notice that these variants are often very close, separated only by a vowel sound; we have included them in the chart so that you can click on them to hear the differences in pronunciation. It is important for students to learn and study the spoken forms aurally, because some spoken Arabic sounds cannot be represented accurately in Arabic script.

The "Ask Your Colleagues" exercises are designed to be done in class using a combination of formal and spoken Arabic that has been very successful in our classrooms. This exercise helps students activate and personalize new vocabulary as they interview their classmates in Arabic. Because they are using the new vocabulary in context, there is a substantial amount of grammar practice that takes place during the time devoted to vocabulary. This combination ensures more active study and, we believe, faster acquisition.

The questions are provided in English for three reasons: (1) to help reinforce the association of words with particular contexts, (2) to force students to produce the new vocabulary in context from scratch rather than reading the Arabic words on the page, and (3) to help students avoid using English, since everyone knows what the questions mean from the outset. Take advantage of that shared knowledge by encouraging your students to work with their partners on the best way to express their thoughts in Arabic.

Teaching Grammar

Before speaking about our approach in teaching and learning grammar, we, as teachers, should ask ourselves an important question: What is the basic grammar of Arabic? What do learners need to know, passively and actively, to produce and comprehend informal Arabic on topics involving daily life? "Informal" is an important distinction because learners' grasp of formal language registers is assumed to follow, not precede, informal registers. Thus the most formal aspects of Arabic grammar—case endings, in particular—are not level-appropriate for elementary- and intermediate-level learners.

What is important for intermediate-level learners is basic sentence structure, especially sentence types, agreement, verb conjugation, noun phrases, and subordination. These structures are not difficult to grasp—in fact, most learners can comprehend these structures in reading and listening long before they have been formally introduced to them, but learners need lots of practice to activate them. Mechanical practice is necessary but not sufficient to reach that goal. The grammar will have been internalized when students use it unprompted in their speech and writing. Accuracy will not be 100 percent. Recall that it is natural for intermediate speakers to make errors even in simple structures. These errors have nothing to do with not knowing or understanding the rules but simply indicates that the structure needs more activation.

At this level of basic grammar, most structures are shared by spoken and formal Arabic. Word-order patterns, including subordinate structures such as indefinite relative clauses, noun phrase grammar, and the basic components of verb conjugation, are all shared grammatical structures. The main differences are in negation, verb mood, and subordination, in which modal particles differ. These variations are quite manageable at the comprehension level, and the degree to which one or both forms are activated will depend on the goals of the instructor and the program.

As in the previous two editions, the sequencing of grammar in *Part One* third edition materials is based not on a predetermined design but, rather, on the story itself, which was written independent of any grammatical considerations. We believe that privileging context in this way yields a more natural sequencing of structures for the learner that she or he can use. Following well-established models of spiraling in language acquisition, most grammar points are presented gradually, with information increasing in level of detail each time according to the language functions appropriate to students' abilities.

Have confidence in your students' ability to comprehend and activate grammar. Keep in mind that the first part happens quickly and the second takes time and practice. It is important that you guide your students to prepare for class by reading the lesson's explanation and by doing the accompanying mechanical drill that helps them begin to use the structure. Outside class, each student can work at his or her pace and be ready to begin using the new structure in class. Their use of this new structure may be tentative at first, but practice, not explanations or lectures, is what will build their confidence.

Our approach also relies on an understanding of interlanguage that says students acquire language by constructing their own internal grammar rather than by internalizing a presentation of grammar. It is the goal of this approach to help learners build their own grammar using induction, analogy, and hypothesis formation and testing. Learning a language involves critical thinking no less than memorization. You can help this process along by asking students questions rather than providing them with answers when they do not know something. Encourage a critical thinking approach to grammar and reward students verbally for asking questions.

Reading for Comprehension

"Reading" for many native speakers of Arabic educated in the Arab world means "reading aloud" because they studied formal Arabic in school, and formal Arabic is most often read aloud. For us, however, reading means reading for comprehension, which is a very different activity that requires different skills. We use the term "reading comprehension" to refer to activities that develop the skills that all fluent readers of Arabic use subconsciously. We are not concerned now with developing the skill of reading texts aloud, which is unrelated to comprehension and, in fact, often interferes with it. Reading aloud helps pronunciation and reinforces vocabulary and structure, and we have provided composed texts for just these purposes in the review drills section of many of the early chapters. Reading activities in this book aim to develop skills such as guessing the meaning from context, using background knowledge to help set expectations about what will be in a text, and using grammatical knowledge to construct meaning. As in previous editions, each chapter in this edition of *Part One* has at least one reading comprehension text. All of the reading texts in this book are authentic—written for educated adult native speakers of Arabic. This is important because the learners using this book are adults and deserve adult reading material.

Make sure your students know that you do not expect them to understand everything in the reading texts, and that they should try to focus on what they *do* understand rather than on what they do not. We want students to approach these texts with an expectation of exploration and discovery, guided with questions like: What kind of text is it, and what clues does it give you as to what kinds of information it gives? Can you guess the meaning of any new words from context? Every piece of information your students can recognize or extract from authentic texts represents a step forward in building students' Arabic language skills.

Reading comprehension texts, thus, are designed to be explored, *not* to be read aloud or read in a linear fashion. In fact, students should be discouraged from reading aloud, even to themselves, and should be encouraged to try to look at phrases or lists. These texts are meant to be skimmed, scanned, and discovered, since their main purpose is to teach strategies and skills necessary for fluent reading. Of course, focusing on close reading and grammatical details is a crucial part of building fluency in reading, and you will notice that these kinds of questions increase as students learn more structure formally. The traditional way to focus on such details is through translation, but we believe that translation of authentic texts at this level is counterproductive because the quantity of unknown vocabulary words would force students to process the text in linear fashion, which is counterproductive to our goal of balancing fluency and accuracy and allowing accuracy to develop gradually.

The reading comprehension exercises included in the book are designed to teach themselves. Your role here is not to explain but to motivate and encourage students and to celebrate with them as they discover the text themselves. We recommend that these exercises be done in class as much as possible, especially at the beginning of the book, until students develop confidence both in themselves and in your expectations of them. (This method also helps prevent students from using the dictionary or asking others about the meanings of unknown words in the text.) Many of these exercises work well when students work in pairs, and this cooperative learning approach helps to create the desired atmosphere of exploration and discovery that makes reading fun.

Each reading comprehension exercise begins with open-ended questions that focus on global comprehension. The key here is to let the students lead by reporting the meanings that they are able to construct. Asking the students specific questions is counterproductive at this stage. Following a global look at the text, second- and third-round questions ask students to focus on specific sections of the text that present them with "muscle-building" exercises that work on bottom-up processing skills. These questions involve guessing the meaning of new words from carefully chosen contexts using contextual and grammatical clues and the Arabic root and pattern system, recognizing and processing grammatical structures in new and authentic contexts, and developing discourse management skills—keeping track of large structural issues, such as recognizing sentence and paragraph structure, identifying parallel constructions, paying attention to connectors, and parsing long sentences in which the subject and predicate or verb may be located far away from each other.

Because the purpose of these reading exercises is to build skills and strategies, we strongly discourage the use of the reading exercises as vocabulary exercises. Each text has been carefully chosen so that students can comprehend a great deal and develop processing skills through reading without any additional vocabulary. Providing lists of all unknown vocabulary in the text will lead students back to linear processing and will not help them develop reading proficiency.

We hope that this new edition will be a useful learning and teaching tool for Arabic, and that those of you who have used previous editions will find the changes we have made helpful in achieving your goals. We wish you a successful, enjoyable, and rewarding experience teaching Arabic!

وبالتوفيق إن شاء الله!

Introduction to the Third Edition for Students

Welcome to the third edition of the textbook *Al-Kitaab fii Ta'allum al-'Arabiyya Part One* and its accompanying companion website **(www.alkitaabtextbook.com)**. These materials aim to help you achieve intermediate-level proficiency in speaking, reading, listening, and writing, and to introduce you to aspects of Arabic culture. Like *Alif Baa*, the book combines both formal (written) and spoken registers of Arabic, with a choice between the dialects of Cairo and Damascus. Many—but not all—of the listening and speaking activities focus on spoken forms of the language, whereas reading, writing, and most grammar components introduce and activate formal Arabic. You will gradually learn to recognize these two types of Arabic and use them in appropriate ways and contexts.

These materials will present you with a range of language variation that may seem challenging at times with formal and spoken varieties included. In dealing with this material, your best strategy is to distinguish between words and concepts that you will learn for active control, such as the vocabulary of a new lesson in the variety you use in class, and those that you are only expected to recognize passively, such as a grammatical ending. Your teacher will help you determine which spoken variety to use and how to distinguish between elements intended for active control and elements that you should learn to recognize when you see and hear them.

Learning Goals

In our experience teaching with this approach and these materials, students reach solid intermediate proficiency in all skills by the end of one year (two college semesters). This means that by the time you finish working through this book, ان شاء الله, you should have acquired the following skills:

- The ability to speak about yourself, your life, and your environment, to initiate and sustain conversations on daily-life topics with educated native speakers who are accustomed to conversing with learners of Arabic as a foreign language, and to paraphrase as necessary to make yourself understood.
- The ability to read simple, authentic texts on familiar topics and understand the main ideas without using the dictionary and with confidence in your ability to guess the meaning of new words from context and other clues.
- The ability to write informal notes and essays on familiar topics connected to daily life.
- The ability to comprehend and produce accurately the basic sentence structures of Arabic.
- Familiarity with the differences in sounds and basic structures between formal and spoken Arabic.
- A general understanding of aspects of Arab culture connected to everyday life, including culturally important expressions commonly used among friends and acquaintances.

Structure of the Book

The chapters in *Al-Kitaab Part One* revolve around the basic story line of Maha and Khalid Abu El-cIla and their extended family, which is presented in two versions, formal and spoken Egyptian. Maha and her family are joined in this third edition by a set of Syrian characters, Nisreen and Tariq al-Nuuri and their extended family, in a new set of videos in spoken Syrian. The plot is the same but Nisreen, Tariq, and their family and friends speak to us only in Damascene Arabic (called Levantine in the book). It is a video story, which means that you will not be reading the basic texts and dialogues but watching and listening to them. This story line is supplemented with different kinds of reading exercises and many speaking and writing activities.

Each chapter contains five main sections that appear roughly in this order:
- Vocabulary, which is presented in three, color-coded varieties (Egyptian spoken, Levantine spoken, and formal/written);
- Story in spoken Arabic, where you will watch a video in your spoken variety;
- Culture, where various aspects of contemporary life and cultural background are discussed;
- Story in formal Arabic, which is the same story you heard in spoken Arabic earlier but is now in formal Arabic;
- Grammar, which focuses on formal Arabic and points out some differences between it and spoken Arabic;
- Reading, which provides authentic texts to develop your comprehension skills;
- Listening, where you will watch a video to practice listening to formal Arabic;
- Dialogue, where you will watch and listen to a video of a situation from everyday life; and
- Review exercises.

Each section is interspersed with mechanical exercises to complete at home and group activities to do in class. Some chapters contain more than one grammar or one culture section.

Learning In and Outside of Class with These Materials

Nobody has ever become fluent in a language simply by attending class. You will reach proficiency in Arabic largely through what you teach yourself. Hence, these materials are designed to teach you how to learn a language. We assume that you have the skills necessary for independent learning and that you will devote approximately two hours outside of class for every hour of classroom instruction. We ask you to do a lot of preparation work outside of class so that you will be ready to interact and carry out tasks in Arabic during class rather than listening to explanations or lectures. This is because the mechanical aspects of language learning are best done outside of class so that everyone can work at her or his own pace. You are expected to prepare for class at home by:

- Listening to the vocabulary on the companion website;
- Reading grammar or other explanations carefully;
- Completing assigned homework exercises with as much effort and concentration as you can; and
- Mentally preparing for active participation in class activities.

It is helpful to use the analogy of playing sports or doing exercise: Your teacher is your coach or personal trainer. He or she shows you what to do and how to do it but the majority of the work falls to you. Homework helps you build and train your "language muscles" so that you are ready to play the game in class. After the first few days you will be able to predict what kinds of questions you will be asked and what kinds of activities you will be asked to perform. Be ready for them by guessing what they will be and practicing beforehand.

The philosophy on which these materials are based places great emphasis on learning aurally (through listening). We often hear students say that they are "visually oriented." This is true for most of us; however, one talent does not preclude the other. We have aural and visual skills, and using both kinds of skills together is more effective than using just one set. Remember that you learned your native language aurally and orally, so you do have the skills to learn words and expressions through listening. For example, the most effective way to memorize vocabulary is to combine two or more activities: Listen and repeat, write and read, listen and write, and so forth. In this way your physical abilities and senses reinforce one another, and words stick in your mind better. In addition, aural and audiovisual input will help you build fluency by focusing on the meaning of phrases and sentences rather than individual words, and this means that you will be able to read, listen, speak, and write more quickly, with greater accuracy, and with better comprehension.

Make the most of class time by being an active learner: Listen to what is being said and how it is being said, and repeat and correct things to yourself. Listening does not have to be a passive activity. While your classmates are talking, take the opportunity to concentrate on the vocabulary or structures they are using and mentally either imitate or try to improve upon their efforts. There is no better drill for practice than to be constantly repeating to yourself correctly formed sentences, and you have to do this kind of drill yourself. If you are mentally tired by the end of class, you are taking full advantage of the opportunities it presents.

Speaking and Writing in Arabic

Like *Alif Baa*, *Al-Kitaab Part One* introduces two varieties of spoken Arabic in addition to a formal register. Your teacher will choose one of the spoken varieties for you to learn alongside the formal register. You will notice that the overwhelming majority of words are shared among all three varieties of Arabic, and that most of the differences involves short vowel sounds—what we might call in English "local accent."

There are differences between formal and spoken Arabic, but you do not need to worry about keeping the two separate now. It is natural to feel confused sometimes and also to mix the forms. With practice and exposure you will learn to mix registers as native speakers do. Your goal at this stage is to focus on accuracy of pronunciation and basic grammatical forms like verb conjugations and gender agreement. These are the kinds of accuracy you need in order to be understood by native speakers who will not have trouble understanding and communicating with you in mixed forms.

Tips for Learning Vocabulary

Because Arabic has a long history and is spoken across a large geographical area, it has an expansive vocabulary. Your biggest challenge in reaching fluency in Arabic is to learn this new vocabulary, and you should devote as much effort as you can to actively acquire the vocabulary in each chapter. "Actively acquiring" means developing the ability to produce the word accurately in the appropriate context without being prompted—that is, without seeing the word in a list or word bank. Put another way, activated vocabulary is vocabulary you own, that you use in the context of your life.

It is crucial that you prepare the lesson's vocabulary before class by listening to the audio An audio of each vocabulary ("في البيت") and doing the drills designated as homework drills by item in a contextualized sentence in formal Arabic is provided as well. These sentences are meant to serve two purposes: (1) To contextualize the new vocabulary, and (2) to give you practice in close listening skills.

As in *Alif Baa*, vocabulary in *Al-Kitaab Part One* is introduced in three color-coded varieties: الفصحى، الشامئ، المصري. Words shared by more than one variety appear in **black**. It is important to remember that the vocabulary list is not a glossary, and that the words given for each variety do not constitute an exhaustive list of equivalents. The vocabulary words presented here are also included because they occur in one of the video segments or reading texts in the chapter. Because most of these texts were originally composed in formal Arabic, the vocabulary lists originated in the formal register. Not all spoken words that are in use are given here. Only those words the actors use in telling the Cairene and Levantine versions of the story are included. These words are listed separately when the word or its pronunciation, as it occurs in the story, differs from the formal word. You will notice that these variants are often very close, differentiated only by a vowel sound; we have included them in the list so that you can click on them to hear the differences in pronunciation. It is important to learn and study the spoken forms aurally because some spoken Arabic sounds cannot be represented accurately in Arabic script.

Another important exercise that will help you learn the vocabulary are the "Ask Your Colleagues" exercises. These exercises are designed to be done in a combination of formal and spoken Arabic. For this activity to be effective, you **must** come to class having already listened at home to the new words in the lesson and having practiced them aloud repeatedly in their various forms (such as those of verb conjugations and the singulars and plurals of nouns). The questions in the exercise are provided in English for three reasons: (1) to help reinforce the association of words with particular contexts, (2) to force you to produce the new vocabulary in context from scratch rather than reading the Arabic words on the page, and (3) to help you avoid using English, since everyone knows what the questions mean from the outset. Take advantage of that shared knowledge to work with your partners on the best way to express your thoughts in Arabic.

Learning Grammar

Much of what we said about activating vocabulary also applies to learning grammar. As with vocabulary, it is important for the initial work to be done outside of class so that you can work at your own pace and class time can be reserved for exercises in which you interact with your classmates. Prepare for class by reading the lesson's grammar explanation and by completing the specified mechanical grammar drills that aim to help you internalize the structure. We are confident that the grammar explanations are clear enough for students to understand without lectures or lengthy presentations in class. It is natural to lack confidence in your complete grasp of grammar, but this does not mean that you need more explanation. Rather, it means you need practice in using the new structures—and this is what the class activities are designed to give you the chance to do. Using the sports analogy again, grammar can be compared to learning a new physical skill: Understanding what your muscles are supposed to do may be helpful at the outset but real results come only with practice.

Many of us find it easier to understand concrete examples than abstract explanations, so the grammar explanations in this book take as their starting point sentences and phrases you already know that contain the grammar point. In other words, the grammar sections do not introduce things you have not seen before, but, rather, they guide you to think about sentences you have already seen or heard and understood, and help you see patterns in them. Your ability to recognize and learn patterns is key to developing your grammar skills in Arabic.

Reading for Comprehension

Reading for comprehension is quite different from reading aloud, and, in fact, it is extremely difficult (if not impossible) to do both at the same time. The reading comprehension activities in this book aim to develop skills such as guessing the meaning from context, using background knowledge to help set expectations about what will be in a text, and using grammatical knowledge to construct meaning. All reading comprehension activities involve authentic texts that are written for adult native speakers by adult native speakers. These texts are meant to be skimmed, scanned, and explored, since their main purpose is to help you develop good strategies and skills necessary for fluent reading. Do not expect to understand everything in these texts, and always focus on what you *do* understand rather than on what you do not. We want you to approach these texts with a sense of discovery. What kind of text is it, and what clues does it give you as to what kinds of information it gives? Can you guess the meaning of any new words from context? Every piece of information you can recognize or extract from authentic texts represents an important step forward in building your Arabic language skills.

Tips for Active Learning

People who seem like gifted language learners have learned to approach language learning actively rather than passively. They think about how to say things in Arabic for fun, they talk to themselves out loud, and they own the vocabulary and grammar they encounter by using it to say and write things that are relevant to their own lives.

Another part of being an active learner is asking questions about what you are learning. Having questions means that you are thinking about the way that Arabic functions, and this is the first step in learning to produce it. In other words, critical thinking skills play a key role in language learning. Critical thinkers have questions and try to reason an educated guess or hypothesis before asking someone else.

Active learning also means learning to work without a safety net. When you are reading, whether in class or at home, whether it is a text or drill, do not write out the meaning of words in English on or near the Arabic. It is very important that you trust your ability to recall meaning with the help of a familiar context—this is how you learned vocabulary in your native language. Keep in mind that you will probably forget and relearn a word several times before you retain it, so go ahead and forget. Forgetting is part of the learning process! You can look it up again if you need to.

The activities that you do in class are designed to provide you with ideas and models for activities you can do with others for further practice. Study in pairs or groups, if that works well for you, and agree to speak Arabic together as much as you can. This is a good way to prepare for class and to review. You can do activities together, such as ask each other questions, brainstorm about assignments, and practice conjugating verbs.

Repetition Is Key

One of the ways you will become fluent in Arabic is by paying attention to and imitating the way ideas are expressed. In order to do this successfully, you must listen, read, and pronounce words and sentences aloud several times. For example, you will notice that the reading and listening exercises in this book instruct you to read or listen not once but several times. The time and effort you put into reading and listening several times will pay off many times over in increased language skills. Not only will you understand more each time you repeat the activity, but you also need to move through several stages of comprehension from general comprehension to more detailed reading. Perhaps the most important reading or listening pass is the one that you do after you have understood as much as possible. This final time, concentrate not on what is being said but on how it is being said. This focus will help you remember the things you have learned about Arabic while reading or listening to the text, and it will give you an opportunity to choose some words and expressions that you want to incorporate into your own speaking and writing.

Memorization

Memorization is central to learning any language. The more you memorize, the more quickly you will learn. If you do not know how to memorize well, ask others how they do it or ask your teachers for help. Experiment with different techniques, and remember that a combination of approaches that use different senses usually works best. Some strategies include:

- Listen to the words and sentences and repeat out loud;
- Write words, phrases, and sentences out by hand and repeat vocabulary over and over;

- Make up your own meaningful sentences with the words so that you own them; and
- Use word-association techniques, such as remembering particular sounds of a word together like the singular and plural forms of a noun or a verb and matching preposition.

Flashcards can be helpful if you use them actively: Rather than just looking at the words, use them in a sentence of your own—a new one each time. Another way to activate vocabulary and help you memorize is to use different forms of the words in different sentences—singular, plural, masculine, and feminine nouns and adjectives, and different verb persons (I, you, she, he, we, and they). Memorize prepositions with their verbs, too, and memorize phrases in addition to single words. Learning language in chunks helps you remember both grammar and vocabulary, so memorize sentences that you like, too. These will serve as good models for your own sentences.

Finally, *Al-Kitaab Part One* is designed to challenge you but not to frustrate you. If you find yourself becoming frustrated—especially if you are having trouble with particular kinds of exercises or with memorizing vocabulary—see your teacher for help. We hope that this new edition of the book will serve as a useful learning and teaching tool for Arabic. We wish you a successful, enjoyable, and rewarding experience learning Arabic!

وبالتوفيق إن شاء الله!

Acknowledgments

We express our deep gratitude to all institutions and individuals who made the production of this book possible. The National Endowment for the Humanities, an independent federal agency, provided the funding for the first edition through a grant to the School of Arabic at Middlebury College, which added matching funds and staff support. The contributions of many colleagues and students who recorded, reviewed, tested, critiqued, and donated materials to the first and second editions live on in this new edition materially or in spirit, and all have played an important role in the continuing evolution of these materials. A special acknowledgment is due to our directors. Ms. Maya Patsalides skillfully and professionally directed the videotaping of all the Syrian video materials included in this volume. We are also grateful to Ms. Nashwa Mohsin Zayid, who directed the Egyptian video scenes of the Maha and Khalid story, and to Mr. Taha Al-Tonsi, who directed the additional Egyptian dialogue scenes at the end of each chapter. We also thank all the actresses and actors who made our characters come to life on the screen in language accessible to beginning students of Arabic— not an easy task for those with no experience in our field.

Sincere thanks go to Michael Heidenreich of the University of Texas Liberal Arts Technology Services (LAITS) for his expert recording and editing of the new audio material. We are grateful to Ghada Hussein and Radwa Al-Barouni, who helped with the recording of new Egyptian and Syrian materials, and to the colleagues whose earlier recordings add to the variety of voices heard on the interactive materials. We also thank Mohammad Abou Braish, who did the graphic design for the reading texts in this edition, and Lucinda Levine for her illustrations throughout, which add both beauty and function to the materials. We also thank ObjectDC, who designed the interior of the book.

Our colleagues at Georgetown University Press were full partners in developing this third edition, and we are grateful to press director Richard Brown and his entire staff for their continued dedication and care in producing these materials. Hope LeGro, director of Georgetown Languages, has been instrumental in helping us to formulate and realize ambitious additions to this third edition.

Finally, we owe a great debt to our skilled and dedicated team of instructors at the University of Texas, Austin, who have been our partners in evolving the pedagogy of these materials in the classroom over the past three years, and without whom this third edition would not have been possible. In particular, the 2008–2010 teams of first-year instructors played a key role in pushing the envelope with integrating spoken Arabic into the formal Arabic classroom and syllabus: Martha Schulte-Nafeh, Laila Familiar, Dina Mostafa, Steve Robertson, Kevin Burnham, Britt Milliman, Cory Jorgenson, Summer Loomis, Tracey Maher, and Drew Paul. We are privileged to work with such talented and devoted teachers. We would like to pay a very special acknowledgment to Hope Fitzgerald, who volunteered to pioneer the new approach you find here as it was still being developed, and who designed and oversaw its highly successful implementation in six sections of first-year Arabic in 2009-2010, a success made possible by her skill, creativity, confidence in her students and her team, enthusiasm, and of course, her patience with us.

And finally, we thank the students who continue to inspire us with their enthusiasm, commitment, and dedication. To all of you,

ألف تحيّة وألف شكر لكم جميعاً

أنا ساكنة في مدينة نيويورك

المفردات

القصة بالعامية: "أنا نسرين" "أنا مها"

القواعد (١):

المؤنّث والمذكّر Gender

النّسبة

السّؤال Interrogatives

القراءة: "تعارف"

القصة بالفصحى: "أنا مها"

الثقافة: الأسماء العربية

القواعد (٢):

الـ

الحوار: "أنا من نفس المنطقة"

تمارين المراجعة

Before you begin, learn to recognize the following key words:

vocabulary	المُفرَدات
formal, written Arabic	الفُصحى
grammar	القَواعِد
sentence	جُملة
culture	الثَّقافة

 المُفرَدات Vocabulary

As in *Alif Baa*, vocabulary in this book will be presented in three varieties: الفُصحى، والشامي، والمصري. Words that are shared among two or three varieties are black in color and listed only in the الفُصحى column. Sometimes words are repeated in all three columns when there is a particular pronunciation difference that we want you to hear. Occasionally, words from spoken Arabic have variant spellings, and these are given as well. Your teacher will decide which variety the class will activate. You will be expected to recognize the formal Arabic words, and you will see and hear them throughout the book.

Always study the new vocabulary first with the audio so that you associate the written form with the correct pronunciation from the outset. Listen to each word several times and repeat aloud with the audio several more, until you can "hear" the word in your mind and say it easily:

Meaning	المعنى	المصري	الشامي	الفُصحى
literature				الأدَب
really?!			والله؟!	والله؟!
United Nations				الأُمَم المُتَّحِدة
which?				أيّ .. ؟
nationality				جِنسِيّة
I study		بادرِس	بِدرُس	أدرُس
I live, reside		ساكِن / ساكْنة	ساكِن / ساكْنة	أسكُن
she lives, resides		ساكْنة	ساكْنة	تَسكُن
he lives, resides		ساكِن	ساكِن	يَسكُن

Meaning	المعنى	المصري	الشامي	الفُصحى
year			سِنة	سَنة
really?! or For real?!				صَحيح؟!
age				عُمر
she works		بِتِشتَغِل	بتِشتِغِل	تَعمَل
he works		بِيِشتَغِل	بيِشتِغِل	يَعمَل
address			عِنوان	عُنوان
Egyptian		مَصري/ مَصريّة	مَصري / مَصريّة	مِصريّ / ة
who?		مين؟	مين؟	مَن؟
area, region		مَنطِقة	مَنطِقة	مِنطَقة
the same				نَفس الـ ..
father				والِد
my father		بابا ، والْدي	بابا	والِدي
mother				والِدة
my mother		ماما ، والْدِتي	ماما	والِدَتي

🎧 Learn This Verb تعلّموا هذا الفعل

Listen to and practice saying and using these forms of the verb "work." Notice that both Egyptian and Levantine varieties have the b-prefix. This prefix is used in these dialects on main verbs, and we will discuss it in more detail in lessons 4 and 9.

	المصري	الشامي	الفُصحى	
	باشتَغَل	بِشتِغِل	أعمَل	أنا
	بِتِشتَغِل	بتِشتِغِل	تَعمَل	أنتَ
	بِتِشتَغلي	بتِشتِغلي	تَعمَلين	أنتِ
	بِيِشتَغِل	بيِشتِغِل	يَعمَل	هو
	بِتِشتَغِل	بتِشتِغِل	تَعمَل	هي

The next chart shows the negation of these forms. Notice that formal and spoken Arabic use different negation particles.

المصري	الشامي	الفُصحى	
ما باشتَغَلش	ما بِشتِغِل	لا أعمَل	أنا
ما بِتِشتَغَلش	ما بِتِشتِغِل	لا تَعمَل	أنتَ
ما بِتِشتَغليش	ما بِتِشتِغلي	لا تَعمَلين	أنتِ
ما بِيِشتَغَلش	ما بِيِشتِغِل	لا يَعمَل	هو
ما بِتِشتَغَلش	ما بِتِشتِغِل	لا تَعمَل	هي

🎧 تمـريـن ١: جُمل المفردات Vocabulary Sentences (في البيت)

Listen to the vocabulary words and the sentences illustrating their usage that you hear by clicking on the button on screen that says "في جملة". Listen to each sentence and write it out to hand in. As you listen and write, pay attention to both the meaning and grammar of what you are hearing, because the relationship between the two will help you write correctly.

🎧 تمـريـن ٢: المفردات الجديدة (في البيت)

This exercise is available online.

تمـريـن ٣: اسألوا زملاءكم Ask Your Colleagues (في الصّف)

This exercise prompts you to activate new vocabulary by using it in conversation with your classmates. The questions below are meant to be used as guidelines, not scripts. Remember that this is not a translation exercise. Do not translate the questions, but rather reformulate them to address your partner: instead of "Who lives and works...", say "Do you live and work. . .? Work at a steady pace, slowly enough to think about all the different things you can say that are appropriate to the context, and quickly enough to get information from several different people. Take some brief notes so that you can report back to the class what you found out, but do not write complete sentences, as it will take time away from speaking. Avoid English, and ask for help if you are stuck or frustrated.

Teacher: The questions are divided into two groups, A and B, so that students hear and ask a variety of questions. Divide the class in half and have the students prepare each set, then find a partner who prepared the other set. Switch partners every five to ten minutes.

If an answer surprises you or is unusual, you can use صحيح؟! or والله؟ to express that.

A. Find out from your classmates in Arabic:

1. In which area of the city do they live? Do they like it?
2. Do they have siblings who study at the same university?
3. Whose father or mother works in an office at home?
4. Who wants to study in Egypt? (If not:) Where?
5. Do they like literature: which literature do they like?

B. Find out from your classmates in Arabic:

1. Who wants to work at the UN?
2. Whose mothers work a lot? Whose fathers drink lots of tea?
3. On (في) which street do they live? Do they like the area?
4. Who likes to live and work in the same area?
5. Whose friend lives in the same house or building?

القصّة بالعاميّة

تمرين ٤: "أنا نسرين" / "أنا مها" 🎧 (في البيت وفي الصف)

In *Alif Baa* you learned to listen to spoken texts in several steps:

First listen: What is being said in general? Get the main topics and ideas, and formulate questions about specific information or expressions for stage two.

Second listen: What specific information can I get out of this text? Focus on answering your questions and finding specific information.

Third listen: How are ideas being expressed? Focus on close listening to details of language use, including focusing on pronunciation and structure.

A. At home, use these strategies to listen to مَها or نِسرين and give in writing as much information as you can, with as much vocabulary as you can, about the following (feel free to use both formal and spoken words and expressions):

١. الاسم: ....

٢. البيت: ....

٣. تعمل: ....

٤. ماما: ....

٥. بابا: ....

6. What new words did you hear? Write them and guess their meaning.

B. In class, discuss with a partner what you remember from the story and reconstruct as much of it as you can. Then, with the sound off, work with your partner to create a new voice-over for the video, one that tells her story in third person. Present your voice-over to the class.

القــواعد (١) Grammar

المُـؤَنَّث والمُـذَكَّر

feminine	مُـؤَنَّث
masculine	مُـذَكَّر

You know that nouns and adjectives in Arabic always carry gender, either مُـؤَنَّث or مُـذَكَّر. It is useful to distinguish between two categories of nouns in Arabic: those that refer to human beings, and those that refer to nonhumans. The gender of human nouns, such as أستاذة or صاحب, including proper nouns, such as مـهـا and محـمـد, follow the gender of the person. In the category of inanimate objects, each noun has its own gender, which does not change. Remember: There is no neutral, nongendered word for "it" in Arabic; you must use هو or هـي depending on the gender of the noun you are referring to. It is important to pay attention to the gender of nouns because the gender of adjectives, pronouns, and (as we will see soon) verbs that refer to them must agree in gender, whether in phrases such as الأدب الإنجـلـيـزيّ, in which both the noun and the adjective are مُـذَكَّر, or in sentences, such as والدتي فلـسـطينيّة, in which both are مُـؤَنَّث. Thus, it is helpful to think about nonhuman nouns as either هو or هـي because this association reinforces the grammatical agreement of the noun and will help your grammatical accuracy when you speak and write.

In unit 6 of *Alif Baa*, you learned that the letter ة (تاء مربوطة) almost always indicates feminine gender[1]. The symbol ة is related to the letter ت, and is pronounced as ت in possessive phrases, such as مدينة نيويورك. In other cases ة is not pronounced, but the فـتـحة that always precedes it is, as in أنـا مصريَّة. We will discuss possessive phrases in lesson 3; in the meantime, pay attention to the pronunciation of ة in the phrases and sentences you learn.

النِّـسـبـة The Nisba Adjective

The word نـسـبة in grammar refers to a type of adjective formed from nouns by adding the suffix يّ for مَـذكَّر or يّة for مـؤنَّث. These adjectives generally indicate origin or affiliation, especially in reference to a place. You have learned several of these already:

أستاذي مصريّ.	قهوة تركيّة وقهوة أمريكيّة.
خبز عربيّ.	والـدتي فلـسـطينيّة.

---

[1] Exceptions: A few masculine nouns, generally Classical words with special meanings, take ة. One is خـلـيـفة caliph.
A few plurals also end in ة. Finally, a handful of nouns are feminine even though they lack ة, for example شَمَس *sun*. These exceptions must be memorized as feminine.

In formal Arabic, the شــدّة on the nisba ending يّ is clearly pronounced, but in spoken Arabic it is not normally pronounced in the masculine.

Learn to recognize both variants. Listen to this chart and compare :

المؤنث	Spoken/Formal المذكر
الأستاذة مصريّة	الأستاذ مصريّ/ مصري
الأستاذة سوريّة	الأستاذ سوريّ / سوري
الأستاذة لُبنانيّة	الأستاذ لُبنانيّ/ لُبناني
الأستاذة مَغرِبيّة	الأستاذ مَغرِبيّ / مَغرِبي

Many family names come from nisba adjectives and refer to the original hometown of the family. Examples include الــفـاســيّ (from المــصريّ (maSr can refer to Cairo), الـبـغـدادي and Fez, Morocco).

Nisbas are usually formed from nouns referring to a place or institution, such as university, library, or house. A few professions are also expressed with nisbas, such as ميكانيكيّ *mechanic* and ساعاتيّ *watch repairer* (from ساعة, plural of ساعات).

To form a nisba adjective from a place noun, follow these steps: (1) Remove all ة, الـ, and final ا or يا from the place name, and (2) add the appropriate nisba ending, يّ or يّة.

أمريكيّ / أمريكيّة	← add nisba ending	أمريك ← remove alif	أمريكا
مكتبيّ / مكتبيّة	← add nisba ending	مكتب ← remove ة	مكتبة
أُردُنيّ / أُردُنيّة	← add nisba ending	أُردُن ← remove الـ	الأُردُن

Now practice by completing the steps for the following:

....	← add nisba ending	....	← remove alif	فَرنسا
....	← add nisba ending	....	← remove الـ	المَكسيك
....	← add nisba ending	....	← remove يا	موريتانيا
....	← add nisba ending	....	← remove الـ, ة	القاهرة

تمرين ٥: النسبة (في البيت) 🎧

Identify the nationality or affiliation of the following people, places, and things:

مثال: هذه طائرة أمريكيّة. (أمريكا)

١. فاس مدينة	(المغرب)
٢. هذه أستاذة	(الجزائر)
٣. "نيكول" بنت	(فرنسا)
٤. "راج" رجل	(الهند)
٥. هذه قهوة	(تُركيا)
٦. "ريتشارد" دكتور	(أوستراليا)
٧. طوكيو مدينة	(اليابان)
٨. سلمى طالبة	(الباكِستان)
٩. مها طالبة	(جامعة)
١٠. هذه ساعة	(الصّين China)

تمرين ٦: النسبة (في البيت) 🎧

This exercise is available online only.

تمـريـن ٧: مَن ؟ ماذا؟ مِن أين؟ (في الصف أو في البيت)

Describe these pictures using what you have learned about gender agreement and nisba adjectives. Challenge yourself and use as many verbs as you can.

السّـؤال Interrogatives

You have learned to use several interrogative particles to ask informational questions:

ما هذا؟   مَن هو؟

وين المكتبة؟   كيفك؟

ايه الأخبار؟   إزّيّك؟

Asking informational questions in Arabic is straightforward and does not differ much from English. In formal Arabic and in most spoken dialects, the interrogative particle comes at the beginning of the sentence:

ما عنوانك؟   أيـن تـسكن؟

شو الأخبار؟   وين بتشتغلي؟

مين بيحبّ الشاي؟

In the Egyptian dialect, however, interrogative particles can come at the end of the question:

تحب تروح فين؟ تشرب ايه؟

The rule of thumb is that the interrogative particle takes the place of the noun it replaces. For example, in the sentence تشرب شاي, we can replace شاي with an interrogative particle and get the question تشرب ايه؟.

Formal Arabic has two words for "what?" One is used primarily in sentences without verbs, and the other is used with verbs. As you have seen, the particle ما is used in questions without verbs:

ما جنسية الدكتورة سارة؟ ما اسم والدك؟

In questions in which verbs are used, ماذا is preferred:

ماذا تعمل والدتك؟ ماذا تشرب في الصباح؟

Prepositions may pair up with interrogative particles. In such phrases, the preposition always comes first:

Meaning	المعنى	المصري	الشامي	الفُصحى
From where?		مِنين؟	مِن وين؟	مِن أينَ ؟
In which?		في أيّ..؟	بِأيّ ..؟	في أيّ..؟
With whom?		مع مين؟	مع مين؟	مَعَ مَن؟

Here are some example sentences:

صاحبتك منين؟ مع مين بتدرسي؟ في أيّ جامعة تدرس؟

مِن أين أنت؟

You have also heard and used many yes/no questions in spoken Arabic. Unlike English, which uses auxiliary, or helping, verbs like "do/does" and "is/are" in addition to intonation to form such questions (as in, "Do you like ice cream?"), Arabic uses the same word order and structure as statements. In other words, there is no difference between the structure of statements and yes/no questions in Arabic. Instead, yes/no questions are normally signaled by intonation in most varieties of spoken Arabic. The following examples illustrate the similar structure of statements and yes/no questions in spoken Arabic. Listen to the difference in intonation:

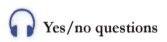 **Yes/no questions**

مها مصرية؟ ⟵ مها مصرية.

أنت طالبة؟ ⟵ أنت طالبة.

As in many languages, falling intonation generally indicates a statement, whereas rising intonation usually signals a question. The exact intonation of an Arabic sentence or question depends on the dialect region. Listen to and imitate the speech of your teacher and native speakers you know.

In formal Arabic, yes/no questions are introduced by the particle هَل (for which there is no English equivalent). This particle has no meaning other than to introduce a yes/no question. Thus in formal contexts you will hear or read the following variants of the example above:

هَل مها مصرية؟

هَل أنت طالبة؟

The following chart summarizes all the interrogative particles you have learned so far:

Meaning	المعنى	المصري	الشامي	الفُصحى
What? (in questions without verbs)		ايه؟	شو؟	ما؟
What? (in questions using verbs)		ايه؟	شو؟	ماذا؟
Which?		أيّ؟	أيّ؟	أيّ؟
Who?		مين؟	مين؟	مَن؟
Where?		فين؟	وين؟	أينَ؟
How?		اِزّايّ؟	كيف؟	كَيفَ؟
(introduces yes/no question)		--	--	هَل؟

تمـريـن ٨: ما السؤال؟ (في البيت)

This exercise is available online only.

تمـريـن ٩: نشاط محادثة (في الصف)

Watch the video "انتي عربية؟" or "تشرّفنا" as a class, if possible. With a partner, continue their conversation. Ask as many questions and use as much new vocabulary as you can.

القراءة:

تمـريـن ١٠: "تعارُف" (في الصف)

Many websites and some magazines provide services so that young people across the Arab world can contact each other. Many young people lack the means or opportunity to travel and meet other young people. They often use these sites and pen-pal connection services to meet other young people and learn about them and where they live by writing letters or chatting online. In the following text, find the kinds of information given.

1. Which attributes are common to many entries?

2. What new words can you guess from context? Start with البلد and الجنس.

التَّعارُف

محمد ود العزَّاز	ريما	محمود عاشور مسعود	حسين الطبّال
الجنسية: سوداني	أنا ريما من السعودية	العمر: 32 سنة ، تاجر	العنوان: ليبيا – طرابلس
من جنوب الوادي	من الرياض، عمري 18	الجنسية: ليبي	العمر: 26 سنة
شكري ابراهيم	**مصري**	**حمد**	**ليبية**
الجنسية: تونسي مقيم في ليبيا	الجنس: ذكر	أنا حمد أبو ربيع	الجنس: فتاة
مواليد: 31/5/1976	العمر : 25	20 سنة	العمر : 18
أعمل فنّي مبردات سيارات	البلد: مصر	أردني من أصل فلسطيني	البلد: ليبيا
هاني	**سعد العتيبي**	**سعودية**	**عبير**
الجنس: ذكر	الجنس: ذكر	الجنس: أنثى	الجنس: أنثى
العمر: 22	العمر: 29	العمر : 22	العمر : 18 عام
البلد: اليمن	البلد:الكــويت	البلد: السعودية– القطيف	البلد: عمان
سامح	**سعودي**	attar	**سوري**
الجنس: ذكر	الجنس: ذكر	الاسم: خير الدين عطّار	الجنس: ذكر
العمر: 20	العمر:22	الجنسية: جزائري	العمر: 29
البلد: السعودية – القطيف	البلد: السعودية ـ الطائف		البلد: سوريا
حبيب	**فتاة**	**فلسطيني**	**سوريّة**
اسمي حبيب	الجنس: فتاة	الجنس: فلسطيني	الجنس: أنثى
عمري 22 ، ذكر	العمر: 22 سنة، فلسطينية	العمر : 26 سنة	العمر:26
السعودية - المدينة المنوّرة	مقيمة في الإمارات	البلد: السعودية	البلد: سوريا
طالب جامعي	الوظيفة : طالبة جامعية	الوظيفة: مبرمج كمبيوتر	الوظيفة: سكرتيرة
طالبة	**بنت**	**كويتية**	**روزاليندا**
الجنس: فتاة	الجنس: أنثى	الجنس: أنثى	الجنس: أنثى
العمر: 14	العمر : 15 سنة	العمر : 18	العمر: 19
البلد: السعودية	البلد: الإمارات – دبي	البلد: الكويت	البلد: لبنان
الوظيفة : طالبة	الوظيفة : طالبة	الوظيفة : طالبة	الوظيفة : طالبة

www.khayma.com/rfh/t3arf.htm

القصة بالفصحى

تمرين ١١: "أنا مها" (في البيت وفي الصف) 🎧

Watch القصة بالفصحى and answer the questions below. The dictation exercise can be completed in the book or online.

1. Listen to Maha tell her story in formal Arabic. What similarities and differences do you hear between formal and spoken Arabic? Write out the phrases that differ.

2. Prepare for class: Write a short biography for Maha with the information you have. Use formal Arabic as much as you can for this formal situation. In class, read your classmates' biographies.

3. Listen again to Maha, and write what she says below or type the missing words in the online exercise:

أنا (١) .... مهـا محمد أبـو العـلا. أنـا (٢) .... ،

(٣) .... في (٤) .... نيـويـورك في (٥) ....

بروكلين. (٦) .... (٧) .... (٨) .... في

(٩) .... (١٠) .... ، و (١١) .... فلسطينية

(١٢) .... في (١٣) .... نيـويـورك.

أنا (١٤) .... في (١٥) .... (١٦) .... ،

و (١٧) .... فيـهـا (١٨) .... الإنجلـيزي.

الثقافة Culture

الأسماء العربية Arabic Names

An Arab's name tells more about his or her family than an American's name. Arabic names usually take one of two formats, illustrated here by two versions of Maha's name:

١. مَها مُحمّد أبو العِلا

٢. مَها مُحمّد يوسف

The first example, مَها is the given name, مُحمّد is her father's first name, and أبـو العـلا is her family name. The second format is used in official documents in Egypt, in particular, and consists of the given name, the father's first name, and the paternal grandfather's first name.

These modern names are shorter versions of the traditional form of Arabic names. Here is an example of the traditional form for the name of a famous poet of the ninth century:

عَلي بن العَبّاس بن جُرَيْج (ابـن الـرّومي)

As you can see, the father's and subsequent ancestral names are separated by ابن son (of) (spelled without the alif in between two names). In addition to these genealogical names, people are usually identified by city of birth, named in a nisba adjective, or by a nickname designating a particular attribute. This poet is known as Ibn al-Rumi because of his Byzantine background (رومّي means *Byzantine*, from الـرّوم).

Most Arab women do not legally take the name of their husbands when they marry. (In some areas, they may be addressed socially by their husbands' family names.) Maha's mother, مَلَك, retains the name of her father and family for life: مَلَك طاهِر دَرويش. Also note that not all female names end in ة. As you learn more names, you will learn to recognize which names are masculine and which are feminine. As in English, a few names may be either gender, such as وَفاء and صَبـاح.

Stereotypical portrayals of Arabs sometimes include characters named Abdul. In Arabic, however, this is only half of a name. The word عَبـد *servant of* must be followed by another word, usually an attribute of God, in order to constitute a proper name. You may have heard some of the following examples:

عـبـد القادِر   عبد الـلّـه   عبد الحَكيم   عبد الجَبّار

In conversation, Arabs tend to address and refer to each other by their first names preceded by a title unless they are close friends. For example, Maha's father might be addressed at work as دكتور محـمـد. In introductions and formal settings both names may be used:

الـدكـتـور محـمـد أبـو الـعـلا.

القواعد ٢ Grammar 2

The Definite Article الـ

In unit 9 of *Alif Baa* you learned that the article الـ makes a noun definite: For example, the indefinite طـالـب *a student* corresponds to definite الـطـالـب *the student*. You cannot assume that all words without الـ are indefinite. Some proper names (e.g., مـصـر, محمود, فرنسا) as well as nouns in one particular grammatical construction (which you will learn in lesson 3) can be definite without it using الـ. However, you can assume that all words with الـ are definite.

In Arabic الـ is used in more contexts than English "the." Notice that Maha says أدرس الأدب *I study literature*, but we do not say in English *I study the literature*. In Arabic, abstract and generic concepts are expressed as definite nouns. Thus we say in Arabic:

أدرس العربية في الجامعة.

أشرب الشاي في الصباح.

أحب القهوة.

The following chart summarizes corresponding English and Arabic usages of the definite and indefinite. In English, singular nouns may be used with (a) the indefinite article "a(n)," as in "a book," (b) the definite article "the," as in "the teacher," or (c) with no article at all, as in "literature". Each of these cases refers to a particular kind of reference: nouns with "a" or "an" are unknown or unspecified ("a book" could be any book); nouns with "the" are known and specific (both speaker and listener know who "the teacher" is); and words with no article are abstract entities or ideas or broad categories (such as "literature," "happiness," and "medicine"). Arabic does not use an indefinite article to express "a" or "an"—this is understood from the absence of the definite article. The definite article ال refers both to specific and abstract or generic entities, as in examples (b) and (c):

(a) *a book*	كتاب
(b) *the teacher*	الأستاذ
(c) *literature*	الأدب

Use this as a rule of thumb to determine where you need to use ال when speaking and writing, and pay attention to the use of ال as given in new vocabulary.

تمرين ١٢: الاستماع الى "الـ" (في البيت) 🎧

Listen to the following phrases and add الـ to the words in which you hear it, leaving the others blank. Remember to listen for the الشدّة that indicates the assimilation of لـ when followed by الحروف الشمسية. (For review, see *Alif Baa*, lesson 9.)

٧. .... تركيـة .... قهـوة			١. .... بـاب .... صغيـر		
٨. .... منهاتن .... منطقة			٢. .... نـور .... صبـاح		
٩. .... طاولة .... نفس			٣. .... قاهرة .... جامعة		
١٠. .... عـربي .... بنك			٤. .... طويـل .... شارع		
١١. .... مهـا .... أسرة			٥. .... سعـودي .... رجل		
١٢. .... مصـري .... طالب			٦. .... طيب .... خبـز		

تـمـرين ١٣: تمرين في "الـ" (في الصف)

Which nouns are definite and which are indefinite in Arabic? Complete the sentences with as many words as you can. Use regular nouns—not proper nouns—and think about where you need to use الـ to refer to a specific item or to a category of things, and where you need an indefinite noun. Note: Not using الـ with things like foods and drinks implies a meaning of "some." For example:

Do you want to drink _some tea_?   عايزة تشربي شاي؟   بدك تشربي شاي؟

١. أحب أدرس .... ولا أحب أدرس ....

٢. عندي .... و ....
عندك .... ؟

٣. أحب .... و ....
ولا أحب .... و ....

٤. أشرب .... و .... ،
ولا أشرب ....

٥. باحب اشوف .... بحب اشوف ....

٦. ما باحبش اشوف .... ما بحب اشوف ....

٧. عايز اسكن في .... بدي اسكن بـ ....

٨. مش عايز اشتغل في .... ما بدي اشتغل بـ ....

الحوار Dialogue

This section contains parallel dialogues in Egyptian and Levantine Arabic so that you can follow the version you are learning. The videos are based on the vocabulary you have been learning, and they are designed to challenge you and push your comprehension skills. You are not expected to reach one hundred percent comprehension; these dialogues are slightly above your level. Rather, approach them with the aim of getting as much out of them as you can.

اللغة والثقافة

Each dialogue contains culturally important expressions that will be explained briefly in this subsection. Read the explanations before you watch the dialogue, and then look for the cues.

The words سيدي and سِتّي come from the formal سَيِّد/ة *ma'am/sir* but are used in this expression to convey friendliness when explaining something, asking a question, or giving an exclamatory tone. While it can have a formal tone to it like "yes ma'am/yes sir," it is often friendlier and conveys to someone you do not know well that you would like to be friendly but still remain polite.

The Egyptian expression رَبِّنا معاك is used to give an encouraging or sympathetic "pat on the shoulder," much like Americans say "Good luck," or even "Good luck with that!" Many Egyptian expressions use the word رَبِّنا *our Lord* as an equivalent to الله. In some parts of the Levant, the word رَبّ tends to be used more by Christians than Muslims.

تـمـريـن ١٤: "أنا من نفس المنطقة" / "أنا من نفس المنطقة" (في البيت وفي الصف) 🎧

1. First listen: Focus on the situation. Who is speaking? What kind of exchange is this?

2. Second listen: Global comprehension. What topics of conversation can you identify?

3. Close listening: Focus on the parts of the conversation that are accessible. Note below the parts of the conversation that you understand, giving as much detail as you can about each speaker in Arabic بالعربي.

الطالب #٢	الطالب #١

تـمـريـن ١٥: نشاط محادثة (في الصف)

Go back to the reading text in تمرين ١٠ and choose one person whose identity you will assume. Prepare to play the role of this person in a pretend virtual chat room. Fill in details from your imagination. Meet and greet!

تـمـارين المراجعة Review Drills

تمريـن ١٦: القراءة الجهرية Reading aloud (في البيت وفي الصف) 🎧

Read the text silently, then aloud several times to practice pronunciation and fluency. When you are ready, record yourself reading it aloud and submit it for your teacher's feedback.

نسرين حَسَن النّوري بنت سورية تسكن في مدينة نيويورك، وهي طالبة في السنة الثالثة في جامعة نيويورك. والدها سوري من مدينة دمشق، ووالدتها فلسطينيّة وجنسيتها سوريّة. صاحبة نسرين اسمها نور وهي من نفس عمرها وتدرس في نفس الجامعة.

درس 2
Lesson 2

أنا فعلاً وحيدة!

المفردات

القصة بالعامية: "أنا فعلاً وحيدة" "أنا فعلاً وحيدة"

الثقافة: شغل البيت

القواعد:

الضمائر Subject Pronouns

الفعل في الجمع Plural Verb Conjugation

الجمع The Plural

القصة بالفصحى: "أنا فعلاً وحيدة"

القراءة: "دراسات الشرق الأوسط"

الاستماع: مع العائلة والاصدقاء

الحوار: "انت دائماً مشغول!" "انت دائماً مشغول!"

"موظفة بالأمم المتحدة" "موظفة في الأمم المتحدة"

تمارين المراجعة

المُفرَدات Vocabulary 🎧

Listen to the new vocabulary alone and in context in sentences (click the في جملة button on the screen). As you listen to the words, listen for the pronunciation difference between formal and spoken Arabic in the sounds ض and ظ, and the vowel sounds in the words الليل الليل and عيلة عيلة:

المعنى	المصري	الشامي	الفُصحى
(nuclear) family	عيلة	عيلة	أُسْرة
people			النّاس
also	كَمان	كَمان	أيْضاً
country			بَلَد
translation (from...to)			التَّرجمة مِن..إلى
translator			مُتَرجِم/ة
specializing/specialist in		مِتخَصِّص/ة في	مُتَخَصِّص/ة في
maternal aunt		خالة	خالة
always	دايماً	دايماً	دائماً
center (noun)			مَركَز
the Middle East			الشَّرق الأوْسَط
busy (with)			مَشغول/ة بِ
work	الشُّغل	الشُّغل	العَمَل، الشُّغل
tomorrow	بُكرة	بُكرة	غَداً
really!, truly			فِعلاً
admission(s)			القُبول
he speaks, talks	يِتْكَلِّم	يِحكي	يَتَكَلّم
he talks about	يِتْكَلِّم عَن	يِحكي عَن	يَتَكَلّم عَن
I have	لِيّ، عَندي	إلي، عِندي	لي، عِندي
language			لُغة
evening	المَسا	المَسا	المَساء
night	الليل	الليل	اللَّيْل
daytime			النّهار
only; lonely (adjective)			وَحيد/ة
employee	مُوَظَّف/ة	مْوَظَّف/ة	مُوَظَّف/ة
today	النّهاردا	اليوم	اليَوم

Notes on Vocabulary Usage

1. The words for family, الأُسرة and العيلة, take singular agreement in Arabic as they do in English:

أسرتي تسكن في مدينة بوسطن.

عيلتي ساكنة ببيت كبير بالشام.

عيلتي ساكنة في منطقة الجيزة.

2. Prepositions with time expressions في and بـ: In general, the preposition في expresses location in space and time in formal and Egyptian Arabic, while in Levantine, بـ normally indicates spatial location. Both Egyptian and Levantine share these expressions with بـ :

الفُصحى	الشامي	المصري	المعنى	Meaning
في النهار	بالنهار	بالنهار		in the daytime
في الليل	بالليل	بالليل		at night

تمـريـن ١: المفردات الجديدة (في البيت) 🎧

Complete the sentences with new vocabulary. Pay attention to grammar for clues to the right answer and make sure the مؤنث/مذكر agreement is correct. You may do this exercise on the website using any Arabic keyboard.

١. روسيا .... كبير جداً.

٢. في الجامعة أدرس .... العربية وأدرس .... الأدب العربي.

٣. هذا مكتب .... في جامعتنا. وهذا ....
دراسات الشرق الأوسط.

٤. أنا أدرس في المكتبة ....

٥. إيران والعراق وتركيا ومصر في ....

٦. هذه .... والدي اسمه صالح وهو

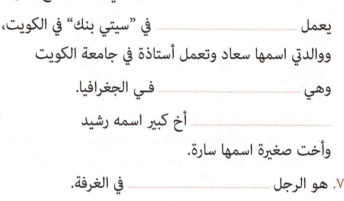

يعمل .... في "سيتي بنك" في الكويت،
ووالدتي اسمها سعاد وتعمل أستاذة في جامعة الكويت

وهي .... في الجغرافيا.

.... أخ كبير اسمه رشيد

وأخت صغيرة اسمها سارة.

٧. هو الرجل .... في الغرفة.

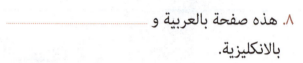

٨. هذه صفحة بالعربية و ....
بالانكليزية.

العائلة العربية	The Arab Family

العائلة العربية

ارتبطت بنية العائلة العربية في الأرياف ارتباطا وثيقا بأسلوب الإنتاج الاقتصادي السائد والعلاقات الاجتماعية التي تشكل الأرض والزراعة ركيزتها الأساسية. وكان النظام القرابي يجد مرتكزاته البنائية في العائلة المتدة التي تعكس ضرورة التماسك والتضامن والتعصب العائلي في مواجهة الأعباء والمشاكل والصراعات مع/وضد العوائل المتدة الأخرى من جهة، ومواجهة الأعباء الضريبية التي تفرضها الحكومات من جهة أخرى. لذلك نجد أن الأسرة المتدة تمثل وحدة بنائية تظهر في وحدة العمل في الأرض التي تحتاج إلى تكثير النسل لرفد الأرض بأيد عاملة كثيرة والزواج المبكر في داخل العائلة. وقد اختلفت النسب بين العائلات المتدة والعائلات النووية تبعا للموقعين الاجتماعي والاقتصادي ومكان إقامة العائلة في المدينة أو الريف. والواقع أن تحولا جوهريا أصاب بنية العائلة العربية فحولها بالتدريج من عائلة ممتدة إلى عوائل نووية، غير أن هذا التحول لم يلغ تماما علاقات القرابة والتعصب لها.

The Arab Family

The construct of the Arab family in the countryside has been deeply connected with the predominant manner of economic production as well as with the social relationships for which the land and agriculture comprise the foundational pillar. The kin system's structural anchors are found in the extended family which reflects the necessity of familial cohesiveness and solidarity in dealing with the problems and conflicts with other extended families on the one hand, and in facing the taxation burdens which the governments levy on them on the other hand. Therefore we find that the extended family represents a structure apparent in the unit of labor in the land. The labor unit requires the proliferation of descendants in order to work the land with many able hands and early marriage. The ratios of the extended and nuclear families have differed according to economic and social standings as well as the place of residence of the family be it in the city or the countryside. Though a core transformation has indeed struck the construct of the Arab family and has gradually transformed it from an extended family into nuclear families, nevertheless this transformation did not utterly efface the relationships of kin and the blood-tie loyalty mindset.

٩. جارتي تشرب القهوة دائماً: في ــــــــــــــــ وفي الليل.

١٠. اليوم عندي امتحان في صف العربية و ــــــــــــــــ عندي امتحان كبير في صف الكمبيوتر.

تمريـن ٢: جمل المفردات (في البيت) 🎧

اكتبوا جمل المفردات من "أسرة" إلى "مشغول بـ".

Listen to the sentences given to illustrate each new formal word and write out the sentences from أسرة to مشغول بـ.

تمريـن ٣: اسألوا زملاءكم Ask Your Colleagues (في الصف)

Use new vocabulary to get information in Arabic from your classmates. Remember to rephrase these questions to address your classmates ("Are you...?") Take notes so you can report to your classmates, but do not write complete sentences, as it will take time away from speaking.

A. Find two people in the class:
1. Who always do their homework at night, not in the daytime.
2. Who are really busy with their job.
3. Who know where the Admissions Office is.
4. Whose mother's brother/sister also lives nearby.
5. Who have a test today or tomorrow.
6. Whose mother/father is a university employee.
7. Who like or want to do translation–which language?

B. Find two people:
1. Who want to study another language–which one?
2. Whose parents really like their jobs.
3. Who like [to read] translation of literature.
4. Who aren't busy with homework.
5. Whose mother is the only girl in her family.
6. Who are majoring in Middle Eastern Studies.
7. Who watch TV in the daytime or at night.

القصة بالعامية

تمرين ٤: "انا فعلاً وحيدة" / "انا فعلاً وحيدة" (في البيت) 🎧

A. Using the listening strategies you have learned, watch and listen to القصة until you can understand the main ideas, then answer these questions in Arabic as much as possible:

عن مها:	عن نسرين:
أ. شغل بابا:	أ. شغل بابا:
ب. شغل ماما:	ب. شغل ماما:
جـ. خالتها:	جـ. خالتها:
د. عيلتها:	د. عيلتها:
هـ. مها مبسوطة؟	هـ. نسرين مبسوطة؟
Guess the meaning:	**Guess the meaning:**
و. وِلاية كاليفورنيا	و. وِلاية كاليفورنيا

B. In class, talk with a partner about what you learned about مها/نسرين.

الثقافة

شغل البيت 🎧

The workings of individual Arab families differ as much as those of American ones. Either partner may be responsible for day-to-day budgeting and financial management, and it is increasingly common for both husband and wife to work outside the home, while extended families often help with daycare. Marriage is seen as a partnership in both cultures; however, in Arab culture, partners' expectations of each other have not changed as drastically as those in the US in recent years. In many families, the responsibilities of each partner remain based on a traditional division of labor (rather than on sharing tasks) in which the wife is responsible for work inside the home, while the husband is expected to be available to run errands outside it. Watch the interviews with some Egyptian women on شغل البيت and الشغل.

"أنا وحيدة"

In Arab culture, spending time by oneself (except when necessary to work or study) is generally viewed as undesirable and to be avoided if possible. Close relations and frequent visits among neighbors, members of the extended family, and friends mean that one is rarely alone for an extended period of time.

تـمـريـن ٥: جمل المفردات (في البيت) 🎧

اكتبوا جمل المفردات من "العمل" إلى "اليوم".

Listen to the sentences given to illustrate each new formal word and write out the sentences from "العمل" to "اليوم".

الـقـواعـد

🎧 Subject Pronouns الـضَـمـائِـر

Arabic has three sets of personal pronouns: subject, object, and possessive. If you are not familiar with these grammatical terms, think of the English pronouns "I," "me," and "my." "I" is the subject pronoun, as in "I live here." "Me" is the object pronoun, as in "he saw me." "My" is the possessive pronoun, as in "my father." In both Arabic and English there is some overlap among these sets. For example, English "you" is both subject—as in, "You are great"—and object—as in, "I love you." Other pronouns change form according to function, such as "he" and "him": We say "He is great" but "I love him." Arabic pronouns show similar overlap and differences.

You have been using Arabic subject pronouns (أنا، أنت، هو، هي) and possessive pronouns (ـي، ـك، ـه، ـها) in the singular. In this chapter we will activate the commonly used plural subject pronouns "we," plural "you," and "they." (The plural possessive suffixes will be introduced in lesson 3.) In addition to these singular and plural pronouns, formal Arabic also has pronouns for the dual (a form used to address or talk about exactly two people or things), as well as feminine plural second-person and feminine plural third-person forms. As these are not used in most urban dialects, they will be introduced later when we get to elements of formal grammar not shared with spoken Arabic. In the meantime, listen to and learn the commonly used pronouns:

المعنى	المصري	الشامي	الفُصحى
I	أنا	أنا	أنا
you (masc. sing.)	اِنتَ	إنتَ	أنتَ
you (fem. sing.)	اِنتي	إنتي	أنتِ
he/it	هُوَّ	هُوّ	هُوَ
she/it	هِيَّ	هِيّ	هِيَ
we	اِحنا	نِحنا	نَحنُ
you (pl.)	اِنتو	إنتو	أنتُم
they	هُمَّ	هِنّ	هُم

تمرين ٦: الضمائر (في البيت) 🎧

Practice using subject pronouns to talk about people and things by completing the following mini-conversations, as the example shows. Since you are writing, use الفُصحى forms.

مثال: "هل أنتِ أستاذة؟" "لا أنا طالبة".

١. "هل .... جوعان يا علي؟"   "نعم، .... جوعان".

٢. "مِن أين أستاذك؟"   " .... مِن مصر".

٣. "هل .... مصرية يا عائشة؟"   "لا. .... سودانية".

٤. "مَن نادية؟"   " .... خالة مها".

٥. "ماذا يعمل والد مها؟"   " .... مترجم في الامم المتحدة".

٦. "في أي صف .... يا شباب؟"   " .... في صف اللغة العربية".

٧. "أين تسكن؟"   "أسكن في منطقة المزّة، و .... منطقة قريبة من جامعة دمشق".

٨. "مَن .... ؟"
   " .... شباب من نيويورك".

الفِعل في الجَمع Plural Verb Conjugation

You have learned a number of verbs in the singular conjugations (أنا، أنتَ، أنتِ، هو، هي). Here we introduce the plural conjugations commonly used in spoken Arabic: نحن، أنتم، هم. Notice that the conjugation for أنتم is closely related to that of أنتَ and that of هم is closely related to هو. Listen to and learn the basic plural conjugation forms for present-tense verbs. You can see in the table below that the Egyptian and Levantine forms end in an alif that is not pronounced. This alif is an old spelling convention that requires that the verb forms for أنتم and هم without ن be written with a final alif, which is not pronounced. (You will see this in formal Arabic as well when we learn more about المضارع in lesson 4.)

المصري	الشامي	الفُصحى	
بِنِشتَغَل	بنِشتِغِل	نَعمَل	نحن
بِتِشتَغَلوا	بتِشتِغلوا	تَعمَلون	أنتم
بِيِشتَغَلوا	بيِشتِغلوا	يَعمَلون	هم

جمع الاسم Noun Plurals

singular	مُفرَد (م.)
plural	جَمع (ج.)

Forming plurals from singular nouns is fairly regular in English: In most cases, we add "s" to the singular to produce the plural. There are exceptions that we memorize, such as "women" and "mice." Forming plurals in Arabic works differently and involves putting the root of the word in a different pattern. There are over ten common plural patterns in Arabic, and you will learn to recognize and even predict them as you acquire more vocabulary. We will introduce several patterns here and in the next lesson. Beginning in lesson 3, the plural of each noun will be introduced in the vocabulary list; it is crucial that you memorize both singular and plural together. In the presentation that follows, plurals will be presented in small groups. Make sure you add all words presented in boxes to your vocabulary study notes or flashcards. From now on, vocabulary lists will indicate the plurals of new words as follows, with the ج standing for plural جمع:

word	كَلِمة ج. كَلِمات

Remember: Memorize the singular and plural together as a unit when you first learn a new word. Repeat them aloud together, and try to use both forms when you speak and write.

Plural Patterns

In *Alif Baa* you saw that roots and patterns constitute the basis of word formation in Arabic, and you practiced identifying the roots of words. This is a skill you should keep working on. After you have identified and isolated the root of a word, everything else you see in that word is part of the pattern. Vowels and any "extra" consonants (other than the root) are thus part of the word's pattern. For example, in the word مَشْغول, the root is ش - غ - ل, and the pattern is مَـ ـْ ـ و . We can represent this and other patterns using a place-holding or generic root, which by tradition is ف - ع - ل, where ف stands for the first consonant in the root, ع for the second, and ل for the third. Thus, the pattern of مَشغول is represented as مَفْعول.

Arabic plurals follow certain patterns that will become fairly predictable when you have acquired a good vocabulary base and learned more about Arabic morphology. We will introduce the most common of these patterns in the next few lessons. To memorize plurals more easily, associate words that have the same pattern together, and use patterns to help you remember pronunciation and spelling. You will notice that Arabic tends to distinguish between human and nonhuman plurals—that is, plurals that refer to human beings and those that refer to animals and inanimate objects. While some patterns overlap, it is often possible to tell whether

a plural noun is human or nonhuman from its pattern. And as you will see in the following section, agreement rules for human plural nouns differ from those for nonhuman plurals.

Two patterns of plural formation in Arabic consist of suffixes: Sound masculine plurals, which refer only to human beings, and sound feminine plurals, which refer primarily to groups of human females and will be introduced in lesson 3.

جمع المُذكّر Human Sound Masculine Plurals
ـ ونَ / ـ ينَ

Examples of sound masculine plurals in Arabic include:

مصريّين	سوريّين	عِراقيّونَ or عِراقيّينَ
		مُتَرجِمونَ or مُتَرجِمينَ

These plurals are called "sound plurals" because the singular stem remains intact. In الفصحى, these plurals take a pair of endings that alternate according to grammatical function: In some cases, you will see or hear the ending ونَ and in others, ـينَ. You will learn these grammatical details later. Note that the final فتحة on both endings is not usually pronounced except in the most formal registers of Arabic. In spoken Arabic only the suffix ‑ يـن (no final فتحة) is used, as the examples show, and so this is the ending that is most often used and heard. Certain categories of nouns regularly take this plural:

a. Most نِسبة adjectives take this plural, with only a few exceptions, including:

أمريكي ج. أمريكان | أميركي ج. أميركان | عربيّ ج. عَرَب

b. Nouns and adjectives referring to people that begin with the prefixes مُ and مَ, such as مَشغول and مُتخصّص, مُترجم, مَبسوط. (Words that begin with the prefix مَ but refer to places, such as مَكتب and مَكتبة, do not take these plural endings.)

c. Adjectives whose singular ends in ـان such as تعبان.

جمع المُذكر

Learn these human plurals. For extra practice go to the map in lesson 1, exercise 6, and form nisba adjectives for as many countries as you can.

الجمع بالمصري	الجمع بالشامي	الجمع بالفصحى	المفرد
مَصريّين	مَصريّين	مِصريّونَ / مِصريّينَ	مِصريٌّ
لبنانيّين	لبنانيّين	لُبنانيّونَ / لُبنانيّينَ	لُبنانيٌّ
سوريّين	سوريّين	سوريّونَ / سوريّينَ	سوريٌّ
عراقيّين	عراقيّين	عراقيّونَ / عراقيّينَ	عراقيٌّ
مُتَرجِمين	مُتَرجِمين	مُتَرجِمونَ / مُتَرجِمينَ	مُتَرجِم
مُوَظَّفين	مُوظَّفين	مُوَظَّفونَ / مُوَظَّفينَ	مُوَظَّف
مُتَخَصِّصين	متخصّصين	مُتَخَصِّصونَ / مُتَخَصِّصينَ	مُتَخَصِّص
مَشغولين	مَشغولين	مَشغولونَ / مَشغولينَ	مَشغول
مَبسوطين	مَبسوطين	ــــــــ / ــــــــ	مَبسوط
حِلوين	حِلوين	ــــــــ / ــــــــ	حِلو
غَريبين	غَريبين	غَريبونَ / غَريبينَ	غَريب

جَمع التَكسير Broken Plurals

These plurals are so named because the stem of the singular is "broken" by shifting the consonants into different syllable patterns so that the pattern of the word changes. These patterns are used in both formal and spoken Arabic, with only slight variations in pronunciation, such as the shifts in some short vowels, ق, and ء that you are already familiar with.

Use your "phonographic memory" (the one you use to remember music) to help you learn these patterns. Read these words aloud:

كِتاب ج. كُتُب

مَدينة ج. مُدُن

The plurals of both nouns contain the same consonants as their singulars but the vowels have changed. These words share the same plural pattern, two syllables, each with a Damma vowel. Using our place-holding root ف – ع – ل, we represent this plural pattern as فُعُل. Two very common plural patterns are أفْعال and فُعول. Listen to and learn the plurals of words you know that take these patterns:

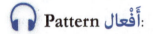 **Pattern** أَفْعال:

أوْلاد	وَلَد
أصْحاب	صاحِب
أسْماء	اِسْم
أعْمال	عَمَل
أشْغال	شُغْل
أشْياء	شَيْء
أخْبار	خَبَر

 **Pattern** فُعول:

بُيوت	بَيْت
دُروس	دَرْس
صُفوف	صَفّ
فُصول	فَصْل
بُنوك	بَنْك
فُلوس	فِلْس

Occasionally, the root of a word can be difficult to identify. The words أخ, خال, باب, and all have و as one of their root consonants. Remember that alif cannot function as a consonant and therefore cannot be part of a root. This و is not visible in the singular, but it appears in the plurals of these words (in fact, looking at the plural can be a good way of determining a root if it is not apparent from the singular).

 Listen and learn:

إِخْوة ← أخ   أخْوال ← خـال   أبْـواب ← باب

These three patterns are not very common. Memorize them as individual words:

جيران ← جار   رِجال ← رَجُل   طُلّاب ← طالِب

Plural Agreement Rules

In many languages, including English, all plural nouns share the same plural agreement rules. Thus, we say in English, "The books? They are on the table," a sentence in which "they" refers to the books; and, in another example, "My friends? They are great!" "they" refers to friends. In Arabic, however, only human plurals are always referred to as "هم." Because nonhuman plurals are usually thought of as a group and not as individuals, they use different agreement rules. The next section introduces the rules for nonhuman plurals.

Rules for plural agreement in Arabic distinguish between human plurals and nonhuman plurals (including animals).

Human Plurals

Human plurals in Arabic take plural agreement (this is not true of nonhuman nouns). In formal Arabic, groups of human females are identified by a regular suffix, ـات. We will return to this plural pattern in lesson 3. Here we will focus on masculine human plurals, which refer to both genders in most forms of spoken Arabic. Following are examples of plural agreement:

أصحابي مشغولين دائماً.   إنتو مبسوطين؟   هم طلّاب قطريّون.

Nonhuman Plural Agreement

The essential agreement rule of nonhuman plurals in modern formal Arabic is that they are always treated as if they were a single group, and they take feminine singular agreement. You saw this when you learned الأمم المتحدة : the word الأمم *nations* is a nonhuman plural noun that is modified by the feminine singular adjective المُتَّحِدة *united*. Remember: In modern formal Arabic, nonhuman plural nouns normally behave like feminine singular nouns. These examples demonstrate:

الأخبار كويسة، الحمد لله!   عندي أخبار منيحة!   البيوت في هذه المنطقة جميلة.

لا أحب الصفوف الكبيرة.

You will notice later that this rule does not always apply in spoken and Classical Arabic.

🎧 تمرين ٧: الجمع (في البيت) 🎧

Describe these groups by using the plural forms of the words in parentheses, as in the example:

مثال: نحـن طلاب أمريـكيـون. (طالـب، أمـريكي)

١. هـم _____ . (صاحب، لبناني)

٢. عندي _____ اليوم! (فصل، صعب)

٣. "هـل أنتم _____؟" (أخ) – "لا، نحـن _____!" (جار)

٤. محـمد وعلي وسعيد _____ . (رجل، يمني)

٥. الناس في هذه البناية _____! (غريب)

٦. هـم _____ في الامم المتحدة! (مترجم، عربي)

٧. نحـن دائماً _____ بالعـمل و _____! (مشغول، تعبان)

٨. في اللغة العربية _____ . (اسم، جميل)

٩. "هل أنتم _____ في مركز الشرق الأوسط؟" -- "لا، نحن _____." (طالب، موظف)

١٠. أنا أردني ولكن لي _____ (خال، فلسطيني)

١١. الرياض ومكّة وجـدّة _____ . (مدينة، سعودي)

🎧 تمرين ٨: نشاط محادثة (في الصف) 🎧

Watch the video "أخبارك ايه؟" "شو أخبارك؟"

Then in groups of two, continue the conversation between نسرين/مها and خالتها. You might want to discuss friends, studies, work, and parents. Use as much new vocabulary and as many plurals as you can.

القصة بالفصحى

تمـريـن ٩: "أنا فعلاً وحيدة" (في البيت) 🎧

Listen to مها tell her story in الفصحى. Watch القصة بالفصحى and answer the questions below. The dictation exercise can be completed in the book or online. Since you know the story, focus here on the structure and pronunciation of formal Arabic.

1. Write out three sentences or phrases that show grammatical agreement with either المؤنث or المذكر.

2. Think about the structure of each sentence you hear. Using any terminology you know, write out and label the parts of two sentences.

3. Fill in the blanks with her exact words. Pay attention to meaning and grammar as you listen and use both to help you write correctly:

مـن وإلى _____ في (٣) _____ (٢) _____ والـدي (١)

، _____ والانجـليـزية و(٦) _____ (٥) _____ (٤)

_____ في مكتب (٩) _____ (٨) _____ و(٧)

_____ (١٢) _____ نيـويورك. (١١) _____ في (١٠)

_____ (١٥) _____ (١٤) دائـماً، ووالـدتي (١٣)

_____ (١٨) _____ و(١٧) _____ في (١٦)

_____ (٢١) _____ . لـي (٢٠) _____ في (١٩)

لـوس أنجـلـوس في ولاية _____ في (٢٣) _____ نادية (٢٢)

في بنك . _____ (٢٥) _____ كـاليـفورنيا، (٢٤)

_____ في (٢٨) _____ (٢٧) _____ أنا (٢٦)

! _____ (٣٠) _____ وأنا (٢٩)

القـراءة

تـمـريـن ١٠: "دراسات الشرق الأوسط" (فـي الـصف)

The Arab Social Science Research website lists various kinds of resources for students and researchers. Unfortunately, the list of academic organizations specializing in the Middle East got mixed up. Please help fix it by working with a partner to match the name of each organization with its Arabic translation. While you are doing so, make a list of all the Arabic words whose meaning you figured out from context.

مراكز دراسات الشرق الأوسط
Middle East Studies Centers, Language, Associations

Arab Social Science Research
بوابة العلوم الإجتماعية العربية

◄ Goethe-Institute Amman, Jordan	◄ جامعة بنسلفانيا، مركز الشرق الأوسط
◄ University of Texas at Austin, Center for Middle Eastern Studies	◄ جامعة طوكيو، دراسات المنطقة الإسلامية
◄ Canadian Committee of the Middle East Studies of North America	◄ جامعة بيرجن - النرويج مركز الدراسات الإسلامية والشرق أوسطية
◄ University of Bergen, Norway, Center for Middle Eastern and Islamic Studies	◄ جامعة دنفر، معهد الدراسات الإسلامية – اليهودية
◄ Warsaw University, Oriental Institute	◄ الجمعية الفرنسية لدراسات العالم العربي والإسلامي
◄ University of Pennsylvania, Middle East Center	◄ جمعية دراسات نساء الشرق الأوسط
◄ University of Michigan, Center for Middle Eastern and North African Studies	◄ جامعة وارسو، المعهد الشرقي
◄ University of London, School for Oriental and African Studies SOAS: Centre of Islamic Studies	◄ معهد الدراسات الدرزية
◄ Australian National University - Centre for Arab and Islamic Studies	◄ جامعة كاليفورنيا، لوس انجيلوس، مركز جي .أي فون جروينباوم لدراسات الشرق الأدنى
◄ University of Cambridge: Middle Eastern and Islamic Studies	◄ معهد جوته في عمان - الأردن
◄ University of Chicago, Center for Middle Eastern Studies	◄ جمعية مكتبيي الشرق الأوسط
◄ Association for Middle East Women's Studies	◄ جامعة ميشيجان، مركز دراسات الشرق الأوسط وشمال افريقيا
◄ University of Tokyo, Islamic Area Studies	◄ جامعة نيويورك، دائرة دراسات الشرق الأوسط: مركز هاكوب كيفوركيان
◄ Institute of Druze Studies	◄ الجمعية الألمانية لدراسات الشرق الأوسط
◄ University of Denver, Institute for Islamic-Judaic Studies	◄ جمعية الدراسات الأرمنية
◄ Middle East Librarians Association	◄ جامعة شيكاغو، مركز دراسات الشرق الأوسط
◄ Society for Armenian Studies	◄ جامعة تكساس في اوستن، مركز الدراسات الشرق أوسطية
◄ University of California, Los Angeles, G.E. von Grunebaum Center for Near Eastern Studies	◄ جامعة كمبردج : مركز الدراسات الشرق أوسطية والإسلامية
◄ New York University, Department of Middle Eastern Studies	◄ جامعة استراليا الوطنية - مركز الدراسات العربية والإسلامية
◄ Association Française pour l'Etude du Monde Arabe et Musulman	◄ اللجنة الكندية لدراسات الشرق الأوسط
◄ German Association for Middle Eastern Studies	◄ جامعة لندن، كلية دراسات الشرق وشمال إفريقيا: مركز الدراسات الإسلامية

الاستـماع: مع العائلة والأصدقاء

🎧 **تمريـن ١١: (في البيت)**

Watch the video "مع عائلة مها" and answer the following questions:

١ – من هي؟ | ٢ – أيـن تـسكـن؟ | ٣ – مـاذا تعـمل؟

🎧 **تـمرين ١٢:** "انت دايماً مشغول!" / "انت دايماً مشغول!" **(في البيت)**

Listen to الحوار in its entirety several times to get a general idea of the content. Listen for words/phrases you recognize, and pay attention to tone of voice as well. What is the relationship between the two speakers? Then listen again and focus on the following questions, answering باللغة العربية in as much detail as you can.

1. What does السِّت want?	1. What does السِّت want?
2. How does الرّاجِل respond?	2. How does الرّجال respond?
3. How is the situation resolved?	3. How is the situation resolved?
4. What do you think the following expressions indicate? Use the context and tone of voice of the speakers to help you.	4. What do you think the following expressions indicate? Use the context and tone of voice of the speakers to help you.
- لأ. النهاردا صعب. أنا مشغول جداً جداً. - انت دايمًا مشغول! ايه دا؟!	- لأ. اليوم صعب. أنا مشغول كتير كتير. - إنت دايمًا مشغول! شو هادا؟!
5. What is the sound she uses to express frustration?	5. What is the sound she uses to express frustration?

الحوار

اللغة والثقافة

In the video you are about to watch in تمرين ١٣, you will hear a new response to the expression تشرّفنا!:

تشرَّفنا :   الشَرَف إلنا / الشَرَف لينا

You will also learn a new expression meaning *not really* or *not very*. Pay attention to the way this expression is used in the scene:

مو كتير / مِش قَوي

🎧 **تـمـريـن ١٣:** "موظفة بالأمم المتحدة" / "موظفة في الأمم المتحدة" (في البيت) 🎧

Use your listening strategies to get as much as you can out of this text.

1. First listen: What is the situation? What can you tell about the speakers?

2. Second listen: Plan your stage-two listening goals for each speaker. Get as much information as you can about where they live and what they do. Who mentions a brother? What do we learn about him?

هو	هي

3. In class, share your information with a partner. How much of the dialogue can you re-create? Make up a new dialogue based on this model.

تـمارين المراجعة Review Drills

🎧 **تـمـريـن ١٤: القراءة الجهرية** Reading aloud (في البيت أو في الصف) 🎧

Read the following passage, first silently for comprehension, then aloud to practice pronunciation. When you are ready, record the passage and submit it to your teacher either on the website or as directed by your teacher.

نادية طاهـر دَرويـش خالـة مـها. تـسكـن الـسيـدة نادية في مدينـة لـوس أنجـلـيـس في بيـت قـريـب من جامـعة كـاليـفورنيا في مدينة لـوس انجـليـس، وتعمـل موظفـة في بنـك كبـير وهـي متـخصّصـة في الـكـومبـيوتـر. وعندها قطة كبـيرة في العمر اسمها "بسبوسة". نادية تحب الـسَّكـن في ولاية كاليـفورنيا وتحب شغلها وتحب بنت أختها نسرين وتتكلم معها بالتليفون دائماً.

تمرين ١٥: السؤال (في البيت) (في البيت) 🎧

Practice asking and answering questions using old and new فصحى vocabulary words:

١. "............................ هذا الكتاب؟" "من المكتبة".

٢. "............................ عندك صف في المساء؟" "لا، عندي صف في النهار".

٣. "............................ تسكن خالتك؟" "خالتي تسكن في مدينة سِياتِل".

٤. "............................ هذه؟" "هذه ترجمة لقصة من الأدب العربي".

٥. "............................ تدرس في الجامعة؟" "أدرس .... الفرنسية".

٦. "............................ هذا الفيلم؟" "طويل!!"

٧. "............................ مكتب القبول؟" "هو في هذه البناية".

٨. "أين السيارة؟" "............................ في شارع قريب".

٩. "............................ محمد؟" "محمد مترجم .... في الأمم المتّحدة".

١٠. "هل أنتِ .... في هذا المكتب؟" "نعم، أهلاً وسهلاً! هل عندك سؤال؟".

3 درس
Lesson 3

عائلة والدي كبيرة

المفردات

القصة بالعامية: "عيلة بابا كبيرة"

الثقافة:

"عَمّ"

عائلة النَّبي مُحَمَّد

القواعد:

الجمع

جمـع المـؤنَّث

الإضافة

ضمائر الملكية Possessive Pronouns

القراءة: "جامعة بيروت العربية" و "جامعة حلب"

الثقافة: الجامعات العربية

القصة بالفصحى: "عائلة والدي كبيرة"

الاستماع: مع العائلة والأصدقاء

الحِوار: "الله يخلّيهن" "صغير وبكرة يكبر"

🎧 المُفرَدات Vocabulary

Listen to the new vocabulary in formal Arabic and your spoken variety. Note the pronunciation of ض in ضابط in the dialects, reflected in an alternate spelling.

المعنى	المصري	الشامي	الفُصحى
history			التّاريخ
now	دِلْوَقتي	هَلَّق	الآن
congratulations!			مَبروك!
response to مَبروك!	اللّه يِبارِك فيك/فيكي	اللّه يبارِك فيك/ لَك	بارَكَ اللّهُ فيك
son[1]	ج. وْلاد	ج. وْلاد	اِبن ج. أبناء
cousin (male, paternal)	ج. وِلاد عَمّ	ج. وْلاد عَمّ	اِبن عَمّ ج. أبناء عَمّ
grandfather	جِدّ ج. جُدود	جِدّ ج. جْدود	جَدّ ج. أجداد
grandmother	سِتّ	سِتّ، تيتة	جَدّة ج. جَدّات
army	جيش ج. جيوش	جيش ج. جيوش	جَيش ج. جُيوش
law (as a field of study)			الحُقوق
actually, in reality	في الحَقيقة	بالحَقيقة	في الحَقيقة
he teaches	بيدَرِّس	بيعَلِّم	يُدَرِّس
religion			الدّين
letter	جَواب ج. جَوابات	مَكتوب ج. مَكاتيب	رِسالة ج. رَسائِل
husband	جوز	جوز	زَوج ج. أزواج
wife[2]	مراة	مَرة	زَوجة ج. زَوجات
married (adj.)	مِتْجَوِّز/ ة ج. -ين	مِتْجَوِّز/مِتْجَوّزة ج. -ين	مُتَزَوِّج/ة ج. -ون/-ين
picture	صورة ج. صِوَر		صورة ج. صُوَر
officer	ظابِط ج. ظُبّاط	ظابِط ج. ظُبّاط (formal word also used)	ضابِط ج. ضُبّاط
medicine (the profession)			الطِّبّ
I know	باعرَف	بَعرِف	أعرِف
science			عِلم ج. عُلوم
political science			العُلوم السِّياسِيّة
anthropology			عِلم الإنسان
psychology			عِلم النّفس

المعنى	المصري	الشامي	الفُصحى
paternal uncle[3]	عَمّ ج. عِمـام (formal word also used)	عمّ ج. عْمـام	عَمّ ج. أعْمـام
(extended) family	عيلة ج. عائِلات	عيلة ج. عيَل	عائِلـة ج. عـائِلات
relative	قَريب ج. قَرايب	قَريب ج. قَرايبين	قَريب ج. أقارِب
college, school (in a university)		كِلِّيّة ج. كِلِّيات	كُلِّيّـة ج. كُلِّيّـات
how many?[4]	كام؟		كَم؟
engineering			الهَندَسة

Notes on Vocabulary Usage

1. The plurals وْلاد أولاد refer to children regardless of gender.

2. The spoken word for wife, مراة مَرة, is only used in possessive constructions (e.g., his wife, your wife, Hussein's wife), and ة is always pronounced as ت .

3. Arabic has very specific terminology to refer to members of العائلة. You have learned four of these words already: ابن عَمّ, عَمّة, خالة, عَمّ, and from them you can extrapolate the rest. Use what you know about المذكر and المؤنث to complete the following diagrams of the father's and mother's sides of the family, including aunts, uncles, their husbands and wives, and cousins.

4. The interrogative particle كام؟ كَم؟ is always followed by a singular noun. In formal Arabic, this noun takes a تنوين فتحة ending: كم طالباً في الصف؟. In spoken Arabic, no endings are used: كام طالب في الفصل؟ عندك كم ولد؟.

Diagram A

في عائلة الوالد

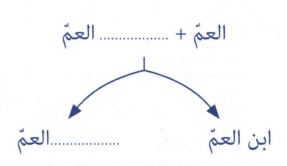

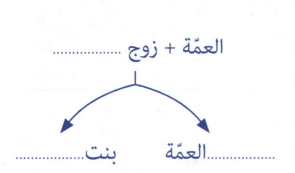

Diagram B

في عائلة الوالدة

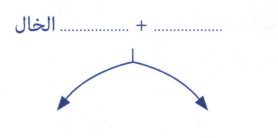

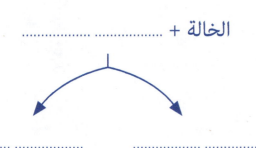

تـمريـن ١: عائلتي (في البيت)

Draw your own family tree, naming all your aunts, uncles, and cousins, and label them with the appropriate Arabic words.

تـمريـن ٢: جمل المفردات (في البيت)

استمعوا الى جمل المفردات واكتبوا الجمل من "التاريخ" إلى "صورة".

Listen to the sentences given to illustrate each new formal word, and write out the sentences from التاريخ to صورة.

تمـريـن ٣: المفردات في جمل (في البيت)

Use old and new vocabulary to write about each picture. Write as much as you can, using all the new vocabulary.

تمـريـن ٤ : اسألوا زملاءكم Ask Your Colleagues (في الصف)

Ask your classmates the questions below from the section you have been assigned by your teacher, and take brief notes so that you can report your findings to the group later. When you are asked a question, volunteer as much information as you can. The goal is to use as much language as possible on these topics. If you say the minimum, you will only get the minimum benefit.

A.

1. Who has a relative who teaches? What does he or she teach? Does he or she like to teach?

2. Who has a friend or relative in the army, and which army? Is he or she an officer? Does he or she like working in the army?

3. Who has lots of aunts and uncles? How many? (Remember to specify which side of the family.)

4. Who is majoring in a science? Who likes to study the sciences?

5. Who sees their cousins a lot? Where?

6. Who is really busy this semester? How many classes do they have?

B.

1. Who likes politics? (Hint: Make the adjective السياسيّة into a feminine noun.) Do they watch the news every day?

2. Who has a stepmother or stepfather? (Hint: Two words.) What does he or she do?

3. Who has letters from their grandparents? Who has text messages from them?

4. Who will go see their extended family soon? (Hint: You can use "close" to mean "close in time.")

5. Who has relatives who know other languages? Which languages?

6. Who doesn't really like their relatives that much?

القصة بالعامية

تمـريـن ٥: "عيلة بابا كبيرة" / "عيلة بابا كبيرة" (في البيت وفي الصف) 🎧

A. At home, listen to نسرين/مها using the strategies you have learned, and answer in Arabic. Write as much as you can about each of these أقارب including الشغل and العيلة:

عن مها: مين همّ؟:	عن نسرين: مين هنّ؟:
أ. محمود	أ. ماهر
ب. عادل	ب. ياسين
جـ. أحمد	جـ. عصام
د. فاطمة	د. أميرة
	هـ. How does Nisreen say feminine *this*?

B. In class, compare your information with a partner's and discuss: Why is نسرين/مها looking at pictures?

تمـريـن ٦: جمل المفردات (في البيت) 🎧

استمعوا الى جمل المفردات واكتبوا الجمل من "ضابط" إلى "الهَندسة".

Listen to the sentences given that illustrate each new formal word and write out the sentences from ضابط to كم.

الثقافة

"عَمّ"

In many parts of the Arab world, it is common to hear the term عَمّ outside the family circle. The words عمّ, عمّة, خال and خالة may refer to and address distant relatives and in-laws as well as close family friends a generation older than the speaker. Mothers-in-law and fathers-in-law are addressed and referred to in many areas as عمّي and مَرة عمّي , and a stepmother may be addressed as خالتي. A man who marries into the family may be addressed by younger members of the family as عَمّي, and a distant female relative may be called عَمّتي. The word عَمّ is also used as a term of respect for an older man of low social status. The exact usage of these terms varies according to regional dialect and local customs.

However, the terms عمّ/ة and خال/ة do not refer to or address spouses of biological aunts and uncles, who are addressed and referred to using terms for "husband of my aunt" and "wife of my uncle":

المعنى	المصري	الشامي	الفُصحى
aunt (married to عمّ)	مِراة عَمّي	مَرة عَمّي	اِمرأة عَمّي
aunt (married to خال)	مِراة خالي	مَرة خالي	اِمرأة خالي
uncle (married to عمة)	جوز عَمّتي	جوز عَمّتي	زَوج عَمّتي
uncle (married to خالة)	جوز خالتي	جوز خالتي	زَوج خالَتي

عائلة النَّبي مُحَمَّد

Arab culture as we know it evolved in the context of Islamic history, and therefore knowledge of Islamic history is important to understanding Arab culture. Non-Muslim Arabs learn this history too—after all, it is a shared history if not a shared religion. The family tree of the Prophet Muhammad is significant for both its religious and historical roles. Many important Muslim leaders and dynasty founders are related to the Prophet by blood or marriage.

prophet	نَبِيّ
caliph	خَليفة ج. خُلَفاء
Shi'ites	الشّيعة
Sunnis	السُّنّة

Read the family tree below and see how much history you can find.

the Rightly-Guided Caliphs (first four after the Prophet's death)	الخُلَفاء الرّاشِدون
the Umayyads, first Islamic dynasty 661-750 (CE)	الأُمَويّون
the Abbasids, second Islamic dynasty 750-1258 (CE)	العَبّاسِيّون
the Hashimites, present-day rulers of Jordan	الهاشِميّون

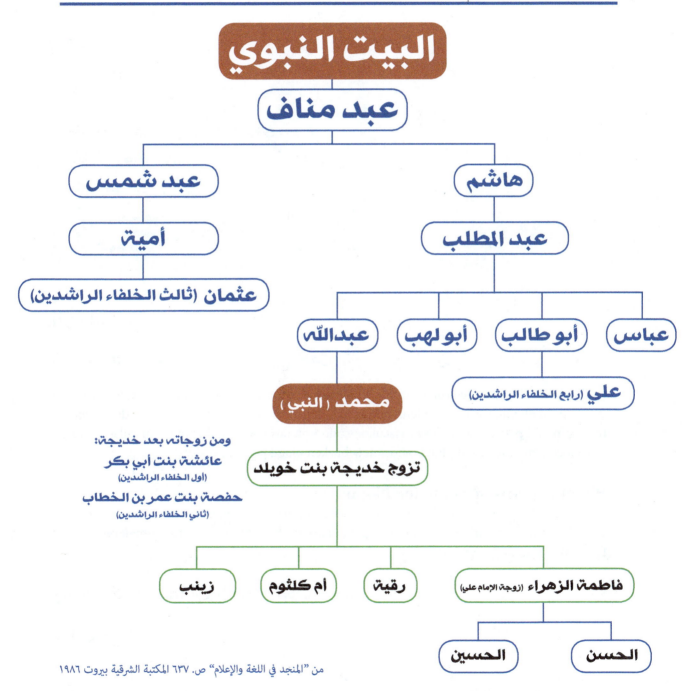

البيت النبوي

من "المنجد في اللغة والإعلام" ص. ٦٣٧ المكتبة الشرقية بيروت ١٩٨٦

تمرين ٧: نشاط قراءة (في الصف)

Use the chart to find these relationships among members of the Prophet's family.

١. النَّبي محمد هو _____ عبد الله.

٢. عبّاس وأبو طالب وأبو لهب هم _____ عبد المطّلب.

٣. علي هو _____ النبي محمد.

٤. الخلفاء الراشِدون هم _____ و _____
_____ و _____ .

٥. أولاد النبي محمد هم _____ و _____
_____ و _____ .

٦. عائشة هي زوجة النبي محمد وهي _____ أبي بكر.

٧. فاطمة الزَّهراء هي _____ علي.

٨. عَبّاس هو _____ النبي محمد.

٩. النَّبي محمد هو _____ الحَسَن والحُسين.

١٠. أُم كُلثوم هي _____ الحسن والحسين.

القواعد

الجمع: جمع المُؤَنَّث (ات-) ووزن فُعَل

We learned some basic rules for masculine plural patterns in lesson 2. Let's continue to learn more about plurals, focusing on feminine plurals in this lesson. In lesson 2 we introduced several broken plural patterns as well as masculine sound plurals and plural agreement rules. Here we introduce feminine sound plurals and a new broken plural pattern, فُعَل.

Plural Patterns of Feminine Nouns

Many—but not all—feminine nouns whose singular form ends in ة take the plural suffix ات–. This includes both human and nonhuman nouns. Remember that nonhuman plurals take feminine singular agreement:

جامعات كبيرة   سيارات يابانية   لغات أوروبية

عائلات عربية   سيّارات صغيرة   حاجات جديدة

Memorize these words as taking ات– plurals:

 Plurals taking ات–

الجمع	المفرد
جامِعـات	جامِعة
سَيّـارات	سَيّـارة
عَرَبيّات	عَرَبيّة
وِلايـات	وِلاية
ساعـات	ساعة
جِنسِيّـات	جِنسيّة
لُغـات	لُغة
كَلِمـات	كَلِمة
صَفَحـات	صَفْحة
طاوِلات	طاوِلة
بِنايـات	بِناية
تَرجَمـات	تَرجَمة
مَكتَبـات	مَكتَبة
سَنَوات	سَنة
حاجات	حاجة

Note, however, that not all singular nouns ending in ة take the plural suffix ات–. Words that have the singular pattern فُعلة or فِعلة form their plurals with فُعَل and فِعَل respectively. Learn these pairs:

 Plurals of the فِعَل and فُعَل patterns

الجمع	المفرد
أُسَر	أُسْرة
غُرَف	غُرْفة
جُمَل	جُملة
أُمَم	أُمّة
قُطَط	قُطّة
قِصص	قِصّة
عِيَل	عيلة
نِمَر	نِمرة
أُوَض	أوضة
إِوَض	أوضة

جمـع المؤنـث: – ات Human Feminine Plurals

Nouns and adjectives that refer to groups of human females are highly regular in formal Arabic. With the exception of the words for women (see below), all the feminine human plural nouns and adjectives you know end in ات–:

الجمع	المفرد
بَنات	بِنت
أخَوات	أُخْت
طالِبات	طالِبة
أُستاذات	أُستاذة
سَيِّدات	سَيِّدة
خالات	خالة
جارات	جارة
فِلِسْطينِيّات	فِلِسْطينِيّة
مُتَرجِمات	مُتَرجِمة
مُتَخَصِّصات	مُتَخَصِّصة
مَشغولات	مَشغولة
لَطيفات	لَطيفة
صَغيرات	صَغيرة

Listen to and memorize the plural forms of "woman," two of which are exceptions to the rules you just learned:

سِتّ ج. سِتّات   مَرَة ج. نِسوان   اِمرَأة ج. نِساء

In urban Arabic dialects, feminine plural agreement with adjectives is rare. Compare these formal and spoken phrases:

بنات مَبسوطين   بنات مَبسوطين   بنات سَعيدات

سِتّات طيِّبين   نِسوان طيِّبين   نساء طَيِّبات

More Broken Plural Patterns with Medial Alif

Many singular nouns that have a long vowel have plural patterns that consist of three syllables, the vowels of which are regular: fatHa, alif, and kasra or ي in that order. Some patterns add consonant و. Words with four root consonants are uncommon but they do exist, and they include words borrowed from other languages. Note that ة does occasionally occur on human plurals, such as دكاترة and أساتذة. Listen to and learn these plurals:

الجمع	المفرد
شَوارِع	شارِع
شَبابيك	شُبّاك
أَساتِذة	أُستاذ
دَكاتِرة	دُكتور
دَفاتِر	دَفتر

تَمريـن ٨: الجمع (في البيت)

List and describe some things one can find in the following, as the example demonstrates:

مثال: في جامعة قَطَر أساتذة قَطَرِيّون و أستاذات قطرِيّات.

١. في عائلتي .... و ....

٢. في صفحتي على *Facebook* .... و ....

....

٣. في الجامعة .... و ....

.... و

٤. في الأمم المتحدة .... و ....

....

٥. في صفّي .... و ....

.... و

٦. في الولايات المتحدة .... و ....

....

٧. في الشارع .... و ....

.... و

تمرين ٩: كم عندك؟ (في الصف)

Find out more information from الجيران في الصف. Remember to use "كم؟" with a singular noun to ask the question and to use a plural noun if the answer is between three and ten. If the question involves a preposition, it goes before كم.

في كم بيت ...؟ ←

1. How many classes do they have? How many male vs. female professors?
2. How many siblings do they have? How many really close friends?
3. How many names do they have?
4. How many cities and states do their relatives live in?
5. How many languages do they know (even a single word)?
6. How many employees does their mother or father work with?
7. How many professors know them?
8. How many cars does your family have?
9. How many rooms are in their house?
10. How many hours do they study at home and at school in a day?

الإضافة

The iDaafa (also called "the construct phrase") is one of the fundamental structures of Arabic grammar. Formally, الإضافة consists of two or more nouns placed together to form **a relationship of possession or belonging.** You have seen many examples of الإضافة, among them:

منطقة بروكلين   مكتب القبول   ولاية كاليفورنيا   جامعة نيويورك

There are three important points to remember about الإضافة:

1. The relationship between the two (or more) nouns may be thought of as equivalent to the formal English use of the word "of" (as in, "the story of the woman" or "the jacket of the boy"). Arabic has no alternative construction for expressing this relationship between nouns. Thus, to say "the woman's story" in Arabic, you must first reconstruct the phrase to "the story of the woman": قصة الإمرأة. Note that many compound words in English are also expressed using الإضافة, for example:

housework   شغل البيت

2. Only the final word in an إضافة can take الـ or a possessive suffix. Study the following examples and note that the first word in each إضافة is **definite by definition** and that is why it cannot take الـ. In the final example, remember that New York is definite because it is a proper noun.

my father's family = the family of my father	عائلة والدي
the professor's office = the office of the professor	مكتب الأستاذة
the student's notebook = the notebook of the student	دفتر الطالب
New York University = The University of New York	جامعة نيويورك

These simple iDaafas all consist of two nouns. Complex iDaafas, on the other hand, contain more than two nouns, in which case all nonfinal nouns behave like the first noun in the phrase and never take الـ. Examine the following إضافة, which contains four nouns:

| Maha's father's cousin = the son of the uncle of the father of Maha | ابن عم والد مها |

Remember that a possessive pronoun can only occur on the final noun in an إضافة. The following phrase will help you remember this rule:

| my telephone number | رقم تليفوني |

3. In الإضافة the ة must always be pronounced as ت on all words in which it appears except the final word in the إضافة.

Listen to the following words, read first in isolation, then as the first part of an إضافة, and compare the pronunciations.

٤. غرفة: غرفة ابن عمّي	١. مدينة: مدينة نيويورك
٥. صورة: صورة والدتي	٢. جامعة: جامعة العين
٦. كلية: كلية العلوم السياسية	٣. عائلة: عائلة والدي

تمـريـن ١٠: الإضافة (في البيت)

This exercise is available online only.

Possessive Pronouns ضمائر المِلِكيّة

You have seen and used several possessive pronouns in Arabic:

ابنها	اسرته	والدي	اسمك	اسمي

Notice that these pronouns are suffixes, and that this order matches that of الإضافة, since nouns with possessive pronouns are kinds of iDaafa constructions. **Remember: ة is written and pronounced as ت when a pronoun suffix is added.**

 The possessive pronouns corresponding to the subject pronouns you know are:

المصري	الشامي	الفُصحى	Subject Pronoun الضمير
ـي	ـي	ـي	أنا
ـكَ	ـكَ	ـكَ	أنتَ
ـكِ	ـكِ	ـكِ	أنتِ
ـهُ	ـهُ ¹	ـهُ	هو
ـها	ـها ²	ـها	هي
ـنا	ـنا	ـنا	نحن
ـكو	ـكُن	ـكُم	أنتم
ـهُم	ـُن (ـهُن)	ـهُم	هم

The pronunciation of some of the vowels in these endings varies slightly among different varieties of Arabic. The spoken endings are fixed for each dialect. In formal Arabic, the pronunciation of words with possessive suffixes varies slightly with the different grammatical endings. For now, learn to recognize the different pronunciations without worrying about the reasons for the differences. Listen to the noun بيت with the three endings that you will see and hear in very formal Arabic:

بيتي	بيتي	بيتي
بيتَكَ	بيتَكَ	بيتَكَ
بيتِكِ	بيتِكِ	بيتُكِ
بيته	بيتَهُ	بيتُهُ
بيتها	بيتَها	بيتُها
بيتنا	بيتَنا	بيتُنا
بيتِكُم	بيتَكُم	بيتُكُم
بيتِهِم	بيتَهُم	بيتُهُم

¹ Final ـه in both Egyptian and Levantine is not pronounced (except in Egyptian if the word is negated).
² This pronoun, and sometimes the plural ـهن, is spelled with ـه even though it is never pronounced, reflecting the relationship with formal Arabic.

Possessive pronoun forms are also used with prepositions. Listen and practice aloud:

المَصري	الشامي	الفُصحى
عَندي	عَندي	عِندي
عَندَك عَندِك	عَندَك عَندِك	عِندَكَ عِندَكِ
عَندُه عَندَها	عَندُه عَندها	عِندَهُ عِندَها
عَندِنا	عَندِنا	عِندَنا
عَندُكو	عَندكُن	عِندَكُم
عَندُهُم	عَندُن	عِندَهُم

Finally, listen to the negation of عند with pronouns in the varieties you are learning[3]:

المَصري	الشامي	الفُصحى
ما عَنديش	ما عَندي	لَيسَ عِندي
ما عَندَكش ما عَندِكيش	ما عَندَك ما عَندِك	لَيسَ عِندَكَ لَيسَ عِندَكِ
ما عَندوش، ما عَندُهوش ما عَندَهاش	ما عَندُه ما عَندها	لَيسَ عِندَهُ لَيسَ عِندَها
ما عَندِناش	ما عَندنا	لَيسَ عِندَنا
ما عَندُكوش	ما عَندكُن	لَيسَ عِندَكُم
ما عَندُهُمْش	ما عَندُن	لَيسَ عِندَهُم

[3] You can see here that some of the Egyptian forms have long vowels in the final syllable. Egyptian stress patterns are very regular and easily identifiable, and you will learn them by listening and imitating.

تمرين ١١: ضمائر الملكية (في البيت) 🎧

This exercise is available online only.

تمرين ١٢: أي شيء؟ (في الصف)

With a partner, take turns saying these sentences to each other. Since they are a bit vague, your partner will ask for clarification by asking: "أي..؟". You must then clarify by using an إضافة, as the example demonstrates:

مثال: "أحب هذا الكتاب!" – "أي كتاب؟" – "كتاب علم النفس".

١. أحب الصور!

٢. أنا متخصص في التاريخ.

٣. يعملون في المركز.

٤. هل تعرفين العنوان؟

٥. ابنتي تتكلّم عن الكلّيّة.

٦. عايز/ة اسكن في منطقة كويسة. / بدي اسكن بمنطقة منيحة.

٧. عايز/ة اشوف البلد. / بدي اشوف البلد.

تمرين ١٣: محادثة "هاي صورة مين؟" / "صورة مين دي؟" (في البيت وفي الصف) 🎧

1. At home, choose some pictures of your family to take to class.

2. In class, watch the conversation between Maha/Nisreen and her father. How does she say "Whose picture is this"? How would you say "What is this a picture of"? Use this construction and other iDaafas to talk about الصور you brought to class with you.

تمـرين ١٤: الإضافة (في الصف)

Read the following sentences describing مها وعائلتها, first silently, then aloud. Pay special attention to the pronunciation of ة in الإضافات.

١. مها بنت مصرية عمرها ٢٠ سنة وهي تسكن في منطقة بروكلين.

٢. والدة مها فلسطينية ولكن عندها الجنسية المصرية.

٣. عائلة والد مها كبيرة ومها لها أقارب كثيرون.

٤. خالة مها تسكن في مدينة لوس أنجليس في ولاية كاليفورنيا وجدتها ساكنة في القاهرة.

٥. والدها من القاهرة، وهو يعمل في قسم الترجمة في الأمم المتحدة.

٦. في الحقيقة، أحمد هو ابن عم والد مها وهو متخصص في العلوم السياسية.

٧. حَنان ابنة عمة مها، وهي أستاذة متخصصة في علم النفس بجامعة الأزهَر في القاهرة وزوجها أستاذ في كليّة الهندسة.

٨. هذه رسالة من زوجة عمها أحمد، وهذه صورة أسرتها.

القراءة

تمـرين ١٥: "جامعة بيروت العربية" و "جامعة حلب" (في الصف)

Following are the listings from two Arab universities. Compare them to see how similar and different their colleges and departments are. Do the colleges or schools have the same departments? Use your grammatical knowledge (of such things as roots and iDaafas) to help you guess the meanings of new words.

كليات جامعة بيروت العربية	كليات جامعة حلب

كليات جامعة حلب

كلية الهندسة
كلية الهندسة المدنية
كلية الهندسة الميكانيكية
كلية الهندسة المعمارية
كلية الهندسة الكهربائية والإلكترونية
كلية الهندسة المعلوماتية
كلية الهندسة التقنية

كلية الطب

كلية طب الأسنان

كلية الصيدلة

كلية التمريض

كلية الزراعة
كلية الزراعة الثانية بإدلب

كلية العلوم
كلية العلوم الثانية بإدلب

كلية الاقتصاد

كلية الفنون الجميلة التطبيقية

كلية الشريعة

كلية الآداب والعلوم الإنسانية
كلية الآداب والعلوم الإنسانية
الثانية بإدلب

كلية الحقوق
كلية الحقوق الثانية بإدلب

كلية التربية

معهد التراث العلمي العربي

المعهد العالي للغات

كليات جامعة بيروت العربية

كلية الآداب
أقسام اللغات
أ- قسم اللغة العربية وآدابها
ب- قسم اللغة الانجليزية وآدابها
جـ- قسم اللغة الفرنسية وآدابها

أقسام العلوم الإنسانية
١- قسم الجغرافيا
٢- قسم التاريخ
٣- قسم الفلسفة
٤- قسم الاجتماع
٥- قسم علم النفس
٦- قسم الإعلام

كلية الحقوق
١- القانون الخاص
٢- القانون العام
٣- العلاقات الدولية والديبلوماسية

كلية التجارة
- المحاسبة
- إدارة الاعمال
- الاقتصاد
- الدراسات المالية والجمركية

كلية الهندسة
أ- قسم الرياضيات والفيزياء الهندسية
ب- قسم الهندسة الكهربائية
جـ- قسم الهندسة المدنية
د- قسم الهندسة الميكانيكية

كلية الهندسة المعمارية

كلية العلوم
- قسم الرياضيات
- قسم الفيزياء
- قسم الكيمياء
- قسم العلوم البيولوجية والبيئية

كلية الصيدلة
- قسم الكيمياء الصيدلية
- قسم التكنولوجيا الصيدلية
- قسم العقاقير
- قسم الميكروبيولوجيا الصيدلية

كلية الطب
١- قسم التشريح الآدمي
٢- قسم الانسجة والخلايا (الهستولوجيا)
٣- قسم وظائف الاعضاء (الفسيولوجيا)
٤- قسم الكيمياء الحيوية الطبية
٥- قسم الامراض (الباثولوجيا)
٦- قسم الادوية (الفارماكولوجيا)
٧- قسم الجراثيم والميكروبات الدقيقة
(الميكروبيولوجيا) والمناعة
٨- قسم طب المجتمع
٩- قسم التوليد وأمراض النساء
١٠- قسم طب الاطفال

الثقافة: الجامعات العربية

Although Arab universities are similar to American universities in many ways, there are some differences. Many Arab universities divide academic fields or subject areas differently from American universities, which group most academic departments together in a school, such as "School of Engineering," "Law School," "School of Nursing," or "College of Arts and Sciences." Arab universities generally use smaller divisions, such as the School (or College) of Humanities كلية الآداب, the School of Commerce كلية التّجارة, and various science and professional schools. Another difference between the two systems of education is that in Arab universities, medicine and law are undergraduate schools, not graduate schools.

The system of education in most Arab countries has traditionally resembled European models rather than the American liberal arts college. By the second year of high school, students must choose to concentrate either in humanities and social sciences or in mathematics and natural sciences. Once the choice is made, the student's choice of college major is limited, so that a humanities major in high school may not enter a science department in college. Each school or department sets its own academic program, including all of the courses the students take in each year of study; students are not allowed to choose electives. In many public universities in the Arab world, courses are one year long and the student's grade is determined solely on the basis of one exam at the end of the year. In recent years, however, the number of private, American-style universities opening all over the Arab world has grown. If you are interested, do a Web search of Arab universities and see what you find.

تمـريـن ١٦: نشاط كتابة (في الصف أو في البيت)

مكتب القبول في جامعتك has asked you to help prepare a handout in Arabic that they can distribute to الطلاب العرب who are interested in applying to the university. Make an outline of its schools and departments.

القصة بالفصحى

تمـريـن ١٧: "عائلة والدي كبيرة" 🎧

There are two parts to this exercise. Watch القصة بالفصحى and answer the questions below. The dictation exercise can be completed in the book or online.

A. As you listen to Maha tell the story in الفصحى, focus on grammar and the use of و. Listen for الإضافة: How many can you find? Then listen to see how many times you hear و in the text. How many times does Maha use this word? Think about how the use of و affects style.

B. Write what Maha says, filling in the blanks below. You will hear some grammatical markings on nouns with possessive suffixes, such as أسرتُه and ابنُها. These vowels represent formal Arabic grammar, and we will come back to them later in this book.

(١) .... والدي (٢) .... ، أعرف (٣) .... من

(٤) .... و(٥) .... (٦) .... (٧) ....

محمود و(٨) .... ، وهذا (٩) .... عادل و(١٠) .... ،

(١١) .... عادل (١٢) .... (١٣) .... في

(١٤) .... وهذا (١٥) .... أحمد و(١٦) .... هو في

(١٧) .... (١٨) .... (١٩) ....

(٢٠) .... (٢١) .... أحمد (٢٢) .... في كلية

(٢٣) .... (٢٤) .... (٢٥) .... القاهرة

وهو (٢٦) .... (٢٧) .... في (٢٨) ....

العين بالإمارات (٢٩) .... (٣٠) .... و(٣١) ....

(٣٢) .... فاطمة و (٣٣) .... وابنها و(٣٤) ....

الاستماع: مع العائلة والأصدقاء

تمريـن ١٨: مع عائلة مها (في البيت) 🎧

Watch the video "مع عائلة مها" and use your listening strategies to get as much information as possible about each speaker. Then, answer the following questions:

١. اسمه: ....

٢. زوجته: ....

٣. أولاده: ....

٤. يسكن في: ....

٥. يعمل في: ....

الحوار

اللغة والثقافة

"الله يخَلّيهُن" / "رَبِّنا يِخَلّيهُم" May God keep them (safe and well)

You have seen that the expression ما شاء الله is often used when seeing or talking about someone's children. You will also hear, and should use, the phrase الله يخَلّيهُن / ربِّنا يِخَلّيهُم to wish others' children well.

بُكرة Tomorrow

The word بُكرة has a cultural dimension beyond its dictionary meaning. In the dialogue you will hear it used to refer not to the literal tomorrow but to a metaphorical one—a day not far off, a day that will come soon. In this sense, بُكرة helps convey a message of "hang in there, it will work out." Conversely, بُكرة can imply a metaphorical tomorrow that will never come: Hence the Egyptian proverb بكرة في المشمش, refers to the apricot season that comes and goes before you know it. بكرة في المشمش means that you will wait and wait but it will never happen.

🎧 تـمرين ١٩: "الله يخَلّيهن" / "صغير وبكرة يكبر" (في البيت)

Use good listening strategies to get as much as you can out of the conversation you will watch in the video clip. Listen for words/phrases you recognize, and pay attention to tone of voice as well.

1. What is the relationship between the two speakers? What kind of conversation is this? After you have formed some ideas, watch several more times to focus on the following questions, and answer باللغة العربية in as much detail as you can.

2. Which aspects of her life does each one talk about? List them here:

الستّ الشابّة:	أم حسن:	المرأة الشابّة:	أم مازن:

الستّ مبسوطة ليه؟	أم حسن زعلانة ليه؟	ليش المرة مبسوطة؟	ليش أم مازن زعلانة؟

تـمارين المراجعة

تـمرين ٢٠: القراءة الجَهريّة (في البيت أو في الصف) 🎧

Read the following passage, first silently for comprehension, then aloud to practice pronunciation. When you are ready, record the passage and submit it to your teacher either online or as instructed by your teacher.

الدكتور عِصام النّوري هو ابن عم الدكتور حسن النّوري، والد نسرين. والدكتور عصام أستاذ في كليّة العلوم السّياسية في جامعة دمشق وهو متخصّص في حقوق الإنسان ولكن يدرّس الآن في السعودية، وهو سعيد في عمله وعنده أصحاب سعوديّون وعرب. والدكتور عصام متزوج وله

ثلاثة أولاد ولكن زوجته تسكن في دمشق مع الأولاد وهو بعيد عن الأسرة ولا يحبّ هذا، ولكن زوجته سعيدة في مدينة دمشق وهي قريبة من عائلتها، والأولاد أيضاً.

درس
4
Lesson 4

كيف أحفظ كل الأسماء؟!

المفردات

القصة بالعامية: «كيف رح احفظ كل الأسامي؟!» «ازيّ احفظ كل الأسامي؟!»

الثقافة: الأكل العربي

الاستماع: «بتحبوا تشربوا شي؟» «تشربوا حاجة الأول؟»

القراءة: «مطعم باب الحارة»

القواعد (١):

الفعل المضارع وتقديم أوزان الفعل The Present Tense Verb

نفي الفعل المضارع

القواعد (٢):

ضمائر النصب Object Pronouns

القصة بالفصحى: «كيف أحفظ كل الأسماء؟!»

القواعد (٣):

الجملة الاسمية

الجملة الفعلية

الاستماع: مع العائلة والأصدقاء

الحوار: «نوّرتي الشام» «نوّرتي مصر»

تمارين المراجعة

 المُفرَدات Vocabulary

Listen to the new vocabulary alone and in context in sentences:

المعنى	المصري	الشامي	الفُصحى
he eats[1]	ياكُل	ياكُل	يَأكُل
yesterday	اِمبارِح	امبارح	أمْس
first			أوّل
primary, elementary			اِبتِدائيّ/ة
I memorize	أحفَظ	اِحفَظ	أحفَظ
sweets, desserts		حِلو	حَلَويّات، حُلو
vegetables			خُضار
school			مَدرَسة ج. مَدارِس
I remember	فاكِر / فاكْرة ج. فاكْرين	بِتذَكَّر	أتَذَكَّر
classmate, colleague (m.)	زِميل ج. زَمايل، زُمَلا	ج. زَمايل	زَميل ج. زُمَلاء
classmate, colleague (f.)			زَميلة ج. -ات
traveling[2]			السَّفَر (من ، إلى)
I travel	آسافِر	اسافِر (عَ)	أُسافِر إلى
salad			سَلَطة ج. -ات
he listens to	يِسمَع	يِسمَع	يَستَمِع إلى
fish			سَمَك
soup			شوربة
friend (m.)	صاحِب ج. أصحاب	رفيق ج. رِفقات	صَديق ج. أصدِقاء
friend (f.)	صاحْبة ج. -ات	رفيقة ج. -ات	صَديقة ج. -ات

المعنى	المصري	الشامي	الفُصحى
childhood			الطُّفولة
restaurant			مَطعَم ج. مَطاعِم
individual (person)			فَرد ج. أفراد
fruits			فَواكِه
before[3]	قَبل + اسم قَبل ما + verb	قَبل + اسم قَبل ما + verb	قَبَلَ (+ اسم)
he reads	يِقرا	يِقرا	يَقرَأ
he says	يِقول	يقول	يَقول
he writes	يِكتِب	يِكتُب	يَكتُب
all (of the ...)	كُل	كِلّ	كُلّ + الجمع
he was[4]	كانْ	كانْ	كانَ
I was	كُنتْ	كِنتْ	كُنتُ
meat			لَحم

Notes on Vocabulary Usage

1. The root that refers to eating is ء ك ل. Remember that hamza is a consonant and can be part of a root. It is also part of the root ق ر ء for words that have to do with reading or reciting. Since the stem vowel in يَقرَأ and the prefix vowel in يَأكُل are fatHa, the hamza is written on alif in these verbs. What happens if we conjugate يَأكُل in first person and add the prefix أ to the root letter أ? Remember that two hamzas combine to make alif madda: آ. Thus, آكُل *I eat*.

2. The word السَّفَر is a noun (gerund), not an adjective (participle). It can be used in sentences like "I love traveling!" However, it cannot be used in sentences corresponding to English "I am traveling," with the verb "to be," because, as a noun, it cannot express an ongoing action that a particular person is in the process of doing.

3. The word قبل is a preposition and can be used before any noun. In order to use a verb after it, we need a word to link them. In spoken Arabic, the linking word ما performs this task. Study these examples:

قَبل ما + verb (no b):

لازم اشوف التليفزيون قبل ما انام !	لازم اشوف التليفزيون قبل ما انام!
بتعملي ايه قبل ما تروحي الفصل؟	شو بتعملوا قبل ما تروحوا ع الصف؟
عايزة تتكلمي مع ماما وبابا قبل ما تسافري؟	بدّك تحكي مع الماما والبابا قبل ما تسافري؟

4. In Arabic, past-tense verbs are conjugated with suffixes (not prefixes like present-tense verbs). The past-tense verb كان was/were uses these past-tense subject suffixes. Listen, repeat aloud, and learn this verb, and notice while you are doing so that the pronouns themselves will help you remember some of the forms 🎧:

المصري	الشامي	الفُصحى	
كُنْت	كِنْت	كُنتُ	أنا
كُنْت	كِنْت	كُنتَ	أنتَ
كُنتي	كِنتي	كُنتِ	أنتِ
كانْ	كانْ	كانَ	هو
كانِتْ	كانِتْ	كانَتْ	هي
كُنّا	كِنّا	كُنّا	نحن
كُنتوا	كِنتوا	كُنتُم	أنتم
كانوا	كانوا	كانوا	هم

تـمـريـن ١: المفردات الجديدة (في البيت) 🎧

Practice using new vocabulary by completing the sentences:

١. هذه صُوَر كل .... عائلتي: أنا ووالدي ووالدتي وأخي وجدّي وجدّتي.

٢. قبل الجامعة، .... طالبة في المدرسة الامريكية في مدينة عمّان.

٣. هل .... الطلاب في صفّكم أمريكيون؟

٤. كل سنة، .... زوجتي الى العراق حيث تسكن عائلتها.

٥. .... في مدينتنا .... عربي ممتاز وأنا اذهب اليه دائماً مع .... ـي ونأكل الحمص والفلافل والتبّولة.

٦. روبرت هو .... ـي من الطّفولة ونحن كنّا في نفس .... الابتدائية.

٧. أنا طالبة في الصف _____ في اللغة العربية واليزابيث وليلى وكريس _____ في الصف.

٨. أنا نَباتِيّ vegetarian لا آكل _____ ولكن آكل _____ و _____ .

٩. _____ الصف كنتُ أدرس في المكتبة.

١٠. أنا مشغولة اليوم: لازم _____ ٤٠ صفحة في كتاب علم النفس، ولازم _____ ورقة لصف الدين ، ولازم _____ كل الكلمات الجديدة لصف اللغة الألمانية.

تـمـريـن ٢: كان (في البيت) 🎧

Situate these actions and states in the past by using the correct form of كان :

١. _____ أسكن في الشرق الاوسط قبل ٥ سنوات.

٢. يا ليلى، أين _____ صباح اليوم؟

٣. والدتها _____ موظفة كبيرة في الامم المتحدة.

٤. أنا وزملائي _____ نستمع الى المحاضرة، وقبل ذلك _____ نأكل في الكافتيريا.

٥. في طفولته _____ ابني يحب الفواكه.

٦. يا شباب، أين _____ في المساء؟

٧. الأولاد _____ يشربون الحليب.

٨. هل _____ تقرأون في السيارة؟

٩. مع مَن _____ تأكل في المطعم يا ابراهيم؟

تـمـريـن ٣: جمل المفردات (في البيت) 🎧

استمعوا الى جمل المفردات واكتبوا الجمل من "يأكل" إلى "سمك".

تـمـريـن ٤: كلمات جديدة وقواعد قديمة (في الصف)

Read these sentences, first silently for meaning, then aloud to a partner.
Pay attention to iDaafas and the pronunciation of ة and الـ .

١. زوجة خالي تُدرِّس في مدرسة ابتدائية.

٢. أحب شوربة الطماطم وسلطة الفواكه في هذا المطعم.

٣. كنت أدرس في مدينة "زيوريخ" في سويسرا في طفولتي.

٤. هذه الإمرأة تعمل في مكتب السفر في الجامعة الامريكية.

٥. أتذكر هذه المدرسة – هي مدرسة أصدقاء طفولتي.

٦. تسكن أسرتي في البيت الأول في شارع "المنصور".

٧. كنت أستمع إلى الراديو في غرفة زميلتي قبل الصف.

٨. كيف أحفظ أسماء كل زملائنا الجُدُد؟!

٩. لا أعرف كل أفراد عائلتي الكبيرة.

١٠. والدة صديقتي تسافر الى أوروبا دائماً.

تـمـريـن ٥: اسألوا زملاءكم (في الصف)

Ask as many زملاء as you can and find out:

A.

1. Who likes to travel? Do they travel every year? Who do they travel with? Where do they want to travel?
2. Who listens to classical music الموسيقى. What else do they listen to?
3. What they remember from their childhood.
4. Who has a problem with their roommate(s)?
5. What restaurants in the university area they like.
6. What they eat every day. What they eat when they have a cold بَرد عنده/ها.
7. What their friends do. Get as much information as you can about their friends.
8. What books they used to read in school.

B.

1. What they remember from their elementary school. Do they remember their first-grade teacher(s)?
2. Who has a roommate or housemate? Get as much information as you can about their roommate.
3. Which member(s) of their family was a student at this university?
4. Where they were before class today.
5. Who is vegetarian نَباتيّ. What do and don't they eat?

6. What they used to watch on TV in their childhood.

7. What music they used to listen to.

8. Whether they like fruit salad. What desserts do they like to eat also?

القصة بالعامية

تمريـن ٦: "كيف رح احفظ كل الأسامي؟!" / "ازايّ أحفظ كل الأسامي؟!"
(في البيت) 🎧

Listen to مها using the strategies you have learned. Write a **short paragraph** for each question. You may use الفصحى and/or المصري words and expressions.	Listen to نسرين using the strategies you have learned. Write a **short paragraph** for each question. You may use الفصحى and/or الشامي words and expressions.
١. مها فاكرة ايه من طفولتها؟	١. شو بتتذكر نسرين من طفولتها؟
٢. مها فاكرة خالد ولّا سامية *more*؟ ليه؟	٢. مين بتتذكر نسرين *more*: طارق ولّا سامية؟ ليش؟
٣. ايه هي مشكلة مها؟	٣. نسرين بدها تشوف طارق ولّا لأ؟ ليش/ليش لأ؟
	٤. شو هي مشكلة نسرين؟
	٥. How does she say *these* (people)?

تمريـن: ٧ جمل المفردات (في البيت) 🎧

استمعوا الى جمل المفردات واكتبوا الجمل من "شوربة" إلى "لحم".

الثقافة: الأكل العربي

The rich regional cuisines of the Arab world reflect the long history of civilization in the Middle East and the Mediterranean and include contributions from Persian, Turkish, and various other cultures. Rice in the Gulf and rice and/or bread in Egypt and the Levant are part of every meal. In North Africa, couscous and bread are staples. You have probably eaten حُمُّص, كَباب, and تَبّولة in a Middle Eastern restaurant. Other popular dishes include salads, vegetable stews flavored with beef or lamb, rice and meat, and various beans and legumes. Most dishes are spiced with garlic, onion, lemon, parsley, and cumin. Watch the slide show to learn the names of some dishes.

الاستماع: مع العائلة والأصدقاء

تمريـن ٨: "بتحبوا تشربوا شي؟" / "تشربوا حاجة الأول؟" 🎧

Watch as طارق/خالد and his friends go to a restaurant. In the Egyptian scene listen for the phrase "bring me." In the Levantine scene you hear a new way to say "please." What do they order? List as many items as you can.

القراءة

تمريـن ٩: مطعم باب الحارة (في الصف)

The next two pages contain excerpts from a menu from مطعم باب الحارة, a Syrian restaurant in Saudi Arabia. Pretend you are there, and take your زملاء to this restaurant. Order a complete meal for everyone, including drinks, appetizers, main dishes and desserts. Your teacher will be your waiter and will be able to explain some of the dishes if you ask بالعربي!

قائمة الطَّعام

الصفحة الرئيسية   باب الحارة
باب الحارة في صور   قائمة الطعام
وجبة اليوم المميزة   طبق اليوم
الأخبار   الحجز
الاتصال بنا   English

المشروبات الباردة

75	اناناس فريش	75	ليمون بالنعنع	75	ليمون فريش
75	تفاح	75	فريز	75	مانجو
50	كولا بأنواعها	75	غريفون	75	برتقال

كوكتيلات

85	كوكتيل فواكه	90	موز وحليب وفريز	85	موز وحليب
90	سلطة فواكه	80	ميلك شيك فريز	80	ميلك شيك شوكولا
				110	سلطة فواكه نستلة+عسل

المشروبات الساخنة

60	قهوة مع الحليب	50	القهوة	50	الشاي بأنواعه
80	كابتشينو	50	كمون	60	اكسبريسو
		60	هوت شوكلت	70	نسكافيه مع حليب

فطور باب الحارة

100	فتة بالدجاج	60	فتة بالزيت	60	فول بالزيت أو اللبن
50	جبنة بيضاء	50	لبنة	50	زيتون مشكل
		50	مربى	50	بيض مقلي

المقبلات الباردة

50	بابا غنوج	50	متبل	50	حمص
50	محمرة	50	حمص بيروتي	125	كبة نية
60	لبنة بالثوم			50	زيتون حلبي

المقبلات الساخنة

50	بطاطا مقلية	25	برك بجبنة 1 قطعة	25	كبة حميص 1 قطعة
100	حمص باللحمة	80	خبز بالثوم 4 قطع	25	جوانح مقلية 1 قطعة

الشوربات

80	شوربة دجاج	80	شوربة عدس	110	شوربة بصل
		80	شوربة ذرة	80	شوربة فطر

السلطات

75	تبولة	75	فتوش	75	سلطة شرقية
75	سلطة زعتر	175	سلطة **باب الحارة**	135	سلطة أرضي شوكي
175	سلطة فرنسية	150	سلطة خس روكفورد	135	سلطة سيزار
75	سلطة سويسرية	85	سلطة معكرونة بالمايونيز	75	سلطة روسية

قائمة الطَّعام

باب الحارة   الصفحة الرئيسية
قائمة الطعام   باب الحارة في صور
الأخبار   وجبة اليوم المميزة
الحجز   طبق اليوم
English   الاتصال بنا

باب الحارة
BAB ALHARA
Restaurant & Café

الوجبات الغربية - اللحومات

فيليه روكفورد	340	فيليه **باب الحارة**	410

الوجبات الغربية - الدجاج

وجبة الشيف	275	دجاج **باب الحارة**	275	كوردون بلو	250
ناغيت	225	شرحات دجاج بالليمون	250	اسكالوب ميلانيز	225
		فخارة **باب الحارة**	250	شرحات دجاج بالفطر	250

المشاوي على الفحم

كباب	180	شقف	225	مشاوي مشكل	210

المعجنات

سباكيتي لولونيز	175	بينيني ارباياتا	200	فرفاللي اسبيناتش	200
بيتزا الفصول الأربعة	150	بيتزا مرغريتا	125	بيتزا **باب الحارة**	175
				بيتزا الكليزوني	150

الكريب

كريب فواكه	85	كريب نيوتيلا مع المكسرات	85	كريب كراميل	85
				كريب زبدة مع مربى	85

البوظة

بنانا سبليت	100	توتي فروتي	90	شوكولامو	75
		جالاكسي	75	بوظة مشكلة	75

أركيلة

أركيلة بأنواعها	100

www.babalhara-rest.com

القواعد ١

الفعل المضارع

verb	فِعل ج أفعال
present or incomplete tense	المُضارع

By now you have seen and heard a number of verbs, among them:

تُسافِر	أحفَظ	أعرِف	أتَذَكَّر	يَستَمِع إلى	يُدرِّس	تعمَل	

These verbs are all مضارع , which is sometimes defined as present tense and sometimes as incomplete tense. المضارع combines both features: It can refer to an incomplete action, usually one taking place in the present, such as "he teaches" or "he is teaching," or a repeated habitual action, such as "she works at the UN" or a state such as "I know." Remember: Any action that stretches over a period of time or takes place repeatedly will involve مضارع because it can express both progressive or ongoing actions ("I am studying") and habitual or repeated actions ("I study" or "I used to study").

In Arabic, the subject of الفعل المضارع is expressed on the verb itself with a prefix or a combination of prefix and suffix, and not with an independent pronoun. Thus, هو يدرس is redundant unless the context calls for some kind of contrastive emphasis (such as "*he* studies") or other stylistic consideration. In the Egyptian dialect, pronoun subjects tend to occur with المضارع more often and are less contrastive than in other varieties.

You have been using verbs for some time now, and you know that the prefixes and suffixes that indicate person remain the same for all مضارع verbs, and the stem of each verb remains constant as well. Once you know the stem of any verb you can easily conjugate it. The table in the next section lists the conjugations of some of the verbs you have learned so far. This is meant to be a review, not a crutch: Verb charts can show you what you need to learn but until you internalize them and have no more need for them, they are not helpful at all in speaking, writing, or understanding what you read and hear.

Main Verbs and Dependent Verbs

In spoken Arabic you have been hearing and using verbs with and without a "بِ" prefix:

بشرب قهوة

باحب آكل حلويات

بدي اروح ع البيت

مش عايز اكتب حاجة!

Notice that the verbs باحب and بشرب in the first two sentences above both have بـ , while the verbs اكتب and اروح in the latter two do not. Notice also that the first two verbs are the main verbs in their respective sentences, while the latter two verbs are dependent on بِدّي / عايز . While these are not verbs grammatically, they may be considered verb-like expressions. The use of بـ indicates that a verb is a main verb. When a verb follows another verb or verb-like expression, it does not take بـ. For now, focus on recognizing this distinction when you hear it and do not worry about producing it. This will come with practice. We will discuss main and dependent verbs in more detail in lessons 9 and 10.

Formal Arabic has the same kind of distinction but with a change in suffix rather than the addition of a prefix. In formal Arabic, the persons أنتَ, أنتِ, أنتُم, and هُم have two variants: one ending in ن and one without it (spelled with a silent alif). Both of these variants are used in formal Arabic; the difference between them is grammatical[1].

The following table presents the prefixes and suffixes for المضارع in all the persons you have learned so far. You are expected to recognize the forms given here in formal Arabic and your dialect, and to choose one set to use.

المصري	الشامي	الفُصحى	
باعمِل/ اعمِل	بعمِل/ اعمِل	أفْعَل	أنا
بتِعمِل/ تِعمِل	بتِعمِل/ تِعمِل	تَفْعَل	أنتَ
بتِعمْلي/ تِعمْلي	بتِعمْلي/ تِعمْلي	تَفْعَلينَ / تَفْعَلي	أنتِ
بيِعمِل / يِعمِل	بيِعمِل/ يِعمِل	يَفْعَل	هو
بتِعمِل/ تِعمِل	بتِعمِل/ تِعمِل	تَفْعَل	هي
بنِعمِل/ نِعمِل	بنِعمِل/ نِعمِل	نَفْعَل	نحن
بتِعمْلوا / تِعمْلوا	بتِعمْلوا/ تِعمْلوا	تَفْعَلونَ / تَفْعَلوا	أنتم
بيِعمْلوا / يِعمْلوا	بيِعمْلوا/ يِعمْلوا	يَفْعَلونَ / يَفْعَلوا	هم

Practice conjugating the new verbs. When studying and learning new verbs, a combination of mechanical and contextual practice usually works best. Practice pronouncing each of the forms aloud, and write them out as you do so to reinforce the sound and spelling of the forms. Then use them in sentences of your own orally and in writing to activate them.

Verb Stems and Their Patterns

While the conjugation prefixes and suffixes remain constant within each variety for all Arabic verbs, the stems themselves take a variety of shapes or patterns. These patterns, however, are limited in number, and learning them is crucial to developing fluency in Arabic. The European tradition of studying Arabic refers to these patterns by number. Several important dictionaries and reference works also use these numbers,

---

[1] This same distinction occurs on the other persons as well in the form of a short Damma or fatHa vowel (such as أفعَلُ or أفعَلَ).The presence or absence of ن and the Damma or kasra depends largely on the presence or absence of certain subordinating or negating particles used in formal Arabic. You will learn these in the later chapters of this book.

so it is helpful to learn them. Here we will introduce four patterns with other patterns to follow in lessons 6 and 8. Spoken Arabic verbs follow these patterns as well, but they do not use the entire set that الفصحى has available. Because of the shifts and omissions of short vowels that occur in informal speech, we will focus here on the patterns in الفصحى.

 Form I or Base Form Verbs: يَفعِل | يَفعَل | يَفعُل

Most of the verbs you have learned so far are Form I verbs. These verbs share the basic stem pattern of two syllables: The first syllable begins with the conjugation prefix and the vowel فتحة in formal Arabic (كسرة or no vowel in spoken Arabic), while the second syllable has the stem vowel, which varies from verb to verb in Form I (it can be فتحة or ضمة or كسرة). Form I is the only verb pattern whose vowels are variable and must be memorized for each new verb; all the other patterns are regular. You can also see that the stem vowels can shift between formal and spoken Arabic: For example, ضمة in formal Arabic often becomes كسرة in spoken Arabic, as happens in the verb يِدرِس.

	يَفعُل		يَفعَل	يَفعِل
أنا	أدرُس		أعمَل	أعرِف
أنتَ	تَدرُس		تَعمَل	تَعرِف
أنتِ	تَدرُسينَ / تَدرُسي		تَعمَلينَ / تَعمَلي	تَعرِفينَ/تَعرِفي
هو	يَدرُس		يَعمَل	يَعرِف
هي	تَدرُس		تَعمَل	تَعرِف
نحن	نَدرُس		نَعمَل	نَعرِف
أنتم	تَدرُسونَ / تَدرُسوا		تَعمَلونَ / تَعمَلوا	تَعرِفونَ/تَعرِفوا
هم	يَدرُسونَ / يَدرُسوا		يَعمَلونَ / يَعمَلوا	يَعرِفونَ/يَعرِفوا

Form II: يُفَعِّل

This pattern has a differently shaped stem: It has three syllables instead of two (including the conjugation prefix), and it has a shadda on the second root consonant. This shadda changes the sound and meaning of the verb, as you can see when you compare يَدرُس with يُدَرِّس. This pair of verbs gives you some idea how the system works: "To teach" is in a sense "to make someone study." We will say more about this relationship in lesson 8.

أنا	أُدَرِّس
أنتَ	تُدَرِّس
أنتِ	تُدَرِّسينَ / تُدَرِّسي
هو	يُدَرِّس
هي	تُدَرِّس
نحن	نُدَرِّس
أنتم	تُدَرِّسونَ / تُدَرِّسوا
هم	يُدَرِّسونَ / يُدَرِّسوا

Form III: يُفاعِل

Like Form II, the Form III pattern also has three syllables, but it has a distinctive alif in the second syllable. The verb يُسافِر is of this form, as is the فصحى verb يُشاهِد to watch:

أنا	أُشاهِد
أنتَ	تُشاهِد
أنتِ	تُشاهِدينَ / تُشاهِدي
هو	يُشاهِد
هي	تُشاهِد
نحن	نُشاهِد
أنتم	تُشاهِدونَ / تُشاهِدوا
هم	يُشاهِدونَ / يُشاهِدوا

Form V: يَتَفَعَّل

The stem pattern of Form V is longer than those of Forms II and III. It resembles the stem of Form II in that its middle root letter takes a shadda, but it contains an additional syllable with the extra consonant ت that is part of the pattern, not the root. Unlike Forms II and III, the vowels of this stem are all فتحة. (The resemblance in form between II and V reflects a relationship in meaning, as you will see later).
The verb يَتَذَكَّر belongs to Form V:

أنا	أتَذَكَّر
أنتَ	تَتَذَكَّر
أنتِ	تَتَذَكَّرينَ/تَتَذَكَّري
هو	يَتَذَكَّر
هي	تَتَذَكَّر
نحن	نَتَذَكَّر
أنتم	تَتَذَكَّرونَ / تَتَذَكَّروا
هم	يَتَذَكَّرونَ / يَتَذَكَّروا

For now, all you need to know about these patterns is that they exist. If you pay attention to the stem shapes of verbs as you learn and study them, you will notice the patterns more and more and remembering verbs will become easier.

Negating the Present Verbs نفي الفعل المضارع

In formal Arabic, الفعل المضارع is negated with لا, which precedes the verb, as the following examples demonstrate:

she does not remember . . .	لا تتذكّر اسمي
he is not working / does not work . . .	لا يعمل في المكتب
we do not study / are not studying . . .	لا ندرس الفرنسية

Formal Arabic has an interrogative particle أ that is used instead of هل in negative questions: The question mark will help you recognize this particle.

Don't you know...?!	ألا تعرفين الموظف الجديد!؟
Don't you remember...?!	ألا تتذكّرون اسمي!؟

 تمـريـن ١٠: الفعل المضارع (في البيت)

This exercise is available online only.

تمـريـن ١١: ماذا يفعلون؟ (في الصف أو في البيت)

Describe what is happening here:

تـمريـن ١٢: ماذا يفعلون؟ (في البيت) 🎧

Figure out what these people must be doing and complete the sentences using verbs you know in the correct form. You may need to add a preposition to some sentences.

١. (نحن) ـــــــــــــــ الأردن كل سنة.

٢. دائماً ـــــــــــــــ الموسيقى في سيارتي.

٣. أخي ـــــــــــــــ هذا الكتاب الآن.

٤. خالتي ـــــــــــــــ لي رسائل دائماً.

٥. هل ـــــــــــــــ اللغة الإيطالية يا رندة؟

٦. أنتم لا ـــــــــــــــ مَن هي؟

٧. من فضلك، مَن ـــــــــــــــ في هذا البيت؟

٨. أنا وأصدقائي دائماً ـــــــــــــــ التلفزيون في المساء.

٩. كيف ـــــــــــــــ كل الكلمات الجديدة يا طلاب؟!

١٠. يا سامي، هل ـــــــــــــــ في النهار أو في المساء؟

١١. يا سارة، هل ـــــــــــــــ القهوة بالحليب والسكر؟

١٢. عمّتي وكل أفراد عائلتها لا ـــــــــــــــ اللحم أو الدجاج أو السمك.

تـمريـن ١٣: اسألوا زملاءكم (في الصف)

Find out who among your زملاء and زميلات does the following. Ask as many people as you can. Take brief notes to report back to class.

Likes to travel?

•···•···•···

•···•···•···

•···•···•···

Teaches or wants to teach?

•···•···•···

•···•···•···

•···•···•···

Eats vegetables every day?

....

....

....

Knows all their cousins?

....

....

....

Remembers all the words from *Alif Baa*?

....

....

....

Studies alone or with friends?

....

....

....

Talks to family members in another language?

....

....

....

Listens to "oldies" music?

....

....

....

Likes to watch videos on the computer?

....

....

....

القواعد ٢

ضمائر النصب Object Pronouns

You have learned to use subject pronouns (أنا، أنت، هي) and possessive pronouns
(ـي، ـك، ـها). The third and final set of personal pronouns in Arabic are object pronouns,
which indicate the object of a verb, as these examples show:

You have to memorize them!	لازم تحفظها!
Who teaches you (f.) Arabic?	مين بيدَرِّسك عربي؟
I don't remember her/it!	لا أتذكّرها!
I love it/him!	بحِبُّه! / باحِبُّه!

The following chart gives pronoun forms that are used as objects of verbs. As you can see,
most of them match the possessive pronoun.

المعنى	المصري	الشامي	الفُصحى
me	ـني	ـني	ـني
you (m.)	ـكَ	ـكَ	ـكَ
you (f.)	ـكِ	ـكِ	ـكِ
him, it	ـهُ	ـهُ	ـهُ
her, it, them[2]	ـها	ـها	ـها
us	ـنا	ـنا	ـنا
you (pl.)	ـكُو	ـكُن	ـكُم
them	ـهُم	ـهُن	ـهُم

It is as important to realize what a crucial role pronouns play in communication as it is to
know the words themselves. Think how strange this sounds in English: "I bought the book at
a sale, and I was very happy because I had wanted to read the book for a long time. When I got
home, I put the book on the table, made myself a cup of tea, and sat down to read the book. I
sat there reading the book for the rest of the day." This passage sounds choppy and disjointed
because there are no pronouns helping it to cohere. Where would you substitute a pronoun for
a noun in this passage to make it sound better? Pronouns play this kind of role in Arabic too,
even more so than in English. Practice using them in the following exercise and whenever you
write.

---

[2] For nonhuman plurals.

تمـريـن ١٤: الضمائر (في الصف)

With a partner, practice using pronouns in context. When you finish these sentences, make up some of your own.

مثال: هذه قطتي وأنا أحبّ(هي)! _____ أحبّها

١. الفارسيّة هي لغة والدتي ونحن نتكلّم(هي) في البيت دائماً. _____

٢. أنا أتذكّر(أنتِ) ولكن لا أتذكّر(هو). _____

٣. هي بنته الوحيدة ولكن لا يحب(هي)! _____

٤. مَن يدرّس(أنتم) العربية؟ _____

٥. سامر وطارق وسوزان هم أولاد جيراننا وأنا أعرف(هم) من طفولتي. _____

٦. أصدقائي يحبون(أنا) وأنا أيضاً أحب(هم). _____

٧. الدكتورة وداد أستاذتنا وهي تدرّس(نحن) علم الإنسان. _____

٨. كيف تتكلّمين معي وأنت لا تعرفين(أنا)؟! _____

القصة بالفصحى

تمـريـن ١٥: "كيف أحفظ كل الأسماء؟!" 🎧

There are two parts to this exercise. Watch القصة بالفصحى and answer the questions below. After listening, complete the first part in the book and the second part in the book or online.

1. Listen to the way in which Maha expresses her story in الفصحى and complete the following:

A. What do these phrases mean, and how are they structured grammatically?

الصف الأول   كل أفراد العائلة

B. Pick out all the إضافة phrases you hear in the text.

٢. استمعوا الى مها واكتبوا ما تقول:

(١) .... سامية (٢) .... (٣) فاطمة

(٤) .... (٥) .... و(٦) خالد

(٧) .... (٨) .... محمود، (٩) ....

في (١٠) .... (١١) .... (١٢) ....

في (١٣) .... الرابع، و(١٤) .... (١٥) ....

(١٦) .... (١٧) .... و(١٨) .

(١٩) .... (٢٠) أحمد ... آه ... اسمها... اسمها...

في (٢١) .... ، لا (٢٢) .... (٢٣) ....

(٢٤) .... (٢٥) .... (٢٦) .

ولا (٢٧) .... كيف (٢٨) (٢٩) ....

(٣٠) .... (٣١) .... السفر (٣٢) .... القاهرة؟!

القواعد ٣

By now you are familiar with basic sentence patterns in Arabic and use them spontaneously. You know that Arabic verbs do not need a separate pronoun subject because the subject marker appears on the verb itself, and thus sentences can begin with verbs. In this section we will introduce the two basic sentence structures of Arabic formally to give you the language to analyze sentences. Such analysis is important for developing reading comprehension, especially because Arabic does not use the verb "to be" in the present tense. In simple sentences this is fairly straightforward, but sentences will soon become more complex, and the ability to analyze them will be useful.

The Nominal Sentence الجـمـلـة الاِسـمِـيّة

noun	اِسـم ج. أَسماء
subject (in الجـمـلـة الاِسـمِـيّة)	مُـبـتَـدَأ
predicate	خَـبَـر

Thus far, most sentences you have seen and heard have a basic sentence structure called in Arabic الجـمـلـة الاِسـمِـيّة, from the word اسـم, which grammatically means noun. الجـمـلـة الاِسـمِـيّة is a sentence that begins with a noun or pronoun. Both formal and spoken Arabic use this structure, which is particularly common in conversational discourse (as distinct from narration). The following six sentences are all جُـمَـل اسـمِـيّة:

٤. هم مشغولون بالعمل	١. مها تسكن في نيويورك
٥. هل الصفوف كبيرة ؟	٢. والدتي تعمل في نفس البنك
٦. بيروت مدينة حلوة	٣. أنا مـن الاسكنِدريّة

Sentences ١ and ٢ in the examples contain verbs. They are still considered جـمـل اسـمـية because they begin with nouns. Sentences ٦ - ٣, however, have no overt verbs because the verb "to be" in the present tense is understood but not expressed in Arabic. To understand this kind of جـمـلـة اسـمية, it is necessary to determine where the meaning "am/are/is" belongs in the sentence, what the subject of the sentence is, and what the predicate of the sentence is. How would you translate sentences ٦ - ٣ above? To do so, you must identify the placement of "am/are/is." What clues help you determine the meaning of each sentence?

The parts of الجـمـلـة الاِسـمـية are called المُـبـتَـدَأ subject and الخَـبَـر predicate (literally, "new information," i.e., what is being related about the subject). In order to understand this type of sentence, you must first identify its two parts, especially in sentences in which the verb "to be" is understood. As you can see in the examples above, الخَـبَـر can be anything—noun, adjective, verb, prepositional phrase, etc. Note that الخَبَر tends to be indefinite when it is a noun or adjective; this clue will help you to identify where the break between the two parts of the sentence lies. Look again at the examples above and identify the parts of speech and definiteness of الخَبَر in each

The following diagrams show the breakdown of الجملة الاسمية:

مها تسكن في نيويورك		أنا مصرية	
تسكن في نيويورك	مها	مصرية	أنا
الخبر	المبتدأ	الخبر	المبتدأ

In this type of sentence, nouns and adjectives in both المبتدأ and الخبر must agree in gender (both مذكر or both مؤنث), and number (both مفرد or both جمع, following the agreement rules you have learned), as the following examples demonstrate. Note, however, that الخبر is usually—but not always—indefinite:

محمد مترجم	الكتب كبيرة
هم متخصصون في الأدب	هي حرّانة
الدروس صعبة !	أنتم مشغولون

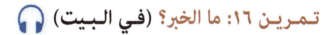

تمرين ١٦: ما الخبر؟ (في البيت) 🎧

This exercise is available online only.

الجملة الفعلية The Verbal Sentence

verb	فِعل ج. أفعال
subject of a جملة فِعلية	فاعِل

The second sentence type, الجملة الفعلية, named for the word فعل verb, is a sentence that begins with a verb. The subject of this verb, الفاعِل (literally, *the doer*), is either contained in the verb itself or is expressed as a noun following the verb. In sentences ١ - ٢, the الفاعِل is contained in the verb itself. In sentences ٣ - ٤, الفاعِل follows the verb.

٣. تستمع زوجتي الى الراديو في الصباح.	١. لا أتذكر كل الكلمات الجديدة.
٤. يعمل والد مها في الامم المتحدة.	٢. يكتبون رسائل الى أفراد العائلة.

Most sentences can be expressed either as a جملة اسمية or as a جملة فعلية. The main difference between the two is word order, which does not affect the basic meaning of the sentence, and the terminology used to name each sentence type[3]. Thus the example of جمل فعلية given above can also be expressed as جمل اسمية. Compare sentences ٥ - ٨ below to ١ - ٤ above:

٧. زوجتي تستمع الى الراديو في الصباح.	٥. أنا لا أتذكر كل الكلمات الجديدة.
٨. والد مها يعمل في الامم المتحدة.	٦. هم يكتبون رسائل الى أفراد العائلة.

These sentences describe the same state of affairs, but they would occur in different contexts and they are analyzed differently and with different terminology. Compare the analysis of sentence ٣, in which الفاعل is double underlined, and ٧, in which الخبر is double underlined:

تستمع: الفِعل / زوجتي: الفاعِل	٣. تستمع زوجتي الى الراديو في الصباح.
زوجتي: المُبتَدأ / تستمع الى الراديو: الخبر	٧. زوجتي تستمع الى الراديو في الصباح.

Both الجملة الاسمية and الجملة الفعلية sentence patterns occur widely in Arabic. The former, الجملة الاسمية, tends to be more common when there are particular topics under discussion because it sets up the topics as the head of the sentence. The latter, الجملة الفعلية, tends to be more common in the narration of events because it organizes sentences around verbs.

---

[3] This difference reflects the fact that each of these two sentence types presents information with a different focus: الجملة الاسمية focuses on a noun, or a topic, whereas الجملة الفعلية focuses on a verb.

When you read and listen to القصة and other texts in Arabic, after you have understood the content, go back and listen or look at the way sentences are structured. Practice identifying both types, الجملة الاسمية, including المبتدأ والخبر, and الجملة الفعلية with its فاعل (and with its object, if the verb takes one). This habit will build fluency in reading and listening comprehension skills over time.

🎧 تمرين ١٧: في جملة اسمية وجملة فعلية (في البيت)

This exercise is available online only.

تمرين ١٨: الجملة الاسمية والجملة الفعلية (في الصف والبيت)

Identify whether these sentences are جملة فعلية or جملة اسمية, and name the parts of each using the Arabic terms الفعل والفاعل or المبتدأ والخبر in these sentences. Also locate any direct objects (the Arabic term is مَفعول بِهِ).

١. تستمع أختي الى الأخبار دائماً.

٢. إخوتي مشغولون بالعمل دائماً.

٣. والدتي متخصصة في الطبّ النِّسائيّ .

٤. تدرّس الأستاذة مَرْيَم اللغة الإسبانية.

٥. هم أساتذة من السودان.

٦. الدروس في الكتاب الأول كانت قصيرة.

٧. هي المرأة الوحيدة في المكتب.

٨. جدّتي تعرف أسماء كل الجيران في بنايتنا.

٩. الناس في مدينة الجزائر يتكلّمون العربية والفرنسية.

١٠. أكتب رسائل تليفونية لأصدقائي في النهار والليل!

الاستماع: مع العائلة والأصدقاء

تـمريـن ١٩: مع عائلة مها (في البيت) 🎧

A director who is collecting film clips for a biographical profile of Maha found this clip in the library. Listen, using the strategies you have learned, then write a script for a voice-over to go with the video in third person ("This is ..."). In class, read your voice-over to a partner, then combine your scripts into a final product to be submitted to the director.

تـمريـن ٢٠: نشاط كتابة (في البيت) ومحادثة (في الصف)

أ. قبل الصف:

On a blank sheet of paper, write as many facts about yourself and your family as you can without revealing your name.

ب. في الصف:

Your teacher will collect everyone's list and redistribute them at random. Your goal is to uncover the identity of the person whose paper you hold. Read it, then ask other students questions based on the information you have until you find the right person.

الحوار اللغة والثقافة

"you have lit up [Cairo, Damascus, ...];" from the word النور, this verb conveys a warm welcome to someone new	نَوَّرتْ/نَوَّرتي (مصر ، الشام ، ....)
response: "[the place] is already lit up by its own people"	مْنَوَّرة بأصحابها / مِنَوَّرة بأهلَها

تمرين ٢١: "نوِّرتي الشام" / "نوِّرتي مصر" (في البيت وفي الصف) 🎧

أ. في البيت:

Watch the dialogue using the strategies you have learned, then answer in as much detail as you can:

1. Describe the situation and people.
2. What do we learn about the new person?

الأسرة: ....

السكن: ....

الدراسة: ....

ب. في الصف: طالب/ة جديد/ة في الكافتيريا

Using the dialogue as a model, act out a similar situation in groups of three or four. Take turns playing the role of an American student studying abroad in an Arab country.

تمارين المراجعة

تمـريـن ٢٢: استماع دقيق (في البيت) 🎧

This exercise is available online only.

تمـريـن ٢٣: القراءة الجَهريّة (في البيت) 🎧

Read the following text first silently for comprehension, then practice reading it aloud. When you are ready, record the text so that your instructor can check your reading.

سامية سَقباني بنت عمة نسرين، وكانت صديقة طفولتها قبل سفر نسرين إلى أمريكا. سامية تسكن مع عائلتها في مدينة دمشق بمنطقة أبو رُمّانة ولها ثلاث أخوات وأخ واحد وهي البنت الكبيرة في الأسرة. وهي الآن طالبة في كلية الهندسة بجامعة دمشق وتدرس الهندسة المَدَنِيّة. سامية تحب السّفر وتحب الاستماع الى الأخبار ، ودائماً تتكلم في السياسة مع أصدقائها وزملائها في الكلية. وهي تكتب رسائل بالـ e-mail الى نسرين.

درس

Lesson 5

الطقس حار جداً في الصيف

المفردات

القصة بالعامية: "ما بحبّ نيويورك" "ما باحبّش مدينة نيويورك"

الثقافة: "شو تشرب؟" "لا.. ولا حاجة"

القواعد (١):

المعرفة والنكرة Definite and Indefinite

هذا / هذه

الأعداد ١١ – ١٠٠

الاستماع: "الطقس اليوم"

القصة بالفصحى: "الجو حار جدًا في الصيف"

القواعد (٢):

تنوين الفتح Adverbs

القراءة: "نيويورك"

الحوار: "لازم اسافر ع باريس" "لازم اسافر باريس"

الثقافة: فيروز وأغنية "حبّيتك بالصيف"

تمارين المراجعة

🎧 Vocabulary المُفرَدات

Listen to the new vocabulary in formal Arabic and your spoken variety.

المعنى	المصري	الشامي	الفُصحى
of _____ descent			مِن أصل (+ nisba adjective)
cold (adj.) (of things)	بَرد	بارِد/بارْدة ، بَرد	بارِد/ة
snow	تَلج	تَلج	ثَلج
very	قَوي	كتير	جِدّاً
weather	الجَوّ	الطَّقس	الجَوّ ، الطَّقس
well (adv.)	كوَيِّس	منيح	جَيِّداً
hot (adj.) (of weather)	حَرّ	شوب	حارّ/ة
the best[1]			أحسَن
sometimes			أحْياناً
autumn			الخَريف
degree			دَرَجة
temperature			دَرَجة الحَرارة
spring (season)			الرَّبيع
humidity			الرُّطوبة
crowding, crowdedness	الزَّحمة	الزَّحمة	الازْدِحام
on account of, because of			بِسَبَب
winter	الشِّتا	الشِّتوِيّة	الشِّتاء
he feels, has feeling of	يِحِسّ بـ	يحِسّ بـ	يَشعُر بـ
sunny	شَمِس	مِشمِس	مُشمِس
summer			الصَّيف
high			عالي/ة
cloudy	مِغَيِّم	مغَيِّم	غائِم
season			فَصل ج فُصول
semester			فَصل دِراسيّ
only	بَسّ	بَسّ	فَقَط
a little bit (adv.)	شوَيّة	شوَيّ	قَليلاً

المعنى	المصري	الشامي	الفُصحى
a lot, much (adv.)	كِتير	كتير	كَثيراً
rain	مَطر	شِتي	مَطَر
as far as __ is concerned[2]	بالنِّسبة لـ __	بالنِّسبة إلـ __	بالنِّسبة لِـ __
loneliness			الوِحدة

Notes on Vocabulary Usage

1. In both spoken and formal Arabic, أَحْسَن is used with an indefinite noun to mean "the best _____" :

جامعتنا هي أحسن جامعة!   أحسن سلطة هي "التبولة"!

أحسن منطقة في "مينيابوليس" هي "ليندن هيلز".

It functions as a noun in this construction and does not take either الـ or ة.

2. The expression بالنِّسبة لـ is one way to express an opinion. Literally it means "in relation to (me/you/her…)." Listen and learn the appropriate forms:

المصري	الشامي	الفُصحى
بالنِّسبة لي	بالنِّسبة إلي	بالنِّسبة لي
بالنِّسبة لَك	بالنِّسبة إلَك	بالنِّسبة لَكَ
بالنِّسبة لِك	بالنِّسبة إلِك	بالنِّسبة لَكِ
بالنِّسبة لُه	بالنِّسبة إلُه	بالنِّسبة لَهُ
بالنِّسبة لْها	بالنِّسبة إلها	بالنِّسبة لَها
بالنِّسبة لْنا	بالنِّسبة إلنا	بالنِّسبة لَنا
بالنِّسبة لْكو	بالنِّسبة إلكُن	بالنِّسبة لَكُم
بالنِّسبة لْهُم	بالنِّسبة إلهُن	بالنِّسبة لَهُم

🎧 تمـريـن ١: الكلمات الجديدة (في البيت) 🎧

Complete the sentences with appropriate formal words from the new vocabulary:

١. عائلتي صغيرة: لي أخت واحدة .... اسمها لينا.

٢. بالنسبة لي، .... هو أحسن فصل، وأنتِ، ما هو أحسن فصل ....؟

٣. باراك أوباما أمريكيّ .... أفريقيّ.

٤. في السعودية .... حارّ جداً في الصيف و ٤٠° – ٤٥°.

٥. الطقس في العراق .... جداً في الصيف وبارد في ....

٦. لا يسكن الناس في منطقة سيبيريا في روسيا كثيراً بسبب .... والطقس البارد.

٧. بِناية "إمباير ستيت" في نيويورك .... جداً.

٨. لا أحب هذا الشارع الكبير بسبب .... الناس والسيارات فيه.

٩. حبيبته في باريس وهو في لبنان، وهو .... بالوحدة!

١٠. في جامعتنا ٣ .... دراسية: الخريف و .... والصيف.

١١. الطقس في عمّان .... اليوم .... ولكن .... في بغداد.

١٢. لا أحب السفر الى فلوريدا في الصيف بسبب الجو الـ .... و .... العالية.

١٣. أنا مشغولة جداً ولا أشاهد التلفزيون ولكن أشاهد .... الأخبار في المساء ....

١٤. بالنسبة لي، جامعتي هي .... جامعة في الولايات المتحدة.

🎧 تمـريـن ٢: المفردات في جمل (في البيت) 🎧

استمعوا الى جمل المفردات واكتبوا الجمل من "من أصل" إلى "الربيع".

🎧 تمـريـن ٣: "شو شوب!" / "الجو حرّ قوي" (في الصف) 🎧

استمعوا وتكلموا: كيف الطقس؟ ازاي الجو؟

Watch people talk about the weather in this video in class, if possible, or as instructed by your teacher. Then, with a partner, make up a dialogue about today's weather.

تمـريـن ٤: اسألوا زملاءكم (في الصف)

A.

1. Where do they go in the summer and why? Do they travel in the winter? Where and why?
2. What are their national/ethnic origins? Do they know a lot about them?
3. Something they always do, something they do a lot, and something they do sometimes.
4. What do they do when (عِندَما) they feel lonely?
5. How is the temperature for them today? How is the temperature in their room or house?
6. What classes do they have for spring semester?
7. Which is the best city in the United States to live in, and why? (Get two reasons.)

B.

1. What is their favorite weather? Their favorite time of year (season)? What (kinds of) weather do they not like?
2. Is this the first semester for them in college? If so, was it a good semester? If not, was their first semester good?
3. What are the best things in this city as far as they are concerned? (Hint: to ask this question, you must choose a specific noun, such as مطعم in أحسن مطعم. Remember to use indefinite nouns. Ask about three different "best" things.)
4. Do they like crowds? Why or why not?
5. Where do they go in the summer and why? Do they travel in the winter? Where and why?
6. What do they do sometimes?
7. What classes do they have for fall/spring semester?

القصة بالعامية

تـمرين ٥: "ما بحبّ نيويورك" / "ما باحبِّش مدينة نيويورك"

(في البيت وفي الصف) 🎧

أ. في البيت:

Listen to مها using the strategies you have learned. Write a **short paragraph** for each question. You may use الفصحى and/or المصري words and expressions.	Listen to نسرين using the strategies you have learned. Write a **short paragraph** for each question. You may use الفصحى and/or الشامي words and expressions.
١. مها بتحب ايه في نيويورك؟ وما بتحبش ايه؟ ليه؟	١. شو بتحب نسرين في نيويورك، وشو ما بتحب؟ ليش؟
٢. مها بتحِسّ بإيه وليه؟	٢. كيف بتحِسّ نسرين وليش؟
٣. مين ليلى؟ و بنعرف ايه عنها؟	٣. مين نور؟ وشو بنعرف عنها؟

ب. في الصف:

With a partner, come up with some ways in which مها/نسرين can improve her outlook on life. Then switch partners and take turns playing مها/نسرين and giving her your suggestions.

تـمرين ٦ : "شو تشرب؟" / "لا.. ولا حاجة" (في البيت وفي الصف) 🎧

Watch the dialogue "لا . . ولا حاجة" and answer:	Watch the dialogue "شو تشرب؟" and answer:
1. مين هم؟ What is the situation?	1. مين هنّ؟ What is the situation?
2. What did she ask him, and what was the response?	2. What did she ask him, and what was the response?
3. What expression did she use with the word شوية, and what do you think it means? What is the response?	3. Notice the word عين ج. عيون eye. It is used in expressions of endearment and to signal one's willingness to do anything for someone. How is it used here?

تمــريـن ٧: المفردات في جمل (في البيت) 🎧

استمعوا الى جمل المفردات واكتبوا الجمل من "الرطوبة" إلى "الوحدة".

القواعد ١

In this section we will review the details of noun phrases in Arabic, focusing on the differences between constructions such as "the big family," "this big family," and "this is a big family" in Arabic.

Definite and Indefinite in Phrases and Sentences المَعرِفة والنَّكِرة

noun-adjective phrase	اسم وصفة
adjective	صِفة ج. –ات
definite noun or adjective	مَعرِفة
indefinite noun or adjective	نَكِرة

In Arabic, noun-adjective phrases such as بيت قديم, and sentences without verbs such as البيت قديم, resemble each other closely. Only the presence or absence of the definite article الـ on the adjective distinguishes one from the other. Keep in mind that all nouns and adjectives in a single phrase must match in definiteness or indefiniteness, whereas sentences usually consist of a definite مبتدأ and an indefinite خبـر (جمل اسمية). Paying attention to definiteness is an important strategy in reading because it helps you recognize the relationships among nouns and adjectives in complex sentences, even when the vocabulary is unfamiliar.

Compare the use of الـ in the three sets below. What do you notice?

A اسم + صفة نكرة		B اسم + صفة معرفة		C Complete Sentences جُمَل	
a small class	صفّ صغير	the small class	الصفّ الصغير	The class is small.	الصفّ صغير
a big city	مدينة كبيرة	the big city	المدينة الكبيرة	The city is big.	المدينة كبيرة
(some) busy students	طلاب مشغولون	the busy students	الطلاب المشغولون	The students are busy.	الطلاب مشغولون

Columns A and B contain noun-adjective phrases that are either completely indefinite (column A) or completely definite (column B). In an indefinite noun-adjective phrase, such as "a big city," all nouns and adjectives must be نَكِرة. In a definite noun phrase, such as "the busy students," both the noun and its adjective(s) must be مَعرِفة. In contrast, column C contains complete جمل اسمية, showing the most common pattern: Definite مبتدأ and indefinite خبر[1].

Remember that possessive suffixes make nouns definite without الـ. For example, صديقي, مدينتنا and اقاربها are all definite. Therefore, the adjective that modifies a noun + possessive suffix must also be definite, and takes الـ:

my Egyptian friend	صديقي المصري
her Palestinian relatives	أقاربها الفلسطينيّون
our beautiful city	مدينتنا الجميلة

تـمريـن ٨: الاسم + الصفة (في البيت)

Complete the sentences below with noun-adjective phrases by matching the nouns and adjectives from the lists with the sentences below. Remember to make the adjectives agree with their nouns and to use الـ where needed. Some sentences will require plural forms.

أسماء:

صديق / ة - موظف / ة - منطقة - بناية - كلب - ابن/ بنت - قطّة - طقس - مدرسة - جار/ة - زميل /ة - جنسيّة - رجل

صفات:

لبناني - عالي - عربي - متخصص - بارد - جميل - جديد - أمريكي - ابتدائي - كبير - صغير - مصري

١. زميلتي تسكن في .... في شارع بيروت.

٢. .... تدرّس في كلية الحقوق.

٣. ابني يسكن في أمريكا وزوجته أمريكية وعنده

....

---

[1] While possible, it is less common that both المبتدأ and الخبر are definite:
Such as, هذه المدرسة هي المدرسة الوحيدة في هذه المنطقة *This school is the only school in this area.* These sentences tend to be emphatic in some way, and, in this example, the pronoun هي acts to separate and highlight both المبتدأ and الخبر.

٤. _____ يشعر بالوحدة.

٥. _____ تتكلم ثلاث لغات.

٦. _____ لا يحبون شغل البيت.

٧. _____ من عائلة كبيرة.

٨. لا نحب _____ في الشتاء!

٩. أختي الصغيرة لمياء عمرها ٩ سنوات وهي تدرس في _____

١٠. في الصورة _____

و _____ .

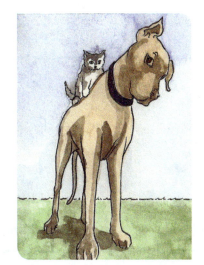

تمـريـن ٩: اسم وصفة أو إضافة؟ (في البيت) 🎧

This exercise is available online only.

هذا / هذِهِ

The demonstratives هذا and هذه are used both in sentences, for example "This is an easy test," and in definite noun phrases, for example, "this test." What differentiates these two constructions? Compare the phrases in A and B:

A	This is a large city.	هذه مدينة كبيرة.
	This is an Italian restaurant.	هذا مطعم إيطالي.
	These are old houses.	هذه بيوت قديمة.
B	this beautiful city	هذه المدينة الكبيرة
	this Italian restaurant	هذا المطعم الإيطالي
	these old houses	هذه البيوت القديمة

You can see that section A contains sentences, whereas section B contains phrases. This distinction is made grammatically by the use of الـ: The definite phrases in B refer to definite, specific entities, and so the nouns and adjectives must be definite. In the sentences in section A, the noun-adjective phrases function as الخبر, and are indefinite. We can, of course, use definite noun-adjective phrases in sentences by adding a خبر, which is usually indefinite:

This big city is very beautiful.	هذه المدينة الكبيرة جميلة جداً.
This Italian restaurant is the best!	هذا المطعم الإيطالي أحسن مطعم!
These old houses are historic.	هذه البيوت القديمة تاريخية.

Demonstrative Pronouns in Spoken Arabic

The following words are commonly used demonstratives in الشامي and المصري[2]:

(also spelled ده) دا	هادا ، هاد	هٰذا
دي	هادي ، هاي	هٰذِهِ

You have heard and used these demonstrative pronouns in sentences like the following

دا مطعم إيطالي.	هادا مطعم طِلياني.
دي صورة حلوة.	هاي صورة حلوة.
دي بيوت قديمة.	هاي بيوت قديمة.

In Levantine Arabic there is an additional short form of the demonstrative pronoun that is used in definite noun phrases: هَـ. This pronoun has no gender and is pronounced as if attached to the definite noun it modifies:

these houses	هالبيوت
this street	هالشارع
this region	هالمنطقة

---

[2] There exist other variant forms in both regions but they are all related to these basic forms.

تمريـن ١٠: ترجِموا إلى اللغة العربية: كيف نقول؟ (في البيت أو في الصف)

1. The old (كبير) man is tired.
2. Is this test hard?
3. This semester is long!
4. This is an easy class!
5. This is a beautiful letter.
6. This is a cold winter!
7. Cairo is a very large city.
8. The new library is very cold.
9. Is your new friend a student here?
10. The short woman is Saudi and the tall one is Kuwaiti.
11. They remember their difficult childhood.
12. I live on (في) this wide street, and overcrowding is a problem.
13. The new student is French of Moroccan origin.
14. I don't feel lonely in my big family.
15. This weather is very hot and sunny!
16. This historic area is very old.

تمريـن ١١: الاسم + الصفة / الإضافة (في الصف)

With a partner, combine the following pairs of words into a phrase and use each in a sentence. Think about whether you want to use صفة + اسم or إضافة and think about the rules for each.

٦. صف + إسبانيّ	١. مدرسة + وحيد
٧. كلية + علوم	٢. طقس + ربيع
٨. سلطة + فواكه	٣. عائلة + صديقة
٩. صورة + حبيب	٤. زميل + جديد
١٠. جيش + العراق	٥. شوربة + بارد

🎧 الأعداد ١١–١٠٠

Learn the numbers from eleven to one hundred. Listen to each of the numbers in the formal Arabic pronunciation, and then listen to the same number as pronounced in your dialect.

٤٠ أَربَعون / أربَعين	٢١ واحِد وعِشرون/ين	١١ أَحَد عَشَر
٥٠ خَمسون / خَمسين	٢٢ اِثنا وعشرون/ين	١٢ اِثنا عَشَر
٦٠ سِتّون / سِتّين	٢٣ ثَلاثة وعِشرون/ين	١٣ ثَلاثة عَشَر
٧٠ سَبعون / سَبعين	٢٤ أربَعة وعِشرون/ين	١٤ أربَعة عَشَر
٨٠ ثَمانون / ثَمانين	٢٥ خَمسة وعِشرون/ين	١٥ خَمسة عَشَر
٩٠ تِسعون / تِسعين	٢٦ سِتّة وعِشرون/ين	١٦ سِتّة عَشَر
١٠٠ مِئة (مائة) [3]	٢٧ سَبعة وعِشرون/ين	١٧ سَبعة عَشَر
	٢٨ ثَمانية وعِشرون/ين	١٨ ثَمانية عَشَر
	٢٩ تِسعة وعِشرون/ين	١٩ تِسعة عَشَر
	٣٠ ثَلاثون/ ثَلاثين	٢٠ عِشرون/ عِشرين

Numbers 11–100 with Nouns

Unlike the numbers from three to ten, which are followed by a plural noun, the numbers from eleven to one hundred must be followed by a singular noun in all varieties of Arabic.[4] In formal Arabic you will see singular nouns that follow numbers eleven to ninety-nine written with تنوين فتحة ending, the same rules that apply to the interrogative كَم؟:

عندي ٢٠ (عشرون) كتاباً من المكتبة.

كم موظفاً يعمل في مكتب القبول؟ -- ١٥ (خمسة عشر) موظفاً

In spoken Arabic the singular noun has no ending:

كم دولار معك؟ -- معي ٣٠ (تلاتين) دولار بس.

عمرك كام سنة ؟ -- عمري ١٩ (تِسَعْتَعْشَر) سنة.

🎧 تمريـن ١٢: الاستماع الى الأعداد (في البيت)

This exercise is available online only.

🎧 تمريـن ١٣: صفحات الكتاب (في البيت)

This exercise is available online only.

---

[3] The alternate (older) spelling مائة for مِئة does not affect its pronunciation.

[4] Formal Arabic imposes agreement rules that affect the gender of the numeral. You will learn these rules later. Spoken Arabic uses fixed forms that vary slightly from dialect to dialect but are easily understood once you know the basic underlying form presented here.

تمـريـن ١٤: بينغو! (في الصف)

Play bingo! Draw up bingo sheets with five rows and five columns containing numbers from one to ninety-nine. One person at a time acts as the caller, calling out numbers at random, and the others check off the numbers they have. The first person to get five straight across or diagonally wins the round.

الاستماع

تمـريـن ١٥: "الطقس اليوم" (في البيت وفي الصف) 🎧

There are two parts to this exercise. Watch the video and complete the activities.

أ. في البيت:

Watch the weather report. Watch it at least once through without stopping to get the main ideas, then make some notes and plan your second listen: What further information can you get? Make a list that summarizes the information you heard, including the name of the city and its weather forecast.

ب. في الصف:

Share and compare your notes with a partner بالعربي. If you could take a trip to some of the cities mentioned in the video, where would you go and what is the weather like there?

القصة بالفصحى

تمـريـن ١٦: "الجو حار جداً في الصيف" (في البيت) 🎧

There are three parts to this exercise. Watch القصة بالفصحى and answer the questions below. The dictation exercise can be completed in the book or online.

1. Listen to Maha tell her story in الفصحى. What فصحى words does she use that differ from dialect words? List them:

2. Listen for Maha's explanation of how she feels. In sentences ١ and ٢ she uses a connecting word that introduces an explanation, similar to "since" or "because" in English. Write what you hear. (Hint: Remember that one-letter particles are connected to the following word.)

١. لا أحب مدينة نيويورك كثيراً، ــــــــــــــــــــــ ـالجو...

٢. أشعر أحياناً بالوحدة في هذه المدينة الكبيرة ــــــــــــــــــــ ـوالدي...

٣. استمعوا الى مها واكتبوا:

(١) لا ــــــــــــــــــــ مدينة نيويورك (٢) ــــــــــــــــــــ (٣)

(٤) ــــــــــــــــــــ (٥) و ــــــــــــــــــــ (٦) فـ ، ــــــــــــــــــــ

(٧) ــــــــــــــــــــ جداً في (٨) ــــــــــــــــــــ و(٩) ــــــــــــــــــــ الرطوبة

(١٠) ــــــــــــــــــــ ، و(١١) ــــــــــــــــــــ جداً في (١٢) .

(١٣) ــــــــــــــــــــ (١٤) ــــــــــــــــــــ (١٥) لي هو

(١٦) ــــــــــــــــــــ (١٧) . ــــــــــــــــــــ أحياناً (١٨) ــــــــــــــــــــ في هذه

(١٩) ــــــــــــــــــــ (٢٠) ــــــــــــــــــــ ، فـ (٢١)

(٢٢) ــــــــــــــــــــ مشغولان (٢٣) ، ولي (٢٤) ــــــــــــــــــــ

(٢٥) ــــــــــــــــــــ فقط (٢٦) ليلى و(٢٧) ــــــــــــــــــــ أمريكية

(٢٨) ــــــــــــــــــــ (٢٩) ــــــــــــــــــــ (٣٠) .

القواعد ٢

تنوين الفتح Adverbs

أيضاً - غداً - دائماً - فِعلاً - شُكراً

قليلاً - كثيراً - جِداً - أحياناً - عَفواً

The words that you see above all share the grammatical ending تنوين الفتح.[5] One of the main functions of this ending is to make a noun or adjective into an adverb, a word that modifies or describes a verb. Most adverbs that end in تنوين الفتح are spelled with alif, which can be written with or without تنوين: ا or أ. In regular, unvocalized texts, the symbol ـً is often omitted, leaving just ا, as in دائما or جدا. Knowing this helps you identify adverbs in texts: Look for words ending in alif: If they are not proper nouns, chances are they should be read with the تنوين ending أـً. A few words that are commonly used as adverbs end in ة. Remember that ة does not take an alif.

---

[5] In addition to its function as an adverb marker, grammatical ending تنوين الفتح has other functions as well, including marking indefinite objects in formal Arabic only. Occasionally you will see and hear nouns marked with the ending in formal contexts. For now, you only need to recognize it as a grammatical ending. We will return to this ending again in lesson 12.

Adverb placement is fairly flexible in Arabic and generally corresponds to English word order, with the exception that in Arabic adverbs tend to follow the verb. In addition, adverbs may also follow the object of the verb or come at the end of the sentence:

أحب الحلويات كثيراً   أصحابي جوعانون دائماً   بنتي تقرأ دائماً

هل تتذكرون هذه الكلمات جيداً؟   لا أدرس جيداً في غرفتي

Like their English equivalents, the adverbs فعلاً ,دائماً ,أيضاً, and المبتدأ may separate المبتدأ and الخبر. Both of these word orders are possible:

أنا تعبانة أيضاً.   or   أنا أيضا تعبانة.

هم بردانون فعلاً.   or   هم فعلاً بردانون.

Note, however, that the adverb جداً must follow the adjective it modifies in formal Arabic:

نحن مشغولون جداً!   هي عطشانة جداً!

تـمريـن ١٧: كتابة (في البيت)

Write ten sentences that describe what your friends and family and others do/do not do, and how much, or how often they do it, by using verbs and a variety of adverbs. Use all of these verbs, and vary the persons to practice all of them:

– يتكلم – يعمل – يشعر بـ – يحبّ – يدرس – يقرأ – يكتب – يستمع الى –

يأكل – يشرب – يتذكر – يدرّس – يسافر – يحفظ – يقول

تـمريـن ١٨: تنوين الفتح (في الصف)

The تنوين الفتح ending may be used on many nouns and adjectives that refer to location in time or space. Rephrase the following underlined phrases by making adverbs out of them. (Remember to drop الـ and use the مذكر forms of the adjectives.)

مثال: زوجي لا يعمل في النهار ◄—— نهاراً

١. لا أشاهد التليفزيون في الصباح.

٢. أدرس في المساء فقط.

٣. هل تسكنون في بيوت قريبة من الجامعة؟

٤. ندرس ساعات طويلة كل يوم.

٥. يسافرون الى مدن بعيدة كل صيف.

٦. هذه المنطقة فيها ازدحام في النهار وفي الليل.

٧. درجة الحرارة في سان فرنسيسكو من ٤٥ إلى ٦٥ في الصيف وفي الشتاء.

تمـرين ١٩: اسألوا زملاءكم (في الصف)

Ask زملاءكم for the following information. Remember to rephrase the questions to use second person with أنتم أنتَ أنتِ. When you find someone who is like you, say وأنا أيضاً.

٦. من يشرب الماء دائماً؟	١. من يكتب رسائل الى اسرته دائماً؟
٧. من لا يتذكر الكلمات أحياناً؟	٢. من تعبان جداً؟
٨. من يسكن قريباً من الجامعة؟	٣. من لا يحب هذه المدينة فعلاً؟ لماذا؟
٩. أين يدرسون جيداً؟	٤. من يسافر بعيداً؟
١٠. ماذا يشربون نهاراً وليلاً؟	٥. من يعمل دائماً؟

القراءة

تمـرين ٢٠: قراءة "نيويورك" (في الصف)

Before you begin to read the following article, take a look at the title and, with a partner, brainstorm what it might be about. What kind of an article do you think it is? What kinds of information do you expect to find in it?

As you read the passage for the first time, remember that you are looking only for things you know. Skip words and strings of words that are unfamiliar and go on to the next sentence. Use your knowledge of sentence structure to identify where each new sentence begins so that you can keep moving. As you have learned to do in listening, work strategically to maximize comprehension. Aim to read with these strategies:

1. Phase One: Skimming and Scanning
Work through the text quickly. Your goal is to identify parts of the text that you will focus on in the second reading. It is not a good idea to write any English (i.e., translations or prompts) on the page. Trust your brain to recall and reconstruct the meanings of the words you have figured out from the context. You might want to mark the sentences or lines you would like to focus on in the next phase.

2. Phase Two: Information Gathering
Before your second reading, compare your notes from phase one with your partner. Go through the text together and focus on the parts that you both identified in the first reading. What is the main topic of each paragraph? List the new words whose meanings you guessed from context, background knowledge, root, and other grammatical clues.

3. Phase Three: Close Reading and Analysis

a. The word تبلغ/يبلغ recurs throughout the text shown on the next page. What kind of word is it? What kind of contexts does it occur in? What do you think it refers to? What other words recur with it and what do you think those words mean? Look at سُكّان (عدد) and مِساحة in particular.

b. Where does the text discuss people? What grammatical forms help you identify the right section? See if you can figure out what the phrase مجموعات عِرقية means.

c. Find at least one example of each of the following. How does recognizing the structure help you guess its meaning?

إضافة   اسم وصفة نكرة   اسم وصفة معرفة

الجملة الاسمية: المبتدأ والخبر   الجملة الفعلية والفاعل

المـعـرفة

الموسوعة الحرة لخلق وجمع المحتوى العربي

نيويورك (مدينة)

مدينة نيويورك

مدينة نيويورك (New York City)، هي أكبر مدينة في الولايات المتحدة الأمريكية، وهي سادسة المدن الكبرى في العالم. تقع على الساحل الشرقي للولايات المتحدة الأمريكية عند مصب نهر هدسون. تبلغ مساحتها ٩٥٦كم²، منها ١٧٤كم² مسطحات مائية. بدأت نيويورك مركزًا صغيرًا للمهاجرين الهولنديين الأوائل، ثم أصبحت الآن مقراً للأمم المتحدة، ومركزًا للتجارة العالمية والمنظمات المالية الضخمة والمصارف والبورصات وشركات الشحن ، كما أصبحت أهم مراكز الثقافة العالمية.

تنقسم المدينة إلى خمس محافظات، هي: مانهاتن، وبرونكس، وكوينز، وبروكلين، وجزيرة ستاتن. وتُعدّ مانهاتن أقدم محافظة بالولاية وأصغرها وأهمها؛ إذ تبلغ مساحتها ٨٨كم²، ويبلغ عدد سكانها نحو مليون ونصف المليون نسمة. وهي تضم أشهر المدارس والجامعات، وبها أكبر المتاجر والمؤسسات المالية في شارعي "وول" و"برود". ومن أشهر مبانيها إمباير ستيت، الذي أنشئ عام ١٩٣١م بارتفاع ٣٨١م، ومبنى مركز التجارة العالمية الذي أنشئ عام ١٩٧٢ بارتفاع ٤١٧م. وكان البرجان من أعلى ناطحات السحاب في العالم، وقد انهار مركز التجارة العالمي في ١١ سبتمبر ٢٠٠١م. وتبلغ مساحة محافظة بروكلين ٢٨٨كم²، وسكانها نحو مليونين وربع المليون نسمة، وهي ميناء ومركز صناعي. أما برونكس، فتبلغ مساحتها نحو ١٤٣كم² ويبلغ عدد سكانها مليونًا ونصف المليون نسمة، وهي منطقة سكنية بالدرجة الأولى. أما كوينز، فهي أكبر محافظة بالمدينة، حيث تبلغ مساحتها ٣٢٦كم²، ويبلغ عدد سكانها نحو مليوني نسمة، وبها مطار لاغورديا ومطار كنيدي الدولي وتعد جزيرة ستاتن أقل المحافظات تطوراً، ومساحتها ١٦٨كم² وسكانها ٣٥٢,٠٠٠ نسمة.

يبلغ المجموع الكلي لسكان مدينة نيويورك نحو ٧,٣٢٢,٥٦٤ نسمة، يمثلون معظم الأعراق والقوميات في العالم؛ فقد هاجر إليها الآلاف من كل أنحاء العالم طلباً للعمل والتعليم والنشاط الثقافي . توجد في المدينة خمس مجموعات عرقية هي: السود، الأيرلنديون، الإيطاليون، اليهود، البورتوريكيون. وهؤلاء يمثلون ٧٥٪ من سكان المدينة، ويُعدّ السود أكبر مجموعة فهم ٢٥٪، ويمثل اليهود ٢٠٪ من جملة السكان، وقد أتوا من أقطار عديدة، أما الإيطاليون، فيمثلون ١٤٪ من السكان، وتبلغ نسبة البورتوريكيين ١٢٪، وقد كان الأيرلنديون يحكمون المدينة في أواخر القرن التاسع عشر وأوائل القرن العشرين، ولكن عددهم انخفض من ٣٠٪ إلى ٩٪. وبالإضافة إلى هذه المجموعات الرئيسية، توجد مجموعات عرقية صغيرة ممثلة في الإنجليز والألمان والروس والصينيين واليونانيين .

وكانت نيويورك مستعمرة هولندية وقد كان اسمها سابقا "نيو امستردام" . وهي أكبر المدن الأمريكية وإحدى أهم مراكز التجارة والمال في العالم. نيويورك هي أيضا أكبر مدن ولاية نيويورك الأمريكية (New York State)، كما تُعدّ المدينة عاصمة اقتصادية للولايات المتحدة لكثرة الشركات والبنوك العالمية فيها. يوجد بها مقر هيئة الأمم المتحدة وسوق الأوراق المالية داو جونز.

http://ar.marefa.org/index.php

تـمريـن ٢١: نشاط كتابة ومحادثة (في البيت والصف)

You have heard مها describe new people twice so far:

لي خالة اسمها نادية.   لي صديقة اسمها ليلى.

This kind of sentence can be used to introduce and describe any new person:

لي صديق يعمل في مطعم "باب الحارة".

لي أخت عمرها ١٩ سنة.

لي عمة تسكن في مدينة واشنطن.

On small cards or pieces of paper, introduce and describe various people in your life in sentences based on these models. Write one sentence on each card. In class, your teacher will collect the cards and mix them together. Take a card from the pile, read it, and find its owner by asking questions. Use the appropriate pronouns for the variety you are learning:

ليك ...؟   إلَك ...؟   لَك ...؟

ليكي ...؟   إلِك ...؟   لَكِ ...؟

These questions give you models to follow:

هل لَكِ أخت اسمها سالي؟   هل لَكِ عمّ يُدرّس في الجامعة؟

إلَك ابن عمّ بيدرس الهندسة؟   إلِك خال ساكن بمدينة نيويورك؟

ليك صاحب بيحبّ السفر؟   ليكي أخ بيشتغل في واشنطن؟

الحوار

اللغة والثقافة

الحمد الله عَ السَّلامة – الله يسَلّمَكِ / حَمد الله عَ السَّلامة – الله يِسَلّمَكِ

السَّلامة here means safety and/or well-being, and this expression is used to welcome someone back from a trip or an illness.

تمـرين ٢٢: "لازم اسافر ع باريس" / "لازم اسافر باريس" (في البيت) 🎧

1. Why does one woman say حمد الله ع السلامة؟	1.Why does one woman say الحمد الله ع السلامة؟
2. How does she describe the place? Give as many details as you can.	2. How does she describe the place? Give as many details as you can.
3. ازّاي كان الجو؟ Compare the weather in both places.	3. كيف كان الطقس؟ Compare the weather in both places.
4. How does the conversation end? What strategies do you hear for ending conversations politely?	4. How does the conversation end? What strategies do you hear for ending conversations politely?

الثقافة: فيروز وأغنية "حَبَّيتَك بالصيف" 🎧

فيروز is a Lebanese singer. She is one of the most famous and popular singers among all generations in the Arab East today because of her beautiful voice and the many different musical

genres in which she sings. These genres range from classical poetry to folk songs to modern "Arabicized jazz." Her career began in the late 1950s and was launched mainly by the musical plays that her husband عاصي الرحباني and his brother منصور wrote. Many of her most famous songs, including the one that you will hear, come from those musicals. The الرحباني brothers were themselves very influential in the field of modern Arabic music and created a school of songwriting that combined elements from folklore, the classical Arabic tradition, and Western music. More recently, her son, زِياد الرحباني, has written songs for her that show the influence of jazz and other Western musical genres while retaining Arabic elements.

فيروز sings most of her songs in the Lebanese dialect, including the following—one of her most famous songs. You can listen to her sing this song by either going to the website: www.youtube.com/watch?v=QPN9yXsSwtY or following the link on the Al-Kitaab website. You can also follow along by reading the lyrics either by going to the website: http://fnanen.net/klmat-aghany/f/fyroz/7bytk-bal9yf.html or by following the link on the Al-Kitaab website.

Pay special attention to the second verse of lyrics and learn some of the new words you hear below. Sing along and enjoy!

I waited for you	نَظَرتك
eyes	عيون
our meeting	مَلآنا
behind, beyond	خَلف

تمـارين المراجعة

تمـرين ٢٣: ضمائر الملكية (في البيت) 🎧

This exercise is available online only.

تمـريـن ٢٤: القراءة الجهرية (في البيت أو في الصف) 🎧

Read the following passage, first silently for comprehension, then aloud to practice pronunciation. When you are ready, record the passage and submit it to your teacher either online or as instructed by your teacher.

نور بوراوي صديقة نسرين في نيويورك وهي تعرفها من الجامعة. ونور أمريكية من أصل عربي ولكن لا تتكلم العربية جيداً بسبب والدها: هو كان يتكلم معها بالإنكليزية فقط في طفولتها ، ولكن هي الآن تدرس اللغة العربية في الجامعة وتتكلم مع نسرين بالعربية أحياناً. وهي جميلة، وكثير من الشباب يحبونها، ولكن، بالنسبة لها، أحسن شاب في كل نيويورك هو ويليام حبيبها وصديقها من أيام المدرسة. والدة نور أمريكية ووالدها تونسي وله أقارب كثيرون في تونس. ونور تحب السفر الى تونس في الصيف بسبب الجو والشمس .. والفواكه الطيّبة والحلويات!. وهي تحب أولاد عمها سارّة وسَوسَن وعامِر، وهم يحبون الكلام معها باللغة الإنكليزية - لغتهم الثالِثة بعد العربية والفرنسية.

درس 6
Lesson 6

معيد بكلّية التجارة

المفردات

القصة بالعامية: "أنا طارق" "أنا خالد"

الثقافة (١): الهوايات

الثقافة (٢): من هو المعيد؟

القواعد (١):

المُثَنَّى

القصة بالفصحى: "أنا خالد"

القواعد (٢):

المصدر

القواعد (٣):

لـماذا؟

القراءة: "روزانا"

الحوار: "ليش بدك تشتغل بشركتنا؟" "ليه عايز تشتغل في شركتنا؟"

تمارين المراجعة

المُفَرَدات Vocabulary 🎧

Listen to the new vocabulary in your spoken variety and in formal Arabic.

المعنى	المصري	الشامي	الفُصحى
after	بَعد	بعد	بَعدَ (+ اسم)
after that	بَعدَ كِدَا	بعد هيك	بَعدَ ذٰلِكَ
commerce, trade			التِّجارة
running			الجَري
he obtains, acquires (a job, degree)[1]	___	___	يحصُل على
to obtain/obtaining	___	___	الحُصول على
lecture, (lecture) class	مُحاضرة ج. ‑ات		مُحاضرة ج. ‑ات
life			الحَياة
he graduates, graduating	يِتخَرَّج	يِتخَرَّج	يَتَخَرَّج ، التَّخَرُّج
I graduated from[2]	اِتخَرَّجْت (من)	تخَرَّجْت (من)	تخَرَّجْتُ (من)
business administration			إدارة الأعمال
he goes to	يِروح	يروح عَ	يَذهَب إلى
dancing			الرَّقص
sports			الرِّياضة
swimming			السِّباحة
week		إسبوع ج. أسابيع	أُسْبوع ج. أسابيع
two years	سَنَتين	سِنْتين	سَنَتانِ ، سَنَتَيْنِ
company	شِرْكة ج. ‑ات	شِرْكة ج. ‑ات	شَرِكة ج. ‑ات
photography			التَّصْوير
graduate fellow, teaching assistant			مُعيد ج. ‑ون / ين
basketball			كُرة السَّلّة
soccer, European football			كُرة القَدَم
in order to, for (the purpose of)	عَشان ، عَلَشان	مِنشان	لِ
because	لإنَّ ، عَشان	لأنَّه	لِأنَّ (+ جملة اسمية)
because of that, for that reason	عَشان كدا	مِنشان هيك	لِذٰلِكَ
why?	ليه؟	ليش؟	لِماذا؟

المعنى	المصري	الشامي	الفُصحى
he plays, playing	يِلعَب ، اللِّعب	يِلعَب ، اللِّعب	يَلعَب ، اللَّعِب
when?	إمتى؟	إيمتى؟	مَتى؟
since, ago[3]	مِن	مِن	مُنذُ
hobby			هِواية ج. ات
day	يوم	يوم ج. إيّام	يَوْم ج. أيّام

أيّام الأسبوع

Learn the days of the week in Arabic by listening to the days in the varieties of Arabic you are learning. As you listen, determine the correspondence between the names of the days in Arabic and English. (Hints: One of the names is a cognate of "Sabbath," and the first day of the week is Sunday. Remember to read right to left.)

يوم السَّبْت	يوم الجُمعة	يوم الخَميس	يوم الأرْبِعاء	يوم الثُّلاثاء	يوم الاثنَيْن	يوم الأحَد
السَّبت	الجمعة	الخَميس	الأرْبَعا	التّلاتا	التّنين	الأحَد
السَّبت	الجُمعة	الخَميس	الارْبَع	التّلات	الاتنين	الحَدّ

Notes on Vocabulary Usage

1. The verb أحصُل على is used in a rather limited sense in Arabic: It means *to obtain* or *acquire* a degree, a job, a scholarship—in general, something you might get from an official agency or institution.

2. The verb تَخَرَّجت is a past-tense verb, as you can tell from its meaning and the pronoun suffix subject ت, which matches the ending on the verb كُنت. The other subject endings you know from the verb كان can be used here as well. For now, learn and practice the singular forms using the table below. Note that the أنتِ suffix in spoken Arabic is spelled two different ways; learn to recognize both:

المصري	الشامي	الفُصحى	
اِتخَرَّجت	تخَرَّجت	تَخَرَّجْتَ	أنتَ
اِتخَرَّجْتِ ، اِتخَرَّجْتي	تخَرَّجْتِ ، تْخَرَّجتي	تَخَرَّجْتِ	أنتِ
اِتخَرَّج	تْخَرَّج	تَخَرَّجَ	هو
اِتْخَرَّجت	تْخَرَّجت	تَخَرَّجَتْ	هي

3. The word مُنذُ signals the occurrence or onset of an action in the past, such as, "She graduated a year ago," or "We have been studying Arabic for one year," or "They have been living in London since 2009." In these sentences, منذ means ago, for, and since, respectively. The main verb can be past or present, depending on whether the action still continues, as in "I have been living here since . . . ," or whether the action occurred once in the past, as in "He graduated a year ago." The English translation of منذ will be clear from context in each case.. The main verb can be in any time frame, and the English translation of منذ will depend on that verb. Notice that the specific time follows منذ:

I have been living in Seattle for the past 3 years.	أسكن في مدينة سياتل منذ ٣ سنوات .
I was living in Dallas 3 years ago.	كنت أسكن في مدينة دالاس منذ ٣ سنوات.
I was with her an hour ago...	كنت معها منذ ساعة، ولكن لا أعرف أين هي الآن.

Use the examples to help you translate these sentences:

أدرس اللغة العربية منذ سنة.   /   أعرف صديقتي رانيا منذ الطفولة.

أختي تتكلم مع صديقها بالتليفون منذ ساعة!   /   تخرّجت من الجامعة منذ سنة.

🎧 الثقافة ١: الهوايات 🎧

ما هواياتك؟

Listen to interviews with some شباب مصريين about their هوايات. Which هوايات are mentioned?

🎧 تـمـريـن ١: المفردات الجديدة (في البيت) 🎧

Complete the sentences using the new formal vocabulary:

١. بنت عمتي نورا طالبة دُكتوراه في قسم علم النفس وهي تعمل _____ في نفس القسم.

٢. " _____ تتخصّصين في العلوم السياسية؟" -- "لأنّي أحب السِّياسة والسياسيين."

٣. تزوجت من شاب فرنسي _____ تحصل على الجنسية الفرنسية.

٤. والدتي تعمل في هذه الشركة _____ ١٢ سنة.

٥. مها هي البنت الوحيدة في أسرتها، و _____ تشعر بالوحدة.

٦. _____ الطلاب في كليّات الحقوق في أمريكا صعبة لأنّهم يدرسون

٣ سنوات بعد _____ على البكالوريوس من الجامعة ودائماً عندهم واجبات وامتحانات.

٧. _____ هي السِّباحة والجري وكرة القدم ولكن زميلتي في البيت

تحب _____ الـ "تانغو" والـ "باليه".

٨. بالنسبة لي، أحسن يوم في _____ هو يوم السبت لأنني لا _____ الى

الجامعة ولكن _____ كرة السلّة مع أصدقائي.

٩. يوم الأربعاء عندي _____ في الجامعة من الصباح الى الساعة ٦ مساءً،

و _____ أذهب الى مركز الرياضة.

١٠. _____ من الجامعة في سنة ٢٠١١ ، وأنا الآن أدرس للحصول على الماجستير في _____

لأعمل في بنك أو في "وول ستريت" إن شاء الله.

١١. " _____ كان أوّل يوم في هذا الفصل الدراسي؟" -- "الخميس ١٩ يناير."

تمـريـن ٢: المفردات في جمل (في البيت) 🎧

استمعوا الى جمل المفردات واكتبوا الجمل من "بعد" إلى "أُسْبوع".

تمـريـن ٣ : اسألوا زملاءكم (في الصف)

Find as many زملاء as you can who:

1. Graduated from college, are graduate fellows now, and are studying to get a دُكتوراه.
2. Still have the same hobbies as they did in their childhood. If not, why not?
3. Graduated from المدرسة one year ago/two years ago/three years ago.
4. Have parent(s) or sibling(s) who have a master's degree ماجستير in business administration.
5. Do not have classes five days a week. Which days do they not have classes?
  Which days do they have the most classes?
6. Have only this class today.
7. Go to lectures just because they want to, not for a class.
8. Remember how the weather was three weeks ago. How was it?
9. Are majoring in business, or want/wanted to major in business.
10. Have lived in the same house for many years. How many years?

القصة بالعامية

تمـريـن ٤: "أنا طارق" / "أنا خالد" (في البيت) 🎧

Listen to خالد, using the strategies you have learned. Write a **paragraph** for each question.	Listen to طارق, using the strategies you have learned. Write a **paragraph** for each question.
١. خالد بيدرس فين؟ وبيدرس ايه؟	١. وين بيدرس طارق؟ وشو بيدرس؟
٢. بيروح الجامعة اِمتى؟ ليه ما بيروحش كل يوم؟	٢. اِمتى بيروح ع الكلية؟ ليش ما بيروح كل يوم؟
٣. المعيد بيعمل ايه؟	٣. شو بيعمل المعيد؟
٤. خالد مشغول؟ ليه/ليه لأ؟	٤. طارق مشغول؟ ليش/ليش لأ؟

الثقافة ٢: من هو المعيد؟ 🎧

Watch the interview with a معيدة مصرية as she explains the معيد system.

تـمـريـن ٥: المفردات في جمل 🎧

استمعوا الى جمل المفردات واكتبوا الجمل من "سنتان" الى "يوم".

القواعد ١

المُثنّى: Preview of the Dual

You heard طارق or خالد use the word "سنتين" referring to "two years." In lesson 5 you heard مها say والدي ووالدتي مشغولان دائماً. Both مشغولان and سنتين have grammatical endings called dual, which indicate specifically *two* human or nonhuman entities. This ending has two forms in الفصحى and one form in most dialects of spoken Arabic, which you heard on the word سنتين in the vocabulary list. These endings are found on the word "two" itself: إِثنان إِتنين. The root that indicates two is ث ن ي , which you see in the Arabic name for the dual: المُثنّى

In spoken Arabic the dual suffix is used mainly on nouns, and it can give the meaning either *two exactly* or *a couple of*, according to context. Both meanings are possible in these examples:

كنت في واشنطن دي سي من أسبوعين.

لازم اذاكر ساعتين قبل ما انام.

In الفصحى, dual endings can occur not only on nouns, but also on adjectives, verbs, and pronouns. We will present these for you to learn actively later. For now, learn to recognize dual suffixes when you see and hear them. It will be easy for you to identify them because they all share the endings ا or ان or ـَين . The following sentences contain examples of different dual suffixes:

هما أختان تدرسان في نفس القسم.

أذهب الى صفَّين فقط في يوم الأربعاء.

هذان البيتان صغيران!

القصة بالفصحى

تـمريـن ٦: "أنا خالد" (في البيت) 🎧

Watch القصة بالفصحى and answer the questions below. The dictation exercise can be completed in the book or online.

1. What makes this version sound more formal than the spoken one? Compare the use of verbs in particular, and list the differences you hear.

2. Listen for the words لـِ, لذلكِ, and لأنّ. What question do these words answer? What implied questions does Khalid answer in this narrative? Write out the questions بالعربية.

٣. استمعوا الى خالد واكتبوا:

أنا خالد (١) _____ أبو العلا ، (٢) _____ في كلية

(٣) _____ (٤) _____ القاهرة، (٥) _____

(٦) _____ (٧) _____ وأدرس (٨) _____

(٩) _____ (١٠) _____ ماجستير في إدارة

(١١) _____ (١٢) . _____ (١٣) _____ ثلاثة

(١٤) _____ فقط في (١٥) _____ ، ولا (١٦) _____

(١٧) _____ (١٨) _____ في (١٩) _____ لا

(٢٠) _____ ، لذلك (٢١) _____ (٢٢) _____ الكلية

(٢٣) _____ (٢٤) _____ (٢٥) _____

(٢٦) _____ فقط.

القواعد ٢

المَصدَر

You heard Khalid use the word الحُصول على with the meaning of "to obtain," which is an infinitive verb form in English:

I am studying (in order) to obtain an MA	أدرس للحصول على ماجستير

This meaning can also be expressed in English as "I am studying for the purpose of obtaining an MA." In formal Arabic الحُصول على means both *to obtain* and *obtaining*. Another word you know that functions similarly is السَّفَر, *traveling* or *to travel*. Both الحُصول على and السفر belong to a class of words known as مَصدَر (ج.) مَصادِر, literally *the source*, since Arab grammarians consider this to be the source form of the verb. As such, المصدر expresses the abstract idea of an action, or an action that has no time reference or tense (this is what "infinitive" means)[1]. Because it is an abstract concept, المصدر will almost always be definite (sometimes as the first word in an إضافة).

The nature of المصدر as a highly abstract kind of word means that it is used more in formal Arabic than in spoken. For example, in lesson 4 you hear Maha say قبل السفر الى القاهرة, whereas in the colloquial stories you heard قبل ما اسافر ع الشام/القاهرة. These two constructions mean the same thing, المصدر is just more formal. Compare the following pairs, which also overlap in meaning:

باحبّ اسافِر	بحبّ اسافِر	أُحِبّ السَّفَر
اسافر بعد ما اتْخَرَّج	بعد ما اتْخَرَّج	بعد التَخَرُّج

Although المصدر often corresponds to an English word ending in "–ing," not all English words ending in -ing can be expressed in Arabic with المصدر[2]. This is because the English suffix –ing has two different functions, only one of which matches that of المصدر. Think about the use of the word "running" in the following sentences:

Running is not just a sport for the young.

I am *running* to catch the bus.

In the first sentence, "running" is a noun. Notice that you can substitute for it other nouns like "basketball" and "soccer" and that it refers to an abstract notion but not an ongoing action (no one is actually running in the first sentence). In contrast, "running" in the second sentence functions as an adjective. Notice that you can substitute for it another adjective, such as "happy," and it pairs up with the verb "to be" to indicate an ongoing action. The Arabic مصدر is a noun, not an adjective, so it cannot be used in sentences such as "I am running." When you practice using المصدر, remember that it cannot take a subject; we cannot say things such as هي السفر الى تونس.

---

[1] المصدر is a noun, not an adjective, and it corresponds in part to what is called a gerund in English grammar. Some English grammars of Arabic call المصدر the "verbal noun" because they view it as a noun that derives from and refers to a verb.

[2] In English grammar these two functions are called "gerund" and "participle." The Arabic مصدر is a gerund in Arabic grammar but it is not a participle. (Arabic has a different set of patterns for participles, which we will present in *Al-Kitaab Part 2*).

Rather, we use المضارع to convey this meaning: تسافر إلى تونس. Use المصدر to say things such as, "I like running," "Getting a degree is important," "Traveling can be fun," and "Learning maSdars is not hard!"

المصدر and Verb Patterns

Can we predict the form of المصدر? In many cases, yes we can, according to the pattern of the verb. In lesson 4 we presented the concept of verb patterns, and you saw four of these patterns, which some English grammars and dictionaries call Form I, Form II, Form III, and Form V. You know that the stem vowels of Form I verbs are unpredictable and must be memorized. Form I مصادر also do not adhere to one fixed pattern, though there are a few very common ones. Hence, the مصدر of each Form I verb must be memorized. Each of the other forms has a fixed مصدر pattern that is regular and predictable, with rare exceptions in a few high frequency verbs. As you learn more verbs and their مصادر, you will see these patterns recurring. We will present the most common of these patterns in the sections that follow.

Form I: Variable

All the patterns listed below are common Form I مصدر patterns. As you listen to each set, pick out the pattern shared among the verbs and المصادر.

الفَعْـل

This pattern is the simplest and most common مصدر pattern of Form I.

الأَكْل	يَأكُل
الرَّقْص	يَرقُص

الفِعْـل الفُعْـل الفَعَـل

Similar to the first pattern, these three مصادر show slight vowel variations. Learning المصادر by listening to them (not reading them) will help you internalize and recall them.

العَمَل	يَعمَل
السَّكَن	يَسكُن
الشُّرْب	يَشرَب
الحِفْظ	يَحفَظ

الفُعـول

In this pattern, the short ضمّة vowel in the first syllable and the long vowel و in the second syllable echo each other.

الشُّعور بـ	يَشعُر بـ
الحُصول على	يَحصُل على
القُبول	يَقبَل

الفِعالة

This pattern is common among "activity" verbs. Note the كسرة vowel in the first syllable.

الدِّراسة	يَدرُس
الكِتابة	يَكتُب
القِراءة	يَقرأ
السِّباحة	يَسبَح

الذَّهاب إلى	يذهَب إلى
المَعْرِفة	يعرِف

الفَعـال / المَفْعِـلة

These two verbs have less common مصدر patterns.

Form II: التَّـفْعيل

The Form II مصدر pattern is highly regular. It has two syllables, the first beginning with ت and the second containing the long vowel ي. You can also see in the examples that المصدر may be used as a regular noun: التصوير means both photography and taking pictures. Recognizing this pattern as a Form II مصدر means that you can derive and use the verb from it, as you see in the chart below. All Form II verbs follow the pattern of يُدَرِّس:

Notice that Form II verbs have a shadda, or **doubled** consonant.

التَّدْريس	يُدَرِّس
التَّصْوير	يُصَوِّر

Form III: المُـفاعَلـة

You know three verbs in this pattern now, shown in the table below. What is the shared pattern among these verbs? What pattern do the first two مصادر share? Note that the verb يسافر has a مصدر that does not fit the pattern (a rare exception).

Form III verbs and مصادر have a distinctive alif. The verb يُسافِر does not use the regular مصدر pattern. It is a rare exception for this form.

المُشاهَدة	يُشاهِد
المُحاضَرة	يُحاضِر
السَّفَر إلى	يُسافِر إلى

Form V: التَّـفَعُّـل

Form V is also a very common verb pattern. What is the pattern you see here? Which verb uses a مصدر that does not fit the pattern?

The verb يَتَكَلَّم has two possible مصدر patterns; the first one is more commonly used, even though it does not fit the pattern.

التَّخرُّج	يَتَخَرَّج
التَّذَكُّر	يَتَذَكَّر
الكَلام (التَّكَلُّم)	يَتَكَلَّم

Form VIII: الاِفْتِعـال

This pattern also has a ت, but it is positioned between the second and third root consonants. Pick out the roots of these two verbs, then look at the shared syllable pattern. What are its distinguishing features?

This pattern has a ت added between the second and third root consonant.
What do you think the verb يَمتَحِن means?

الاِسْتِماع إلى	يَسْتَمِع إلى
الاِمْتِحان	يَمتَحِن

Beginning in lesson 7, the مصدر form will be given along with المضارع of each new verb so that you can memorize both المضارع and المصدر together. We will return to the root and pattern system of Arabic verbs in lesson 8.

المصدر والإضافة

While it is part of the verb system, المصدر behaves grammatically like a noun; it can be a subject, object, or predicate of a sentence, or it can be the object of a preposition, as these examples show.

١. السفر بالأوتوبيس صعب!

٢. لا أحبّ السباحة في الشتاء.

٣. أحسن هواية بالنسبة لي هي الرقص!

٤. هل تأكل قبل الذهاب الى الصف؟

We noted before that المصدر is normally definite, and in the examples we have seen so far, المصادر have all had الـ. But المصدر can also occur in an إضافة, and, in fact, it must be the first term of an إضافة if its action is carried out on an object. For example, the verbs يقرأ and يكتب usually involve reading and writing *something*. In order to express this *something* with المصدر, we use an إضافة:

writing the homework (literally, *the writing of the homework*)	كِتابة الواجب
watching television (literally, *the watching of the television*)	مُشاهَدة التليفزيون

تمريـن ٧: المصدر (في البيت)

What are they talking about? Use an appropriate مصدر to express the action, adding words as you need them. Remember to decide if المصدر is definite with الـ or because it is in an إضافة :

مثال: لا أحب كتابة الرسائل.

١. هل تحبّون .... في نيويورك؟

٢. نستمع الى الكلمات قبل .... ـها.

٣. أصدقائي مشغولون بـ .... واجباتهم.

٤. أذهب الى المكتبة لـ ....

٥. .... بالوحدة صعب جداً.

٦. هل تدرس لـ .... على الدكتوراه؟

٧. أختي تحبّ .... الناس بكاميرتها الجديدة.

٨. أستاذتنا لا تحبّ .... في الصباح.

٩. أنا وأصدقائي نذهب الى المطعم اللبناني لـ .... الفلافل والحمص.

١٠. هل تحبّون .... الأفلام العربية؟

تمريـن ٨: المصدر والفعل المضارع (في الصف)

How would you express the following in Arabic? In some cases you will use المصدر and in others الفعل المضارع; determine which is correct for each context and translate:

1. I like to travel because traveling is great. I'm traveling to Paris today!

2. We're studying Arabic, and we like studying Arabic.

3. My brother isn't in school now; he's working.

4. Getting a job is hard these days.

5. I sometimes study at home, but studying at the library is best.

6. My father doesn't like writing email letters.

7. When are you all graduating?

8. She is not speaking with her mother.

9. Don't you like watching movies?

10. My friends are traveling to Europe this week.

11. Why aren't you all eating?

تـمـريـن ٩: مصادر جديدة من مفردات قديمة (في الصف)

This exercise is a purely mechanical one whose aim is to help you develop a feel for the مصدر patterns. To get the most benefit out of it, practice saying the words you see and the new words you write out loud.

Each column in the chart below represents a مصدر pattern. Underneath it, you see a list of familiar words, each of which can be made into a مصدر of the form given. Find the root in each word, then put it into the pattern to form new مصادر:

التَّفَعُّل Form V	المُـفَـاعَـلة Form III	التَّفْعيل Form II
يعرف	صديق	جديد
القبول	رسالة	وحيد
شمس	يتذكّر	علم
قريب	بعيد	أحسن
متخصّص	أحفظ	صحيح

تـمـريـن ١٠: المصدر والهوايات (في الصف)

With a partner, read the following text and find out which people match your interests. Then find a new partner and compare notes. After you finish, see how many new words you can find that you think are مصادر, vowel them, and, if you know الجذر, guess what they mean.

الاسم	السن	الهوايات	العنوان
هبة الله مصطفى	٢٤	القراءة، سماع الأغاني، المراسلة	٢ ش د. أحمد إبراهيم – مدينة نصر – القاهرة
باسم حسن حامد	٤	القراءة، سماع الأغاني، الرسم، المراسلة	٧١١١٣ ش الشرقاوي – أحمد سعيد
مؤمن درويش	٢٢	المراسلة، الرسم، الرياضة	العزيزة – المنزلة – دقهلية
محمد صبري	١٦	الرسم، سماع الأغاني، الموسيقى	أسيوط – ٧١١١٤
ثريا محمد جمال	١٨	القراءة، سماع الأغاني، الموسيقى	٢٢ ش جمال عبد الناصر القبلي، نبين الكرم – المنوفية
نهى أحمد السيد	١٧	القراءة، سماع الأغاني	٧ ش عمر بن أبي ربيعة الحضرة القبلية – الإسكندرية
محمود محمد أحمد	٨	الرسم، الكمبيوتر، القراءة، المراسلة	٣ ش أحمد ياسين، فيصل – مدينة النور – القاهرة
فريد صقر سيد	٤	السباق الدراجات، الرسم، سماع الأغاني، السباحة	٩ ش جامع خضر، طوسون، شبرا
فاطمة صبري رشدي	٢	القراءة، الدينية والأدبية والشعر	قنطرة غمرة رقم ٧١ عمارة القاهرة كود بريد ١٢٧١
مي عبد المنعم خاطر	٩	الرحلات، النت، المراسلة	١ سكة سندوب – مشعل منزل أبو نمرة رقم ١ المنصورة
محمود صلاح سالم	٦	القراءة في مجال السياسة الدين	كفر الشيخ – الكتالة – عمارة رفاعي عطوان
محمد زكريا عامر	٥	جمع العملات، المراسلة كرة القدم	الدقهلية – منزل منشأة – برج التحرير – الإسكندرية
هند محمد عطية	٢	السباحة، الرياضة، سماع الموسيقى	١٢ ش محطفى كامل – فلتنج – برج التحرير – الإسكندرية
أحمد محمد الشناوي	١٧	الإسكواش، السباحة	١٧ ش عبد المنعم حداد – كفر الزيات، العربية للأنابيب
سمر محمد حسين	٣	مراسلة البنات فقط الكمبيوتر	١٥ ش مصطفى كامل – سموحة – شقة ٢ – ٤ – الإسكندرية
ربيع أحمد ملوخية	١٧	سماع الموسيقى والقراءة	٢١ ش مالك حفني، فيكتوريا، الإسكندرية
دينا محمد إبراهيم	٣	سماع الأغاني والموسيقى والسباحة	محافظة الغربية – قطور – الجيش – كفر الزيات
أحمد محمد شاهين	١٧	المراسلة، الإنترنت، الشطرنج	٢٨ ش ابن خلدون – روض الفرج
رشا صبري حافظ	١٨	الموسيقى، القراءة	٩ ش يوليو – مجمع السلام – مكتب ٥٠،٧٥ بورسعيد
نشوى عبد اللطيف	١٧	الرسم، سماع الأغاني	١٢ ش ابن الفرات شبرا – مصر
هالة عادل سعد	١٧	مشاهدة كرة القدم، الكمبيوتر	ش سعد زغلول بجوار السجل المدني، دمنهور
محمود محمد جمال	١٧	كرة القدم، كرة السلة، المراسلة	٢ ش السلاح من المحكمة – ص ب ١١١١٢، طنطا
رفعت يونس	١٢	كرة السلة، الموسيقى الأجنبية	٥ ش حفني الطردي، النيل، القاهرة ش ٣
حسين صبري ٢ حسين	٥١		

القواعد ٣

لِماذا؟

why?		لِماذا؟
because		لِأَنَّ
in order to, for the purpose of		لِ
because of		بِسَبَب

For the first time we will begin to work with complex sentences, that is, sentences that contain more than one clause. As we move beyond simple sentence patterns, it will become increasingly important for you to think grammatically about sentence construction. The structures of Arabic sentences are easy to understand and produce if you learn to think according to a step-by-step construction process in which each component of the sentence tells you what kind of grammatical structure comes next. This information will be given to you in the vocabulary lists and grammar sections of each chapter as we proceed through the book. For example, in this chapter you saw: (لِأَنَّ + جملة اسمية). This information reminds you that the very next element in any sentence with لِأَنَّ must be a noun heading a sentence and cannot be a verb—we cannot say in formal Arabic, for example, لِأَنَّ أدرس.

You have seen three ways to answer the question لِماذا why?, or to give information about reasons or purposes, and we will present the rules for their usage one at a time below. While the meanings of these particles are similar, their grammatical usages are quite distinct, and two of them have limited uses. Memorize the way in which each word or particle is used grammatically in addition to its dictionary meaning.

١. لِأَنَّ + جملة اسمية because

The most widely used construction for giving a reason is لِأَنَّ because it is used in both formal and spoken Arabic and because it introduces a complete sentence. (The other possible constructions, لِ and بِسبب, are more limited in grammatical context and meaning.) لِأَنَّ may be used to give any kind of sentence-length explanation, such as "because the weather is cold" or "because she is sick."

In formal Arabic, لِأَنَّ has one hard and fast rule: It must be followed by a جملة اسمية. In the first example below, the sentence الجو فيها بارد has a clear مبتدأ and خبر:

لا تحب "شيكاغو" لِأَنَّ الجو فيها بارد في الشتاء .

In the next sentence, لِأَنَّها. Where is الخبر? the المبتدأ is the pronoun ـها on لِأَنَّها. Where is الخبر?

لا تذهب الى الكلية هذا الأسبوع لِأَنَّها مريضة.   because she is sick

In الفصحى, if the جملة اسمية that follows أنّ begins with a pronoun, the pronoun must be attached to لأنّ, as it is in the immediately preceding example. The same pronouns that function as the object of a verb are attached to لأنّ, too:

because I . . .	لأني / لأنَّني	لأنَّ + أنا
because you . . .	لأنَك / لأنَّكِ	لأنَّ + أنتَ/أنتِ
because he/it . . .	لأنَّهُ	لأنَّ + هو
because she/it/they . . .	لأنَّها	لأنَّ + هي
because we . . .	لأنَّنا	لأنَّ + نحن
because you . . .	لأنَّكُم	لأنَّ + أنتم
because they . . .	لأنَّهُم	لأنَّ + هم

٢. لِ + المصدر / المضارع in order to

The particle لِ introduces a reason or purpose for doing something and corresponds to the English *in order to* or *for the purpose of* [3]. In this construction, لِ may be followed either by المصدر or by الفعل المضارع. Both constructions give the same basic meaning, but المصدر tends to be a bit more formal in style than المضارع. The following pairs of examples are equivalent in meaning:

أدرس لأحصُل على البكالوريوس.	=	أدرس لِلحصول على البكالوريوس.
يذهبون إلى المكتبة لِيدرسوا.	=	يذهبون إلى المكتبة لِلدراسة.
تستمع إلى الـ iPod لِتحفَظ الكلمات.	=	تستمع إلى الـ iPod لِحِفْظ الكلمات.

Notice in the preceding examples that the alif on الـ has been dropped in the words لِلحصول and لِلدراسة. This rule applies whenever لِ is prefixed to a word beginning with الـ:

لِ + القراءة ⟶ لِلقراءة   لِ + الكلام ⟶ لِلكلام

٣. بسبب + اسم because of

The word بِسَبَب (preposition بِ and noun سَبَب *reason*) has restricted usage because it can only be used as the first part of an إضافة and cannot be followed by a sentence. Explanations with بسبب are short and to the point:

because of the overcrowding	لا أحب نيويورك بسبب الازدحام
because of the beautiful weather	نحب الصيف بسبب الجو الجميل

---

[3] Do not confuse "in order to" with infinitive "to" in phrases such as "I like to read." Always ask yourself: does this "to" answer the question لماذا؟

تـمريـن ١١: لماذا؟ (في البيت)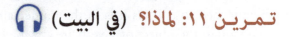

This exercise is available online only.

تـمريـن ١٢: لماذا؟ (في البيت وفي الصف)

What would you like to do and why? On five 3x5 cards or slips of paper, write five different things you would like to do that you can express in Arabic, and why you would like to do them. Be creative and use all the constructions we have learned to answer لماذا؟ Bring them with you to class. In class, have everyone mix all the cards in a bag from which each person will draw out one at a time. Find the author of each wish by asking زملاءك *"Do you want to ..?"* until you have found the person who wrote the card.

القراءة ٣

تـمريـن ١٣: "روزانا" (في الصف)

The BBC Arabic Service regularly produces human interest stories. The following text is taken from their series on girls and young women in the Arab world[4]. Use good reading strategies to get as much as you can out of the text:

1. First reading: Scan the text. How is the text arranged? What helps you divide it up into parts for closer reading?

2. Second reading: Focus on the words you know.
    a. What do we know about her?
    b. What are the important things in her life?

3. Third reading: Close-read the text.
    a. How many مصادر can you identify?
    b. How many dual words can you find?
    c. Where does she talk about the future? What does she hope for the future?
    d. List any words you have guessed from contextual or grammatical clues:

---

[4] Artwork has been substituted for original photographs.

اسمي رُوزانا، عمري ٢١ سنة، طالبة في مجال علم النفس التربوي، ومتزوجة ولديَّ طفل. أريد أن أتكلم عن حياتي الحالية وكيف أوازن بين مسؤولياتي المختلفة.

هذه كليتي وهي جزء كبير من حياتي لأن التعليم من أساسيات الحياة وان شاء الله سأتخرج بعد عام.

أهم شخصين في حياتي هما زوجي وابني، لأنهم أسرتي وسبب سعادتي، ومن دونهم اشعر بالضياع.

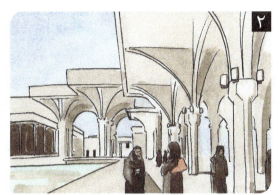

وهذه صورة اخوتي في منزل والدتي. أما الكرسيان والطاولة، فهي قطع أثاث من بيت أبي. وأعتز بها كثيرا، لأنني أتذكر إخوتي من أبي وأهل والدي فور رؤيتها لأن هذا الأثاث تنقل مع أبي.

هذه صورة لنا مع صديقتي التي اعتبرها أساسية في حياتي، فهي أيضا من أقاربي ووُلِدنا في نفس العام.

وهذه مكتبتي في البيت أنا وزوجي. وتـمثل حبي للقراءة، وهي مفيدة جدا لأنها تجعلنا أكثر انفتاحا. وهذه الصورة هي مذكراتي. والكتابة جزء كبير من حياتي لأنها طريقة للتعبير عن نفسي. ومن أحلامي أيضا أن أصبح كاتبة في المستقبل.

زوجي يعمل ويكمل دراسته بالإضافة إلى كونه زوج وأب.

http://news.bbc.co.uk/hi/arabic

الحوار

اللغة والثقافة

In contexts such as an interview, when one party is expected to make an offer but does not want to do so on the spot, she or he can say إن شاء الله خير *hopefully it will work out well* as a noncommittal but polite good wish. The phrase إن شاء الله خير expresses a wish that things go well without promising anything specific. It can also be used to wish people luck.

You know that the title إستاذ / أُستاذ is often used as a respectful term of address to a teacher. Here you will see it used in addressing an educated person or white-collar employee in a professional context.

تمريـن ١٤: "ليش بدك تشتغل بشركتنا؟" / "ليه عايز تشتغل في شركتنا؟" (في البيت) 🎧

Listen to the dialogue using the strategies you have learned, and answer بالعربي as completely as you can.	Listen to the dialogue using the strategies you have learned, and answer بالعربي as completely as you can.
1. What is the situation? شو هاد؟	1. What is the situation? ايه دا؟
2. What experience and skills does غَسّان mention?	2. What experience and skills does طارق mention?
الدراسة الشغل شو كمان؟	الدراسة الشغل ايه كمان؟
3. Do you think غسّان will succeed? ليش؟	3. Do you think طارق will succeed? ليه؟
4. How many past tense verbs can you hear? Write them down. When do they use the past tense?	4. How many past tense verbs can you hear? Write them down. When do they use the past tense?
5. Write two new words or expressions you heard and what you think they mean. See if you can find the word for "salary."	5. Write two new words or expressions you heard and what you think they mean. See if you can find the word for "salary."

تمارين المراجعة

تمـرين ١٥: ما هي الكلمة الغريبة؟ (في البيت)

This exercise is available online only.

تمـرين ١٦: هذا/ هذه (في البيت)

This exercise is available online only.

تمـرين ١٧: القراءة الجهرية (في البيت أو في الصف)

Read the following passage, first silently for comprehension, then aloud to practice pronunciation. When you are ready, record the passage and submit it to your teacher, either online or as instructed by your teacher.

اسمي أسامة ماهر النوري وأنا أخو طارق. عمري ثماني عشرة سنة. وأنا طالب بَكالوريا في مدرسة يوسف العَظمة في مدينة دمشق. أحب مدرستي وأساتذتي ولكن الدروس طويلة والامتحانات كثيرة، ولذلك أشعر بالتَّعَب دائماً ...حياة طالب البكالوريا فعلاً صعبة جداً. عندي هواية واحدة فقط هي الرّياضة، وأنا ألعب كرة القدم وكرة السلّة مع زملائي كل يوم جمعة وأحياناً بعد الصفوف يوم الاثنين. في الصيف أعمل في التجارة مع خالي عبد السَّلام في سوق الحَميدِيّة ، وأنا أعمل معه منذ كان عمري ١٤ سنة لأنّي أحب حياة السّوق وأحب مشاهدة الناس وازدحامهم في شوارعه وأحب أيضاً أكْل الحلويات الطيّبة في مطاعمه والكلام مع التُّجّار من كل مدن سوريا.

درس 7
Lesson 7

الله يرحمها

المفردات

الثقافة: الثَّانوية العامّة

القصة بالعامية: "أنا أكبر واحد" "أنا أكبرهم"

الاستماع: "ميّت من الجوع" "حاموت من الجوع!"

القواعد:

أفعَل The Superlative

الجملة الاسمية: الخبر المُقَدَّم Fronted Predicate

القصة بالفصحى: "أنا أكبرهم"

القراءة: "النعي"

الاستماع: مع العائلة والاصدقاء

الحوار: "يا لطيف!" "يا ساتر يا ربّ!"

تمارين المراجعة

المُفرَدات Vocabulary 🎧

Listen to the new vocabulary in your spoken variety and in formal Arabic.

المعنى	المصري	الشامي	الفُصحى
first (adj.)			أولى (مؤنث) (مذكر: أوّل)
secondary	ثانوي	ثانوي	ثانَويّ/ة
crazy			مَجنون/ة ج مَجانين
accident	حادْثة ج. حَوادِث	حادِث ج. حَوادِث	حادِث ج. حَوادِث
saddening, distressing[1]	بيزَعِّل	بيزَعِّل	مُحزِن/ة
foreign affairs	الخارْجيّة	الخارْجيّة	الخارْجيّة
May God rest her soul	الله يِرحَمها	الله يِرحَمها	رَحَمَها الله
(future tense prefix)[2]	حَـ	رَح ، حَـ	سَـ
hospital			مُسْتَشْفى ج مُسْتَشْفَيات
preparatory (school, referring to middle school or junior high school)			إعدادِيّ/ة
general, public[3]			عامّ /ة
to live	بِيعيش	يْعيش	يَعيش
economics, economy			الاِقتِصاد
the biggest or oldest			أكْبَر (+ اسم نكرة)
he died	ماتْ	ماتْ	ماتَ
she died	ماتِت	ماتِت	ماتَت
money	فِلوس	مَصاري	مال ج. أموال
there is	فيه	فيه	هُناك
ministry			وِزارة ج. - ات

Notes on Vocabulary Usage

1. The words مُحزِّل، بيزَعِّل، مُحزِن describe something that makes you sad or upset. In formal Arabic you might be زَعلان because of something that is مُحزِن, and in spoken Arabic you are حَزين/ة because of something that بيزَعِّل. Notice that the formal word is an adjective, whereas spoken Arabic uses a Form II verb to convey the meaning: *it makes one* زعلان/ة. It is common in spoken Arabic for verbs to be used to describe feelings. English speakers use "sad" to describe both a person with the feeling of sadness (sad child) and a situation or thing that makes the person sad (sad news), but in Arabic these meanings are conveyed by different patterns. The state of "being sad/happy/hungry," etc., corresponds to the use of a Form I verb, and the idea of "making (someone) sad/happy/hungry," etc., corresponds to the use of a Form II verb.

2. The future tense is indicated by a prefix on المضارع:

المُستَقبَل The Future

حَ	رَح or حَ	سَ
حاروح معاك المستشفى.	حَروح معك ع المستشفى.	سَأذهب معك إلى المستشفى.
حَيتخرّجوا السنة دي؟	رَح تِتخرّجوا هالسنة؟	هل سَتَتَخرّجون هذه السنة؟
حاكُل مع اصحابي المسا.	حآكُل مع رفقاتي المسا.	سآكُل مع أصدقائي هذا المساء.

3. The adjective عامّ refers to things in the public sector, such as:

المكتبة العامّة *public administration* الإدارة العامّة | العمل العامّ *public service* | *public administration*

It is not, however, used to refer to what we, in the United States, call "public schools."

🎧 تمـريـن ١: المفردات الجديدة (في البيت) 🎧

Practice using the new vocabulary by writing the correct formal word in the correct form to complete the sentences.

١. في مدينة نيويورك مكتبة _____ كبيرة وممتازة فيها كتب بلغات كثيرة.

٢. وزارة _____ الأمريكية تريد موظفين يتكلمون اللغة العربية للعمل في السِّفارات *embassies* الأمريكية في البلاد العربية.

٣. مات ناس كثيرون في _____ سيارات هذه السنة، هذا شيء _____ فعلاً !!

٤. الطقس _____ في هذه الأيام: أسبوع برد وثلج وأسبوع حرارة ورطوبة!!

٥. ما عندي وظيفة ، وكثير من الناس في بلدنا لا يعملون بسبب _____ .

٦. اسمي غسّان وأنا طالب في السنة _____ (فرِشمَن) في الجامعة الأمريكية في الكويت. والدي موظف في _____ العمل *Labor* الكويتية ووالدتي طبيبة، وهي تعمل في _____ كبير في مدينة الكويت. أنا _____ ولد في الاسرة ولي أخت وأخ صغيران. أختي عمرها ١٥ سنة

وهي طالبة في مدرسة ــــــــــــــــ للبنات وأخي عمره ١٢ سنة وهو طالب في مدرسة ــــــــــــــــ .

نحن ــــــــــــــــ في الكويت منذ ١٠ سنوات وقبل ذلك كنّا في السعودية.

جدّي يسكن معنا في البيت لأن جدتي ــــــــــــــــ منذ سنة.

تـمـريـن ٢: المفردات في جمل 🎧

استمعوا الى جمل المفردات واكتبوا كل الجمل من "أُولى" إلى "وِزارة".

تـمـريـن ٣: اسألوا زملاءكم (في الصف)

A. Find out from الزملاء and take brief notes to report:

1. What are they going to do this week?
2. Whose car died this year?
3. Who was in a car accident this year? Where? Was it a big one?
4. How is the US economy [doing] now as far as they are concerned?
5. Who would like to work for the State Department? Why?
6. Who is a freshman (hint: what year of college)?
7. Who has been in the hospital? How many days or weeks were they there?
8. Who has lived in the same house since childhood?
9. What crazy things have they done in their life?
10. Do they go to the public library in their hometown?

B. With a partner, list in Arabic the full names of all the schools where each of you has studied. Think about how you would order the nouns and adjectives.

الثقافة: الثّانَوِية العامّة 🎧

International Baccalaureate, High School Diploma

In many Arab countries, الثانويّة العامّة refers to both the last year of high school and the set of examinations students take at the end of that year. The exams are cumulative, covering all subjects studied throughout high school, and students' scores on these exams determine whether or not they will graduate and in what college they may enroll. Cutoff scores are very high for entering medicine, engineering, and the sciences in general. Students face tremendous pressure to perform well on these exams, and this pressure can affect the entire family. Watch the interviews in  "ما هي الثانويّة العامّة بالنسبة لك؟" to hear people describe how these exams affect family life.

القصة بالعامية

تـمريـن ٤: "أنا أكبر واحد" / "أنا أكبرهم" (في البيت) 🎧

Listen to خالد, using the strategies you have learned. Write a **paragraph** for each question.	Listen to طارق, using the strategies you have learned. Write a **paragraph** for each question.
١. مين في عيلة خالد وبنعرف ايه عنهم؟	١. مين بعيلة طارق وشو بنعرف عنهن؟
٢. الوالد بيشتغل فين؟ والوالدة؟	٢. وين بيشتغل الوالد؟ والوالدة؟
٣. مين عايش مع العيلة دلوقتي؟ ليه؟	٣. مين ساكن مع العيلة هلّق؟ ليش؟
٤. خالد زعلان ليه؟	٤. ليش طارق زعلان؟

تـمريـن ٥: "ميِّت من الجوع" / "حاموت من الجوع!" (في البيت) 🎧

Watch الجدة? What do they ask المدرسة. What do they ask الجدة? What do you think the title of this scene means? With a partner, create a scene in which you are as hungry as they are and decide what to do about it.

القواعد

The Superlative أفعَل

You have learned two words that have superlative meaning: أكبر (ولد) and أحسن (فصل). Notice that these words share a pattern: The words are two syllables, each with fatHa vowels, and the first syllable begins with alif. The shape and name of this pattern is أَفْعَل. These words can function as either comparative adjectives or superlatives, each of which has a different grammatical construction. Here we will focus on their use as superlatives.

Superlatives may be formed from simple adjectives like بارد and كبير, صغير, صعب by using the root of the adjective: Extract the root and insert it into the pattern أَفْعَل. Grammatically, you may use any أفعل word with a following اسم نكرة indefinite noun to give the superlative meaning:

ما هي أَحسَن جامعة بالنسبة لك؟   روسيا هي أَكـبَر بلد في أوروبا .

Remember:
To give the superlative meaning, use an indefinite noun following the أفعَل word.

تمـرين ٦: "أفعل" (في البيت) 🎧

This exercise is available online only.

تمـرين ٧: "أفعل" (في الصف)

With a partner, come up with a list of "top ten" categories to poll your زملاء about, using as many different أفعل words as you can. Some examples might include best film, biggest restaurant, and hardest day of (in) the week. Then poll as many people as you can in the time allotted and report back to the class.

Fronted Predicate الخبر المُقَدَّم :الجملة الاسمية

Expressing possessive and "there is/there are" types of sentences in Arabic is not difficult. You have been doing so since *Alif Baa* with عندي and فيه / فيه. In this section we will first present an overview of possessive sentences, then show you the grammatical structure of these kinds of sentences, which are considered to be جمل اسمية in Arabic grammar.

You have seen both لـ and عند used to indicate possession, as in:

لي خالة اسمها نادية.   عندي سيّارة جديدة.

These words overlap somewhat in meaning but لـ tends to be more formal and abstract than عند, and it is used in cases where the possession is figurative, as in human relationships, or to indicate figurative belonging.

It is important to keep in mind that عند is only used for **human** possessors. When you are describing what a place (such as "my house") or an abstract entity (such as "my family") or an institution (such as "our university") *has*, you should use فيه/فيها:

بيتي فيه أربع غرف.   or   في بيتي أربع غرف.

أسرتي فيها ثلاث بنات وولد.   or   في أسرتي ثلاث بنات وولد.

في قسمنا عشرة أساتذة متخصصون في لغات الشرق الأوسط.

If the entire sentence is very abstract, لـ may be used but not عند:

هذه المدينة لها تاريخ طويل.   or   لهذه المدينة تاريخ طويل.

Like عند, ‍لـ is often used with pronoun objects. Listen to and learn the pronunciation of ‍لـ with pronouns in the variety of Arabic your class is using, and learn to reocgnize the formal set.

المصري	الشامي	الفُصحى
لِيَّ	إلي	لي
ليك	إلَك	لَك
ليكي	إلِك	لَكِ
ليه	إله	لَهُ
ليها	إلها	لَها
لينا	إلنا	لَنا
ليكو	إلكُن	لَكُم
ليهم	إلهُن (إلُن)	لَهُم

These prepositions are used to express "to have," which is a verbal concept in English, but they are not themselves verbs. The prepositions عند and ‍لـ are not verbs but prepositions and thus function differently in sentences than the way we use "to have", which is a verb, in English. While the English verb gets a subject (I have, she has), the Arabic prepositions occur in prepositional phrases with pronouns, as you saw above, or with nouns. The sentences in which they occur are a kind of جملة اسمية in which the order of المبتدأ and الخبر is reversed. To understand how this kind of sentence works, think of a grammatical translation for two of the original examples given above:

At-me is a new car.	عندي سيّارة جديدة.
Belonging-to-me is an aunt named Nadia.	لي خالة اسمها نادية.

Here المبتدأ cannot occur at the beginning of the sentence because an Arabic sentence may not begin with an indefinite noun. For this reason, the prepositional phrase خبر jumps in front of المبتدأ so the order of المبتدأ and الخبر is reversed.

The reversed جملة اسمية is used to express possession and the existential construction there is/there are هُناك / فيه / فيه. These sentences begin with a خبر that usually consists of a prepositional phrase or the word هناك there, as the following examples demonstrate:

There are many people on this street.	في هذا الشارع ناس كثيرون.
There is only one daughter/girl in our family.	في أسرتنا بنت واحدة فقط.
There are many Egyptians in the Emirates.	هناك مصريون كثيرون في الإمارات.

In spoken Arabic such sentences are often preceded by a sentence topic, but the basic reversed جملة اسمية remains its core. Compare the following sentences with the formal ones just above:

فيه ناس كتير في الشارع دا.	فيه ناس كتير بهالشارع.
فيه بنت واحدة بس في عيلتنا.	فيه بنت واحدة بس بعيلتنا.
فيه مصريين كتير في الإمارات.	فيه سوريين كتير بالإمارات.

The important thing to remember when reading these kinds of sentences is that you need to find the break between المبتدأ and الخبر because this is where the meaning "there is" or "there are" fits into the sentence. In English, this break is clearly marked by the verb "to be," but in Arabic it is not. Which part of the sentence is المبتدأ (what the sentence is about)? Which part is الخبر, and what is it saying about المبتدأ? The following diagrams show the grammatical structure of reversed جملة اسمية. Study the examples:

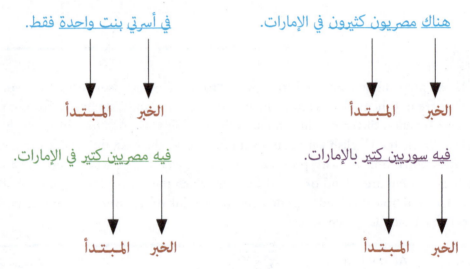

These existential sentences may be negated with the verb لَيْسَ in formal Arabic or with the negative particles ما / ما –ش in spoken Arabic. Choose one variety to learn, and be able to recognize the others:

المعنى	المصري	الشامي	الفُصحى
there is not	ما فيش	ما فيه	لَيسَ هناك
she/he/it does not have	ما فيهوش / ما فيهاش	ما فيه / ما فيها	لَيسَ فيه/ فيها
she/he/it does not have (abstract)	ما لُهش / ما لْهاش	ما لُه / ما لها	لَيسَ له / لَها

أمثلة:

الأوضة دي ما فيهاش شباك!	هالأوضة ما فيها شباك!	هذه الغرفة ليس فيها شباك!
ما عنديش قطة.	ما عندي بسّة.	ليس عندي قطة.
مافيش فصول النهاردا عشان التلج!	مافيه صفوف اليوم منشان التلج!	ليس هناك صفوف اليوم بسبب الثلج!

ما كان / ما كانش. In this جمل اسمية These may be put in the past with كان or negative past ما كانش or negative past ما كان / ما كانش. In this kind of sentence, كان occurs at the beginning of the sentence, and is not conjugated[1]:

كان عندي سيارة بس هلّق ما عندي.	كان عندي سيارة ولكن ليس عندي سيارة الآن.
ما كانش فيه فصول النهاردا عشان الثلج.	ما كان هناك صفوف اليوم بسبب الثلج.
كان إلكن رفقات كتير إيام المدرسة؟	هل كان لكم أصدقاء كثيرون في أيام المدرسة؟
كان ليكو أصحاب كتير أيام المدرسة؟	

We suggest that you memorize a model sentence for each pattern rather than try to remember these rules. At the same time, it is a good idea when you are reading to identify المبتدأ والخبر of existential sentences so that you remember to identify the logical place of the verb "to be."

تـمـريـن ٨: أين المبتدأ؟ (في البيت)

This exercise is available online only.

تـمـريـن ٩: ترجموا الى اللغة العربية (في البيت)

Remember to use فيه/فيها and لـ to describe places and عند or لـ for people.

1. There are no students of Arab descent in our class.
2. Thankfully, there was no traffic (overcrowding) in the streets.
3. I had no time for studying and now I have a big exam!
4. This area does not have many restaurants.
5. They have no money because they are college students.
6. In his childhood, Beirut did not have McDonald's restaurants, and now it has seven.
7. Last week we had lots of homework.
8. They had two sons and three daughters, but the oldest son died.
9. She didn't have office hours yesterday so she wasn't in her office.
10. Last Thursday, we had a crazy day at work.

---

[1] The reason usually given for this is that when كان or any verb precedes its grammatical subject and is separated from it by another word or words, the verb does not have to agree with its subject. We might also think of كان here as putting the sentence as a whole in the past, and that is why it must precede and why it does not agree with any particular part of the sentence.

تمـريـن ١٠: الجملة الاسمية: خبر مقدم مع النَّفي (في البيت)

What do or did these people and places not have? Write out your answers in full sentences, using the written form.

مثال: الطلاب في مصر ليس عندهم محاضرات يوم الجمعة .

١. هذا المطعم ....

٢. خالد ....

٣. أمس، أنا وأصدقائي ....

٤. غرفة صفنا ....

٥. "يا طلاب، لماذا .... في الأسبوع الماضي؟"

٦. إخوتي ....

٧. هذه الجامعة ....

٨. السنة الماضية، ....

تمـريـن ١١: الجملة الاسمية (في الصف)

Identify المبتدأ والخبر in the following sentences by single-underlining المبتدأ and double-underlining الخبر (ignore interrogative particles, adjectives, and adverbs):

١. عندهم محاضرات اليوم.

٢. في هذه الصورة كل الموظفين في مركزنا.

٣. هناك شركات وبنوك أمريكية كثيرة في دُبي.

٤. هل عندك امتحان يوم الأربعاء؟

٥. في مدينة بوسطن ٢٥ جامعة وكلية.

٦. لنا أصدقاء لبنانيون وفلسطينيون.

٧. في هذا البيت غرف كبيرة جداً.

٨. هناك مستشفيات صغيرة في هذه المنطقة.

٩. في حياتهم مشكلة كبيرة.

١٠. عندها هوايات كثيرة.

الكتابة

تمـرين ١٢: نشاط كتابة عن مدينتك بالجملة الاسمية (في البيت)

Write a paragraph of at least fifty words describing what your مدينة has to offer, using فيها and الجملة الاسمية with fronted خبر.

القصة بالفصحى

تمـرين ١٣: "أنا أكبرهم" (في البيت) 🎧

Watch القصة بالفصحى and answer the questions below. The dictation exercise can be completed in the book or online.

1. Listen to خالد tell his story بالفصحى. Fill in the chart with information about the people he talks about:

العمر (approximate)		المدرسة	الاسم

2. Analyze the word order of each sentence خالد says, and determine whether it is:

جملة اسمية   جملة فعلية   جملة اسمية خبر fronted

3. استمعوا إلى خالد واكتبوا ما يقول:

والدي (١) _____ في (٢) _____ (٣) _____ ووالدتي،

الله (٤) _____ ، (٥) _____ ، (٦) _____ في

(٧) _____ (٨) _____ (٩) لي .

(١٠) _____ ، أنا (١١) _____ ؛ عادل طالب في (١٢) _____

(۱۳) _____ ، ووليد طالب في (۱٤) _____ (۱٥) _____ بـ

(۱٦) _____ (۱۷) _____ . وعبد المنعم طالب في (۱۸) _____

(۱۹) _____ (۲۰) _____ (۲۱) _____ .

(۲۲) _____ (۲۳) _____ معنا (۲٤) _____

(۲٥) _____ والدتي، الله (۲٦) _____ في (۲۷) _____

(۲۸) _____ ثلاث (۲۹) _____ .

القراءة

تمرين ۱٤: النَّعي (في الصف)

The following text is taken from the obituary pages of the Egyptian newspaper *Al-Ahram*. Before you read the passage, brainstorm with a partner: What kinds of information do you expect to find? When you have some ideas, skim over the text and identify its parts.

1. Scan: How is the text organized? What kinds of information does it provide about the deceased? Check all the parts you are able to identify. After you finishing scanning, share what you found with your partner and develop a reading plan for phase two.

2. Read: Follow your plan to find more information in the text. Use your grammatical skills to see if you can identify the following words:

deceased _____

daughter _____ (formal word used in newspapers)

sister _____ (While أخت can be either full or half-sister, this word specifies full sister.)

3. What information can you find about the funeral?

4. Analyze: Go through the text again and examine the use of و. One of the most important functions of و is to signal punctuation. و is used instead of a comma to list things, instead of a semicolon for listing phrases, and instead of a period to mark the beginning of a new sentence. Look for two of these functions of و in the text and practice skimming through each section و by و .

بسم الله الرحمن الرحيم

"يا أيتها النفس المطمئنة
ارجعي إلى ربك راضية مرضية"
صدق الله العظيم

انتقلت إلى رحمة الله تعالى
المرحومة علية محمد حسين أبو العلا
كريمة المرحوم محمد حسين أبو العلا
عضو مجلس النواب السابق
زوجة المرحوم لواء شرطة محمود محرم

والدة

الأستاذ محمد جمال محرم عضو مجلس ادارة البنك المصري الخليجي ورئيس الغرفة التجارية الأمريكية زوج السيدة هيام محمد الشرقاوي ووالدة السيدة مرفت محرم.

وجَدَّة

كل من السيدة هنا جمال محرم حرم الأستاذ محمود سلامة مدير شركة فيرومصر والسيدة هند جمال محرم حرم الأستاذ تميم السعدي المدير بشركة هيكله والأستاذ كريم رجب المدير بشركة شورى الدولية.

وشقيقة

كل من المرحوم الأستاذ أحمد محمد حسين أبو العلا مدير عام شركة البحر الأحمر للتأمين والأستاذ المرحوم محمد حسين أبو العلا عضو مجلس الأمة السابق.

وعمة وخالة

كل من الكاتب والمؤلف صلاح أحمد حسين والمرحومة منى أبو العلا والسيدة آية أحمد أبو العلا رئيس مجلس إدارة بيريوس للتأمين والدكتور أيمن أحمد حسين أبو العلا رئيس مجلس إدارة كير اند كيور والمرحوم عماد أبو العلا والأستاذ علاء أبو العلا المدير بفنادق سفير والسيدة فاتن حسين.

وزوجة عم

كل من الدكتورة نادية محرم والأستاذ طارق محرم المحامي والدكتور حازم محرم رئيس مركز النيل للأشعة.

وزوجة خال

كل من السيدة سناء بركات والسيدة هناء بركات والأستاذ رفيق بركات والدكتورة هبة بركات.

والجدة الروحية

لكل من الدكتور أحمد صلاح بأمريكا والأستاذ شريف طنطاوي المدير بأوراسكم والمهندس وليد صلاح والسيدة أميرة عبد الجواد والسيدة ياسمين أيمن والمخرج عمرو صلاح والسيدة انجي عبد الجواد والسيدة سلمى أيمن والآنسة هبة محسن عبد الحميد ومحمد حسام وحكم صلاح وكريم أيمن وياسمين علاء وسارة ونرمين ومحمد مجدي.

وابنة عم وخال

الدكتور صلاح عبد المتعال وإخوته ومحمد عبد الصالحين وإخوته.

وقريبة ونسيبة

عائلات محرم وأبو العلا والشرقاوي وسلامة والسعدي ورجب وراشد وعبد المعز وغريب وعبد المتعال والشحات وجميع عائلات الفشن والشريعي وطنطاوي وعبد الجواد وعبد الرحيم والشوربجي وزكي وعبد الوهاب وسعادة وعمر والحفناوي وحبيب وطه والقشيري والأسيوطي وفاضل.

وشيعت الجنازة يوم السبت والعزاء بجامع عمر مكرم الاثنين للرجال والسيدات.

تلّغرافياً ٩ شارع عبد المنعم رياض

ونسألكم الفاتحة

الاستماع: مع العائلة والأصدقاء

تـمـريـن ١٥: "مع زميلة مها" (في البيت) 🎧

استمعوا واكتبوا:

Watch the video "مع زميلة مها" and write a جملة طويلة for each of the first two questions.

١. من يتكلم؟ الاسم والعائلة والدراسة :

٢. كيف تعرف مها؟ هل هي صديقة مها؟ لماذا ؟

3. You hear the speaker use a new word to describe مها. Identify the root, and write the word. (Hint: Identifying the root before you write will help you hear the word better.) Before you look it up in the glossary, think: What meaning am I expecting?

الحوار

اللغة والثقافة: !Bad News

When someone looks or sounds زعلان or says directly or indirectly that something bad has happened, the appropriate response is the question: خير؟ or خير إن شاء الله؟, meaning *I hope it's good news?* In *Alif Baa* you learned that the expression لا إله إلا الله is often said upon hearing very bad news. A similar expression is used in both formal and spoken Arabic: لا حَولَ ولا قُوّةَ إلّا بالله *There is no power or strength save in God.* Spoken Arabic has several expressions that are phrased as a plea to God to lighten the catastrophe or misfortune. Some of them are:

O Kind One (lessen the blow)! يا لَطيف!

O Protector (protect us all)! ياساتِر!

اللغة والثقافة: ?Do You Want or Need Anything

بَدّك شي؟ عايز/ة حاجة؟ / عاوز/ة حاجة؟[2]

As you watch the video, notice that the caller asks the other person if she wants (or needs) anything before ending the conversation. This is both polite and a convenient way to signal that you are leaving. This expression is also used to address another person who is there when leaving the house, or in any situation where you are excusing yourself from or leaving family or friends.

---

[2] The word عاوز/ة is just an alternate pronunciation of عايز/ة. You will hear both pronunciations in Egypt.

تمرين ١٦: "يا لطيف!" / "يا ساتر يا ربّ!" (في البيت وفي الصف) 🎧

A. Use good listening strategies and answer as completely as you can:

١. هم زعلانين ليه؟	١. ليش هنّ زعلانين؟
٢. بنعرف ايه: فين – مين – إمتى – ليه؟	٢. شو بنعرف: وين – مين – ايمتى – ليش؟
How does the conversation end? ٣.	How does the conversation end? ٣.

B. In class: Bad news is difficult, but it is important to be prepared to respond to it. Practice by making up some bad news about fictional characters to tell your partner.

تـمارين المراجعة

تمرين ١٧: مراجعة مفردات (في البيت)

Complete the sentences below, using an appropriate word from your vast vocabulary:

١. في الأسبوع سبعة _____ وأحسن يوم ،بالنسبة لي، هو _____ .

٢. ادريس أستاذ في _____ ثانوية في مراكش وهو _____ في التاريخ الأوروبي.

٣. هذا الأسبوع أنا _____ !!!

عندي امتحان كبير في اللغة الروسية يوم

الاثنين ولازم _____ كل الكلمات

الجديدة و _____ اليها على الـ

iPod. وعندي امتحان في علم الإنسان يوم

الثلاثاء ولازم _____ ١٠٠ صفحة

في الكتاب وأيضاً لازم _____

ورقة لصف الدين ليوم الخميس.

٤. _____ من الجامعة منذ أسبوعين فقط ولا _____ ماذا أعمل

بحياتي الآن؟!!

٥. صديقي رشيد أمريكي من _____ عربي وهو _____ مع أسرته

_____ الآن في قطر _____ والده يعمل هناك.

٦. آلاسكا .... ولاية في الولايات المتحدة ولكن قليل من الناس

يعيشون فيها .... الطقس ....

٧. سلوى هي بنت خالتي ولكن، في الحقيقة، هي صديقتي و ....

لأننا من نفس .... (١٧ سنة) ولأننا ندرس في نفس المدرسة.

٨. في الجيش السوري .... كثيرون متخصصون بالهندسة.

٩. الطقس في الكويت .... جداً في الصيف و .... يسافر كثير

من الكويتيين الى لبنان وسوريا .... الطقس هناك أجمل.

١٠. هواياتي .... و .... و ....

تمـريـن ١٨: القراءة الجهرية (في البيت أو في الصف) 🎧

Read the following text, first silently for comprehension, then practice reading aloud. When you are ready, record yourself reading it aloud and submit it for your teacher's feedback either online or as instructed by your teacher.

ريم عَلوان طالبة في جامعة نيويورك حيث تدرس الكيمياء الحَيَوِيّة ، وهي زميلة مها وتعرفها من الجامعة حيث كانت تدرس معها في صف تاريخ الشرق الأوسط. ولكن ريم ، في الحقيقة، لا تعرف مها جيّداً لأن مها لا تتكلم مع الطلاب في الجامعة كثيراً وتذهب الى بيتها بعد المحاضرات كل يوم. بالنسبة لريم، مها انسانة غريبة لأنّها لا تعرف كيف تعيش حياتها . وريم دائماً تتكلم مع مها ولكن مها لا تستمع الى كلامها!!

والد ريم ووالدتها عراقيان: والدها من مدينة بغداد وهو الآن موظف في شركة متخصصة في التَّكنولوجْيا الطِّبِّيَة في نيويورك، ووالدتها من مدينة الموصل وهي دكتورة أمراض نسائية وتعمل في مستشفى في منطقة "برونكس".

ريم تحب مدينة نيويورك كثيراً ودائماً تقول لها: "صحيح نيويورك مدينة مجنونة ولكن أحبّها بكل جُنونها".

تمـريـن ١٩: ماذا يفعلون؟ 🎧

This exercise is available online only.

درس 8
Lesson 8

المستقبل للتجارة

المُفْرَدات Vocabulary 🎧

Listen to the new vocabulary in formal Arabic and your spoken variety.

المعنى	المصري	الشامي	الفُصحى
mother	أُمّ ج. أُمَّهات	إمّ ج. إمّات	أُمّ ج. أُمَّهات
after (followed by verb)[1]	بعد ما	بعد ما	بَعدَ أَنْ (+ فعل)
I obtained	—	—	حَصَلْتُ على
government			حُكومة ج. – ات
I entered	دَخَلْت	دَخَلْت	دَخَلْتُ
to enter	يُدخُل	بِدخُل	يَدخُل ، الدُّخول
(nation-) state			دَولة ج. دُوَل
international			دُوَليّ ، دَوَليّ / ة
to study, go over material review lessons	يِذاكِر ، المُذاكرة	—	يُذاكِر ، المُذاكَرة
president, head			رَئيس ج. رُؤَساء
prime minister			رَئيس الوُزَراء
opinion about			رَأي ج. آراء (في)
he refused	رَفَض	رَفَض	رَفَض
to refuse	يُرفُض	يِرفُض	يَرفُض ، الرَّفض
he wanted to[2]	كان عايز	كان بِدُّه	أرادَ أَنْ (+ فعل مضارع)
he wants to	عايز	بِدُّه	يُريد أَنْ (+ فعل مضارع)
to help (someone) with	يِساعِد... في ، المُساعْدة	يْساعِد... في ، المُساعَدة	يُساعِد... في ، المُساعَدة
throughout (time period)	طول	طول	طِوال
thanks to			بِفَضل (+ اسم)
future			مُسْتَقبَل
as	زَيّ ما	مِتل ما	كَما (+ فعل)
he joined, entered (school, army, political party)	—	—	إلتَحَقَ بِ
to join, enter	—	—	يَلتَحِق بِ ، الالْتِحاق بِ
like	زَيّ	مِتل	مِثل
past, last (week, year, etc.)			الماضي/ة

المعنى	المصري	الشامي	الفُصحى
I succeeded in, passed	نَجَحْت في	نَجَحْت بِـ	نَجَحْتُ في
to succeed, pass	يِنجَح في	يِنجَح بِـ	يَنجَح في ، النَّجاح

Notes on Vocabulary Usage

1. The prepositions قبل and بعد are used with both nouns and verbs. However, since it is not grammatically possible for a preposition to precede a verb directly, we must use a linking particle. In spoken Arabic this particle is ما:

بعد ما اتخرّج من الجامعة ، بدي اشتغل سنة أو سنتين قبل ما ادخل برنامج ماجستير.

بعد ما انجح في الامتحان ان شاء الله وقبل ما اشتغل، عايزة اسافر واشوف بلاد بعيدة.

The linking particle ما also appears as part of other expressions with prepositions, such as كما, مِتِل ما, زَيّ ما *as, like:*

لا أنام كما أريد.   ما بنام متل ما بدي.   ما باَمْشِ زيّ ما انا عايز

2. The formal verb أراد – يُريد can be used with either a مصدر or the linking particle أنْ followed by a مضارع verb. This particle is not used in spoken Arabic, and in formal Arabic it serves to link the main and dependent (infinitive) verb. Compare:

أريد أن أدخل كلية الحقوق بعد التخرّج.

بدي ادخل كلية الحقوق.

عايز ادخل كلية الحقوق.

Similarly, the verb رَفَضَ and other verbs that have to do with likes, dislikes, wishes, and so forth, can be used with either a following مصدر or with أنْ + المضارع:

رفض أخي الصغير أكْل الخضار.   =   رفض أخي الصغير أن يأكُل الخضار.

أرفُض المُذاكرة يوم الجمعة بالليل!   =   أرفض أن أذاكِر يوم الجمعة بالليل!

🎧 تمـرين ١: المفردات الجديدة (في البيت)

Practice using new vocabulary. Remember to put each word in its correct form for the context.

١. جدتي مريضة جداً ولكن لا .... الذهاب الى المستشفى كما قال لها الطبيب.

٢. مروان هو صديقي من أيام الطفولة وأحبّه _____ أخي. نحن الآن في نفس المدرسة الثانوية وفي نفس الصف، وفي _____ نريد أن _____ بكلية الهندسة في الجامعة إن شاء الله.

٣. في الولايات المتحدة هناك وظيفة الرئيس وهناك وظيفة الوزراء ولكن ليس هناك وظيفة _____ كما في _____ مثل بريطانيا وفرنسا ومصر والهند.

٤. والدي لا يحب _____ أمّي بشغل البيت و _____ أن يعمل أيّ شيء anything في البيت ولذلك هي دائماً زعلانة منه.

٥. كان عندنا امتحان في الاقتصاد في الأسبوع _____ ، والامتحان كان صعباً جداً ولكن _____ فيه ، الحمد لله، وحصلت على درجة "A".

٦. ما _____ـكم في السياسة الاقتصادية للحكومة العراقية الجديدة؟

٧. _____ على البكالوريوس في العلوم السياسية منذ سنتين ، وأدرس الآن للحصول على الماجستير في الدراسات _____ في SAIS في جامعة جونز هوبكنز في تخصُّص السياسة الخارجية.

٨. مدينة واشنطن هي مركز الحياة السياسية في الولايات المتحدة. فـ _____ الأمريكي يسكن في البيت الأبيض، كما تعرفون، وكل مكاتب _____ الأمريكية هي في واشنطن أيضاً.

٩. كل طلاب المدارس الثانوية في مصر مشغولون هذه الأيام بـ _____ لامتحانات الثانوية العامة.

١٠. لا أريد أن أعيش في هذا البلد _____ حياتي ؛ أريد أن أسافر وأشاهد الناس في بلاد ومدن بعيدة وجديدة.

١١. ابنتي وعائلتها يسكنون في كندا بعيداً عنا ولكن، _____ Skype والإنترنت، أتكلم معهم كل أسبوع لأعرف أخبارهم.

١٢. تريد ابنتي أن تعمل في الأمم المتحدة _____ تتخرّج من الجامعة.

🎧 تمـريـن ٢: المفردات في جمل 🎧

استمعوا الى جمل المفردات واكتبوا الجمل من "أم" إلى "يرفض".

تـمـريـن ٣: أوزان المفردات الجديدة (في البيت أو في الصف)

Complete this chart with new verbs and their مصادر by listing them with the appropriate pattern (ignore the verb أراد، يُريد, which does not fit any of these patterns):

المصدر	الفعل الجديد	Pattern	Form
		يَفعُل	Form I
		يَفعُل	
		يَفعَل	
		يُفاعِل	Form III
		يُفاعِل	
		يَفتَعِل	Form VIII

تـمـريـن ٤: اسألوا زملاءكم (في الصف)

Practice using the new vocabulary with a partner. One person asks the questions in A and the other asks the questions in B. If you have time, try the two extra challenge questions.

A.

1. In their opinion, who should be able to join the army?
2. Do their parents help them with (في) things? What?
3. Are they or any of their friends majoring in international studies? Will the major help them get a good job?
4. What do they think of your university president?
5. What are three things they don't have now but want in the future?
6. Will they study a lot tonight? How many hours?
7. What do they refuse to eat or drink and why?

B.

1. Do they know any people who refuse to travel? Why?
2. Are they like their mother or their father? How?
3. What restaurants, in their opinion, will succeed in this area?
4. What is something big they succeeded in? Thanks to what did they succeed?
5. What does their mother tell them about their future—does she have an opinion?
6. What does a prime minister do? Do they know any governments that have a prime minister?
7. To whom do they go for help with something?

*Extra challenge

1. Should international studies majors have to study languages? For how many years? Should they have to study abroad? Why or why not?

2. After they graduate, do they want to join the government? What do they want to do?

الثقافة

التَّقْدير Evaluation

In many Arab universities, التقدير is an evaluation of a student's overall performance based on his or her performance on the comprehensive exams given at the end of the school year. Scores are given for exams in each subject, then a تَقْدير is given based on the exam scores, ranging from مُمتاز *excellent* to جَيِّد جدًا *very good* to جَيِّد *good* to مَقبول *acceptable* (i.e., passing), to the failing grades of ضَعيف *weak* or ضعيف جدًا. The overall تقدير is recorded on the diploma.

القصة بالعامية

تمريــن ٥: "المستقبل للتجارة" / "المستقبل للتجارة" (في البيت)

Watch خالد, using the strategies you have learned. Write a **short paragraph** for each question. You may use الفصحى and/or المصري words and expressions.	Watch طارق, using the strategies you have learned. Write a **short paragraph** for each question. You may use الفصحى and/or الشامي words and expressions.
١. خالد طالب كويس؟ ليه/ليه لأ؟	١. طارق طالب منيح؟ ليش/ليش لأ؟
٢. خالد كان عايز يدرس ايه؟ وليه ما درسهوش؟	٢. شو كان بده يدرس طارق؟ وليش ما درس هالشي؟
٣. ايه رأي الوالد في مستقبل خالد؟	٣. شو رأي البابا بمستقبل طارق؟
٤. في رأيكم، خالد زعلان لأنه ما دخلش قسم الأدب؟ ليه/ليه لأ؟	٤. برأيكن، طارق زعلان لأنه ما دخل قسم الأدب؟ ليش/ليش لأ؟

تمريــن ٦: "الأدب ما إله مستقبل" / "الأدب مالهوش مستقبل" (في البيت)

شاهدوا الفيديو بالعامية

Watch the exchange between طارق/خالد and his father with your teacher. Then, with a partner, pretend you are friends of طارق/خالد. As his friends, your role is to give him your honest opinion about what is best for him. What will you say to him?

تـمـريـن ٧: المفردات في جمل (في البيت) 🎧

استمعوا الى جمل المفردات واكتبوا الجمل من "أراد أنْ" إلى "ينجح".

القواعد ١

الفعل الماضي Past Tense

In lesson 4 you learned that المضارع describes incomplete and habitual actions, similar to the English present tense. To describe past completed actions and events, Arabic uses الفعل الماضي, of which you have seen several examples:

دَخَلْتُ كلية التجارة   تَخَرَّجتُ منذ سنتين   ماتَت والدتي، الله يرحمها

While المضارع is conjugated mainly with prefixes, الماضي is conjugated with suffixes. Each verb tense has its own stem, المضارع and الماضي, and the two stems are similar but not identical. You must memorize both stems for each verb. الماضي stem vowels are highly regular in the sense that most الماضي verbs have only fatHa vowels. Since الماضي in third-person masculine singular (هو) is the simplest and most basic, the only conjugation suffix being a final fatHa vowel in formal Arabic, it is considered to be the dictionary form or the citation form of the verb.

You know the suffixes for الماضي from the verb كان. The following table shows the conjugation of الماضي using the verb "to do" in our three varieties:

الفعل الماضي 🎧

عَمَلْت	عمِلْت	فَعَلْتُ	أنا
عَمَلْت	عمِلْت	فَعَلْتَ	أنتَ
عَمَلْتِ، عَمَلْتي	عمِلْتِ، عمِلْتي	فَعَلْتِ	أنتِ
عَمَل	عمِل	فَعَلَ	هو
عَمَلَت	عمِلْت	فَعَلَتْ	هي
عَمَلْنا	عمِلْنا	فَعَلْنا	نحن
عَمَلْتم	عمِلْتوا	فَعَلْتُم	أنتم
عَمَلوا	عمِلوا	فَعَلوا	هم

Remember that the alif on the plural ending وا is a spelling convention only and is not pronounced.

As you can see, the conjugation of الماضي in spoken Arabic is quite similar to formal, except that spoken Arabic drops a couple of the final short vowel vowels and the م on the أنتم form.

Conjugating الماضي with Stems with Roots Containing Vowels

You learned to conjugate the verb كان with two stems, كان and كُنْـ. This same pattern holds for verbs whose root contains a و or ي that appears as an alif in الماضي.[1] For these verbs, you will memorize two الماضي stems, one for third person and the other for first and second person. Learn the stems of the verb أراد in formal Arabic:

🎧 Verb Stems أراد

(نحن) أَرَدْنا	(أنا) أَرَدْتُ.
(أنتم) أَرَدْتُم	(أنتَ) أَرَدْتَ (أنتِ) أَرَدْتِ
(هم) أرادوا	(هو) أرادَ (هي) أرادَتْ

الماضي Negation نَفي

In formal Arabic الماضي and المضارع use different negation particles. In lesson 4 you learned to negate المضارع with لا in formal Arabic, as in لا أعرف. There are two ways to negate the past tense in formal Arabic; the one we will use for now is ما + الماضي. The following examples demonstrate:

I did not graduate . . .	ما تَخرَّجتُ من الجامعة.
Why were you not . . .	لماذا ما كنت في الفصل؟
She did not enter (go to) . . .	جدتي ما دَخَلَت الجامعة.

---

[1] There are historical and linguistic reasons for this phenomenon, some involving the avoidance of long vowels in closed syllables in الفصحى.

تمــرين ٨: ماذا فعلوا؟ (في البيت) 🎧

Practice narrating and describing past events in الفصحى using the verbs in parentheses:

١. الحمدلله! _____ أختي في كل امتحاناتها. (نجح)

٢. بعد التخرج من الجامعة _____ ابن خالي بالجيش. (التحق)

٣. كم سنة _____ الأدب الفرنسي يا سميرة؟ (درس)

٤. هل _____ مع أصدقائكم الى المطعم الجديد؟ (ذهب)

٥. _____ المدرسة الابتدائية وعمري ٦ سنوات. (دخل)

٦. كيف _____ عنوان بيتنا يا سامية؟ (عرف)

٧. يوم السبت الماضي، أنا وزملائي _____ طوال النهار. (عمل)

٨. في الحقيقة، أنا ما _____ معها منذ أسبوعين. (تكلم)

٩. _____ ابن عمّي السفر إلى تونس ولكن والدته _____
(أراد، رفض)

١٠. الموظفون ما _____ في مكاتبهم يوم الجمعة. (كان)

١١. ما _____ كرة القدم منذ سنة! (لعب)

١٢. لا أتذكّر متى _____ هذه القصة. (قرأ)

تمــرين ٩: اسألوا زملاءكم: ماذا فعلوا؟ (في الصف)

Practice narrating and describing past events by asking your classmates these questions. Then report what you found out to the class.

١. كم كلمة جديدة حفظوا؟

٢. متى تخرجوا من المدرسة الثانوية؟

٣. أيّ فيلم شاهدوا؟

٤. ماذا عملوا الصيف الماضي؟

٥. مع من تكلّموا بالتليفون اليوم؟

٦. هل استمعوا الى الاخبار أو الطقس اليوم؟

٧. في أيّ شيء نجحوا؟

٨. راحوا فين السبت الماضي؟ راحوا مع مين؟ شافوا مين؟

وين راحوا السبت الماضي؟ مع مين راحوا؟ مين شافوا؟

القصة بالفصحى

تـمريـن ١٠: "المستقبل للتجارة" 🎧

Watch القصة بالفصحى and answer the questions below. The dictation exercise can be completed in the book or online.

1. How many جمل فعلية do you hear خالد use? Write the verb in each جملة فعلية you hear.
2. All verb forms (and some other words) have been removed from the text. Focus your attention on following the thread of narration by listening for verbs and add them, in the forms you hear, into the spaces below. In addition, listen for المصدر and note how it is used.

بعد (١) _____ (٢) _____ الثانوية العامة ، (٣) _____

(٤) _____ (٥) _____ (٦) _____ كلية الآداب

(٧) _____ (٨) _____ محمد، لكن والدي (٩) _____ ذلك،

و(١٠) _____ (١١) _____ (١٢) _____ بكلية

(١٣) _____ (١٤) _____ (١٥) _____ و الدتي،

(١٦) _____ دراسة (١٧) _____ في رأيهِ (١٨) _____ لها

(١٩) _____ (٢٠) _____ و (٢١) _____ .

فَ (٢٢) _____ (٢٣) _____ كلية كما (٢٤) _____ هو

والمرحومة (٢٥) _____ و (٢٦) _____ والحمد لله في (٢٧) _____

و (٢٨) _____ (٢٩) _____ تقدير (٣٠) _____ جداً

(٣١) _____ (٣٢) _____ الدراسة (٣٣) _____ الله

و (٣٤) _____ (٣٥) _____ (٣٦) _____ لي

(٣٧) _____ في .

الكتابة

تـمـرين ١١: لماذا فعلت هذا؟ (في البيت)

Give several reasons or purposes for the following actions and situations. Write a paragraph-length sentence for each:

١. لماذا اِلتحقت بهذه الجامعة؟ ولماذا دخلت هذا الصف؟

٢. لماذا (ما) سافرت هذه السنة؟

٣. أيّ لغة درست في المدرسة الثانوية؟ لماذا؟

القواعد ٢

الجذر والوزن

root	جَذر
pattern (grammatical term)	وَزن ج. أوزان

You have learned that roots and patterns play an important role in Arabic. The root, الجَذر, is a group of three consonants that gives the core meaning to a family of words.[2] You use roots to help you remember words and guess the meaning of new words in reading. You know that the order of these consonants is critical to the integrity of الجذر: د-ر-س is not equivalent to س-ر-د, and ك-ت-ب is different from ك-ب-ت. You have seen that و and ي can be part of الجذر, because they function as consonants as well as vowels. Alif, on the other hand, can never be part of الجذر, but hamza can, as in the root ق - ر - ء that has to do with reading.

You have begun to see that the pattern, الوَزن, adds grammatical meaning to the semantic core of الجذر. The way this works will become clearer gradually as you learn more words. You have been introduced to several verbal أوزان, numbered according to the system followed in many grammars and dictionaries. You have also seen that various kinds of words, such as plurals, adjectives, and المصدر, tend to share certain patterns. The next section will give you strategies for identifying الجذر and الوزن of both new and familiar words.

---

[2] Some roots consist of two consonants and others consist of four. Two-consonant roots are rare and probably very old, while four-consonant roots occur regularly in many dialects and also in formal Arabic. Four-consonant roots have a very limited number of patterns, however.

الجذر والوزن Identifying

Every Arabic word (except one- and two-letter prepositions) consists entirely of a جذر and a وزن. The ability to identify each component is an important skill that will serve you well in vocabulary learning as well as in speaking, reading, listening, writing, and, in particular, spelling. Identifying الجذر is also important for using Arabic dictionaries, the vast majority of which do not list words alphabetically but, rather, list them according to الجذر. For example, to find the word مشغول, you must know to look it up under ش-غ-ل.

Identifying الجذر is a skill that takes practice. To identify الجذر, look for three core consonants. The following cases are straightforward:

الكلمة	دُخول	مِثل	بارِد	وِزارة	أكْبر
الجذر	د-خ-ل	م-ث-ل	ب-ر-د	و-ز-ر	ك-ب-ر

The جذر of other words may be less obvious. How can you identify الجذر of the following words, which have more than three letters?

الاقتصاد   يلتحق   مستقبل   مشغول

First, eliminate any verb or pronoun prefixes and suffixes and الـ. Second, look for long vowels—especially alif (but not hamza!)—and the consonants م, س, ت, and ن. These letters often belong to الوزن. If there are more than three letters, eliminate those first. Eliminating these letters from the previous words, we are left with الجذر:

الكلمة	مشغول	مستقبل	يلتحق	الاقتصاد
الجذر	ش – غ – ل	ق – ب – ل	ل – ح – ق	ق – ص – د

Keep two final points in mind. First, if in looking for الجذر you see only two consonants, the second consonant may have a شدّة. This is called a doubled (or geminate) root. For example, الجذر of the word عمّ is ع-م-م, and that of صفّ is ص-ف-ف.[3] Second, sometimes the plural of a noun or المضارع stem of a verb will clarify a missing letter of its جذر. For example, only two consonants appear in the word خال. However, the plural أخوال shows a third root letter: و. Similarly, الجذر of the verb عاش (الماضي) يعيش (ع-ي-ش) is visible in المضارع but not in الماضي. You can practice this skill by identifying الجذر of new and old vocabulary or by looking up words you already know in an Arabic–English dictionary (the glossary in this book does not contain enough words to be useful for practicing this skill).

---

[3] Do not confuse the شدّة here with the شدّة in words like يدرّس, which already have three clear root consonants. The latter شدّة is part of الوزن.

Once you have identified الجذر, you can work out الوزن. You have seen that أوزان are identified using the consonants ف-ع-ل as a neutral جذر. The following أوزان are familiar to you from your vocabulary:

يَرفُض	يَدخُل	يَحصُل	يَدرُس	وزن يَفعُل:
وَحيد	صَغير	كَبير	جَميل	وزن فَعيل:
سِياسة	وِزارة	تِجارة	دِراسة	وزن فِعالة:

Remember that the extra letters found in longer verb أوزان include shadda, long vowels ا-و-ي, and consonants أ-ت-س-م and occasionally ن. Examples of أوزان that contain these letters include:

مُسْتَفْعَل	اِفْتِعال	يُفَعِّل	مَفْعول	فَعْلان	أَفْعال	الوزن
مُسْتَقْبَل	اِمْتِحان	يُدَرِّس	مَشْغول	تَعْبان	أَوْلاد	مِثال

Most longer أوزان are related to verbs. In lessons 4 and 6 you saw five verbal أوزان, and you learned that the common verb أوزان are numbered I to X (IX وزن being rare). The following chart shows these أوزان, but since you have not learned verbs in all of them yet, we will focus for now on the أوزان in red.

أوزان الفعل

المصدر	المضارع	الماضي	الوزن
(varies)	يَفْعَل/يَفْعُل/يَفْعِل	فَعَل/فَعُل/فَعِل	I
تَفعيل	يُفَعِّل	فَعَّل	II
مُفاعَلة	يُفاعِل	فاعَل	III
إفعال	يُفعِل	أَفْعَل	IV
تَفَعُّل	يَتَفَعَّل	تَفَعَّل	V
تَفاعُل	يَتَفاعَل	تَفاعَل	VI
اِنْفِعال	يَنْفَعِل	اِنْفَعَل	VII
اِفْتِعال	يَفْتَعِل	اِفْتَعَل	VIII
اِسْتِفْعال	يَسْتَفْعِل	اِسْتَفْعَل	X

Each of these أوزان adds an aspect of meaning to the verb. As you learn more verbs, you will develop an understanding of how the various أوزان relate to each other. For now, look at the relationship between wazn I and wazn II in the chart below. You can see that wazn II adds a causative element to wazn I:

	وزن II فَعَّلَ ، فَعَّل		وزن I فَعَلَ/فَعِلَ ، فِعل	الجذر
to teach - have someone study	دَرَّسَ ، دَرِّس	to study	دَرَسَ ، دَرَس	د-ر-س
to have, make someone drink	شَرَّبَ ، شَرِّب	to drink	شَرِبَ ، شِرب	ش-ر-ب
to make someone upset	زَعَّلَ، يْزَعِّل / يِزعَّل	to get upset	زِعِل ، يِزعَل	ز-ع-ل

In subsequent chapters we will expand on this and other أوزان meanings. In the meantime, it will be helpful to incorporate الوزن into your study of vocabulary by grouping together and practicing out loud words of the same وزن, because this will help your pronunciation, reading, spelling, and vocabulary retention by making it easier to remember the exact shape and sound of a word. Remembering words by their وزن and جذر is an efficient way to memorize and retain large amounts of vocabulary.

تمريـن ١٢: الجذر (في البيت) 🎧

This exercise is available online only.

تمريـن ١٣: الجذر (في البيت) 🎧

This exercise is available online only.

دراسة الفعل: الماضي والمضارع والمصدر

Beginning in the next chapter, new verbs will be presented in dictionary format, with all three stems of the verb given together: الماضي والمضارع والمصدر. The format in the vocabulary lists will look like this:

to enter	دَخَلَ، يَدخُل، الدُّخول

Note that "to enter" is not a translation of دَخَلَ, just a way of listing the meaning of the stem. دَخَلَ here represents the dictionary form of the verb. **Memorize all three forms together** by repeating them aloud so that you have each stem at instant recall. After you memorize the stems, you will be prepared to practice using the verbs in context in all of their various conjugations.

The following charts contain all the verbs you have learned according to وزن, with وزن I in groups according to the stem vowels. Listen to the audio and repeat aloud until you can hear the pattern, noted in red below, that is shared among the members of each group. Examples of the patterns fall beneath each.

وزن I

المصدر	المضارع	الماضي
الـفَـعْـل الـفَـعَـل الـفِـعـالة الـفُـعـول	يَـفْـعُـل	فَـعَـل
الأَكْل	يَأْكُل	أَكَل
الرَّفْض	يَرفُض	رَفَض
الرَّقْص	يَرقُص	رَقَص
السَّكَن	يَسكُن	سَكَن
الدِّراسة	يَدرُس	دَرَس
الكِتابة	يكتُب	كَتَب
الشُّعور بـ	يَشعُر بـ	شَعَر بـ
الحُصول على	يَحصُل على	حَصَل على
الدُّخول	يَدخُل	دَخَل
الكَوْن	يكون[4]	كان ، كُنْت
القَوْل	يَقول	قال ، قُلْت
المَوْت	يَموت	مات ، مِتّ
--	يروح / يِروح	راح ، رِحْت / رُحْت
--	يشوف / يِشوف	شاف ، شِفْت / شُفْت

[4]The مضارع of كان is used in future and infinitive contexts (will be and to be), which you will see soon.

المصدر	المضارع	الماضي
المَفْعِلة الفَعْل	يَفعِل	فَعَل
المَعرِفة	يَعرِف	عَرَف
العَيْش	يَعيش	عاش ، عِشْت
الحَكي	يِحكي	حَكَى

المصدر		المضارع	الماضي
الفُعْل الفِعل الفَعَل الفَعل		يَفعَل	فَعِل
Few Form I stem vowels are predictable, but if الماضي has a كسرة vowel فَعِل then the stem vowel of المضارع will be فتحة.	الشُّرب	يَشرَب	شَرِب
	الحِفظ	يَحفَظ	حَفِظ
	العَمَل	يَعمَل	عَمِل
	اللَّعِب	يَلعَب	لَعِب

المصدر	المضارع	الماضي
الفِعل الفِعالة الفَعال	يَفْعَل	فَعَل
الفعل	يَفعَل	فَعَل
القراءة	يَقرَأ	قَرَأ
السِّباحة	يَسبَح	سَبَح
الذَّهاب إلى	يَذهَب إلى	ذَهَب الى
النَّجاح	يَنجَح	نَجَح

وزن II

المصدر	المضارع	الماضي
التَّفعيل	يُفَعِّل	فَعَّل
التَّدريس	يُدَرِّس	دَرَّس
التَّصوير	يُصَوِّر	صَوَّر
—	يُزَعِّل / يِزَعِّل	زَعَّل

وزن III

المصدر	المضارع	الماضي
المُفاعَلة	يُفاعِل	فاعَل
المُشاهَدَة	يُشاهِد	شاهَد
المُساعَدة	يُساعِد	ساعَد
المُذاكَرة	يُذاكِر	ذاكَر
السَّفَر الى*	يُسافِر إلى	سافَر الى
المُحاضَرة	يُحاضِر	حاضَر

* This مصدر is an exception to the usual pattern rules.

وزن IV

المصدر	المضارع	الماضي
الإِفْعال	يُفْعِل	أَفْعَل
الحُبّ*	يُحِبّ	أَحَبّ
الإرادة	يُريد	أراد / أرَدت

* This مصدر is an exception to the pattern.

وزن V

المصدر	المضارع	الماضي
التَّفَعُّل	يَتَفَعَّل	تَفَعَّل
التَّذَكُّر	يَتَذَكَّر	تَذَكَّر
الكَلام* ، التَكَلُّم	يَتَكَلَّم	تَكَلَّم
التَّخَرُّج	يَتَخَرَّج	تَخَرَّج
التَّخَصُّص	يَتَخَصَّص	تَخَصَّص
الزَّواج* ، التَّزَوُّج	يَتَزَوَّج	تَزَوَّج

* This مصدر is an exception to the pattern.

وزن VIII

المصدر	المضارع	الماضي
الافْتِعـال	يَفْتَعِل	افْتَعَل
الاسْتِماع الى	يَستَمِع الى	اسْتَمَع الى
الالْتِحاق بـ	يَلتَحِق بـ	الْتَحَق بـ
(الاشْتِغال)	يَشْتَغِل	اشْتَغَل
الامْتَحان		
الاقتِصاد		

تمرين ١٤: المصدر (في الصف)

Design an opinion poll for your class about a wide range of actions and activities, using as many different مصادر as you can. Remember to use an إضافة where necessary. Here are some ideas to get you started:

مثال: ما رأيهم في الالتحاق بالجيش؟ ما رأيهم في (+ مصدر)

مثال: هل يرفضون مشاهدة كرة القدم؟ ماذا يرفضون؟

مثال: هل يحبون المذاكرة؟ ماذا (لا) يحبون؟

تمرين ١٥: نشاط كتابة (في البيت)

Write a short قصة about each sequence of pictures (go from right to left). Use as many verbs in الماضي as you can. A time frame is given for each set of pictures.

١. يوم السبت الماضي

٢. منذ ثلاثة أسابيع

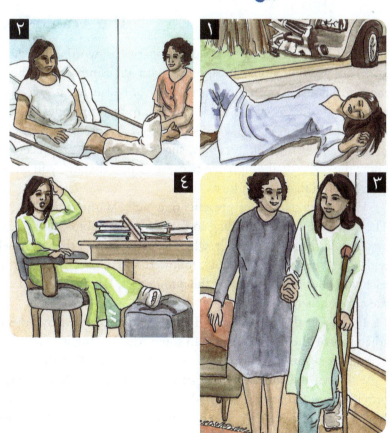

٣. السنة الماضية

القاموس العربي The Arabic Dictionary

You know by now that Arabic dictionaries list words according to الجذر. The consonants of الجذر are listed in alphabetical order, with alif representing the consonant hamza (remember that the alif itself cannot be part of a root because it is a vowel). Thus, in the dictionary, the root ء – ر – ب precedes ب – ر – د which in turn precedes ب – ر – ز.

Doubled roots, such as ح – ق – ق of حقيقة, are usually listed according to the alphabetical order of the first two letters only, such that ح – ق – ق precedes ب – ق – ح. Make sure you know the order of the alphabet because to find the جذر you are looking for, you must look for each letter in that جذر in turn.

Each dictionary entry presents one جذر. Within this entry, the first section lists the verb. The verbs are listed according to form. Some Arabic–English dictionaries use the numbering system with Roman numerals, while others write out the verb itself. Form I is listed first, along with the stem vowel of المضارع, followed by Forms II through X. Some dictionaries spell out each verb, but others give just the number (II, III, IV . . .) and assume that the user can derive the correct form.

Following the verb, you will find nouns, followed by adjectives, then مصادر and verbal adjectives of the derived forms. In some Arabic–English dictionaries, internal vowels are given in transliteration like this: *sakana u* (سكن *sakan*). Here the vowel *u* means that the vowel of المضارع stem is Damma: يَسكُن, and المصدر is given in parentheses. Each noun entry should provide its plural form, and good dictionaries will give prepositions and idiomatic expressions as well. It is important to pay attention to these pieces of information when looking up the meaning of a word—sometimes a preposition can change the meaning of a word entirely (for an example, read through the entry of رغب in your dictionary).

تمـريـن ١٦: مع القاموس (في البيت وفي الصف) 🎧

Practice using القاموس by looking up the following words with a partner. First, identify their جذر. If it is familiar, think about what the approximate meaning of the new word will be. Then arrange the words in alphabetical order by الجذر and write the word and الجذر in the spaces provided. Finally, look up the words in alphabetical order and write their meanings.

مَتاعِب - مُساعِد - مَعْمَل - حَقّ - أَديب - مُذَكِّرات - تَفْسير - تَدريجِيّاً - تَمويل - مُراسِل

الكلمة	الجذر	Alphabetical Order by الجذر
١.		١.
٢.		٢.
٣.		٣.
٤.		٤.
٥.		٥.
٦.		٦.
٧.		٧.
٨.		٨.
٩.		٩.
١٠.		١٠.

القراءة ١

"السيرة الذاتية لوزراء حكومة الرفاعي" (في الصف)

تـمـريـن ١٧: السيرة الذاتية لوزراء حكومة سمير الرفاعي في الأردن (في الصف)

When a new حكومة is announced, people want to know about the ministers involved. The Jordanian newspaper الرأي published these short biographies of the new ministers in December 2009. With a partner, read through them. For each, determine what the person's new job is, and what his or her qualifications are for the position. At home, after you have finished, choose two or three unfamiliar words that seem important because they recur in the text, and look them up in the dictionary.

السيرة الذاتية لوزراء حكومة سمير الرفاعي

نائب رئيس الوزراء - الدكتور رجائي المعشر

ولد في عمان ١٩٤٤، وحاصل على دكتوراه إدارة أعمال من جامعة ايلينويز في امريكا وشغل المناصب التالية :

- مدير دائرة في الجمعية العلمية الملكية - ١٩٧٦ووزير الاقتصاد الوطني — ١٩٧٦ وزير الصناعة والتجارة مرتين - مدير عام في عدة شركات خاصة - ١٩٨٨ وزير تموين وصناعة .

الداخلية - نايف القاضي

ولد في حوشا ١٩٤٤ وحصل على البكالوريوس في العلوم السياسية من جامعة بغداد ١٩٦٩ وشغل منصب وزير للداخلية في حكومة عبد الرؤوف الروابدة عام ١٩٩٩ .

الخارجية - ناصر جودة

ولد في عمان ودرس المرحلتين الابتدائية والإعدادية ثم انتقل إلى بريطانيا حيث أكمل المرحلة الثانوية من دراسته ، وأكمل دراسته الجامعية في جامعة جورج تاون الأمريكية .

عمل في بداية حياته العملية بين عامي ١٩٨٥ و ١٩٩٢في الديوان الملكي الهاشمي العامر في المكتب الصحفي لجلالة المغفور له جلالة الملك حسين ثم كسكرتير خاص لسمو ولي العهد .

عين وزيرا للإعلام وناطقا رسميا باسم الحكومة عام ١٩٩٨ ثم عمل في القطاع الخاص بعد استقالة الحكومة ١٩٩٩ . وفي عام٢٠٠٥ عاد إلى العمل العام عندما عين ناطقا رسميا باسم الحكومة ثم وزيراً للدولة لشؤون الإعلام والاتصال ووزيراً للخارجية ٢٠٠٩ .

التعليم العالي - الدكتور وليد المعاني

ولد في الكرك، عام ١٩٤٦، متزوج وله أربعة أبناء (ولدان وبنتان)، حاصل على بكالوريوس الطب والجراحة (مرتبة الشرف الثانية) ١٩٦٩ ودبلوم الجراحة العامة ١٩٧٠ من مصر.

حصل الدكتور المعاني على وسام الكوكب الأردني من الدرجة الأولى ، وهو عضو زمالة ايزنهاور، الولايات المتحدة الأمريكية، ١٩٨٣ .

يومية عربية سياسية
تصدر في عمان - الأردن

الأثنين ٤ كانون ثاني ٢٠١٠م
آخر تعديل : ٢٠١٠/١/٤ ١١:١٤ م

الاحتلال يعتقل ٦ مواطنين في الخليل وجنين

بحث تفصيلي / الأرشيف
أخبار اليوم

المؤسسة الصحفية الأردنية

Jordan Times
مجلة حاتم للأطفال
منبر الرأي

الصفحة الرئيسية
محليات
إقتصاد
رياضة
عربي دولي
مقالات
وفيات
أبواب
ثقافة وفنون
تحقيقات
كاريكاتير
صحافة عربية وعالمية

محليات

وزير المالية - محمد ابو حمور

ولد في السلط عام ١٩٦١، حاصل على دكتوراه اقتصاد / مالية عامة من جامعة SURREY في بريطانيا ١٩٩٧ وماجستير اقتصاد من الجامعة الاردنية ١٩٨٩ وبكالوريوس اقتصاد جامعة اليرموك ١٩٨٤ ، وهو متزوج وله اربعة اطفال .

وزيرة السياحة والآثار - مها الخطيب

حاصلة على ماجستير في الإدارة العامة من الجامعة الأمريكية في بيروت ، متزوجة ولها ولدان وبنت.

عملت من ٢٠٠٠ إلى ٢٠٠٧ مديرة لمؤسسة نهر الاردن ومن عام ٢٠٠٦ مستشارة لجلالة الملكة رانيا العبد الله. مديرة برنامج اصلاح القطاع العام الذي كان موجوداً آنذاك في وزارة التنمية الإدارية.

التخطيط - الدكتور جعفر حسان

يحمل الدكتور جعفر حسان درجة الدكتوراه ودرجة الماجستير في العلوم السياسية والاقتصاد الدولي من معهد الدراسات الدولية بجامعة جنيف في سويسرا، ودرجة الماجستير في الإدارة العامة من جامعة هارفارد ودرجة الماجستير في العلاقات الدولية من جامعة بوسطن. وكان حصل على درجة البكالوريوس في العلاقات الدولية من الجامعة الأمريكية في فرنسا بتفوق.

وبدأ حياته العملية في وزارة الخارجية في العام ١٩٩١. وانتدب للعمل في الديوان الملكي ، حيث عمل مساعدا خاصا لسمو الأمير طلال بن محمد . وشغل موقع مدير دائرة الشؤون الدولية في الديوان الملكي منذ العام ٢٠٠٦ إلى حين تسليمه حقيبة التخطيط والتعاون الدولي.

وحسان من مواليد السوق خريبة عام ١٩٦٨، ومتزوج وله ابنة، ويتقن اللغات الإنجليزية والفرنسية والبلغارية.

شؤون رئاسة الوزراء - جمال الشمايلة

ولد في المفرق ١٩٥٧، وهو متزوج ، وله بنت وولد.
حاصل على بكالوريوس علوم سياسية - جامعة ولاية كاليفورنيا عام ١٩٨١ .
عمل ملحقاً في وزارة الخارجية وسكرتيراً خاصاً لرئيس الوزراء، وعمل في عدة مناصب في وزارة الخارجية وسفيراً لدى دولة الإمارات .

www.alrai.com/paper.php?news_id=308003

الاستماع: مع العائلة والاصدقاء

تمرين ١٨: "مع عائلة خالد" (في البيت) 🎧

استمعوا واكتبوا:

١. من يتكلم؟ من هو بالنسبة لخالد؟

٢. لماذا هو زعلان؟

٣. ماذا يريد أن يعمل بعد التخرج؟

٤. ماذا يحب أن يفعل ولماذا؟

القراءة ٢

نشاط قراءة ومحادثة وكتابة

تمرين ١٩: استمارة الالتحاق بوحدة اللغة العربية (في الصف)

You may be interested in studying in an Arab country. The following is an application to one such study-abroad program. Read through it with a partner and, as you do so, fill out the form for her or him by asking questions بالعربي. Guess what you can from context and الجذر, and skip the questions for which you cannot make a reasonable guess.

بسم الله الرحمن الرحيم
المملكة العربية السعودية
جامعة الملك سعود

معهد اللغة العربية

ص.ب -4274 الرياض 11491

استمارة ترشيح
بوحدة اللغة والثقافة
بمعهد اللغة العربية

١. اسم الطالب (مطابقاً لجواز السفر): ....

٢. الجنسية: .... ٣. الديانة: ....

٤. (أ) تاريخ الـميلاد: .... (ب) مكان الـميلاد: ....

٥. العمر: .... ٦. الحالة الاجتماعية: متزوّج أعزب

٧. الجنس: .... ٨. المهنة: ....

٩. العمل الحالي: ....

١٠. إذا كنت قد درست في بلاد عربية من قبل فاذكر:

(أ) اسم البلد: ....

(ب) اسم المدرسة أو الجامعة: ....

(ج) تاريخ التخرّج: ....

١١. اذكر اللغات التي تعرفها ومدى معرفتك بها من ناحية فهم الكلام، والتحدّث، والقراءة، والكتابة، مع ذكر المستوى إذا كان ممتازاً أو جيّداً أو مـتوسّطاً.

(أ) لغتك الأم: ....

(ب) لغات أخرى:

الكتابة			القراءة			التحدّث			فهم الكلام			اللغة
ممتاز	جيّد	متوسّط	ممتاز	جيّد	متوسّط	ممتاز	جيّد	متوسّط	ممتاز	جيّد	متوسّط	

التقدير العام	المؤهل العلمي	التخصّص	مدة الدراسة	تاريخ التخرّج	تاريخ الالتحاق	اسم المدرسة، المعهد، الكلية، أو الجامعة

الحوار
اللغة والثقافة

to provide a (good) atmosphere	عمل جَوّ

This expression can be used to describe any kind of positive atmosphere. It may be calm, pleasant, festive–anything appropriate to the circumstances.

🎧 تـمريـن ٢٠: "شو رأيك بامتحانات..؟" / "ايه رأيك في امتحانات..؟" (في البيت) 🎧

استمعوا الى الحوار بالمصري واكتبوا جملة طويــــــلة لكل سؤال:	استمعوا الى الحوار بالشامي واكتبوا جملة طويـــــلة لكل سؤال:
١. هو مين ؟ بيتكلّم مع مين ؟ عن إيه؟	١. مين هنّ؟ عن شو بدها تحكي ؟ شو بيقول هو؟
٢. عمل ازاي؟ بفضل ايه؟	٢. كيف عمل؟ بفضل شو؟
٣. هو عاوز يدرس إيه في الجامعة؟ ليه؟	٣. شو بدّه يدرس بالجامعة؟ ليش؟
٤. بيقول ايه عن السفر؟	٤. شو بيقول عن السفر؟

تماريـن المراجعة

تـمريـن ٢١: معرفة ونكرة، مؤنّث ومذكّر 🎧 (في البيت) 🎧

This exercise is available online only.

تـمريـن ٢٢: ضمائر النصب (في البيت) 🎧

This exercise is available online only.

تـمريـن ٢٣: القراءة الجهريّة (في البيت أو في الصف) 🎧

There are two parts to this exercise:

1. Read the text silently first, then aloud several times to practice pronunciation and fluency. When you are ready, record the passage and submit it to your teacher, either online or as instructed by your teacher.

Notice this word:

if	إذا (+ الماضي)

عادل محمود أبو العلا هو أخو خالد وهو طالب في الثانوية العامة ولكنّه، مثل كل الشباب في عمره، لا يحب المذاكرة ولكن يحب الإستماع الى الموسيقى والكلام مع أصدقائه ساعات طويلة في غرف الـ "chat"على الإنترنت. عادل يريد الإلتحاق بالجامعة في المستقبل القريب ليكون مع أصدقائه، فأصدقاؤه دخلوا الجامعة منذ سنة، أمّا هو، فما نجح في امتحانات الثانوية العامة في السنة التي ماتت فيها أمه، الله يرحمها، ولذلك ما تخرّج السنة الماضية.

إذا نجح عادل في الثانوية العامة هذه السنة إن شاء الله وحصل على تقدير جيّد فهو يريد أن يدخل كلية التجارة مثل خالد، ويريد أيضاً أن يعمل في شركة أمريكية بعد التخرّج. ولذلك فهو يدرس اللغة الإنجليزية ويشاهد البرامج التّلفزيونية باللغة الإنجليزية على "يوتوب" ويكتب رسائل بالإنكليزية إلى شباب كنديين وأمريكيين يعرفهم من الإنترنت.

2. Grammar review: In the above text, find and circle two examples of each of the below:

١. الاسم + الصفة

٢. المصدر

٣. الإضافة

٤. الجملة الاسمية / المبتدأ والخبر

٥. الجملة الفعلية

جدّتي توقظني في السّادسة والنصف

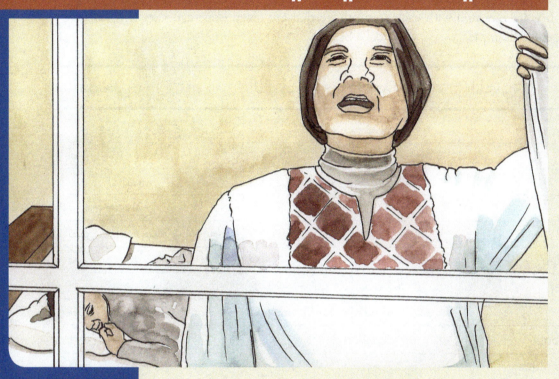

المفردات

القصة بالعامية: "ستي بتفيّقني" "ستي بتصحينا"

الثقافة: "صباح الخيرات" "صباح الفل يا حاجّة"

"هل تدخّنون أمام الأسرة؟"

القواعد (١): المضارع المرفوع و"بــ" + الفعل المضارع

القصة بالفصحى: "جدّتي توقظني في السادسة والنصف"

القواعد (٢): الأعداد الترتيبية Ordinal Numbers

القراءة: "من برامج التليفزيون"

الاستماع: مع العائلة والأصدقاء

الحوار: "الله يساعدني عليها" "رايحة على فين؟"

تمارين المراجعة

Vocabulary المُفرَدات 🎧

استمعوا الى المفردات الجديدة بالفصحى والعامية.

Notice that verb entries now include الماضي والمضارع والمصدر. Take time to practice all of them aloud in different contexts, and memorize all three together so that you can recall them easily. Pay attention to prepositions and memorize them with the verbs. Prepositions that are obligatory are repeated with each stem; those that are given once can vary according to context (see, for example, نَزَلَ في and نَزَلَ من below).

المعنى	المصري	الشامي	الفصحى
other	تاني/ة	تاني/ة	آخَر ، مؤنث: أُخرى، ج. آخَرون
or			أو
to begin	بَدَأ ، يِبدَأ	بَدا ، يِبدا	بَدَأَ، يَبدَأ، البَدء
program			بَرنامَج ج. بَرامِج
some (of)[1]			بَعض + (اسم جمع في اضافة)
then, بعد ذلك	بَعدين	بَعدين	ثُمَّ
newspaper	جَريدة ج. جَرايد	جَريدة ج. جَرايد	جَريدة ج. جَرائِد
to sit	قَعَد، يُقعُد، القُعاد	قَعَد، يِقعُد، القَعدة	جَلَسَ، يَجلِس، الجُلوس
around, about	حَوالي	حَوالي	حَوالَيْ
to leave (a place)	خَرَج، يُخرُج	طِلِع، يِطلَع	خَرَجَ من، يَخرُج من، الخُروج من
special; (its) own; private			خاصّ/ة
to smoke	دَخَّن ، يِدَخَّن	دَخَّن، يدَخِّن	دَخَّنَ، يُدَخِّن، التَّدخين
sixth (adj.)			سادِس/ة
chess			الشَّطرَنج
to be able to	قِدِر ، يِقدَر	قِدِر ، يِقدِر	اِستَطاعَ، يَستَطيع (+ أن/المصدر)
noon	الضُّهْر	الضُّهْر	الظُّهْر
afternoon	بَعد الضُّهْر	بَعد الضُّهْر	بَعدَ الظُّهْر
dinner	العَشا	العَشا	العَشاء
the world			العالَم
to return	رِجِع ، يِرجَع	رِجِع عَ، يِرجَع عَ	عادَ الى، يَعود الى، العَوْدة الى
eye			عَيْن ج. عُيون

المعنى	المصري	الشامي	الفُصحى
lunch	الغَدا	الغَدا	الغَداء
favorite			مُفَضَّل/ة
to eat breakfast	فِطِر، يِفطَر، الفِطار	فِطِر، يِفطَر، الفْطور	فَطَرَ، يَفطُر، الفُطور
club (e.g., sports, social)			نادي (نادٍ) ج. نَوادي (نوادٍ)
to leave (the house), to stay (in a hotel)[2]	نِزِل، يِنْزِل من، يِنزِل في	طِلِع، يِطلَع من، نِزِل، يِنزِل بـ	نَزَلَ، يَنْزِل، النُّزول من، في
half	نُصّ	نِصّ	نِصف
subject, topic			مَوضوع ج. –ات، مَواضيع
to wake (someone) up	صَحّى، (صَحّيت)، يِصَحّي	فَيَّق، يفَيِّق	أَيْقَظَ، يوقِظ

Notes on Vocabulary Usage

1. The word بَعض is used in الإضافة with a plural noun or pronoun:

بعض الناس ينامون بعد الظهر وبعضهم لا يفعلون ذلك.

بعض الناس بيناموا بعد الضهر وبعضُن لأ.

بعض الناس بيناموا بعد الضهر وبعضهم لأ.

In spoken Arabic the word بَعض alone means *each other*:

انا ورفقاتي بنشوف بعض بالجامعة وبالنادي.

انا واصحابي بنشوف بعض في الجامعة وفي النادي.

2. The spoken expressions for "to leave the house" present an interesting case study on language and culture. The Egyptian and Levantine verbs in the vocabulary list, يِنزِل and يِطلَع, are actually opposite in meaning: يِطلَع means *to go up* or *to ascend*, whereas يِنزِل means *to descend* or *to go down*. It seems as if the Egyptian verb reflects the reality of life in Cairo, where almost everyone lives in tall apartment buildings and literally *goes down* to leave the house. Levantine يِطلَع, on the other hand, is used for going out in general and may reflect a figurative ascendance into public space. In all three varieties, however, نزل في means *to stay in (a hotel)*.

تعلموا هذا الفعل 🎧

(١)

المضارع		الماضي	
نَعود	أعود	عُدنا	عُدتُ
تَعودونَ / تَعودوا	تَعود	عُدتُم	عُدتَ
	تَعودينَ / تَعودي		عُدتِ
يَعودونَ / يَعودوا	يَعود	عادوا	عادَ
	تَعود		عادَت

(٢)

المضارع		الماضي	
نَستَطيع	أَستَطيع	اِستَطَعنا	اِستَطَعتُ
تَستَطيعونَ / تَستَطيعوا	تَستَطيع	اِستَطَعتُم	اِستَطَعتَ
	تَستَطيعينَ / تَستَطيعي		اِستَطَعتِ
يَستَطيعونَ / يَستَطيعوا	يَستَطيع	اِستَطاعوا	اِستَطاعَ
	تَستَطيع		اِستَطاعَت

تـمـريـن ١: استطاع وعاد (في البيت) 🎧

Use the verbs عاد and استطاع to complete the following sentences. Choose the correct verb for each blank and put it in the correct form.

١. أنا لا .... شُرب القهوة قبل الفطور.

٢. الطلاب .... كتابة واجباتهم على الكمبيوتر.

٣. صديقتنا تريد الذهاب معنا الى السينما لكنها لا ....
بسبب مرض ابنتها.

٤. أنت طالب جديد هنا؟! (نحن) .... مساعدتك!

٥. متى .... من عملكم اليوم؟

٦. الأسبوع الماضي ما .... الخروج من البيت بسبب الثلج.

٧. كل يوم تخرج زوجتي من البيت حوالي الساعة ٧ صباحاً ولا ....
قبل الساعة ٨ مساءً.

٨. سافرنا إلى دمشق و ــــــــــ إلى بيروت في نفس اليوم.

٩. كيف ــــــــــ الى البيت أمس--بالأوتوبيس أو بسيارتكم؟

🎧 تمريـن ٢: المفردات الجديدة (في البيت)

اكتبوا كلمة من الكلمات الجديدة في كل جملة.

١. كان عمّي، الله يرحمه، ــــــــــ حوالي ٣٠ سيجارة كل يوم.

٢. هناك محاضرة غداً في المساء ولكن لا أعرف ما هو ــــــــــ المحاضرة.

٣. هذا الكتاب صعب ولا أريد قراءته، أريد قراءة كتاب ــــــــــ .

٤. كل يوم بعد أن نَنتَهي finish من عملنا أنا وزوجي في الساعة السادسة مساءً
ــــــــــ في غرفة الجلوس في بيتنا نقرأ ــــــــــ ونتكلم عن يومنا
أو نشاهد الأخبار وبعض ــــــــــ في التلفزيون ثم نأكل ــــــــــ .

٥. ابنة عمّي سَحَر دكتورة متخصّصة في أمراض diseases ــــــــــ .

٦. كل يوم (أنا) ــــــــــ أولادي في الساعة ٦،٠٠ صباحاً وآكل
معهم، وبعد ذلك (هم) ــــــــــ من البيت في
الساعة ٧،٠٠ ويذهبون الى مدارسهم. يوم الجمعة ليس هناك مدارس ، والحمد لله،
لذلك يبدأ يومنا في الساعة ٨ صباحاً. وفي الساعة ٢ ــــــــــ نذهب
كلنا الى المطعم لنأكل ــــــــــ ، والمطعم ــــــــــ عند أولادي هو
"بيتزا هت".

٧. لا نستطيع الدخول الى هذا النادي لأنّه ــــــــــ وليس لكل الناس.

٨. بعد التخرّج من الجامعة أريد العمل في الحكومة ــــــــــ في واحدة من
الشركات الأمريكية في منطقة الخليج Gulf.

٩. ــــــــــ دراسة اللغة العربية في الخريف الماضي والآن أستطيع القراءة
والكتابة والكلام بها! هذا شيء ممتاز فعلاً!

١٠. من هواياتي المفضّلة ــــــــــ وأنا ألعبه
أحياناً بعد الشغل مع ــــــــــ
زملائي الموظفين.

١١. في المستقبل أريد أن أسافر الى كل

بلاد ....

تـمـريـن ٣: المفردات في جمل (في البيت) 🎧

استمعوا إلى جمل المفردات واكتبوا الجمل من "آخر" إلى "الشطرنج".

تـمـريـن ٤: اسألوا زملاءكم (في الصف)

A.

1. Who leaves his or her house/room before eating breakfast? Who doesn't eat breakfast?
2. Who reads newspapers on the internet? Which paper/s?
3. Who wakes up his or her roommate in the morning? Whose roommate wakes her or him up instead?
4. Do many of his or her friends smoke? When did they start smoking? Do they think smoking is problem? Why or why not?
5. Who has joined a student club? Which one? Why?
6. What do they do first after they go back home in the evening/at night?
7. What subjects have they not studied that they would like to study in the future?
8. Who knows how to play chess? Who in their family knows how to play chess?
9. Is there a special chair or room or building they like to sit in to study?

B.

1. Does his or her dog or cat wake them up sometimes?
2. Does he or she prefer classes before 2 pm or after? Why?
3. Who thinks that paper newspapers have no future because of the internet? Is reading newspapers online like reading paper? Why or why not? Are his or her eyes tired after reading a lot either online or in a paper?
4. Where do they eat lunch?
5. What would they say to a friend who started smoking?
6. What, in his or her opinion, is the best restaurant where you can eat breakfast all day and all night?
7. Does he or she go back to their parents' home a lot? What do they do there?
8. Are student clubs good for universities? Why or why not?
9. Does he or she like one-hour classes or hour-and-a-half classes? Why?

القصة بالعامية

تمريـن ٥: "ستّي بتفيّقني" / "جدّتي بِتصَحّيني" (في البيت) 🎧

Listen to خالد, using the strategies you have learned. Write a **paragraph** to answer each question from 1 to 3, and write what you hear for 4 and 5.	Listen to طارق, using the strategies you have learned. Write a **paragraph** to answer each question from 1 to 3, and write what you hear for 4 and 5.
١. ايه رأيك في برنامج خالد؟ ايه هي الحاجات الكويسة فيه؟ مين عنده برنامج أحسن: أنت أو خالد؟ ليه؟	١. شو رأيك ببرنامج طارق؟ شو هي الأشيا المنيحة فيه؟ مين عنده برنامج أحسن: أنت أو طارق؟ ليش؟
٢. خالد لازم يعمل بعض الحاجات لأنه عايش مع عيلته- ايه هي؟	٢. فيه اشيا طارق لازم يعملها لأنّه ساكن مع عيلته – شو هي؟
٣. امتى بيروح خالد النادي؟ هل بيروح في نفس الوقت كل يوم؟ ليه؟ بيعمل ايه بالنادي؟	٣. اِمتى بيروح طارق ع النادي؟ هل بيروح بنفس الوقت كل يوم؟ ليش؟ شو بيعمل بالنادي؟
٤. ازاي بيقول خالد *to eat lunch*؟	٤. كيف بيقول طارق *to eat lunch*؟
Listen for الوزن and الجذر to help you write the new verb:	Listen for الوزن and الجذر to help you write the new verb:
٥. استمعوا للأفعال:	٥. استمعوا للأفعال:
Notice that Khalid uses the بـ prefix on some of the verbs. Which ones? List as many as you can. What might the بـ indicate here?	Notice that Tariq uses the بـ prefix on some of the verbs. Which ones? List as many as you can. What might the بـ indicate here?

الثقافة

"صباح الخيرات" / "صباح الفل يا حاجّة" 🎧

Watch الجدة طارق / خالد try to wake up الجدة. In the Egyptian version, what verb does repeat, and what does it seem to mean? What do her hand gestures signal?

هل تدخّنون أمام الأسرة؟ 🎧

Watch the interviews to hear what young smokers say about smoking around their parents.

تمريـن ٦:المفردات في جمل 🎧

استمعوا إلى جمل المفردات واكتبوا الجمل من "استطاع" إلى "أيقظ".

القواعد ١

المضارع المرفوع و"بـ" + الفعل المضارع

In English, present-tense verbs take slightly different forms depending on whether they are habitual, as in "she *plays* chess," progressive or stative, as in "she *is playing* chess," or subordinate to another verb (also called auxiliary), as in "she *wants to play* chess" or "she *might play* chess." Both formal and spoken Arabic distinguish the main verb of a clause or sentence from a dependent or subordinate verb (as in the last example above), but they each do this in different ways: Formal Arabic adds a suffix to المضارع, while spoken Arabic adds the prefix بـ to the main verb. Here we will focus on the formal suffix and spoken prefix بـ to mark habitual or recurring action on the main verb[1]. We will return to dependent or subordinate verbs in lesson 10.

بالشامي وفي المصري

In the story you heard طارق / خالد use many verbs with the بـ prefix. This prefix signals that an action takes place repeatedly or continuously—that it is taking place. As such, it is used on main verbs in the sentence:

باحب اصحابي كتير.	بحب رفقاتي كتير.
باشرب قهوة قبل الفطار.	بشرب شاي بعد الغدا.
هو دايماً بيزعَّل مراته!	الاخبار هالأيام بتزعِّل.

Verbs occur without this prefix when they are subordinate to a main verb or an expression that functions like a main verb, such as بدّ and عايز and auxiliaries like لازم and ممكن:

لازم اشوف الموظف في مكتب القبول.	ممكن اقعد معكن؟
عايز اتكلم مع حضرتك في موضوع السفر.	بدي ارجع ع البيت لأني تعبانة شوي.

Remember: In Egyptian and Levantine, the prefix بـ indicates main verb status and habitual or repeated action.

 في الفصحى

When we introduced المضارع conjugation in lesson 4, we noted that the forms for أنتِ, أنتم, and هم in formal Arabic include two variants, one with ن and one without it:

تفعلينَ ، تفعلي	أنتِ
تفعلونَ ، تفعلوا	أنتم
يفعلونَ ، يفعلوا	هم

---

[1] Levantine dialects are distinguished from Egyptian (and most other Arabic dialects) in having an additional prefix that signals progressive action: عَم بدرُس *I am studying* (as distinct from بِدرُس *I study*). You have heard طارق use this construction a couple of times. For now, recognize that this عَم signals an ongoing action and we will return to it again later.

The form with ن is the main verb form in formal Arabic, and this is called المضارع المرفوع. In other persons the مرفوع marker is the suffix ـُ. This ضَمّة vowel will not appear in unvocalized texts, and you will only hear it spoken in very formal contexts. When المضارع is the main verb in its sentence or clause, it normally takes this form. The next chart gives the endings of المضارع المرفوع using the verb يفعل as a model:

	يفعلُ / تفعلُ	تفعلُ / تفعلينَ	أفعَلُ	Singular
	يفعلونَ	تَفعَلونَ	نفعلُ	Plural

You will hear these endings in formal and prepared speech such as news broadcasts. There are two other endings that الفعل المضارع can have in الفصحى, as well, whose form and function you will learn in lessons 10 and 13.

تمـريـن ٧: المضارع المرفوع (في البيت وفي الصف)

Part A of this exercise focuses on formal Arabic, and part B focuses on spoken Arabic. As you work, think about the changes you are making to move from one register to the other.

A. في البيت Put the verbs in parentheses in the correct مضارع form and write all short vowels on each verb.

١. كل أسبوع _____ كرة السلة مع أصدقائي ثم _____ كلنا الى مطعم و_____ العشاء . (لعب، ذهب، أكل)

٢. كثير من الناس _____ الجرائد و _____ الى الأخبار على الإنترنت. (قرأ، استمع إلى)

٣. أنا _____ من المكتب في حوالي الساعة الخامسة والنصف مساءً ولكن زوجي لا _____ العودة قبل الثامنة. (عاد، استطاع)

٤. كل ساعة أو ساعة ونصف _____ هذه الموظفة من مكتبها لـِ _____ سيجارة أمام *in front of* البناية. (خرج، دخّن)

٥. كثير من رؤساء دول العالم _____ الى نيويورك كل سنة للكلام أمام الأمم المتحدة. (سافر)

٦. كل يوم عندنا مشكلة مع التلفزيون في بيتنا: زوجي _____ مشاهدة الأخبار دائماً، والأولاد _____ مشاهدة برامج الصغار، وأنا لا _____ أي شيء. (أراد، أحبّ، شاهد)

٧. ابني لا _____ العربية وأفراد عائلتي في الأردن لا _____ الفرنسية لذلك أترجم لهم كل شيء. (تكلّم، تكلّم)

B. With a partner express the sentences aloud in part A in the dialect you are studying.

تـمـريـن ٨: ماذا أفعل أحياناً أو دائماً؟ (في الصف)

Do you and your زملاء have similar lifestyles? In groups of three, using the questions below as prompts, find several things you all do and several more that not all of you do. Discuss your activities with each other in the dialect you are learning, then write up your findings in formal Arabic, using المرفوع endings as appropriate.

١. ماذا تفعلون في الصباح؟   ٢. ماذا تفعلون بعد الظهر؟

٣. ماذا تفعلون يوم الأحد؟   ٤. مع من تخرجون يوم الجمعة أو يوم السبت؟

٥. أين ومتى تأكلون الغداء والعشاء؟

القصة بالفصحى

تـمـريـن ٩: "جدّتي توقظني في السادسة والنصف" (في البيت) 🎧

استمعوا الى خالد بالفصحى واكتبوا:

1. Mention something خالد does that you do not do:

أ. في الصباح ....

ب. بعد الظهر ....

ج. في المساء ....

2. Order the following activities according to what خالد does:

يفطر   يعود الى البيت   جدته توقظه   يقرأ الجرائد   يخرج من البيت

يلعب الشطرنج   يأكل الغداء   يدرس في المكتبة   ينزل والده وإخوته

١. ....

٢. ....

٣. ....

٤. ....

٥. ....

٦. ....

٧. ....

٨. ....

٩. ....

3. Write what خالد says بالفصحى, paying special attention to the way he expresses the time. You may need to add a و, which is written as part of the word that follows it:

أ. "في الأيام التي أذهب فيها الى الجامعة، (١) _____ (٢) _____ البيت (٣) _____ الساعة (٤) _____ صباحاً."

ب. "لكن جدّتي توقظني (١) _____ في(٢) _____ (٣) _____ لِ (٤) _____ معهم."

جـ. محاضراتي (١) _____ في (٢) _____ (٣) _____ (٤) _____ ، لذلك (٥) _____ قبلها (٦) _____ في _____ (٧) _____ (٨) _____ أو ثلاث ثمّ أتناول (٩) _____ .

Complete these اسم وصفة phrases with attention to grammar:

د. أذهب مع (١) _____ (٢) _____ (٣) _____ لنلعب الشطرنج (٤) _____ (٥) _____ .

هـ. "أساعد (١) _____ قليلاً في (٢) _____ في . (٣) _____ (٤) _____ ، أذهب الى (٥) _____ (٦) _____ وأدرس في المساء."

4. Khalid introduces a new topic, يوم الجمعة, using a topic switcher. Write below what he says:

أمّا... ، فّ... ...,... *as for*

ماذا يَقول خالد عن يوم الجمعة ؟

"أمّا (١) _____ (٢) _____ ,فـ (٣) _____ (٤) _____ (٥) _____ !"

5. Watch the video ماذا تفعلون في النادي؟ and prepare to discuss it in class.

القواعد ٢
Ordinal Numbers الأعداد التَّرتيبيّة

| عَدَد ج. أعداد | number |

You have learned the cardinal (counting) numbers from ١ to ١٠٠. Arabic also has ordinal numbers that are easily derived from the cardinal numbers through the وزن and جذر system: Simply put الجذر of the cardinal number into وزن فاعِل/ة (see the chart below). This combination produces the ordinal numbers from second to tenth.

Note that the Arabic word for "first" is derived from a different جذر than that of واحد , just as English "one" and "first" do not resemble each other, and that الجذر of "six" is really س – د – س and not س – ت – ت, which is a later development of the counting-number six.

The cardinal numbers from one to ten have masculine and feminine forms. Formal Arabic has special rules about their use, which you will learn later.

مؤنث	مذكر	العدد
الأولى	الأوَّل	واحِد/ة
الثّانية	الثّاني	إثنان/ اِثنَين
الثّالثة	الثّالث	ثَلاث/ة
الرّابعة	الرّابِع	أربَع/ة
الخامسة	الخامِس	خَمس/ة
السّادسة	السّادِس	سِتّ/ة
السّابعة	السّابِع	سَبع/ة
الثّامنة	الثّامِن	ثَماني/ة
التّاسعة	التّاسِع	تِسع/ة
العاشِرة	العاشِر	عَشْر/عَشَرة
الحاديةَ عَشْرة	الحادي عَشر	أحَدَ عَشر
الثّانيةَ عَشرة	الثاني عَشر	إثنا عَشر
الثّالثةَ عَشرة	الثالِث عَشر	ثَلاثةَ عَشر

أمثلة:

نحن في الأسبوع الخامس من هذا الفصل الدراسي.

أسكن في غرفة ٤١٣ وهي الغرفة الثانية بعد غرفة الجلوس.

معظم الموظفين يخرجون من مكاتبهم للغداء في الساعة الثانية عشرة.

تـمـريـن ١٠: الأعداد الترتيبية (في البيت)

Create an ordinal number from the numeral in parentheses to designate the correct
order or place in a sequence. Use the numeral in parentheses, if given; otherwise,
use any appropriate number.

١. بعض زملائي طلاب في السنة _____ في الجامعة.

٢. عندنا ٣ امتحانات كبيرة في هذا الصف: امتحان في الأسبوع _____ (٤)
وامتحان في الأسبوع _____ (٩) ثم امتحان في الأسبوع _____ (١٣).

٣. اللغة العربية هي لغتي _____ .

٤. عنده ولد من زوجته _____ وولدان من زوجته _____ .

٥. يوم الخميس هو اليوم _____ في الأسبوع.

٦. جورج واشنطُن كان الرئيس _____ للولايات المتحدة.

🎧 What Time Is It? "الساعة كام؟" "قَدّيش الساعة؟" "كم الساعة؟"

In spoken Arabic cardinal numbers are used to tell time, but in formal Arabic the ordinal
numbers are used with the exception of ١,٠٠. In the audio listen to the different time examples
and repeat them aloud, focusing on الفصحى and the dialect you are learning.

الساعة واحْدة	الساعة واحْدة	الساعة الواحِدة	١,٠٠
الساعة اتنين	الساعة تِنْتين	الساعة الثّانية	٢,٠٠
الساعة أربعة ونُصّ	الساعة أرْبَعة ونُصّ	الساعة الرّابعة والنّصف	٤,٣٠
الساعة عشرة ونُصّ	الساعة عَشْرة ونُصّ	الساعة العاشِرة والنّصف	١٠,٣٠
الساعة حِداشر	الساعة إدَعش	الساعة الحادِيةَ عَشْرة	١١,٠٠
الساعة اِتناشَر ونُصّ	الساعة تْنَعش ونُصّ	الساعة الثّانيةَ عَشْرة والنصف	١٢,٣٠

To give more exact times, the following words are used in formal and spoken Arabic, which you can hear on the audio. Listen to them, repeat each aloud, and learn. Notice that the roots of "a quarter "and "a third" come from "four" and "three"—this will help you remember them:

Expressions for Telling Time

minute	دَقيقة ج. دَقائِق دقيقة ج. دقايِق دِقيقة ج. دَقايِق
quarter	رُبع
third	ثُلُث تِلت تِلت
less (literally: except)	إلّا

The word إلّا is used to give times such as "five of ten" or "five until ten." The Arabic way of phrasing this is literally "ten less five minutes":

الساعة عَشْرة إلّا خمسة	الساعة عَشْرة إلّا خَمسة	الساعة العاشرة إلّا خَمس دَقائِق	
الساعة واحِدة وخمسة	الساعة واحدة وخمسة	الساعة الواحِدة وخَمس دَقائِق	١،٠٥
الساعة اِتنين ورُبع	الساعة تِنتين ورِبع	الساعة الثّانية والرُبع	٢،١٥
الساعة ثَّمانية وتِلت	الساعة ثمانة وتِلت	الساعة الثامِنة والثُلُث	٨،٢٠
الساعة عَشّرة إلّا تِلت	الساعة عَشّرة إلّا تِلت	الساعة العاشِرة إلّا ثُلثاً	٩،٤٠
الساعة اِتناعشر إلّا عَشَرة	الساعة تتّعش إلّا عَشَرة	الساعة الثانية عَشّرةَ إلّا عَشَر دقائِق	١١،٥٠

تمـريـن ١١: في أي ساعة؟ (في البيت)

This exercise is available online only.

تمـريـن ١٢: في أي ساعة؟ (في الصف)

A. Ask زملاءك في أي ساعة يفعلون هذا؟
Be sure to specify مساءً, or صباحاً , بعد الظهر

ينامون	يأكلون الغداء
يشاهدون التليفزيون	يعودون الى البيت
يلعبون الرياضة	يأكلون العشاء
يتكلّمون مع أصدقائهم بالتليفون	يذهبون الى الجامعة
يقرأون أو يستمعون الى الأخبار	يدرسون في غرفهم
يبدأون العمل	يذهبون الى المكتبة

B. Did they do any of these things at another time yesterday أمس ؟

القراءة: نشاط قراءة

تمـريـن ١٣: "من برامج التلفزيون" (في الصف)

In what follows there is some information about satellite television programming
في العالم العربي. Be sure to read both pages about programming.

A. With a partner find programming that will tell you about:

٢. آراء الشباب العرب.	١. البرامج العائلية.

٣. الثقافة العربية (specify which aspects).

٥. مستقبل العمل في منطقة الشرق الأوسط.	٤. المرأة العربية.

٦. برامج الأولاد.

B. How many new words in the text in Part A can you guess using context in addition
to الوزن والجذر? List them here.

من تلفزيون دبي

إقتصاد الخليج

يعرض: يوم الجمعة
٢١:٠٠ UAE | ٢٠:٠٠ KSA

يعاد: السبت والجمعة
١٢:٠٠ UAE | ١١:٠٠ KSA

برنامج اقتصادي اسبوعي يتناول أهم المواضيع الاقتصادية في العالم بما في ذلك الاقتصاد العربي والمحلي.

مسلسل عجيب غريب

يعرض: من الأحد إلى الخميس
١٥:٣٠ UAE | ١٤:٣٠ KSA

يعاد: من الأحد إلى الخميس
٠٢:٣٠ UAE | ٠١:٣٠ KSA

يحكي مسلسل الست كوم "عجيب غريب" في جزئه الأول قصة عائلة مكونة من الأب والأم وعدد من الأولاد مع جدتهم .

من تلفزيون الآن في دبي

برنامج يومي يعرض آخر وأحدث الألبومات الموسيقية والاغاني والفيديو.
مدة العرض : ٤٥ دقيقة
وقت العرض : من الأحد الى الخميس ١٣:١٥ مساء بتوقيت السعودية .

أول برنامج سعودي منوع للشباب يناقش القضايا الهامة والحساسة التي تهم الشباب السعودي مثل: الواسطة، علاقة الابناء بالأهل، الزواج والطلاق المبكر، الى جانب أحدث اخبار الموسيقى والسينما والسيارات .

من تلفزيون عجمان

كرتون أطفال : من ١٧:٣٠ وحتى ١٩:٠٠ :
تقدم القناة الرابعة مجموعة رائعة من برامج الكرتون للأطفال، قصص يعشقها الأطفال ويحبون مشاهدة أبطالها.

برامج وثائقية الساعة ١٩:٠٠ :
يوميا نصف ساعة من البرامج الوثائقية المميزة من بينها مجلة عن فرنسا، التكنولوجيا في اليابان، وآخر أخبار الرياضة العالمية.

الأحد: Music Mix :
مزيج رائع من الأغاني الإنجليزية والهندية والعربية والتي يطلب المشاهدون سماعها.

الأربعاء: شو ع بالك ؟
للموسيقى العربية والفيديو كليب وقع خاص في نفوس الشباب والمشاهدين. البرنامج يقدم آخر الأغاني العربية المصورة وأخبار النجوم ويلتقي بهم في الأستديو.

من تلفزيون المنار في لبنان

المنار الصغير

فترة يومية ومنوعة لأطفال المنار مدتها ساعة كاملة تقدم مجموعة من البرامج الخاصة بأطفالنا وهي "لوز وسكر" ، "العم وضّاح" ، "بيت بيوت"، بالإضافة إلى مجموعة مميزة من برامج الرسوم المتحركة وأغاني الأطفال واستعراض صور أصدقاء المنار الصغير والإصدارات الخاصة بالأطفال.

من تلفزيون الشارقة

صباح الشارقة

برنامج مباشر يتناول مواضيع تهم المرأة والشباب ، يتخلل البرنامج عدة فقرات منها : الصحف اليومية المحلية ، رياضية ، دينية .

يعرض: يومياً عدا الجمعة ١٠:٠٠

وللشباب رأي

برنامج أسبوعي .. يتناول قضايا الشباب ، ويطرحها للنقاش على الشباب لأخذ آرائهم حول هذه القضية ومناقشتها .

يعرض: الثلاثاء ٢٠:٤٥ U.A.E   ويعاد: الأربعاء ١١:٤٥ U.A.E

ملح وسكر

برنامج طبخ ، يهم في المقام الأول أغلب رَبّات البيوت .. حيث يقدم لهن كيفية طبخ ألوان كثيرة من الأكلات العربية وغير العربية .

يعرض: يوميا ١٩:١٥ U.A.E   ويعاد: يوميا ١١:١٥ U.A.E

يوم جديد

برنامج تلفزيوني إذاعي مباشر صباحي يشتمل على فقرات متنوعة منها نقل مباشر لحركة السير والازدحام في شوارع الشارقة ..... حركة الطيران ..أين تذهب اليوم؟ ...آخر الأخبار المحلية والعالمية وأخبار الرياضة.

يعرض: يوميا عدا الجمعة والسبت ٠٦:٤٥ U.A.E

من تلفزيون الوطن في الكويت

صباح الوطن الأربعاء ٠٨:٠٠

برنامج صباحي من الساعة الثامنة حتى الساعة الحادية عشرة يشهد العديد من اللقاءات مع شخصيات المجتمع الكويتي التي تسلط الضوء على الحياة اليومية للأسرة الكويتية. كما يتضمن البرنامج فقرات منوعة مثل : المطبخ مع الشيف "هنوف الهلبان" والفقرة الرياضية والاقتصادية وشارع هوليوود والعديد من التقارير اليومية على الواقع اليومي للكويت.

اليوم السابع

برنامج سياسي واجتماعي واقتصادي يتناول قضايا الساعة التي تعيشها الساحة الكويتية من خلال استضافة المختصين والمسؤوليين الحكوميين من وزراء وأعضاء مجلس الأمة والناشطين بمختلف المجالات.

الاستماع: مع العائلة والأصدقاء

تمرين ١٤: مع زميل خالد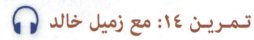

Watch the video "مع زميل خالد" and answer the questions below.

أسئلة:

١. من هو سامي؟

٢. ماذا يعمل؟

٣. لماذا يذهب الى الجامعة كل يوم؟

٤. ما هواية سامي المفضّلة؟

٥. ماذا يكتب؟ : ـــــــــــــــــــ . ما معنى هذه؟

تمرين ١٥: نشاط محادثة (في الصف)

A tray of بقلاوة is missing and believed stolen from the department office. Investigators from each class will interrogate everyone. With a partner, construct your alibi for the past 24 hours. Make sure you both know your story because you will be interrogated separately!

الكتابة

تمرين ١٦: نشاط كتابة (في البيت) 🎧

Watch the video and then write a story describing يوم في حياة الأستاذة كريستن.

الحوار

اللغة والثقافة: يا سَلام!

The expression يا سَلام! can convey a range of emotions from pleasure to surprise to anger. How it is intended depends on the tone with which it is said. Watch the following dialogue in Drill 17: How is it used here?

تمـريـن ١٧: "الله يساعدني عليها" / "خير، رايحة على فين؟" (في البيت) 🎧

استمعوا الى الحوار بالمصري واكتبوا فَقرة paragraph لكل سؤال:	استمعوا الى الحوار بالشامي واكتبوا فَقرة paragraph لكل سؤال:
١. هي رايحة فين ومع مين وحترجع إمتى؟	١. هي وين رايحة ومع مين وإيمتى رح ترجع؟
٢. ابنهم فين -- ليه مش في البيت؟	٢. وين ابنُن -- ليش مو بالبيت؟
٣. هو زعلان ليه في رأيك -- في الحقيقة؟	٣. ليش هو زعلان برأيك --بالحقيقة؟
٤. ايه رأيك: الستّ عندها حق ولّا الرّاجِل؟ ليه؟ عندها حَقّ she is right	٤. شو رأيك: المرة عندها حقّ ولّا الرِّجّال؟ ليش؟ عندها حَقّ she is right

تـمارين المراجعة

تمـريـن ١٨: معرفة الجذر في الاستماع (في البيت) 🎧

This exercise is available online only.

تمـريـن ١٩: مفردات 🎧

This exercise is available online only.

تمـريـن ٢٠: كم؟ (في البيت) 🎧

This exercise is available online only.

تمـريـن ٢١: القراءة الجهرية (في الصف أو في البيت) 🎧

Read the following passage, first silently for comprehension, then aloud to practice pronunciation. When you are ready, record yourself reading it aloud and submit it for your teacher's feedback either online or following your teacher's instructions.

سامي مُصطفى واحد من زملاء خالد وأصدقائه في الجامعة وهو يعمل معيداً في قسم الاقتصاد بكلية التجارة. برنامج سامي في الكلية ليس فيه أي تدريس أو محاضرات في هذا الفصل الدراسيّ لأنّه مشغول بكتابة رسالة الماجستير وموضوع رسالته هو "البنك الدوليّ والاقتصاد في بلاد العالم الثالث". بيت سامي صغير وليس فيه مكان للدراسة ، ولذلك يذهب الى مكتبة الجامعة يوميّاً - إلّا يوم الجمعة - حيث يقرأ ويكتب ويعمل على الكومبيوتر. وفي يوم الأربعاء بعد الظهر يذهب سامي مع خالد وبعض زملائهم الآخرين الى النادي حيث يجلسون الى المساء يتكلمون عن الحياة والمستقبل وأخبار الكليّة والبلد والناس. خالد يحب الشّطرنج كثيراً، امّا سامي، فهو يحب شُرْب القهوة والكلام مع البنات!

بيت العائلة

المفردات

القصة بالعامية: "بيت العيلة" "بيت العيلة"

الثقافة (١): بيت العائلة

القواعد (١):

"إذا" و "لو" Conditionals

"أفعل" The Comparative

المضارع المنصوب

الثقافة (٢): جامع الحسين

القصة بالفصحى: "بيت العائلة"

القواعد (٢):

القراءة: "معيشة جلالة الملك اليومية" و "برنامج الإمام الخميني"

الحوار: "قولوا إن شاء الله"

تمارين المراجعة

🎧 Vocabulary المُفرَدات

استمعوا الى المفردات الجديدة بالفصحى والعامية.

المعنى	المصري	الشامي	الفصحى
late	مِتأَخَّر/ة	مِتأَخِّر/ة	مُتَأَخِّر/ة ج. -ون ، -ين
if[1]	لَوْ (+ الفعل الماضي)	إذا (+ الماضي أو المضارع)	إذا (+ الفعل الماضي)
match, game (sports)	ماتش ج. -ات		مُباراة ج. مُبارَيات
mosque			جامِع ج. جَوامِع
to come	جا (جيت)، بيجي	إجا (إجيت)، بِجي	جاءَ (جِئتُ)، يَجيء إلى، المَجيء إلى
salary		مَعاش ج.-ات	مُرَتَّب ج. -ات
rest period, break			اِستِراحة ج. -ات
quickly, in a hurry		بِسرعة	بِسُرْعة
to stay up late	سِهِر ، يِسهَر	سِهِر ، يسهَر	سَهِرَ، يَسْهَر ، السَّهَر
to become	بَقى ، يِبقى	صار، يصير	أصبَحَ، يُصْبِح
to wake up	صِحي (صِحيت)، يِصحى	فاق (فِقت) ، يفيق	صَحا (صَحوتُ)، يَصحو
frankly, honestly			بِصَراحة
(ritual) prayer			الصَّلاة
to pray, do ritual prayers	صَلّى، (صَلّيت)، يِصَلي	صَلّى، (صَلّيت)، يصَلي	صَلّى (صَلَّيتُ)، يُصَلّي، الصَّلاة
usually			عادةً
to understand	فِهِم، يِفهَم	فِهِم، يِفهَم	فَهِم، يَفهَم ، الفَهم
to meet	قابِل، يِقابِل	قابِل، يقابِل	قابَلَ، يُقابِل ، المُقابَلة
interview			مُقابَلة ج. -ات
more	أكتر	أكتر	أكثَر
to be[2]	يِكون	يكون	يَكون
(a) night			لَيلة ج. ليالي (لَيالٍ)
tonight			اللَّيلة

المعنى	المصري	الشامي	الفُصحى
to enjoy			اِستَمْتَع بـ ، يسْتَمْتِع بـ ، الاسْتِمتاع بـ
going well	ماشي	ماشي	--
it is possible to[3]	مُمكِن / قِدِر، يِقدَر	مُمكِن / قِدِر، يِقدِر	يُمْكِن أنْ
boring			مُمِلّ/ة
king			مَلِك ج. مُلوك
to sleep, go to sleep	نام (نِمت)، يِنام ، النَّوم	نام (نِمت)، يْنام ، النَّوم	نامَ (نِمْتُ)، يَنام ، النَّوم
(fixed) time, appointment	مَعاد ج. مَواعيد		مَوعِد ج. مَواعيد
time			وَقت ج. أوقات
since	من ساعة ما	مِن وَقت ما	مُنذُ

Notes on Vocabulary Usage

1. The words إذا and لَو both mean "if" in Arabic. The verb following إذا or لَو should be in الماضي, and, in this case, الماضي does not give a past tense meaning but a conditional one. We will present an overview of conditionals in Arabic in the القواعد section of this lesson.

2. You know that the verb "to be" is used in الماضي to put sentences into past, and that present tense sentences with "is," "are," and "am" are normally expressed without a verb in Arabic. However, the present tense of كان is needed in two types of situations: One situation is the habitual, for a recurring but not permanent state:

عادةً تكون هذه الموظفة في مكتبها قبل الساعة ٨٫٣٠ صباحاً.

الاستاذ بيكون بمكتبه كل يوم.   /   عادةً بيكون فيه أخبار الساعة ١٢ الضُّهر كل يوم.

The other situation in which يكون is found is in a subordinate clause, such as for example after أنْ:

أين الأستاذة؟ -- يمكن أن تكون في مطعم الجامعة.

وين الأستاذة؟ -- ممكن تكون بالصف.

الساعة ١٠ كلنا لازم نكون في الأوتوبيس.

3. The formal Arabic expression يُمكِن أنْ is impersonal, meaning that the verb يُمكِن is fixed, and not conjugated for person. However, the logical subject can be expressed by a pronoun object:

is possible for me/you/him/her ... to	يُمكِنُني ، يُمكِنُكَ ، يُمكِنُهُ

لا يمكنها أن تسهر الليلة لأنها تسافر في الصباح.

يمكنك الجلوس على هذا الكرسي.

هل يمكنكم أن تجيئوا معي الى النادي؟

تعلّموا هذه الأفعال

Listen to the verbs نام وجاء وصَحا in الفصحى and your dialect repeatedly until you can pronounce them easily. Then practice by making up questions and answers by yourself or with a study partner. Notice that المضارع verbs in the dialects have been recorded with بـ because this is the way they occur when they function as the main verbs in sentences. We will discuss when this بـ is left off the spoken مضارع later in this chapter.

نام ، يَنام

الماضي

نِمت	نِمت	نِمتُ	أنا
نِمت	نِمت	نِمتَ	أنتَ
نِمتي	نِمتي	نِمتِ	أنتِ
نام	نام	نامَ	هو
نامِت	نامِت	نامَت	هي
نِمنا	نِمنا	نِمنا	نحن
نِمتوا	نِمتوا	نِمتُم	أنتم
ناموا	ناموا	ناموا	هم

المضارع

بانام	بنام	أنام	أنا
بِتنام	بِتنام	تَنام	أنتَ
بِتنامي	بِتنامي	تَنامينَ / تَنامي	أنتِ
بينام	بينام	يَنام	هو
بِتنام	بِتنام	تَنام	هي
بِننام	بِننام	نَنام	نحن
بِتناموا	بِتناموا	تَنامونَ / تَناموا	أنتم
بيناموا	بيناموا	يَنامونَ / تَناموا	هم

جاء ، يَجيء

الماضي

جيت	إجيت	جِئْتُ	أنا
جيت	إجيت	جِئْتَ	أنتَ
جيتي	إجيتي	جِئْتِ	أنتِ
جا (جَه)	إجا	جاءَ	هو
جَت	إجِت	جاءَت	هي
جينا	إجينا	جِئْنا	نحن
جيتوا	إجيتوا	جِئْتُم	أنتم
جُم	إجوا	جاءوا (جاؤوا)	هم

المضارع

بآجي	بِجي	أجيء	أنا
بِتيجي	بِتيجي	تَجيء	أنتَ
بِتيجي	بِتيجي	تَجيئينَ / تَجيئي	أنتِ
بِيِجي	بيجي	يَجيء	هو
بِتيجي	بِتيجي	تَجيء	هي
بِنِجي	بِنجي	نَجيء	نحن
بِتيجوا	بِتجوا	تَجيئونَ/ تَجيئوا	أنتم
بِيِجوا	بيجوا	يَجيئونَ/ يَجيئوا	هم

صحا ، يَصحو

الماضي

صِحيت	فِقت	صَحَوْتُ	أنا
صِحيت	فِقت	صَحَوْتَ	أنتَ
صِحيتي	فِقتي	صَحَوْتِ	أنتِ
صِحي	فاق	صَحا	هو
صِحْيِت	فاقِت	صَحَت	هي
صِحينا	فِقنا	صَحَوْنا	نحن
صِحيتوا	فِقتوا	صَحَوْتُم	أنتم
صِحْيوا	فاقوا	صَحَوْا	هم

المضارع

أنا	أَصحو	بفيق	باصحى
أنتَ	تَصحو	بتفيق	بِتصحى
أنتِ	تَصحينَ / تَصحي	بتفيقي	بِتصحي
هو	يَصحو	بيفيق	بِيصحى
هي	تَصحو	بتفيق	بِتصحى
نحن	نَصحو	بنفيق	بِنصحى
أنتم	تَصحونَ /تَصحوا	بتفيقوا	بِتصحوا
هم	يَصحونَ / يَصحوا	بيفيقوا	بِيصحوا

تـمـريـن ١: كلمات جديدة وقواعد قديمة (في البيت) 🎧

اكتبوا كلمة من الكلمات الجديدة في كل جملة.

١. زميلتي التحقت بالجيش منذ ٤ سنوات

و ـــــــــــــــ ضابطة ، وهي سعيدة بحياتها لأن

عندها وظيفة ممتازة و ـــــــــــــــ ممتاز.

٢. أصحو ـــــــــــــــ في الساعة السادسة صباحاً ،

ولكن اليوم صحوت في السابعة والنصف

لأنني ـــــــــــــــ ليلة أمس الى الساعة الواحدة

بسبب ورقة صف علم الإنسان.

٣. ما رأيكم أن ـــــــــــــــ كلّـكم الى بيتي للعشاء

ـــــــــــــــ السبت ثم نشاهد ـــــــــــــــ كرة القدم؟

٤. مريم: "كيف كانت المحاضرة؟"

محمود: "تريدين رأيي؟ ـــــــــــــــ ، المحاضرة كانت طويلة

و ـــــــــــــــ جداً وما ـــــــــــــــ بها".

٥. مصر وسوريا وتونس دول عربية فيها رؤساء ولكن السعودية والأردن

والمغرب فيها ـــــــــــــــ .

٦. أنا عادةً _____ في الساعة الحادية عشرة ليلاً ولكن زوجي

لا _____ ـه النوم قبل الساعة الواحدة صباحاً .

٧. كانت القصة صعبة قليلاً ، وفي الحقيقة ما كان عندي إلا ساعتان لقراءتها،

لذلك قرأتها _____ وما _____ كل شيء فيها. إذا كان عندي

_____ اليوم في المساء أريد أن أقرأها أكثر.

٨. هذا _____ في مدينة الرياض في السعودية

يذهب اليه الناس كل يوم لـ _____ .

٩. أمس زوجتي كان عندها _____ مع طبيبتها

في الساعة الخامسة بعد الظهر ولكنها كانت

_____ بسبب حادث سيارة وازدحام

كبير في الشوارع.

١٠. ابني يحب أن _____ الأول في كل شيء إلا في الدراسة!

١١. الموظفون في كل وزارات الدولة عندهم _____ للغداء ، وهي تكون عادةً

من الساعة ١٢ ظهراً الى ١ بعد الظهر.

١٢. عندي أخبار ممتازة! _____ العمل مع رئيس الشركة أمس كانت ناجحة

جداً واليوم قال لي انني حصلت على الوظيفة.

🎧 تمريـن ٢: المفردات في جمل (في البيت)

استمعوا الى جمل المفردات واكتبوا الجمل من "متأخّر" إلى "عادةً".

تمرين ٣: الجذر والوزن (في البيت أو في الصف)

A. Identify الوزن والجذر of all the new verbs by completing the chart:

المصدر	المضارع	الماضي	الوزن
			I فَعَلَ ، يفعل
			II فَعَّلَ، يُفَعِّل، التَّفعيل
			III فاعَلَ، يُفاعِل، المُفاعَلة
--			IV أفعَلَ، يُفعِل، الإفعال
			X اِستَفعَلَ، يَستَفعِل، الاسْتِفعال

B. Expand your vocabulary! Use الجذر or words you know to figure out the approximate meaning of the underlined words in each sentence.

١. عندي موعد مع الدكتور ولا أعرف ماذا سأفعل إذا <u>تَأخَّر</u> الأوتوبيس!!

٢. السفر والشطرنج والسينما هوايات <u>مُمتِعة</u>!

٣. أحب صديقي لأنه رجل <u>صَريح</u>.

٤. هل كلامي <u>مَفهوم</u> بالنسبة لكم؟

٥. سيارة "فيراري" الإيطالية <u>سَريعة</u> جداً.

٦. أحبّ بيتي وأشعر <u>براحة</u> كبيرة فيه.

تمريـن ٤: اسألوا زملاءكم (في الصف)

A.

1. Do they have breaks during their school days? What do they do during these breaks?

2. Do they enjoy traveling? Why or why not? What things do they enjoy?

3. When they come home late, what is "late"?

4. Did they sleep well last night, and did they stay up late in order to study?

5. Do they wake up at a set time every day? What do they do if they wake up late?

6. What time do they usually wake up in the morning and go to sleep at night?

7. What is a good salary for a job on campus, in their opinion? Have they had a job with a good salary?

B.

1. Do they stay up late at night more often because of homework or to enjoy themselves with friends?

2. How many job interviews have they had? Do they usually do well in job interviews? How?

3. Do their friends come to their room or house a lot? Did someone come over last night?

4. Do they have any appointments this week? When? How do they remember appointments?

5. Do they enjoy watching basketball, football, or soccer games more?

6. What are three boring things, in their opinion?

7. If they stay up late, are they tired the next day?

***Extra challenge:**

1. Do they want to become a parent? When?

2. Have they ever asked for a raise? How?

تمريـن ٥: كلمات جديدة + المصدر (في البيت)

Use المصدر to list things you do and do not enjoy and can and cannot do.
(Use this exercise to review old vocabulary.)

أستمتع بـ :

١. ....

٢. ....

٣. ....

لا أستمتع بـ :

١. ....

٢. ....

٣. ....

يمكنني:

١. ....

٢. ....

٣. ....

لا يمكنني:

١. ....

٢. ....

٣. ....

القصة بالعامية

تمرين ٦: "بيت العيلة" / "بيت العيلة" (في البيت)

استمعوا إلى خالد:	استمعوا إلى طارق:
Write a فقرة **paragraph** for questions 1-3 and write what you hear for 4-5.	Write a فقرة **paragraph** for questions 1-3 and write what you hear for 4-5.
١. خالد بيعمل ايه ليلة الخميس ويوم الجمعة؟	١. شو بيعمل طارق ليلة الخميس ويوم الجمعة؟
٢. ليه برنامج يوم الجمعة خاص بالنسبة لخالد؟	٢. ليش برنامج يوم الجمعة خاص بالنسبة لطارق؟
٣. ايه هوّ "بيت العيلة"؟ ايه رأي خالد في بيت العيلة؟ ليه؟	٣. شو هوّ "بيت العيلة"؟ شو رأي طارق ببيت العيلة؟ ليش؟
٤. ازاي بيقول خالد to watch TV؟	٤. كيف بيقول طارق to watch TV؟
Listen for الوزن and الجذر to help you write the new verb:	Listen for الوزن and الجذر to help you write the new verb:
٥. استمعوا للأفعال:	٥. استمعوا للأفعال:
Which verbs have بـ and which do not? Write as many as you can, and for those that do not have بـ give the reason why:	Which verbs have بـ and which do not? Write as many as you can, and for those that do not have بـ give the reason why:

الثقافة ١

ما هو بيت العائلة بالنسبة لك؟ (في البيت)

Watch the interviews about بيت العائلة. To what extent do people's experiences and situations differ? Are the differences comparable to those you would find in your country?

تمرين ٧: المفردات في جمل (في البيت)

استمعوا الى جمل المفردات واكتبوا الجمل من "فهم" إلى "منذ".

القواعد

Conditionals "لو" و "إذا"

The words إذا and لَو are used in formal and spoken Arabic to express conditions, as we do in English with "if." In formal Arabic, the two words differ in the kind of condition they express: إذا is used in conditions that are possible and لَو is used in conditions that are impossible. In spoken Arabic, the distinction between possible and impossible conditions is less important, and each region has a preferred word: Egyptians tend to use لَو and Levantine speakers prefer إذا.

In formal Arabic, conditionals have rather strict rules. Here we will focus on the rules for إذا, which must be followed by الماضي, because الماضي is the conditional tense—that is, الماضي in this case does not have a past meaning but rather a conditional one. The result clause—what happens if the condition is met—is signaled in formal Arabic by فَ. Study the examples, and compare them with the examples from spoken Arabic, which show more flexibility:

إذا نجحت في صف الفيزياء فيمكنني أن أتخرج في ديسمبر!

إذا بدك تاكل شي حلو لازم تروح ع المطعم اللبناني الجديد!

لو دخلت كلية الحقوق، عايز اتخصص في حقوق الإنسان.

إذا ما استطعت أن أنام فسأقرأ بعض القصص.

إذا ما قدرت انام رح اقرا بعض القصص.

إذا ما قدرتش انام حاقرا شوية قصص.

In Levantine, الماضي is not obligatory and its use signals a greater "iffiness" than a sentence without it. In Egyptian, الماضي is normally used except in existential sentences. Examples:

إذا ما فيه وقت هلّق، ممكن نروح بعدين.

إذا بتقدر تيجي معنا رح اكون مبسوط كتير!

إذا ما قدرت تنام ممكن تحكي معي.

لو مافيش وقت دلوقت ممكن نروح بعدين.

لو قدرت تيجي معانا حاكون مبسوط قوي!

لو ما قدرتش تنام ممكن تتكلم معايَ.

تمـريـن ٨: ماذا سنفعل إذا.. (في الصف)

Find out from زملائك what they would or will do if:

1. They didn't have classes tomorrow due to the weather.
2. They got a check شيك for $500.
3. Someone they don't know wants to become their friend on Facebook.
4. They are very tired but have a big exam or paper tomorrow.
5. Their friend had a problem and asked them to stay up late to help him/her with it.
6. They meet someone special.
7. Their best friend got so busy they didn't have time for them.

The Comparative "أَفْعَل"

You have seen words with وزن "أَفعَل" used in the superlative in different situations that we have discussed, such as:

أكبر بلد في العالم

أحسن هواية بالنسبة لي

ألطف رجل قابلته

In the story, you heard طارق / خالد use an أفعَل word in another sense: أكثر meaning *more*. In fact, all أفعَل words can be used in the comparative sense as well as the superlative, but the different meanings are distinguished by different grammatical structures. To give the superlative meaning, أفعَل words such as أحسن, أكبر, أصغر, and act like nouns and function as the first term of an إضافة:

ألطَف رجل   أحسَن هواية   أكبر بلد

In contrast, the comparative is an adjective and follows the noun it describes in a noun-adjective construction. Contrast these comparatives and superlatives in meaning and form:

a better day	يوم أحسن	*the best day*	أحسن يوم
more delicious food	أكل أطيب	*the most delicious food*	أطيب أكل
a larger mall	مركز تجاري أكبر	*the largest mall*	أكبر مركز تجاري
a larger number of . . .	عدد أكبر من . . .	*the largest number possible*	أكبر عدد ممكن

To express an explicit comparison, use the preposition مِن:

هل الجو في تونس أحسن من الجو في مصر؟

ما أكلت أي شيء أطيب من أكلك يا أمي!

أخي أصغر مني في العمر ولكنه أطول مني.

To express comparison with adjectives such as النسبة and those with longer أوزان like وزن أفعل, that cannot fit into أكثر, we use مفضّل or متأخر or مشغول:

هذه الترجمة أكاديمية أكثر.

من مشغول أكثر: نحن أو أنتم؟

صحيح أني متأخرة ولكن الأستاذة متأخرة أكثر منّي!

هذا البرنامج مفضّل اكثر من البرامج الأخرى.

تمـريـن ٩: أفعل من ... (في البيت)

Yesterday you were in a great mood and everything was superlative. Today you are more down to earth and want to correct the wildly exaggerated things you wrote and said. Make these statements more realistic by toning them down to comparisons as the example shows:

مثال:

والدي أطول رجل في العالم!   ←   والدي أطول من معظم الرجال.

١. هذه كانت أطول مباراة كرة شاهدتها في حياتي!

٢. أمس أكلت أحسن بيتزا في العالم!

٣. هذا كان أصعب واجب في هذا الفصل الدراسي!

٤. هذا الجو أبرد جو في التاريخ!

٥. أكبر مشكلة عندي هي سيارتي!

٦. هي أجمل امرأة في العالم!

٧. هذا أسهل درس في الكتاب كله!

٨. درجة الحرارة في غرفتي أعلى درجة في كل بيوت الطلاب في أمريكا!

تمـريـن ١٠: أفعل للمقارنة (في الصف)

Compare with your classmates the following aspects of حياة الطلاب:

المطاعم في منطقة الجامعة   البيوت والمناطق السَكَنية

المراكز التجارية   الموسيقى   الصفوف والأقسام

المضارع المنصوب

In formal Arabic, there are two ways to express a subordinate verb (i.e., a dependent or infinitive verb): المصدر and a form of المضارع called المضارع المنصوب[1]. You have seen المصدر used to express the infinitive verb in constructions like

لا يمكننا الخروج   أستطيع الجلوس في غرفتي.

and with لـ *in order to*, as in:

أسهر لمذاكرة المفردات.   يدرس للحصول على دبلوم

This same meaning may also be expressed by أنْ followed by الفعل المضارع, as you have seen in:

يمكننا أن نسهر = يمكننا السَّهَر.

كنت أريد أن ألتَحِق بالجيش = كنت أريد الالتحاق بالجيش.

Likewise, the phrase "in order to" may also be expressed using لـ followed by المضارع or المصدر as in:

نعود الى البيت لنأكُل الغداء = لأكْل الغداء.

نسهر لنشاهد التليفزيون = لمشاهدة التليفزيون.

Remember that these constructions are equivalent in meaning:

المصدر = أنْ + المضارع   /   لـ + المصدر = لـ + المضارع

---

[1] This form of the verb is often called the subjunctive in English treatments of Arabic grammar, and it shares some features of subjunctives in other languages. It mainly serves as a subordinate, nonfinite verb form.

While المصدر tends to be more formal than المضارع, both constructions are widely used in formal Arabic. Study these examples:

أريد أن أستمع الى موسيقى جديدة = أريد الاستماع الى موسيقى جديدة.

نستطيع أن نخرج مع أصدقائنا = نستطيع الخروج مع اصدقائنا.

لا أحب أن أدخل المُستشفَيات = لا أحب دخول المستشفيات.

When المضارع is used with لِ or أنْ, it takes a form called المضارع المنصوب. In unvoweled texts, you will not notice anything different about المضارع المنصوب, except in the forms for persons انتِ, انتم, and هم, which do not take final ن. The مضارع منصوب forms for the other persons take a final فتحة vowel, which is indicated only in fully vocalized texts. The chart that follows shows المنصوب suffixes:

نريد أنْ نذهبَ	أريد أنْ أذهبَ
تريدون أنْ تذهبوا	تريد أنْ تذهبَ تريدين أن تذهبي
يريدون أنْ يذهبوا	يريد أنْ يذهبَ تريد أنْ تذهبَ

As a rule of thumb, you can use أنْ in most cases where we use an infinitive in English, such as with these verbs:

استطاع   يمكن   يحبّ   أراد   رفض

There is one important exception, however: We do not use أنْ with verbs of beginning:

بدأنا ندرس اللغة العربية في الخريف الماضي.

بدأت أقرأ قصة جديدة ليلة أمس وأنا أستمتع بها كثيراً.

In formal Arabic, قبل and بعد must be followed by either المصدر or the linking word أنْ. The phrase قبل أنْ must be followed by المضارع المنصوب.

before we travel	قبل أن نُسافِرَ	=	*before traveling*	قبل السَّفَر
after we graduate	بعد أن نتخرّجَ	=	*after graduating*	بعد التخرّج

بالشامي وفي المصري

In spoken Arabic, neither المصدر nor أن is used. The difference between the main verb and a subordinate verb is expressed by the presence or absence of the prefix بـ . Main verbs, which in formal Arabic take المرفوع form, take بـ in spoken Arabic, while subordinate verbs, which take المنصوب in formal Arabic, have no بـ prefix in the dialects. The following examples demonstrate:

بدي إسهر الليلة لأنُّه ما عندي دروس بكرة!

ممكن تيجي معي عند الدكتور؟

عايزة اسهر الليلة عشان ما عنديش محاضرات بكرة!

ممكن تيجي معايا عند الدكتور؟

With prepositions, the linking word ما is used:

قبل ما اسافر   بعد ما نتخرّج

تـمـريـن ١١: اسألوا زملاءكم: قبل أو بعد؟ (في الصف)

اسألوا زملاءكم What do they do first? With a partner, order these activites by asking each other what you do first, then write your partner's answer. Remember to phrase your questions to your partner in second person and write about her or him in third.

مثال:

آكل الغداء   —   أذهب الى الصف   ⟵   آكل قبل أن أذهب إلى الصف.

⟵   أذهب الى الصف بعد أن آكل.

١. أقرأ قليلاً   —   أنام.

٢. ندرس الكلمات الجديدة   —   نشاهد الفيديو.

٣. أخرج من البيت   —   يخرج زميلي من البيت.

٤. أبدأ عملي كل يوم   —   أتكلّم مع زملائي في المكتب.

٥. آكل العشاء   —   أذهب الى المكتبة.

٦. أعود الى البيت   —   تعود والدتي.

٧. أصحو   —   أشرب القهوة.

٨. أفطر   —   أستمع إلى الأخبار.

تمـريـن ١٢: من المصدر الى المضارع المنصوب (في البيت)

Read each sentence and identify المصدر, then rewrite using المضارع المنصوب.

١. تريد الحكومة الحصول على مساعدات مالية من البنك الدولي.

٢. لا يمكنني الذهاب الى النادي اليوم.

٣. يريدون السكن بعيداً عن هذه المنطقة.

٤. لماذا لا تستطيعين الخروج معنا؟

٥. لا أريد التأخّر عن موعدي!

٦. لماذا ترفضون مشاهدة هذا الفيلم؟

٧. يريد الكلام مع أمه بالتليفون.

٨. لا أحب الأكل بسرعة.

٩. هل يمكنك مساعدتنا؟

١٠. تريد العمل في وزارة الخارجية بعد التخرُّج.

١١. خالد يدخّن سيجارة بعد نزول والده.

الثقافة ٢

🎧 جامع الحسين (في الصف)

الإمام الحسين: هو ابن الإمام علي (الخليفة الرابع وابن عم النبي محمد) والسيدة فاطمة الزهراء (بنت النبي محمد).

جامع الحسين هو جامع كبير في مدينة القاهرة في منطقة اسمها "الحسين"، وهي منطقة قريبة من جامع الأزهر. عاش الحسين في "المدينة" ومات في سنة ٦٨٠ في مدينة كربلاء في العراق. ويمكنكم أن تشاهدوا صوراً بالفيديو لجامع الحسين.

Hussein's importance to Muslims lies in his opposition to the rule of the Umayyad dynasty and his assassination at the hands of Umayyad soldiers. Shi'ites (الشّيعة) commemorate his assassination every year on عاشوراء, the tenth day of the Islamic month مُحَرَّم. Shi'ites consider الحسين to be the third إمام, or leader, after his father الإمام علي and his older brother الإمام الحَسَن.

القصة بالفصحى

تـمـريـن ١٣: "بيت العائلة" (في الصف) 🎧

استمعوا الى خالد بالفصحى واكتبوا بالفصحى:

١. لماذا يوم الخميس خاص بالنسبة لخالد؟ ماذا يريد أن يفعل مساء يوم الجمعة؟
اكتبوا ما يقول: أحب عائلتي ولكني أستمتع أكثر ....

.... هل تفهمون .... ؟

٢. استمعوا الى خالد واكتبوا ما يقول :

(١) .... الخميس (٢) .... (٣)

(٤) .... (٥) .... التليفزيون أو(٦) ....

(٧) .... مع أصدقائنا، لذلك (٨) .... (٩)

.... يوم الجمعة، فـ(١٠) .... (١١) .... والحمد لله هو

(١٢) .... (١٣) . ... مع والدي و(١٤) ....

(١٥) .... الجمعة في (١٦) .... الحسين، ثم

(١٧) .... (١٨) .... إلى البيت لنتناول (١٩)

قبل (٢٠) .... (٢١) .... (٢٢) .... كرة القدم

التي(٢٣) .... (٢٤) .... في التليفزيون يوم

(٢٥) .... وفي (٢٦) .... التي ليست فيها

(٢٧) .... ، (٢٨) .... (٢٩)

و(٣٠) .... أو (٣١) .... بعد (٣٢) ....

أمّا (٣٣) .... (٣٤) .... فـ(٣٥)

(٣٦) .... (٣٧) .... (٣٨) .... بيتنا،

(٣٩) .... أقامت معنا (٤٠) .... (٤١) .... بيت

(٤٢) .... (٤٣) ، .... إليه كل يوم (٤٤) .... كل

(٤٥) .... العائلة.

3. (في الصف) Listen to the particles and linking words that خالد uses to make his speech cohesive. How does he link sentences together? How do we know he is changing topics? Giving explanations? Does he use الجملة الفعلية or الجملة الاسمية more?

4. Notice that Khalid says: يجيء إلَيْهِ. In formal Arabic, the pronunciation of vowels on pronouns sometimes varies. The following grammar section will explain some of the changes you will hear.

القواعد ٢

In formal Arabic, the pronunciation of possessive pronoun endings ـهُ and هُم shifts to ـهِ and هِم when immediately preceded by a kasra or ي. Read the following examples, first silently for meaning, then aloud to practice the kasra vowels:

يجيئون إلَيْهِ كثيراً. ←	يجيئون إلى بيتنا كثيراً.
استمعنا إلَيْهِم. ←	استمعنا إلى زملائنا.
كتبت الكلمات علَيْهِ. ←	كتبتْ الكلمات على الدفتر.

Another pronoun whose pronunciation changes is the suffix of الماضي for أنتم. In this case, the subject ending تُم (for أنتم) adds a long vowel و for ease (and beauty) of pronunciation:

قابلتُموها ←	قابلتُم + ـها
درّستُموني ←	درّستُم + ـني

Finally, note that the silent alif that is written on the plural suffix وا on verbs is dropped when an object pronoun is added:

أقاربي تذكّروني. ←	أقاربي تذكّروا + أنا
هل تريدون أن تقرأوه؟ ←	هل تريدون أن تقرأوا + هو؟

القراءة: الملك فؤاد والخميني

تمـريـن ١٤: "معيشة جلالة الملك اليومية" و "برنامج الإمام الخُميني" (في الصف)

The following texts are taken from official biographies of famous persons. The first is an excerpt from a 1931 official biography of King Fuad of Egypt. The language is somewhat flowery but very accessible. The second is a biography of Imam Khomeini, leader of the Iranian Revolution of 1979 and Supreme Leader of the Islamic Republic of Iran from 1979 until 1989.

Working with a partner, each of you read one of the texts, using good reading strategies and the guidelines below. Then discuss them together and compare.

A. Read through your text. Follow the daily activities of these famous people by looking for words you know and can guess the meaning of from الجذر or context.

B. Discuss: How many similarities can you find between the lives of these two people?

C. Write the new words whose meaning you guessed from الجذر, context, or both.

الإمام الخُميني

جلالة الملك فؤاد

معيشة جلالة الملك اليومية

قال جلالة الملك مرة لجماعة من أخصائه : " اني أستيقظ عادة الساعة الخامسة صباحاً ولكني لا أغادر الجناح الخاص بي الا بعد ذلك بوقت طويل ".

وبعد الاستيقاظ يدخل جلالة الملك الحمام ، ويرتدي ملابسه على الاثر ، ثم يقوم ببعض الحركات الرياضية ، ويجلس بعد ذلك الى المائدة ليفطر فطوراً خفيفاً جداً،وبعد الفراغ من الأكل يعكف جلالته على العمل فيجلس في احدى قاعات الجناح الخاص به و يبدأ في تصفح الجرائد والمجلات ، ومن البديهي ان الجرائد المصرية هي التي تهمه أكثر من غيرها. فيؤتى لجلالته بالجرائد اليومية العربية والافرنجية حال صدورها.

ويتلقى جلالة الملك عشر جرائد يومية ونحو عشرين مجلة فرنسية وأربع أو خمس جرائد يومية ونحو عشرين مجلة انجليزية ، وكثيراً من الجرائد والمجلات الايطالية، وبهذه الطريقة يتمكن جلالة الملك من متابعة الحالة العامة فى العالم كله .

وفي منتصف الساعة الحادية عشرة يبدأ جلالة الملك باستقبال الزائرين وكثيراً ما تدوم المقابلات والتشريفات حتى الساعة الثانية بعد الظهر بلا انقطاع ويستقبل جلالته الزائرين عادة في مكتبه الواسع الذى يشرف على سراي عابدين.

وبعد انتهاء المقابلات يتناول جلالة الملك طعام الغداء ثم يستقبل في الحال رؤساء الديوان الملكي ويدرس معهم المسائل التى يعرضونها عليه فيصدر اليهم تعليماته ويوقع المراسيم والاوامر حتى منتصف الساعة الرابعة بعد الظهر إذ يعود جلالته الى مقابلاته الرسمية.

وبعد انتهاء المقابلات الرسمية يجتمع جلالة الملك بكبار موظفي السراي ويشتغل معهم حتى ساعة متأخرة ، وكثيراً ما يظل جلالته حتى الساعة الثامنة في مكتبه ... ثم يدخل جلالة الملك جناحه الخاص ليتعشى عشاء خفيفاً وليمضي فترة من الزمان مع أفراد أسرته الكريمة.

من كتاب "جلالة الملك بين مصر وأوروبا"، تأليف: كريم ثابت، دار الهلال، القاهرة، ١٩٣١.

البرنامج اليومي للإمام الخُمَيْني

الإمام الخميني (رضوان الله تعالى عليه) له برنامج يومي ثابت ينظم من خلاله شؤونه اليومية.

تُحدّثنا السيدة زهراء ابنة الإمام (رضوان الله تعالى عليه) عن هذا البرنامج اليومي:

1- عند الساعة الثانية بعد منتصف الليل يستيقظ الإمام الخميني ليقوم بأعمال التهجد والعبادة وأداء صلاة الليل ويستمر حتى طلوع الفجر.

2- صلاة الفجر والدعاء حتى طلوع الشمس.

3- استراحة حتى الساعة السادسة.

4- المشي لمدة نصف ساعة يشتغل خلالها بذكر الله.

5- تلاوة القرآن، وكان محافظاً على تلاوة القرآن.

6- ثم يتناول الإفطار قبل الساعة السابعة.

7- في الساعة السابعة يدخل إلى غرفة الاستقبال وتبدأ اللقاءات (لمدة ساعتين) للتواصل الدائم مع الناس. يعيش هموم الناس وقضاياهم.

8- في الساعة التاسعة يمارس الإمام رياضة المشي لمدة نصف ساعة يشتغل خلالها بذكر الله.

9- في التاسعة والنصف يدخل إلى غرفته الخاصة لقراءة التقارير التي ترسل إليه من أنحاء البلاد.

10- استراحة القيلولة؛ ما بين العاشرة وعشر دقائق إلى الساعة الحادية عشرة والنصف يأخذ قسطاً من الراحة.

11- صلاة الظهر والعصر.. في الساعة (11،30) يستعد للصلاة: يبدأ بالوضوء. ثم يتلو القرآن، ثم يؤدي صلاتي الظهر والعصر.

12- الجلوس مع أفراد العائلة ..في الساعة (12،55) ينتهي من الصلاة فيجلس للتحدث مع أفراد عائلته (لمدة عشر دقائق).

13- تناول طعام الغداء.. في الساعة الواحدة وخمس دقائق، وبعد الانتهاء، يتحدث مع العائلة لمدة عشر دقائق.

14- قراءة التقارير الخبرية .. والاستماع إلى أخبار الساعة الثانية.

15- الاستراحة حتى الساعة الرابعة.

16- في الساعة الرابعة يمارس رياضة المشي لمدة نصف ساعة، يشتغل بذكر الله.

17- قبل غروب الشمس يجدد الوضوء ويبدأ بتلاوة القرآن إلى أن تغرب الشمس، فيتهيأ لإقامة صلاتي المغرب والعشاء.

18- المطالعة والقراءة (يدخل غرفته الخاصة). يهتم بقراءة الكتب المطبوعة حديثا ويهتم بقراءة الصحف والمجلات ويتابع برنامج التلفاز ويستمع إلى الأخبار بدقة ويستمع إلى التقارير الخبرية ويتابع المقابلات والتصريحات.

19- ثم يمارس بعض التمارين الرياضية لمدة ربع ساعة.

20- تناول طعام العشاء في الساعة التاسعة.

21- بعد الانتهاء من العشاء يقوم ببعض الأعمال الخاصة به تستمر إلى العاشرة أو العاشرة وعشر دقائق.

22- بعدها يذهب إلى غرفته للنوم إلى الثانية بعد منتصف الليل.

الحوار

اللغة والثقافة: بنت حلال، ابن حلال

حَلال means literally *"legally permissible"* and, by extension *"a good person."*
The بنت حلال، ابن حلال implication is that this is the person you will marry.

تـمـريـن ١٥: "قولوا إن شاء الله" / "قولوا إن شاء الله" (في البيت)

استمعوا الى الحوار بالمصري واكتبوا فَقرة paragraph لكل سؤال:	استمعوا الى الحوار بالشامي واكتبوا فَقرة paragraph لكل سؤال:
١. مين هو ؟ عرفنا إيه عن دراسته؟	١. مين هو ؟ شو عرفنا عن دراسته؟
٢. بيعمل ايه كل يوم؟	٢. كيف برنامجه اليومي؟
٣. هو مبسوط في الشغل ولّا لأ؟ ليه؟	٣. هو مبسوط بشغله؟ ليش/ليش لأ؟
٤. يعني ايه "عمل بزنس صغير"؟ إيه هو ؟	٤. شو يعني "عمل بزنس صغير" ؟ شو هو هالبزنس؟
٥. بيقول ايه عن المستقبل؟	٥. شو بيقول عن المستقبل؟

تمارين المراجعة

تـمـريـن ١٦: المصدر (في البيت)

This exercise is available online only.

تمـريـن ١٧: ترجموا الى اللغة العربية (في البيت)

1. My grandfather used to have beautiful pictures of old Kuwait.
2. Did you have a doctor's appointment this week?
3. There are no classes today because of the snow!
4. She doesn't have any time today, so we can't sit and chat with her.
5. The members of my family do not have opinions like mine.
6. Do you have any news from your family in Yemen?
7. My new roommate has a sister who works for the Ministry of Labor.
8. I don't like this job because it has no future.
9. There are good Chinese restaurants in this area.
10. Our city has more than five sports clubs.

تمـريـن ١٨: القراءة الجهرية 🎧 (في البيت أو في الصف)

Read the following passage, first silently for comprehension, then aloud to practice pronunciation. When you are ready, record the passage and submit it to your teacher, either online or as directed by your teacher.

اسمي أمل ناصر الحكيم ..... وانا جدة طارق ... أسكن الآن في بيت ابني ماهر، وهو بيت جميل فعلاً ولكنّه ليس بيتي. بيتي الآن فارِغ لا يسكن فيه أحد، ولكن إن شاء الله في المستقبل يسكن فيه طارق وزوجته. والبيت فيه غرفة جلوس واسعة وثلاث غرف نوم كبيرة وبلكون كبير، وهو في منطقة الصالحية القريبة من وَسَط المدينة. كان زوجي عاصي، الله يرحمه، يعمل في تجارة القُطن ونجح فيها وتعلّم منه ابني ماهر، وهو كان يعمل في نفس التجارة مع والده قبل أن يشتغل في الحكومة. في البداية كنا كلّنا زعلانين لأننا كنا نريد أن يكون ماهر تاجراً للقطن مثل والده ولكن يوم التاجر طويل وليس فيه استراحة، وماهر كان يريد أن يكون عنده وقت لأسرته، ولذلك دخل العمل الحكوميّ وأصبح موظفاً في وزارة الاقتصاد.

بعد أن ماتت زوجة ابني أم طارق الله يرحمها في حادث محزن جداً جئت لأسكن مع ماهر والأولاد في هذا البيت. لا أريد أن أكون سيّدة البيت لأنّ سيّدة البيت ليست هنا ولكن ،على الأقلّ، أستطيع أن أساعد ماهر والأولاد في شغل البيت وفي حياتهم اليوميّة.

أما ابني الكبير حسن فيسكن بعيداً عنا في أميركا . . . كان لا يحب التجارة منذ صِغَرِه .. وطارق مثله تماماً – لا يحب التجارة ولا يستمتع بأي شيء فيها. ولكنه أيضا لا يريد أن يعمل في الحكومة لأنّ عمل الحكومة مملّ ولأن مرتبات الموظفين في رأيه ليست جيّدة. بصراحة، لا أفهمه!

أشعر بالخجل أحياناً

المفردات

القصة بالعامية: "أحياناً بحسّ بالخجل" "بدّي اقلّك شي"

"باحسّ بالخجل أحياناً" "عايزة أقولك حاجة" "حضرتك مين؟"

القواعد (١): قال، يقول لـ بالعامية

الثقافة: كيف هي صداقاتك وعلاقاتك؟

القواعد (٢): جملة الصفة

القصة بالفصحى: "أشعر بالخجل أحياناً"

القواعد (٣): أوزان الفعل

القراءة: "برنامج تركيا"

الاستماع: مع العائلة والأصدقاء

الحوار: "شو بدّي اعمل؟" "اعمل ايه في المشكلة دي؟"

تمارين المراجعة

المُفرَدات Vocabulary 🎧

استمعوا الى المفردات الجديدة بالفصحى والعامية.

المعنى	المصري	الشامي	الفُصحى
someone	حَدّ	حَدا	أحَد
no one	ما حَدِّش	ما حَدا	لا أحَد
sea			بَحر ج. بِحار
to exchange (news, opinions, etc.)			تَبادَل ، يَتَبادَل ، التَّبادُل
between, among[1]	بين	بين	بَيْنَ
mountain			جَبَل ج. جِبال
(an) experience	تَجرُبة ج. تَجارُب (formal word also used)		تَجْرِبة ج. تَجارِب
to gather together	اِتجَمَّع، يِتْجَمَّع	تجَمَّع، يِتْجَمَّع	تَجَمَّع، يَتَجَمَّع، التَّجَمُّع
tour			جَولة ج. - ات
shyness, embarrassment			الخَجَل
she got engaged to[2]	اِتخَطَبِت لِ	اِنْخَطَبِت لَ	خُطِبَت لِ
tourism			السِّياحة
market[3]			سوق ج. أسواق
pharmacy			صَيدَلِيّة ج. - ات
several	كام + مفرد	كَم + مفرد	عِدّة (+ اسم جمع نكرة)
to get to know, meet	اِتْعَرَّف، يِتْعَرَّف على	تعَرَّف، يِتْعَرَّف على	تَعَرَّف على، يَتَعَرَّف على، التَّعَرُّف على
emotional, romantic			عاطِفيّ/ة ج. -ون/ين
most (of)			مُعظَم (+ اسم جمع)
relationship, relations (between)			عَلاقة ج. - ات (بَيْنَ)
when[4]	لَما	لَما	عِندما (+ جملة فعلية)
expensive			غالي/ة (غالٍ)
hotel			فُندُق ج. فَنادِق
to be cut off	اِنقَطَع، يِنقِطِع / اِتقَطَع، يِتْقِطِع	اِنقَطَع، يِنقِطِع	اِنقَطَع، يَنْقَطِع، الاِنقِطاع

المعنى	المصري	الشامي	الفُصحى
once, (one) time; pl. times[5]			مَرّة ج. – ات
together	مع بعض	مع بعض	مَعاً
of, among (quantity)[6]			مِن
engineer			مُهَنْدِس ج. – ون/ين

Notes on Vocabulary Usage

1. Like English "between," the preposition بَينَ can indicate either a location, a relationship, or a difference between two things or parties. If one or both of these two parties is a pronoun, the word بين is repeated, as the examples show:

كانت بَيني وبينَه علاقة طيبة ثم انقطعت.

تعرف أين فندق "ريتز"؟ شركتنا بينه وبين الشارع الخامس.

2. The verb "to get engaged" is used in the feminine only, reflecting the traditional passive role of women in arranging marriage. For the man, the verb خَطَبَ *to ask for someone's hand in marriage* is used. This verb gives you a preview of what the passive looks like in Arabic.

3. The word سوق is usually مؤنث in formal Arabic but can be مذكر, perhaps influenced by spoken Arabic usage, in which it is normally مذكر.

4. The words عِندَما and لَمّا are used in narratives, not interrogatives: "When (something happened), (something else happened)." As in English, these sentences have two clauses and they usually match in tense:

عندما أسهر كثيراً، لا أنام جيّداً.	عندما ذاكرت الدرس مرةً ثانية، فهمته أكثر.
لمّا بسهر كتير، ما بنام منيح.	لمّا درست الدرس كمان مرة، فهمته أكثر.
لمّا باسهر كتير، ما بانامش كويس.	لمّا ذاكرت الدرس تاني، فهمته أكثر.

But notice that sentences about the future only use future marking in the result clause (as in English):

عندما أعود الى البيت سآكل العشاء ثم سأنام.

لمّا ارجع ع البيت رح اتعشى وبعدين رح انام.

لمّا ارجع البيت حاتعشى وبعدين حانام.

5. Two forms are used in Egypt for the verb "to be cut off." In Cairo, اِتقَطَع بِتقِطِع is more common.

6. The preposition مِن can be used with numbers to specify part of a group:

هو واحد من أصحابي.

ثلاثة من المهندسين ماتوا في الحادث، الله يرحمهم.

عدد من طلاب الصف ما جاءوا اليوم.

The nonspecific words كل, مُعظَم, بعض, and عِدّة, however, may not be followed by مِن but instead function as the first word in an إضافة:

قرأت كل الجرائد لأفهم الأخبار أكثر.

الرؤساء تكلّموا عن عدّة مواضيع سياسية واقتصادية.

بعض الفنادق كان فيها "ديسكو" وكنا نذهب إليها ونرقص الى ساعة متأخرة من الليل!

هل معظم المدارس في المغرب تدرّس العلوم باللغة الفرنسية؟

تـمريـن ١: الكلمات الجديدة (في البيت) 🎧

اكتبوا كلمة من الكلمات الجديدة في كل جملة.

١. كل يوم، نخرج أنا وأولادي من البيت _____ في الساعة السابعة صباحاً.

٢. لا _____ في عائلتي يعرف السباحة إلا أنا ولذلك لا نذهب الى البحر كثيراً.

٣. في الإسكندرية نزلنا في _____ "هيلتون" ليلتين فقط. الـ "هيلتون" ممتاز ولكن _____ جداً: ٢٠٠ دولار لكل ليلة!!

٤. لا أحب أن أتكلم كثيراً ولذلك أشعر بـ _____ أحياناً عندما أتكلم في صفّ العربية.

٥. "روميو وجولييت" قصّة _____ كتبها "شِكسبير" وكان هناك فيلم عنها، وأنا شاهدت الفيلم ثلاث _____ .

٦. في هذه الصورة نشاهد ــــــــــــ المُتَوَسِّط Mediterranean قرب اسبانيا ونشاهد أيضاً واحداً من ــــــــــــ الكثيرة في اسبانيا. وهذه الصورة من صديقتي وفاء وهي تعمل في مكتب لِـ ــــــــــــ والسفر في تونس.

٧. الصيف الماضي عملتُ مُتَدَرِّبة intern في قسم العلاقات الدولية في وزارة الخارجية في واشنطن، وكانت هذه ــــــــــــ ممتازة لأنني ــــــــــــ على موظفين كثيرين في الحكومة.

٨. ابنتي لـ ــــــــــــ ممتاز يعمل في مكتب للهندسة في دبي، وبعد سنة تزوّجت وسافرت مع زوجها الى دبي وعاشت هناك ــــــــــــ سنوات بعد زواجها.

٩. الشباب في هذه الأيام ــــــــــــ الرسائل والأخبار مع أصدقائهم على الإنترنت.

١٠. ــــــــــــ العلاقات الديبلوماسية بين إيران والولايات المتحدة لسنوات طويلة.

١١. أول شيء أحب أن أفعله ــــــــــــ أسافر الى مدينة جديدة هو أن أعمل ــــــــــــ سريعة بالأوتوبيس السياحي في المدينة لأتعرّف على ناسها ومناطقها وشوارعها.

١٢. هذه صورة لـ ــــــــــــ الحميدية في دمشق.

١٣. أريد أن أصوّركم ، هل يمكن أن ــــــــــــ معاً في وسط الغرفة؟

تمـرين ٢: كلمات جديدة وقواعد قديمة (في البيت) 🎧

This exercise is available online only.

تمـرين ٣: الجذر والوزن (في البيت)

Identify الوزن والجذر of all the new verbs in the vocabulary list by completing the chart:

المصدر	المضارع	الماضي	الوزن
الخُطوبة	يَخطُب	خَطَبَ	I فَعَلَ ، يَفعُل ، الفُعولة
			V تَفَعَّلَ ، يَتَفَعَّل ، التَّفَعُّل
			VI تفاعَلَ ، يَتَفاعَل ، التَّفاعُل
			VII اِنفَعَلَ ، يَنْفَعِل ، الاِنفِعال

تمـرين ٤: المفردات في جمل 🎧

استمعوا الى جمل المفردات واكتبوا الجمل من "أحد" إلى "صيدلية".

تمـرين ٥: اسألوا زملاءكم (في الصف)

Prepare to discuss the following topics with your زملاء. Choose three topics to ask about, but be prepared to answer all questions:

1. Your family is coming to visit. Get your classmates' suggestions for
- the best hotel in town
- touristy things they can do
- restaurants that are not too (= very) expensive.

2. How/when/where did they meet their husband/wife/girlfriend/boyfriend? Where are good places to meet people? Do they think it is hard to meet people these days? Are people more or less romantic than they were thirty years ago?

3. Who do they exchange news with most often, a family member or a friend? What kinds of news do they exchange with that person? Do they swap opinions with their parents about politics?

4. Are they enjoying their college experience? What experiences are best so far (الى الآن)? Have they been lonely or shy more? Have they had or do they want the experience of studying abroad (بالخارج)? Why or why not?

5. In their opinion, are relations between Iran and the US/Europe, and China (الصّين) and the US better than last year? Will they get better? Do they think that relations between the US and any other country will be cut off? Which country?

القصة بالعامية

تمـريـن ٦: "أحياناً باحِسّ بالخجل" / "باحِسّ بالخجل أحياناً" (في البيت) 🎧

استمعوا الى خالد واكتبوا فقرة لكل سؤال:	استمعوا الى طارق واكتبوا فقرة لكل سؤال:
١. أصحاب خالد متخصصين في ايه؟	١. رفقات طارق بشو متخصصين؟
٢. ازاي علاقة خالد بأصحابه؟ ليه؟	٢. كيف علاقة طارق مع رفقاته؟ ليش؟
٣. ازاي علاقات خالد مع البنات؟ ليه؟	٣. كيف علاقات طارق مع البنات؟ ليش؟
٤. خالد إنسان عاطفي؟ ليه/ليه لأ؟	٤. طارق إنسان عاطفي؟ ليش/ليش لأ؟

تمـريـن ٧: "بدّي أقولّك شي" / "عايزة اقولك حاجة" (في الصف) 🎧

في الصف، شوفوا خالد وصاحبته وبعدين اتكلموا مع بعض:	في الصف، شوفوا طارق ورفيقته وبعدين احكوا مع بعض:
رأيكو ايه في البنت؟ هي زعلانة عشان حتتجوّز شاب تاني؟ ليه؟ المهندس أحسن من خالد؟ ازاي؟ هل خالد زعلان عشان بيحب البنت أو عشان عايز قصة حب؟	شو رأيكن بالبنت؟ هي زعلانة لأنّها رح تتجوز شاب تاني؟ ليش؟ المهندس أحسن من طارق؟ كيف؟ هل طارق زعلان منشان بيحب البنت أو منشان بدّه قصة حب؟

القواعد ١

قال، يقول لـ بالعامية

In the scene in exercise 7 you heard the girlfriend say, "عايزة اقولك حاجة" "بدّي قلّك شي".
How would you translate this into English? Notice that the verb قال is often used with the preposition لـ to express "to tell someone (something)." The preposition لِـ in this case indicates the person to whom you are saying something, and it most often occurs with a pronoun. In spoken Arabic, this لـ is usually pronounced as if it is part of the verb, as you heard.

"حضرتك مين؟" 🎧

Listen to another example when you watch the video scene "حضرتك مين؟". How does Maha use قال لـ, and what does it mean? Listen for لـ and pronouns when you hear the verb قال، يقول. You will soon hear it on other verbs as well. You can learn this pronunciation by imitating the speakers you hear doing it and practicing on your own.

الثقافة: كيف هي صداقاتك وعلاقاتك؟ 🎧

Watch the interviews with بعض الشباب المصريين about their friendships. How do their ideas compare to your own?

تمـريـن ٨: المفردات في جمل (في البيت) 🎧

استمعوا الى جمل المفردات واكتبوا الجمل من "عدّة" إلى "مهندس".

القواعد ٢

جملة الصفة

In lesson 5 you practiced introducing and describing friends and relatives with sentences like these:

لي صديقة اسمها ليلى.

لي صديق يدرس تاريخ الشرق الاوسط.

In this chapter, خالد uses a similar sentence to explain the end of his relationship:

خُطِبَت لِمهندس يعمل في السعودية.

These sentences introduce and describe new entities (animate or inanimate). Since they are unknown to the reader/listener, these nouns are presented as indefinite: *a friend, a girl, a professor*, etc. Because they have some importance to the conversation, however, they need to be further defined—more information needs to be added. The defining sentences that further identify and describe these indefinite nouns are joined to the noun directly, just like an indefinite adjective (صفة =); hence their name, جملة الصفة. These phrases normally begin with a verb, as you can see in the examples above and below:

(١) صديقي حامد استاذ يدرّس الادب العربي في جامعة القاهرة.

... *a professor who teaches*

(٢) تعرّفنا على امرأة تعمل في قسم اللغات.

... *a woman who works*

(٣) هذه صورة عمرها أكثر من ١٠٠ سنة.

... *a picture whose age is*

The sentences that describe indefinite nouns are complete sentences that could stand on their own but, in the context of the larger sentence, need to be linked in some way back to the noun[1]. The noun they describe is the topic of جملة الصفة, so it lies outside the structure of the sentence. In order to link the sentence back to it, the sentence needs a pronoun that stands in its place within جملة الصفة. Often, when جملة الصفة is a جملة فعلية, this pronoun is in the verb, itself, because the topic noun is also the subject of the verb that begins جملة الصفة. This is the case in the examples (١) and (٢) above and repeated here:

صديقي حامد استاذ يدرّس الادب العربي . . .

... *a professor [who] (he) teaches*

تعرّفنا على امرأة تعمل في قسم اللغات . . .

... *a woman [who] (she) works*

---

[1] Formal English has a similar construction with "who" and "that," as in, "a woman *who* teaches," or "an idea *that* influences people." In Arabic definite nouns are linked in this way with the words الذي / التي اللي اللي (note the الـ in each of them, reminding you it is definite), which you have heard in passing and will activate soon. Except for the addition of the definite linking word, the structure of the sentences is the same for those using definite and those using indefinite, as well as for both spoken and formal Arabic.

Notice that English requires the use of "who" in this case, while Arabic requires that no linking word be used.

If the noun being described is the object of the verb—such as مباراة in شاهدنا مباراة, or the object of a preposition, such as سوق in ذهبت الى سوق --the link is provided through a matching pronoun that fills the hole left by the topic noun. Compare the original sentence to the جملة صفة formed from it:

استمتعت بـمباراة. ←——— شاهدت مباراة استمتعت بها.

I saw a game I liked [it].

دخّنت سيجارة. ←——— هذه أول سيجارة دخّنتها.

This is the first cigarette I smoked [it].

ذهبت الى سوق. ←——— هذا أكبر سوق ذهبت إليه!

This is the biggest market I've ever been to [it]!

It is important to learn to recognize this structure, especially when reading. Your clue is the indefinite noun: Any indefinite noun followed by a verb is very likely to be a جملة صفة. Practice recognizing and forming جملة صفة in the exercises that follow.

🎧 تمريـن ٩: جملة الصفة (في البيت)

This exercise is available online only.

تمريـن ١٠: ترجمة جملة الصفة (في الصف)

Familiarize yourself with the structure of جملة صفة in Arabic by changing the structure of the following English sentences to an Arabic structure as in the example. Remember to use pronouns that refer back to the noun being described when needed. Work in English first to identify where the linking pronoun belongs, then ترجموا هذه الجمل الى اللغة العربية.

Example: I saw a movie I didn't like. ——→ I saw a movie I didn't like *it*.

1. He's in love with a woman he met last week!
2. I've watched every game they played this year.
3. I remember that from a book I read.
4. Last year I had a roommate who used to sleep all the time.
5. I don't enjoy every sports game I go to, but I enjoy most of them.
6. She is busy with friends who came Thursday night.
7. We want a government that listens to people.
8. I live in an area that has good schools.
9. She got engaged to a man who lives in Morocco.
10. They're talking about a new story she wrote.

تمرين١١: أين جملة الصفة؟ (في الصف)

اقرأوا للفهم أولاً، ثم لمعرفة أين جمل الصفة:

Underline all جمل الصفة you can find. Remember that the best clue is an اسم نكرة followed by a verb.

هل تريدون أن تستمعوا الى قصة تحبونها؟ لي صديق يعيش في مدينة بوسطن حيث يدرس في جامعة تعرفونها جيداً. وهذا الصديق يسكن في بيت ليس فيه "گراج"، وعنده سيارة لا تعمل جيداً، ولكنه يحب أن يذهب بسيارته الى السوق البعيد. ومرّة، عندما كان في السوق، وأراد أن يعود الى بيته، ماتت سيارته. الحمد لله، شاهدته امرأة تعمل في السوق، وساعدته على الكلام مع AAA. بعد ذلك، تكلّم صديقي مع المرأة التي ساعدته بالتليفون وبدآ يخرجان معاً. هل هذه بداية علاقة عاطفية يمكن أن تصبح علاقة زواج في المستقبل؟ لا أحد يعرف!

تمرين ١٢: كتابة جملة الصفة (في البيت)

Imagine that you have an interesting story or something important to say about a person or thing. Use the prompts below to build your story, beginning with جمل الصفة. Make as many جمل فعلية as you can.

١. أريد الحصول على عمل
....

٢. هو رئيس
....

٣. أمس تعرّفت على رجل
....

٤. قرأت قصة
....

٥. هذه شركة
....

٦. عندما كنا في نيويورك، نزلنا في فندق
....

القصة بالفصحى

تمـريـن ١٣: "أشعر بالخجل أحياناً" (في البيت) 🎧

Watch القصة بالفصحى and answer the questions below. The dictation exercise can be completed in the book or online.

1. You know the word صيدليّة. خالد uses a closely related word in this video. Listen for it, then write the phrase in which it occurs and guess its meaning:

_____

_____

2. خالد says: "اثنان منهم تخرّجا" To what do you think the ending on this verb refers?

3. Listen for all the quantities خالد uses (including words like "some" and "most") and write them out. Include any nouns that indicate "one" but do not have an article.

4. Listen to خالد again and focus on his use of و to mark new sentences and lists. Identify each و and the two or more phrases or sentences it connects.

5. استمعوا إلى خالد واكتبوا ما يقول. Make sure to include all و you hear—you will not find separate blanks for و and لـ because, being one-letter words, they are written as part of the following word with no space in between.

(١) _____	(٢) _____	(٣) الآن كانوا _____
في (٤) _____	(٥) الثانوية.	(٦) _____ تخرّجا
من كلية (٧) _____	(٨) ، _____	(٩) _____ كلية
(١٠) _____	(١١) ، _____	(١٢) _____ كلية
(١٣) _____	(١٤) ، _____	(١٥) _____ كلية
(١٦) _____	(١٧) _____	(١٨) نجلس _____.
(١٩) _____	(٢٠) كل _____	(٢١) _____ الأخبار
(٢٢) _____	(٢٣) _____	(٢٤) أشعر _____.
(٢٥) _____	(٢٦) لأنه ليست _____	(٢٧) _____
(٢٨) _____	(٢٩) مثلهم.	(٣٠) _____ طالباً في
(٣١) _____	(٣٢) _____	(٣٣) ، _____
(٣٤) _____	(٣٥) _____	(٣٦) في _____
(٣٧) _____	(٣٨) _____	معاً
(٣٩) _____	(٤٠) _____	(٤١) ثم ، _____
(٤٢) _____	(٤٣) _____	(٤٤) _____ خُطِبَت
(٤٥) _____	(٤٦) _____	بالسعودية.

القواعد ٣
أوزان الفعل

وزن VI ووزن VII

The vocabulary in this chapter introduces you to verbs from two new patterns you have not seen before:

🎧

VI تَفَاعَلَ، يَتَفاعَل، التَّفاعُل   تَبادَلَ، يَتَبادَل، التَّبادُل

VII اِنفَعَل، يَنفَعِل، الانفِعال   اِنقَطَعَ، يَنقَطِع، الانقِطاع

What are the distinguishing characteristics of each? The wazn VI stem begins with ت and all its short vowels in الماضي and المضارع are fatHa, like wazn V, but it also has alif like wazn III. This resemblance seems not to be accidental because wazn VI shares aspects of meaning with both of these other awzaan. Wazn VII, on the other hand, is unique in having a ن².

Form and Meaning in أوزان الفعل

The meanings of verbal awzaan will take some time to acquire completely, in part because the system itself is not an exact science--language changes over time--and in part because you need more vocabulary to see how the principles work in practice. We will be talking about the meanings of the awzaan extensively throughout *Al-Kitaab Part 2*. There are, however, several basic principles that you can start paying attention to now.

The first principle is that the awzaan have meanings that relate to each other, not to an abstract reference point. For example, wazn VII is related in meaning in a certain way to wazn I; wazn VI is related to wazn III, and so forth. We will talk about these relationships in more detail in the coming sections and chapters. The second principle is that, in general, the longer and more complex the wazn, the more abstract the meaning. For example, wazn X is quite abstract, and the awzaan with shadda reflect some kind of extension or intensification of meaning. The third principle is that each wazn relates to one or two other awzaan in form and meaning. For example, II and V both have shadda, and III and VI both contain alif. Pairs that relate in meaning include I and II, and I and VII. In this chapter we will take a look at the pairs I and II, II and V, and I and VII. Note that you can listen to and practice all of the examples given below in your audio.

---

² A trick to help you remember the number of this wazn is to remember that the sound of "nuun" in انفعل matches the "n" in "seven."

The most basic aspect of the relationship between wazn I and wazn II is that wazn II adds a causative meaning to the wazn I meaning, as in "to make or cause (someone or something) to perform X action," where X represents the meaning of wazn I.

I فَعَلَ، يَفْعِل، المَفْعِلة	عَرَفَ، يَعْرِف، المَعْرِفة

to know

II فَعَّلَ، يُفَعِّل، التَّفْعيل	عَرَّفَ، يُعَرِّف، التَّعْريف بـ

to introduce someone to someone;
to make someone know someone | something

This relationship between verbs is very common in spoken Arabic. In lesson 7 you heard these verbs used in الحوار:

I فِعِل، يِفْعَل	زِعِل، يِزْعَل

to become or be upset

II فَعَّل، يِفَعِّل	زَعَّل، يِزَعِّل
فَعَّل، يِفَعِّل[3]	زَعَّل، يِزَعِّل

to make (someone) upset

Almost any transitive wazn I verb can potentially be made into wazn II in spoken Arabic: For example, "to give someone something to eat or drink," "to make someone understand," "to make someone die (of boredom or laughter)," and so forth. Again, as you learn more verbs, this relationship will become clearer.

The relationship between wazn II and wazn V is similarly close: Wazn II is transitive, in other words something that one does to someone or something else, and wazn V is reflexive, or something that one does to oneself. The following examples demonstrate:

II فَعَّلَ، يُفَعِّل، التَّفْعيل	عَرَّفَ، يُعَرِّف، التَّعْريف بـ

to introduce someone to someone else (to make someone know someone)

V تَفَعَّلَ، يَتَفَعَّل، التَّفَعُّل	تَعَرَّفَ، يَتَعَرَّف، التَّعَرُّف على

to become acquainted with, to get to know
(to make someone known to yourself)

II فَعَّلَ، يُفَعِّل، التَّفْعيل	ذَكَّرَ، يُذَكِّر، التَّذْكير بـ

to remind someone of something

V تَفَعَّلَ، يَتَفَعَّل، التَّفَعُّل	تَذَكَّرَ، يَتَذَكَّر، التَّذَكُّر

to remind yourself of something, to recall, remember

---

[3] Egyptian dialect also has the pattern فَعِّل يِفَعِّل; you will learn more about this later.

Sometimes wazn II and wazn V may be formed from a noun. From the word سوق we get:

II فَعَّلَ، يُفَعِّلُ، التَّفعيل   سَوَّقَ، يُسَوِّق، التَّسويق

to market (something)

V تَفَعَّلَ، يَتَفَعَّلُ، التَّفَعُّل   تَسَوَّقَ، يَتَسَوَّق، التَّسَوُّق

to take oneself to market, to go shopping

The relationship of wazn I and wazn VII is very straightforward: Wazn VII is the passive of wazn I, when the meaning of wazn I allows a passive. The verb اِنقَطَعَ is related to the verb قَطَعَ to cut (something):

I فَعَلَ، يفعَلَ، الفَعْل   قَطَعَ، يَقطَعَ، القَطْع

to cut

VII اِنفَعَلَ، يَنفَعِلِ، الاِنفِعال   اِنقَطَعَ، ينقَطِع، الاِنقِطاع

to be cut

Only a minority of wazn I verbs, though, have meanings that can be made passive, so wazn VII is relatively rare.

We will return to the relationship between forms III and VI later when you know more verbs. For now, we note that the meaning of the wazn VI verb you learned in this chapter, تَبادَل, is an excellent example of the reciprocal meaning that VI often has with each other. It is helpful to use this meaning as a reminder to think of this form as "the *each other* wazn." Now listen to all of these new forms on the audio.

النخبة للسياحة والسفر
Elite Travel & Tourism

برنــامج تركيا ١٣ يـوم ١٢/ الليـلـة
مرسين – ألانيا – انطاليا - بامو كالة – بورصة – يالوا –
استانبول – كبادوكيا - مرسين

البرنامج

اليوم الأول : **دمشق - مرسين**	التجمع في تمام الساعة ٩،٣٠ مساءً أمام وزارة السياحة والانطلاق في تمام الساعة العاشرة إلى حدود باب الهوى، ثم التوجه إلى منطقة الحربيات لتناول الفطور والتمتع بمناظر الشلالات، المتابعة إلى مدينة مرسين الساحلية والوصول ظهرا إلى الفندق، استلام الغرف ووقت حر للاستراحة والاستجمام ،عشاء على أنغام الموسيقى التركية .
اليوم الثاني: **مرسين - ألانيا-** **انطاليا**	الإفطار وتسليم الغرف والانطلاق باكراً إلى أنطاليا على أروع الطرق الجبلية الساحلية ، الاستمتاع بالمناظر الطبيعية الساحرة للجبال الخضراء والبحر الأزرق الصافي ، التوقّف في بعض الاستراحات ، الوصول إلى ألانيا والتوقف فيها ثم المتابعة إلى أنطاليا، وصول الفندق للعشاء والمبيت .
اليوم الثالث: **أنطاليا**	الإفطار، الانتقال لزيارة شلالات أنطاليا الشهيرة (دودان) وشلالات كورشونلو ثم عودة إلى الفندق ووقت حر أو الذهاب إلى شواطئ أنطاليا الجميلة، مساءً عودة إلى الفندق للعشاء والمبيت.
اليوم الرابع : **أنطاليـا-** **بامو كالة**	الإفطار وتسليم الغرف ثم التوجه إلى قلعة القطن (بامو كالــة)، والوصول إلى الفندق ، استلام الغرف ثم التوجه إلى السبخات الكلسية ، عودة في المساء إلى الفندق للعشاء والمبيت.
اليوم الخامس : **بامو كالة –** **بورصة**	الإفطار، وتسليم الغرف ثم التوجه إلى مدينة بورصة العاصمة الأولى للدولة العثمانية والوصول إلى الفندق ، وبعد استلام الغرف وقت حــر للتسوق في أسواق بورصة الشهيرة ثم عودة إلى الفندق للعشاء والمبيت.
اليوم السادس : **بورصةـ يالوا -** **استانبول**	الإفطار، وتسليم الغرف والصعود بالتلفريك إلى الجبل العظيم (أولوداغ) والاستمتاع بأجمل المناظر الطبيعية وتناول وجبة غداء على الطريقة التركية ،ومن ثم التوجه إلى مدينة يالوا لمشاهدة حمامات الرمال الشهيرة.

وقضاء وقت ممتع في حدائقها وحماماتها ثم المتابعة لركوب العبّارة واجتياز بحر مرمرة وصولاً إلى استانبول، التوجه إلى الفندق لاستلام الغرف والعشاء والمبيت.

اليوم السابع : **استانبول**	الإفطار، القيام بجولة في استانبول تشمل (جامع السلطان أحمد، قصر التوب كابي، السوق المغطى، ميدان سباق الخيل) ثم عودة إلى الفندق للعشاء والمبيت .
اليوم الثامن : **استانبول**	الإفطار، جولة بحرية لزيارة جزر استانبول (الأميرات) وصولا إلى أكبر هذه الجزر جزيرة بيوك أضة، زيارة الجزيرة والقيام بجولة في عربات الخيل للتعرف على معالم الجزيرة ومشاهدة الفيلات الخشبية وتناول المأكولات البحرية في الجزيرة ، ثم عودة إلى الفندق للعشاء والمبيت .
اليوم التاسع : **استانبول**	الإفطار، ثم قضاء وقت حر للتسوق في أسواق استانبول الشهيرة، جولة بحرية في مضيق البوسفور بالمركب والاستمتاع بمنظر غروب الشمس، ثم عودة إلى الفندق، عشاء ومبيت.
اليوم العاشر : **استانبول- بولو -** **كبادوكيا**	الإفطار وتسليم الغرف ثم التوجه إلى كبادوكيا عبر سلسلة جبال بولو الرائعة والتمتع بأجمل المناظر الطبيعية ثم المتابعة الى مدينة كبادوكيا والوصول الى المدينة والتوجه الى الفندق واستلام الغرف، عشاء ومبيت.
اليوم الحادي عشر: **كبادوكيا**	الإفطار، والقيام بجولة بوادي غورمي حيث مداخن الجنيات، وفي المساء عودة الى الفندق للعشاء والمبيت .
اليوم الثاني عشر : **كبادوكيا -** **مرسين**	الإفطار وتسليم الغرف، ثم التوجه إلى مدينة مرسين ووقت حر للتسوق والغداء (على حساب المشترك) ثم التوجه إلى الفندق واستلام الغرف ، وقت حر للعشاء والمبيت.
اليوم الثالث عشر : **مرسين – دمشق**	الإفطار وتسليم الغرف، ثم التوجه إلى مدينة انطاكية ، وقت حر للتسوق والغداء لمن يرغب ثم المتابعة للعودة إلى الوطن .

السعر يتضمن: الإقامة في الفنادق مع وجبتي الإفطار والعشاء . - التنقلات في بولمان حديث ومكيف .

نتمنى لكم قضاء رحلة سعيدة

http://alnokhbatours.com/turkey.htm#prog3

القراءة

تـمـريـن ١٤: "برنامج تركيا" (في الصف)

1. Using good reading strategies, take a global look at the text. What kind of text do you think it is? How does this text relate to the map? What information do you expect to find on closer reading?

2. Find as many places mentioned as you can on the map. Using the map and the text, as well as any background knowledge you have, describe what people will see بالعربية.

3. Discuss بالعربية: Would you enjoy taking this trip? لماذا أو لماذا لا؟

4. Use your grammatical knowledge to increase your comprehension:

    a. What can you guess about the meaning and grammatical form of المبيت؟
    b. What do you think تسليم الغرف and استلام الغرف mean? What helped you guess? What kinds of words are these? How are they related?
    c. A number of other words are repeated in this text. How many of them can you guess?

5. How many of the new words you identified are مصادر؟ See how many مصادر you can identify by وزن and pronounce them out loud. Why would this text have a lot of مصادر in it? What contextual and grammatical clues (such as the preposition إلى, which indicates motion toward) help you guess their meaning? At home, practice identifying وزن and جذر and using the dictionary by looking up some of the new words that seem important.

الكتابة

تمـريـن ١٥: نشاط كتابة (في البيت)

Write about أصدقائك from any standpoint you wish. Use connectors such as و, ولكن, and لأنّ to make the sentences flow together. If you are talking about friends one at a time, you can introduce the last one with the topic switcher أمّا – فـ:

أمّا صديقتي .... فهي ....

الاستماع: مع العائلة والأصدقاء

تمـريـن ١٦: مع أصدقاء خالد (في البيت) 🎧

شاهدوا واكتبوا:

١. من يتكلم؟ من هو بالنسبة لخالد؟　　٢. ماذا يعمل؟ اين يعمل؟

٣. ما هو برنامجه اليومي؟　　٤. ماذا يفعل يوم الاثنين؟

٥. هل هو مثل خالد؟ لماذا / لماذا لا؟

الحوار

اللغة والثقافة

just between you and me	بيني وبينك

تمـريـن ١٧: "شو بدّي اعمل؟"　/　"اعمل ايه في المشكلة دي؟" (في البيت) 🎧

استمعوا الى الحوار بالمصري واكتبوا فقرة لكل سؤال:	استمعوا الى الحوار بالشامي واكتبوا فقرة لكل سؤال:
١. ليه بيقول فيه مشكلة؟ ايه هي المشكلة؟	١. ليش بيقول فيه مشكلة؟ شو هي المشكلة؟
٢. مين هو مروان؟ هل مروان مشكلة كمان؟	٢. مين هو مروان؟ هل مروان مشكلة كمان؟
٣. ازاي كانت قصة الحب بينه وبين مراته رنا؟	٣. كيف كانت قصة الحب بينه وبين مرته رنا؟
٤. لازم يعمل ايه في رأيك؟	٤. شو لازم يعمل في رأيك؟

تـمارين المراجعة
تـمرين ١٨: حروف الجرّ 🎧

This exercise is available online only.

تـمرين ١٩: المضارع المنصوب والمرفوع (في البيت) 🎧

This exercise is available online only.

تـمرين ٢٠: القراءة الجهرية (في البيت أو في الصف) 🎧

Read the text silently first, then aloud several times to practice pronunciation and fluency. When you are ready, record yourself reading it aloud and submit it for your teacher's feedback, either online or as instructed by your teacher.

طارق عبد الكريم واحد من أصدقاء خالد المفضّلين. تخرّج من كلية السياحة والفنادق منذ سنتين ثم حصل على عمل بمرتّب جيد في مطعم فندق "رَمسيس هيلتون". طارق يعمل ستة أيام في الاسبوع من الساعة السادسة صباحاً الى الساعة الرابعة بعد الظهر ولذلك يبدأ يومه في الساعة الرابعة عندما يصحو من النوم ويشرب القهوة ويفطر فطوراً خفيفاً، ثم ينزل من البيت في الخامسة. وفي الساعة الخامسة بعد الظهر يعود طارق إلى البيت بعد يوم طويل ويشاهد التلفزيون بعد أن يأكل العشاء مع عائلته وقبل أن ينام.

يوم الاثنين هو يوم الاستراحة الاسبوعية عند طارق وبالنسبة له هو أفضل يوم بين كل أيام الأسبوع، لأنه يستطيع أن ينام فيه كما يريد ولأنه يذهب فيه أيضاً لمقابلة خالد والأصدقاء الآخرين في النادي حيث يتجمّعون بعد الظهر ويلعبون الرياضة والشطرنج ويتكلمون عن أخبارهم. طارق يحب خالد كثيراً ولكن، في رأيه، خالد خجول جداً ولا يريد أن يدخل تجربة أخرى بعد انقطاع العلاقة مع البنت التي كان يخرج معها. أما طارق، فهو يحب التجارب العاطفية ويستمتع بها كثيراً.

أصعب قرار في حياتي

المفردات

القصة بالعامية: "أصعب قرار في حياتي" "أصعب قرار في حياتي"

القواعد (١):

المستقبل والنفي

القصة بالفصحى: "أصعب قرار في حياتي"

القواعد (٢):

الاسم المنصوب

الجملة الفعلية Verb-Subject Agreement

الاستماع: مع العائلة والاصدقاء

القراءة: "الجامعة الأمريكية بالقاهرة توفر منحاً لطلابها"

الحوار: "حياتنا كلها صارت بالبيت" "حياتنا كلها بقت في البيت"

الثقافة: أغنية "زوروني" لِفيروز

تمارين المراجعة

المُفرَدات Vocabulary 🎧

استمعوا الى المفردات الجديدة بالفصحى والعامية.

المعنى	المصري	الشامي	الفُصحى
to take	خَد، ياخُد	أخَد، ياخُد	أخَذَ ، يَأخُذ ، الأخْذ
the last ...[1]			آخِر
all together	مع بَعض	مع بَعض، كِلّنا سَوا	جَميعاً
vacation (from work)	أجازة ج. -ات	إجازة ج. - ات	إجازة ج. - ات
director			مُدير ج. -ون، -ين ، مُدَراء
to visit[2]	زار، يزور	زار، يزور	زارَ، يَزور، الزِّيارة
= ما سافر	ما سافِرش	ما سافَر	لم يُسافِر
in addition to			بِالإضافة إلى
of course, naturally			طَبْعاً
holiday, vacation (official)	أجازة ج.-ات	عطلة ج. عِطل	عُطلة ج. عُطَل
to learn of, know[3]	عِرِف، يعرَف	عِرِف بـ ، يَعرِف	عَلِمَ بـ، يَعْلَم بـ ، العِلم بـ
I was appointed	اتْعَيّنْت	تْعَيّنْت	عُيِّنْتُ
to be absent from, miss	غاب (غِبت)، يِغيب عن	غاب (غِبت)، يغيب عن	تَغَيّبَ عن، يَتَغَيّب عن، التَّغَيُّب عن
coming, next (week, year, etc.)	جايّ/ة	جايي/ة	قادِم/ة
to decide to	قَرَّر، يِقَرَّر (+ المضارع)	قَرَّر، يْقَرِّر (إنّ)	قَرَّرَ، يُقَرِّر (+ أنْ /المصدر)
decision			قَرار ج. -ات
comparative			مُقارَن/ة
to spend (time)[4]	قَضى، يِقَضي	قَضّى، يِقَضّي	قَضى، يَقْضي، القَضاء
scholarship award, grant, fellowship			مِنْحة ج. مِنَح
here	هِنا	هون	هُنا
there	هِناك	هِنيك	هُناك
= مَوت			وَفاة

Notes on Vocabulary Usage

1. The words آخِر and أوَّل are superlative in meaning and function, even though they do not appear to match وزن أفعَل. They therefore must be followed by an indefinite noun. The resulting phrase is indefinite in Arabic even though the English equivalent is definite. In the following examples, note that أول and آخِر are followed by جملة صفة, and pick out the pronoun that refers back to the phrase:

آخِر فيلم شاهدناه كان طويلاً جدًا ومملّاً.

أوّل كتاب قرأته بالعربية كان قصة لنجيب محفوظ.

آخر شي قريته كان الجريدة.

أول مرّة شفته فيها كانت من ٣ سنين.

2. The verb يزور takes a direct object, just like its English counterpart:

زرت جدي وجدتي واستمتعت بالزيارة كثيراً.

بدي ازور ستّي وجدّي بالجبل يوم السبت، ورح آخد لهن معي شويّة فواكه وحلو.

عايزين تزوروا عمّ نبيل في اسكندرية وتنزلوا البحر؟

3. The verbs عَرَف and عَلِمَ بِـ overlap in meaning, but عَلِمَ بِـ tends to be more formal. The past tense of these verbs means "found out" or "learned of". Like other verbs referring to states of being, such as نام, these verbs signal an entry into a state, for example, of knowing or sleeping. Study the examples:

عندما علمت بنجاحي في الامتحان كنت سعيدة جداً طبعاً!

When I learned of …

نمت قبل ما احكي معها.

I fell asleep before …

عرفت خبر وفاة ستّي لمّا كنت في القاهرة.

I learned the news of …

4. The verb قَضّى، يَقضي / قَضى، يقَضي must be followed by a period of time, such as:

قضينا أسبوعاً على البحر وكانت أحسن استراحة!

سنقْضي سنة كاملة في تونس ندرس اللغة العربية.

قَضّيت وقت حلو كتير مع رفقاتي.   حنقَضّي الأجازة كلها في البيت عشان جوزي مريض.

For reasons we will see later in this chapter, in formal Arabic the word signaling the period of time must be منصوب .

تعلموا هذه الأفعال

زار، يَزور

المضارع المرفوع		الماضي	
نَزورُ	أزورُ	زُرنا	زُرتُ
تَزورونَ	تَزورُ تَزورينَ	زُرتُم	زُرتَ زُرتِ
يَزورونَ	يَزورُ تَزورُ	زاروا	زارَ زارَت

قَضى، يَقضي / قَضّى، يقَضّي

الماضي

قَضّيْت	قَضيت	قَضَيْتُ
قَضّيْت	قَضيت	قَضَيْتَ
قَضّيتي	قَضيتي	قَضَيْتِ
قَضّى	قَضى	قَضى
قَضّت	قَضّت	قَضَت
قَضّينا	قَضّينا	قَضَيْنا
قَضّيتوا	قَضّيتوا	قَضَيْتُم
قَضّوا	قَضّوا	قَضَوْا

المضارع

بَاقَضي	بقَضي	أقضي
بِتقَضي	بِتقَضي	تَقضي
بِتقَضي	بِتقَضي	تقضينَ
بيقَضي	بيقَضي	يَقضي
بِتقَضّي	بِتقَضّي	تَقضي
بِنقَضي	بِنقَضّي	نَقضي
بِتقَضّوا	بِتقَضّوا	تَقضونَ
بيقَضّوا	بيقَضّوا	يَقضونَ

تـمـريـن ١: الوزن والجذر (في البيت)

Identify الوزن والجذر of all the new verbs by completing the chart:

المصدر	المضارع	الماضي	الوزن
			I فَعَلَ، يَفعِل
			II فَعَّلَ، يُفَعِّل، التَّفعيل
			V تَفَعَّلَ، يَتَفَعَّل، التَّفَعُّل

🎧 تـمـريـن ٢: المفردات الجديدة (في البيت)

اكتبوا كلمة من الكلمات الجديدة في كل جملة.

١. بدأت غادة العمل في الشركة قبل ١٥ سنة، وفي السنة الماضية أصبحت

_____ للشركة بفضل عملها الممتاز.

٢. _____ يوم في الدراسة هو ١٧ ديسمبر ثم تبدأ _____ .

سأذهب لزيارة عائلتي كما أفعل كل سنة ولكن سأعود في _____

بداية يناير.

٣. في الأسبوع _____ سنسافر في جولة سياحية الى تركيا وسـ _____

هناك عشرة أيّام.

٤. كيف _____ بخبر حصولي على المنحة؟ أنا ما قلت هذا لأحد!

٥. فاطمة _____ أولادها إلى المدرسة بسيارتها كل يوم صباحاً.

٦. نريد أن _____ تونس مرة ثانية لأنَّ _____ نا الأولى اليها

كانت قصيرة جداً.

٧. كثير من الموظفين _____ عن أشغالهم أمس بسبب الطقس المثلج.

٨. أصبح محمد السادس ملكاً للمغرب بعد _____ والده الملك الحسن الثاني.

٩. ــــــــــــــ والدتي العودة إلى العمل بعد الانقطاع عنه سنوات طويلة ،

ووالدي كان سعيداً بهذا ــــــــــــــ .

١٠. يريد المدير أن يقابل المهندسين ــــــــــــــ ولا يريد أن يقابلهم واحداً واحداً.

١١. الدكتورة سعاد متخصصة في السياسة ــــــــــــــ وتدرس السياسة العربية-

الأوروبية. وهي تتكلم اللغتين الانكليزية والفرنسية ــــــــــــــ اللغة العربية.

قبل سنتين حصلت على ــــــــــــــ "فولبرايت" للدراسة في الولايات المتحدة،

وبعد عودتها ــــــــــــــ رئيسة لقسم العلوم السياسية في الجامعة.

تمرين ٣: المفردات في جمل (في البيت) 🎧

استمعوا الى جمل المفردات واكتبوا الجمل من "أخذ" الى "عُيِّنت".

تمرين ٤: كلمات جديدة وقواعد قديمة (في البيت)

Complete these sentences using at least one new كلمة in each sentence. Remember to pay attention to the grammatical structures you need to use with بسبب , أنْ , لأنّ, and.

١. لماذا قرّرتم أن ــــــــــــــ ؟

٢. زملاؤنا يريدون أن ــــــــــــــ .

٣. هل علمتم بـ ــــــــــــــ ؟

٤. من فضلك ، هل يمكنك أن ــــــــــــــ ؟

٥. صديقي يشعر بالخجل لأنّ ــــــــــــــ .

٦. انقطعت العلاقات بيننا بسبب ــــــــــــــ .

٧. لا نستطيع أن ــــــــــــــ لأنّ ــــــــــــــ .

٨. في المستقبل ســـ ــــــــــــــ .

تمـريـن ٥: اسألوا زملاءكم (في الصف)

اسألوا زملاءكم في هذه المواضيع:

1. Who will be coming to visit them or who will they visit on their next vacation?
What do they do when people visit them in the middle (= half) of the semester?

2. How many hours per day do they spend studying? Taking a break? Working?

3. Is it a problem when students miss class a lot? Why/why not?

4. What was the best decision they ever made (= took) in their lives? How did they decide?
Who helped them decide? What and when will their next big decision be?

5. Do they remember where they were when they learned of September 11?
Do they think that young children should learn of news like this? Why or why not?

6. Do they know of any scholarships for summer language study?
Where is the best place to get information on scholarships?

7. What do they take with them when they leave the house in the morning?

القصة بالعامية

تمرين ٦: "أصعب قرار في حياتي" / "أصعب قرار في حياتي" (في البيت) 🎧

استمعوا الى القصة بالمصري واكتبوا فقرة لكل سؤال: Give as many details as you can.	استمعوا الى القصة بالشامي واكتبوا فقرة لكل سؤال: Give as many details as you can.
١. مين هو واسمه ايه؟ بنعرف ايه عنه؟	١. مين هو وشو اسمه؟ شو بنعرف عنه؟
٢. ازاي جا أمريكا؟	٢. كيف إجا ع أميركا؟
٣. قال لنا إيه عن آخر مرة سافر فيها مصر؟	٣. ليش فيه صور بالأبيض والأسود والناس فيها زعلانين؟ إمتى كان هادا؟
٤. ليه هو مبسوط من الزيارة دي لـمصـر؟	٤. ليش هو مبسوط من هالزيارة للشام؟
٥. للكلام في الفصل: في رأيكم، محمد عايز يرجع مصر؟ ليه/ليه لأ؟	٥. للحكي بالصف: برأيكن، هو بده يرجع ع الشام؟ ليه/ ليه لأ؟
	في الصف: شوفوا فيديو "مبروك!": إمتى كان هادا؟ شو بتقول مريم؟ كيف بيقول حسن "عندي أخبار ممتازة"؟

تمرين ٧: جمل المفردات 🎧

استمعوا الى جمل المفردات واكتبوا الجمل من "تغيّب" الى "وفاة".

القواعد ١

المُستَقبَل

You know that the prefixes سَـ حَـ حَـ and رَح indicate future time in our three varieties of Arabic. In formal Arabic, the prefix سَـ has a long form, سَوْفَ, which overlaps with سَـ in meaning but belongs to a high literary register. Grammatically, both سَـ and سَوْفَ require the verb to be مضارع مرفوع. The following chart shows the conjugation of المستقبل in الفصحى using the verb يفعل as an example:

المضارع المرفوع	
سَنَفعَلُ / سَوفَ نَفعَلُ	سَأَفعَلُ / سَوفَ أَفعَلُ
سَتَفعَلونَ / سَوفَ تَفعَلونَ	سَتَفعَلُ / سَوفَ تَفعَلُ
	سَتَفعَلينَ / سَوفَ تَفعَلينَ
سَيَفعَلونَ / سَوفَ يَفعَلونَ	سَيَفعَلُ / سَوفَ يَفعَلُ
	سَتَفعَلُ / سَوفَ تَفعَلُ

The expression إن شاء الله *God willing,* is often used when talking about the future to express the hope or wish that something will happen, much the way American English speakers use the word "hopefully," as these examples show:

أمثلة:

سوف أتخرّج بعد سنة إن شاء الله .

سأسافر الى بعض البلاد العربية السنة القادمة إن شاء الله.

نفي المستقبل

In formal Arabic, the future is negated with the particle, لَن, which indicates specifically and emphatically that an action **will not** happen. Note that لن must be followed by المضارع المنصوب, even when its verb is the main verb of the sentence, and that لن **never occurs with** سَـ or سوف. Only one of these particles may be used at a time. The following chart shows future negation using the verb يفعل as an example:

لَن نَفعَلَ	لَن أَفعَلَ
لَن تَفعَلوا	لَن تَفعَلَ
	لَن تَفعَلي
لَن يَفعَلوا	لَن يَفعَلَ
	لَن تَفعَلَ

In spoken Arabic, we use مش and ما to negate المستقبل:

ما رح آخد عطلة هلّق لأنّه فيه شغل كتير بالشركة.

مش حاخد أجازة دلوقتي عشان فيه شغل كتير في الشركة.

The verb كان is used in talking about the future. Learn the formal conjugation:

لَن نَكونَ	لَن أكونَ		سَنَكونُ	سَأكونُ
لَن تَكونوا	لَن تَكونَ لَن تَكوني		سَتَكونونَ	سَتَكونُ سَتَكونينَ
لَن يَكونوا	لَن يَكونَ لَن تَكونَ		سَيَكونونَ	سَيَكونُ سَتَكونُ

تـمريـن ٨: قراءة المستقبل (في الصف)

In Arab culture fortunes are told in several ways. One of the most common is the reading of the coffee grounds left in the cup, الفنجان, after drinking Arabic/Turkish coffee. Have a cup of coffee and see if you can tell the fortunes of your classmates and let them read yours for you.

تـمريـن ٩: ماذا سيفعلون أو لن يفعلوا؟ (في البيت) 🎧

Practice المستقبل and its negative using the word in parentheses, as in the example. Decide whether the sentence calls for a positive or negative verb and write its appropriate form, including the correct منصوب or مرفوع suffixes on all verbs.

مثال: أصدقائي سَيَذهَبونَ إلى السينما اليوم. (ذهبوا)

١. _____ أختي من الجامعة بعد ثلاث سنوات إن شاء الله. (تخرّجَت)

٢. هل _____ في مباراة كرة القدم غداً يا أحمد؟ (لعِبتَ)

٣. هل _____ رئيس الوزراء إلى فرنسا في الأسبوع القادم؟ (سافر)

٤. لن _____ مرّة اخرى كما سهرنا أمس!! (سهِرنا)

٥. _____ بالوحدة إذا عِشتِ بعيداً عن عائلتك وأصدقائك. (شعرتِ بـ)

٦. غداً، _____ إخوتي في المذاكرة ثم _____ إلى النادي.

(ساعدتُ، ذهبتُ)

٧. لن _____ إلى تلك المدينة مرّة أخرى! (عُدنا)

٨. صديقتي _____ الجامعة في أوّل السنة القادمة إن شاء الله . (دخلت)

٩. في أيّ ساعة _____ من البيت غداً؟ (نزلتم)

١٠. _____ على زميلتي الجديدة عندما تجيء الى الغرفة اليوم. (تعرّفتُ)

١١. أختي لن _____ في اليوم لأنّ ابنها مريض. (زارت)

١٢. عندما أتخرج، إن شاء الله، _____ ماذا أريد أن أعمل. (قرّرتُ)

١٣. لن _____ السفر إلى مصر هذه السنة. (استطعنا)

١٤. لن _____ قبل الساعة الحادية عشرة يوم السبت ! (صحَوتُ)

١٥. عندما يسافرون الى عمّان، _____ في فندق "عمان ماريوت". (نزلوا)

١٦. أنتم تعملون كثيراً جداً، وإن شاء الله _____ إجازة قريباً! (أخذتم)

القصة بالفصحى

تمـرين ١٠: "أصعب قرار في حياتي" (في البيت) 🎧

استمعوا الى محمد بالفصحى واكتبوا:

١. كيف يقول بالفصحى "قرّرت إنّي اعيش هون" "قرّرت أعيش هنا" ؟

٢. القواعد: Listen to find the following structures:

أ. كم جملة فعلية يقول محمد هنا؟ List the verbs and their subjects?

ب. أين جملة الصفة؟ _____

٣. أيّ اجازة أخذ محمد وملك؟ _____

٤. استمعوا إلى محمد واكتبوا ما يقول:

أنا اسمي (١) .... أبو العلا. (٢) .... (٣) ....

الكثير (٤) .... (٥) .... مها، (٦) ....

(٧) .... قسم (٨) .... (٩) ....

(١٠) .... (١١) .... و (١٢) ....

(١٣) .... أ (١٤) .... ، و (١٥) .... الماجستير

(١٦) .... (١٧) .... (١٨) .... للدكتوراه

(١٩) .... (٢٠) .... كاليفورنيا في سانتا بربارا.

بعد (٢١) .... (٢٢) .... الدكتوراه في (٢٣) ....

(٢٤) .... (٢٥) .... (٢٦) .... هنا.

(٢٧) .... (٢٨) .... هذا (٢٩) ....

(٣٠) .... في (٣١) .... ، فأنا (٣٢) ....

(٣٣) .... (٣٤) .... (٣٥) ....

و (٣٦) .... (٣٧) . ... (٣٨) ....

(٣٩) .... فيها مصر (٤٠) .... (٤١) .... ثلاث

(٤٢) .... ، عندما (٤٣) .... (٤٤) ....

(٤٥) .... (٤٦) .... (٤٧) .... محمود،

وكانت (٤٨) .... (٤٩) .... جدا، ولم (٥٠) ....

ملك ومها (٥١) .... هذه (٥٢) .... (٥٣) ....

(٥٤) .... ، و (٥٥) .... (٥٦) .... في القاهرة،

أنا وملك (٥٧) .... (٥٨) .... السّنوية،

ومها (٥٩) .... (٦٠) .... أ (٦١) .... محاضراتها

(٦٢) .... (٦٣) .... (٦٤) ....

(٦٥) ....

القواعد ٢

الاسم المنصوب

In the story you heard محمد use the formal grammatical ending تنوين فتحة:

عُيِّنتُ معيداً.

سنسافر جميعاً.

ستتغيَّب أسبوعاً عن محاضراتها.

You know that this ending marks adverbs, such as أحياناً and عادةً. The words marked with this ending in the sentences above, however, are not adverbs. Rather, they play other roles in these sentences. Here we will discuss some of these additional roles that المنصوب indicates on nouns. These uses of تنوين are limited to formal Arabic.

Recall that only indefinite nouns take tanwiin. The المنصوب ending can be definite, in which case it is a single fatHa, or indefinite, in which case it is tanwiin fatHa. In both cases, the noun is called اسم منصوب[1]. If the noun is indefinite, the منصوب ending will be either اً or ةً. If the noun is definite, the منصوب ending will be ـَ . The indefinite اسم منصوب is the only grammatical ending that is visible in ordinary, unvoweled print, because of the final alif:

عينت معيدا or معيداً

عندما كنت طالبا or طالباً

Remember that the double fatHa of تنوين may or may not be marked on the alif and that if you see alif at the end of a word and it is not a proper noun, it probably indicates المنصوب.

Why do some nouns get منصوب endings? In Mohammad's sentence عينت معيداً, the word معيداً is the direct object of the verb عُيِّنت. In the sentence سنسافر جميعاً the word جميعاً refers to how they will travel. And in the sentence ستتغيَّب أسبوعاً عن محاضراتها the word أسبوعاً answers the question how long she will be away. Together, these examples show that the منصوب ending on nouns indicates the direct object, *what?* and other additional information about how the action of the sentences took place, as in "*when?*," "*how?*," and "*for how long?*" In formal Arabic, الاسم المنصوب signals an answer to one of these questions. It may function as a direct object of the verb or as another kind of qualifier, as in "how" or "for how long?" These examples demonstrate:

ماذا قرأت؟ قرأت كتاباً غريباً!	كم يوماً ستتغيب؟ سأتغيَّب يوماً واحداً فقط.
كيف ستعيش هناك؟ سأعيش وحيداً.	ماذا شاهدت؟ شاهدت فيلماً جديداً.

---

[1] Remember that we used the term المضارع المنصوب to refer to the مضارع verb with فتحة endings (such as أنْ يذهبَ), as distinguished from the ضمّة endings of المضارع المرفوع (يذهبُ). Both الفعل المنصوب and الاسم المنصوب share the فتحة vowel.

تـمريـن ١١: الاسم المنصوب (في الصف)

• These sentences are missing the grammatical markings needed in formal Arabic. Which nouns and adjectives need to be marked as منصوب? Remember that the tanwiin fatHa only occurs on indefinite nouns. With a partner identify and mark all the nouns, then read the sentences aloud to each other.

١. عندما كان والدي طالب، عُيّن معيد في القسم. ثم بعد أن تخرّج أصبح أستاذ في جامعة "ويليام أند ماري".

٢. قررنا أنا والعائلة أن نسافر الى البحر في العطلة ونقضي أسبوع هناك ثم نزور صديق يعيش في الجبال.

٣. عملت خالتي مديرة لمستشفى في بغداد عدة سنوات ثم قررت أن تعمل أستاذة في كليّة الصيدلة في الجامعة.

٤. في جولتنا شاهدنا جامع قديم عمره ٥٠٠ سنة وسوق كبير من أيّام العُثمانيين.

٥. آسفة، أخذت موعد مع الدكتور ولا يمكنني أن أتأخّر. سأتغيّب ساعة واحدة.

Subject–Verb Agreement: الجملة الفعلية

By now you have seen many examples of الجملة الفعلية, sentences that begin with verbs. In some جمل فعلية, the subject of the verb is contained in the verb itself, as in:

أسكن في مدينة نيويورك.

نسهر لنشاهد التليفزيون.

هل تفهمون ما أقصد؟

In other جمل فعلية, the subject, الفاعِل, is expressed independently and follows the verb:

(١) لم يسافر الأولاد مع أمهم.

(٢) يجيء كل أفراد العائلة إلى البيت.

(٣) استمتع الطلاب بالمحاضرة أمس.[2]

(٤) تجمّع الناس في بيوتهم ليستمعوا الى الرئيس.

---

[2]Notice the placement of the subject in these sentences: When the verb phrase includes a preposition, the subject normally occurs between the verb and its preposition.

Note that the verbs in these sentence examples are all singular, even though the subjects are plural. Formal Arabic grammar stipulates that in الجملة الفعلية, **whenever a verb precedes its subject** and that subject is a separate noun (i.e., not part of the verb), **the verb must always be singular.** Compare sentences (٤), (٣), (٢), (١) above with the following:

(٥) الأولاد لم يسافروا مع أمهم.

(٦) كل أفراد العائلة يجيئون إلى البيت.

(٧) الطلاب استمتعوا بالمحاضرة أمس.

(٨) الناس تجمّعوا في بيوتهم ليستمعوا الى الرئيس.

The verbs in sentences 1–4 precede their subjects, while those in 5–8 follow their subjects. The first four are examples of جملة فعلية; the last four are examples of جملة اسمية.

Although الجملة الفعلية has special plural and singular agreement rules, the verb should agree with its subject in gender. Thus, when the subject of a جملة فعلية is a nonhuman plural or a human feminine plural, the verb must be feminine singular (هي):

رفضت النساء المصريات قرار الحكومة الجديد في موضوع حقوق المرأة.

حصلت بعض الطالبات على منح للدراسة في الخارج.

تبادلت الحكومة السعودية والحكومة الصينية في الأسبوع الماضي عدّة رسائل دبلوماسية.

Remember: A verb that precedes its subject must be singular.

تمـرين ١٢: الجملة الاسمية والجملة الفعلية (في البيت)

This exercise is available online only.

الاستماع: مع العائلة والأصدقاء

تمرين ١٣: أحب عملي كثيراً (في البيت) 🎧

شاهدوا واكتبوا:

١. من يتكلم؟ من هو؟ ماذا يعمل؟ أين؟

٢. ما هي مشكلة شغله؟

٣. ماذا يقول عن محمد؟

٤. كيف العلاقة بينه وبين محمد؟

الكتابة

تمرين ١٤: نشاط كتابة (في البيت)

Write an essay of approximately one hundred words about your favorite vacation. You may want to address the following points:

* أين قضيت العطلة؟	* متى أخذت العطلة ؟
* لماذا استمتعت بها؟	* من كان معك؟

In your paragraph, use الجملة الفعلية and as many connecting words as you can. Connectors you have learned include the following:

Function	Connector
Links events in chronological order	ثُمَّ
Begins all related sentences (except those beginning with ثم or فَ)	و
Introduces an explanation or result (like the English words "since" or "so")	فَ
Links two related actions	كما، وبالإضافة الى ذلك
Helps order events chronologically	بعد أنْ
Helps order events chronologically; must be followed by المضارع	قبل أنْ

القراءة

تمـريـن ١٥: "الجامعة الأمريكية بالقاهرة توفر منحاً لطلابها" (في الصف)

اقرأوا وتكلّموا:

The following guidelines are designed to help you develop reading strategies for reading the language used in the media, in particular. Though they are numbered like steps in order, they do not all have to be done separately. In fact, as your reading skills improve, you will synthesize these strategies and use them in different ways to serve your reading goals. In general, news articles tend to have a predominance of الجمل الفعلية. Use this information to help you skim through texts and divide them up mentally into smaller units. Then, you can decide which of those units will yield more relevant or accessible information upon close reading. Keep in mind that journalists everywhere are trained to fit all of the basic information into the first sentence of the article. It is usually helpful to look at the first sentence of each paragraph to see if you can get a general idea about the topic of that paragraph, without spending too much time on it.

1. Find the basic information of this article in its first sentence by looking for the answers to the questions below.

من؟   ماذا؟   أين؟   متى؟

2. Map out the structure of the article mentally by looking at the beginning of each paragraph: What is the topic of each one, as far as you can tell?

3. Plan a strategy for reading each section of the article according to what information you think you can get out of it. Look for the following information: How many programs are mentioned? At whom are they aimed? What are some of the things they offer these students? How many students are affected? What kinds of students are mentioned?

4. Use grammar and context together to help you guess the meanings of new words. Identify the kind of word first—noun, verb, adjective. Then, look to the context for semantic clues to the meaning of the phrase as a whole. Find two verbs that mean "to offer," and guess the meaning of the following phrases:

المعونة المالية   التفوق، الطلاب المتفوقين

5. After you have completed the above in class, at home choose three words that you do not know that you think will increase your understanding of the article, or a part of it, and look them up. Have an idea of what you are looking for before you go to the dictionary, otherwise you may get lost in a sea of English synonyms. Did you choose well? What did these three words add to your comprehension of the article?

الجامعة الأمريكية بالقاهرة

الجامعة الأمريكية بالقاهرة توفر منحاً لطلابها تقدر بـ ١٨ مليون دولار

القاهرة - محرر مصراوي - أعلنت الجامعة الأمريكية بالقاهرة الأحد أنها تقوم سنوياً بتخصيص ١٨ مليون دولار للمنح الدراسية والمعونات المالية التي تقدمها لطلابها لمساعدتهم على تحمل نفقات تعليمهم.

وقال الدكتور أشرف الفقي نائب رئيس الجامعة لشئون الطلاب أن حوالي ٧٠ ٪ من طلبة الجامعة الأمريكية بالقاهرة يتلقون مساعدة مالية بصورة أو بأخرى وذلك عن طريق المنح الدراسية أو المعونات المالية. وأضاف أن الجامعة تلتزم بتقديم الفرصة للطلاب الحاصلين على درجات أكاديمية مرتفعة لتلقي تعليمهم بالجامعة الأمريكية بالقاهرة.

وتعتبر المنحة المقدمة من الجامعة الأمريكية للطلبة الحاصلين على الثانوية العامة من المدارس الحكومية - والتي يتم دعمها جزئياً عن طريق مشاركة الشركات والأفراد- من أنجح برامج المنح التي تقدمها الجامعة. وهذه المنحة تتكفل سنوياً بنفقات تعليم ٢٠ من طلاب الثانوية العامة المتفوقين من خريجي المدارس الحكومية والذين ليس لديهم الموارد المادية للالتحاق بالجامعة الأمريكية بالقاهرة.

وأكد الفقي أن البرنامج - والذي بدأ عام ١٩٩٠ - قد أعطى الفرصة لأكثر من ٢٠٠ طالب للدراسة بالجامعة. "في الواقع إنّ ٨٠ بالمائة من طلاب هذه المنحة قد تخرجوا من الجامعة بتفوق وحصلوا على أعلى الدرجات مع مرتبة الشرف."

وهناك أيضاً برنامج إعداد القادة والتنمية الذي تدعمه الحكومة المصرية والأمريكية والذي يوفر منحاً دراسية شاملة المصروفات الدراسية والإقامة بسكن الطلاب التابع للجامعة الأمريكية لـ ٥٨ طالباً- شاباً وفتاة- من كل محافظة من محافظات مصر. ويستفيد أيضاً طلاب برنامج إعداد القادة والتنمية بفرصة السفر إلى الخارج للدراسة لمدة تيرم دراسي واحد. ويوجد حالياً ٢٣٨ طالباً بهذا البرنامج يدرسون بالجامعة الأمريكية بالقاهرة بالإضافة إلى ٥٨ طالباً سيلتحقون بالبرنامج هذا العام.

بالإضافة إلى ذلك هناك برنامجان موجهان لطلاب الجامعة الأمريكية بالقاهرة الحاصلين على درجات أكاديمية متميزة وهما منحة الإنجاز التي تقدم لأول ٢٥ بالمائة من الطلاب المقيدين بالجامعة والتي تتيح للطلاب تخفيض٣٠٪ من المصروفات الدراسية وكذلك منحة الإمتياز التي تمنح في بداية كل عام دراسي للطلاب الخمسة الأوائل الحاصلين على أعلى الدرجات على المستوى المحلي أو الإقليمي في شهادة إتمام الدراسة الثانوية باختلاف أنواعها. وهذه المنحة تمنح الطالب تخفيضاً قدره ٤٠ ٪ بالإضافة إلى منحة الإنجاز.

ويضيف الفقي أن الطلاب المتفوقين في الرياضة سواء المحلية أو الدولية أو المشاركين في الأنشطة الثقافية لديهم الفرصة للحصول على تخفيض قدره ١٥ ٪ في المصروفات الدراسية.

www.masrawy.com/News/Egypt/Politics/2009/july/19/american_university.aspx

الحوار

اللغة والثقافة

مو مَعقول!	مش مَعقول!	literally, *not reasonable!*

This expression is used much like the English expressions: *"That's crazy!" "That's insane!"* or *"That's ridiculous!"*

يا ريت!	يا ريت!	*I wish!*

تمـريـن ١٦: "حياتنا كلها صارت بالبيت" / "حياتنا كلها بقت في البيت" (في البيت) 🎧

استمعوا الى الحوار بالمصري واكتبوا فقرة لكل سؤال:	استمعوا الى الحوار بالشامي واكتبوا فقرة لكل سؤال:
١. مين بيتكلم؟ بيتكلموا عن ايه؟	١. مين عم يحكي؟ عن شو عم يحكوا؟
٢. حيعملوا ايه في أجازة العيد؟	٢. شو رح يعملوا بعطلة العيد؟
٣. رنا مش مبسوطة ليه؟ هي عايزة ايه؟	٣. ليش رنا مش مبسوطة؟ شو بدها؟
٤. في رأيك، ناصر حيقول ايه لمّا صاحبه يتكلم معاه؟	٤. برأيك، شو رح يقول ناصر لمّا رفيقه يحكي معه؟

الثقافة 🎧

أغنية "زوروني" لِفيروز

Learn some of the new words you hear in the song below. Sing along and enjoy.

كلمات جديدة:

بالمَرَّة	*completely*
حَرام	*Shame (on you)! It's not right!* (expression)
تِنسوا	*you forget*

 فيروز sings most of her songs in the Lebanese dialect, including the following. Search online for the lyrics to this song, then learn them while you watch فيروز perform the song.

تـمارين المراجعة

تمـريـن ١٧: حروف جر وضمائر (في البيت) 🎧

This exercise is available online only.

تمـريـن ١٨: النفي بالفصحى والعامية (في البيت ثم في الصف)

A. في البيت Negate these فصحى sentences using لن, لا, or ليس. Remember to write the correct منصوب or مرفوع endings. Also remember that ليس normally comes at the beginning of the sentence it negates.

B. في الصف Rephrase each of the sentences in the dialect you are learning, then negate them.

١. هذا أخي.

٢. هذا أول كتاب أقرأه باللغة العربية.

٣. سيكون عندنا عطلة طويلة في الربيع وسأسافر فيها الى لبنان.

٤. يحب معظم الأولاد أن يأكلوا الخضار والفواكه.

٥. سيزورني كل أفراد عائلتي عندما أسافر للدراسة في مصر السنة القادمة.

٦. يحصل خالد على تقدير "ممتاز" دائماً.

٧. السفر من بيروت إلى دمشق يأخذ وقتاً طويلاً.

٨. أستطيع السهر كل يوم لأن أول صف لي يبدأ في الساعة التاسعة.

٩. لي أعمام كثيرون يعيشون في هذا البلد.

١٠. تتغيّب مريم عن صفوفها أحياناً بسبب ابنها الصغير.

١١. سنسافر هذه السنة إلى الجزائر ان شاء الله.

١٢. يخرجون من البيت قبل الساعة السابعة صباحاً.

١٣. في غرفة صفّنا شبابيك كثيَرة.

تمـريـن ١٩: "الـ" في الاستماع (في البيت) 🎧

This exercise is available online only.

تمرين ٢٠: جملة الصفة (في الصف)

Work with a partner to describe what is happening in each of these pictures using what you've learned about جملة الصفة.

تمرين ٢١: القراءة الجهرية (في البيت أو في الصف) 🎧

Read the following passage, first silently for comprehension, then aloud to practice pronunciation. When you are ready, record the passage and submit it to your teacher either online or as instructed by your teacher.

أميرة عاصي النوري عمة نسرين وهي كذلك زوجة السيد محمد علي النوري، ابن عمها وأحد تُجّار الشام المعروفين. والسيد محمد يتاجر بالقطن مثل والده وجده، وهو مثلهم ناجح في شغله الى درجة كبيرة. والسيدة أميرة سعيدة في حياتها معه ولها منه أربعة أولاد: رامي، الكبير وهو يعمل مع والده في التجارة، وغادة، متزوّجة ولها ابن عمره سنة واحدة، ودُنيا، طالبة هندسة في جامعة دمشق، وسامية، الصغيرة، طالبة في المدرسة الثانوية. أميرة تقضي يومها في شغل البيت، وفي زيارة الأصدقاء والأقارب، وهم أيضا يزورونها طبعاً. وأحيانا تأخذ الغداء الى بيت بنتها غادة، المشغولة بابنها الصغير .

طبعاً السبب الحقيقي لهذه الزيارة هو مشاهدة الولد، أول حفيد للسيدة أميرة وزوجها! والولد اسمه عاصي على اسم جده، وهو أجمل ولد في العالم في رأي أمّه وجدته. وبالإضافة الى كل هذا فالسيّدة أميرة مشغولة بمستقبل أولادها الآخرين، فهي تريد أن تُزوّج ابنها رامي، وهذا لن يكون سهلاً لأنّ رامي يريد شابة جميلة ومتعلمة ومن عائلة شامية قديمة وعندها فلوس. ودنيا تتكلم فقط عن الهندسة وتجربة العمل في الخارج، ولا تريد أن تتزوج. آه، بنات اليوم!!! أما سامية الصغيرة فتريد أن تخرج دائماً مع أصحابها لأنّها تحب السَّهر والحفلات والرّقص. السيّدة اميرة تشعر بأن سامية ستجيء إليها في المستقبل القريب وتقول لها إنّها على علاقة عاطفية مع واحد من أصدقائها الشباب. هذه ستكون مشكلة المشاكل! ولكن "كل شي بيجي من الله منيح" كما يقولون.

درس

لماذا قررت البقاء في أمريكا؟

المفردات

القصة بالعامية: "ليش قررت ابقى بأمريكا؟" "ليه قررت اعيش في أمريكا؟"

القواعد (١):

"أنّ" و "إنّ" Sentence Complements

القصة بالفصحى: "لماذا قررت البقاء هنا؟"

القواعد (٢):

نفي الماضي: لم + المضارع المجزوم

مراجعة المضارع المرفوع والمنصوب والمجزوم

القراءة: "أرغب في الحصول على منحة دراسية"

الاستماع: مع العائلة والاصدقاء

الحوار: "انت بس ارجع" "انت بس ارجع"

تمارين المراجعة

المُفرَدات Vocabulary 🎧

استمعوا الى المفردات الجديدة بالفصحى والعامية.

المعنى	المصري	الشامي	الفصحى
finally, at last			أخيراً
in front of, before	قُدّام	قِدّام	أمامَ
not to[1]	--	--	أَلّا (أَنْ + لا)
magazine, journal			مَجَلَّة ج. - ات
dream	حِلم ج. أحلام	حِلم ج. أحلام	حُلْم ج. أحلام
= عاد ، يعود	رِجِع ، يِرجَع	رِجع ، يرجَع ع	رَجَعَ ، يَرجِعُ، الرُّجوع من / إلى
to desire, wish to	--	--	رَغِبَ في، يَرغَبُ في، الرَّغبة في
continues to, is still[2]	لِسّه	بَعد (+ pronoun)	ما زالَ (ما زِلْتُ)
theater			مَسرَح ج. مَسارِح
to encourage (someone) to	شَجَّعَ ، بِشَجِّع	شَجَّع ، يشَجِّع	شَجَّعَ ، يُشَجِّع، التَّشجيع على
to think that, believe[3]	اِفتَكَر، يِفتِكِر إنّ	ظَنّ (ظَنّيت)، يظِنّ انّه (إنّو)	ظنَّ أنَّ (ظَنَنْتُ أنَّ)، يَظُنّ أنّ
it means[4]			يَعني
longing for one's native land; feeling of being a stranger; homesickness			الغُربة
opportunity, chance			فُرْصة ج. فُرَص
nice to have met you!			فُرْصة سَعيدة!
to fail (at, in)	فَشَل ، يِفشَل بـ	فِشِل، يِفشَل بـ	فَشَلَ، يَفْشَل، الفَشَل في
to dismiss, fire (from a job)	فَصَل ، يِفصِل	فَصَل ، يِفصِل	فَصَلَ، يَفصِل، الفَصل
to think about (doing something)[5]	فَكَّر، يِفَكَّر	فَكَّر، يفَكِّر	فَكَّرَ، يُفَكِّر، التَّفكير في (+ المصدر/أنْ)
to settle down, become stable			اِسْتَقَرَّ، يَسْتَقِرّ، الاِسْتِقرار
article (e.g., in a newspaper)			مَقالة ج. -ات
likewise, also	كَمان	كَمان	كَذلِكَ
appropriate, suitable (for)			مُناسِب/ة (لِ)
to finish (something)	خَلَّص ، يِخَلَّص	خَلَّص ، يخَلِّص	اِنتَهى، يَنتَهي، الاِنتِهاء مِن

الفُصحى	الشامي	المصري	المعنى
وَجَدَ ، يَجِد	لَقى (لْقيت)، يلاقي	لَقى (لْقيت)، يِلاقي	to find
لم أجِد = ما وَجَدتُ	ما لْقيت	ما لْقيتش	I did not find
وَظيفة ج. وَظائِف	وَظيفة ج. وَظايِف	وَظيفة ج. وَظايِف	position, job

Notes on Vocabulary Usage

1. The particle أَلّا consists of the particles لا + أنْ and functions as the negation of أنْ:

قرّرت أَلّا أعيش في بيت الطلاب.

أفكّر أَلّا أسافر الى الشرق الأوسط هذه السنة لأن السفر أصبح غالياً.

2. In English we express the continuation of an action into the present with the adverb "still," as in, "Are you still angry with me?" In formal Arabic this concept is expressed with the verb ما زالَ[1]. As a verb, it must be conjugated for person. The following chart gives the conjugation of the verb ما زالَ:

 ما زالَ

ما زِلنا	ما زِلتُ
ما زِلتُم	ما زِلتَ / ما زِلتِ
ما زالوا	ما زالَ / ما زالَت

On the following page you will see more examples of this concept.

---

[1] This idiom is actually composed of the verb زال and the negative ما (lit., to not cease).

أمثلة

ما زالوا زعلانين مني!   أكلنا ولكن ما زلنا جوعانين!

Notice that ما زالَ behaves like the verbs كان and بدأ in that all of them can be followed by a noun or an adjective or a verb:

عندما كنت طالبة كنت رياضيّة وكنت ألعب كرة القدم،

I used to be athletic and I used to play ...

والآن ما زلت رياضيّة وما زلت ألعب السلّة.

I am still athletic and I still play.

بدأت تتغيّب عن الصف منذ أسابيع وتكلّم الأستاذ معها ولكنها ما زالت تتغيب.

She began to miss class ... but she still misses class.

كانوا يتبادلون الرسائل وما زالوا يتبادلون الرسائل الى الآن.

They used to exchange letters ...and they still exchange letters.

Note that in spoken Arabic different constructions are used to express this concept:

هو لِسّه بيحبّها!	بعده بيحبّها!	ما زال يحبها!
احنا كلنا بس لِسّه جعانين!	أكلنا بس بعدنا جوعانين!	أكلنا ولكن ما زلنا جوعانين!
هم لسّه زعلانين مني؟	بعدهن زعلانين مني؟	ما زالوا زعلانين مني؟

3. In English we use the verb "to think" to mean two different kinds of activities: To give opinions and to consider, ponder, or mull over a matter or a course of action. In Arabic each of these activities is expressed by a different verb. To give an opinion or express a belief, one of the most widely used verbs is ظنّ، يَظُنّ أنّ. Note that الماضي has two stems:

ظَنَنّا أنَّ	ظَنَنْتُ أنَّ
ظَنَنْتُم أنَّ	ظَنَنْتَ أنَّ ظَنَنْتِ أنَّ
ظَنّوا أنَّ	ظَنَّ أنَّ ظَنَّت أنَّ

Levantine speakers share the verb يَظُنّ with formal Arabic, whereas Egyptian speakers are more likely to use اِفْتَكَر، يِفْتِكِر to express a belief.

أَظُنّ أنّ هذا الموضوع صعب جداً.

بظنّ إنّه هالموضوع صعب كتير.

بافْتِكِر إنّ الموضوع دا صعب قوي.

To express thinking as a process, the verb فَكَّر في is used in all three of our varieties. Notice the use of preposition في about (something).

أريد أن أفكِّر في الموضوع أكثر قبل أن أقرِّر.

بدي افكِّر بالموضوع أكثر قبل ما اقرر.

عايزة افكَّر في الموضوع أكثر قبل ما اقرر.

4. You will often hear native speakers use يعني in conversation as a filler similar to the English "you know" or "like."

تعلموا هذه الأفعال 🎧

اِنْتَهى من، يَنْتَهي من

المضارع المرفوع		الماضي	
نَنْتَهي من	أَنْتَهي من	اِنْتَهَيْنا من	اِنْتَهَيْتُ من
تَنْتَهونَ من	تَنْتَهي من تَنْتَهينَ من	اِنْتَهَيْتُم من	اِنْتَهَيْتَ من اِنْتَهَيْتِ من
يَنْتَهونَ من	يَنْتَهي من تَنْتَهي من	اِنْتَهَوْا من	اِنْتَهى من اِنْتَهَتْ من

In formal Arabic verbs whose جذر begins with و lose the و in the present tense of I وزن:

وَجَدَ، يَجِد 🎧

المضارع	
نَجِد	أَجِد
تَجِدونَ	تَجِد تَجِدينَ
يَجِدونَ	يَجِد تَجِد

The spoken verb meaning "to find" comes from a فصحى root, ²ل-ق-ي:

لقى، يلاقي

المضارع		الماضي		
بالاقي	بلاقي	لَقيت	لَقيت	أنا
بِتلاقي	بِتلاقي	لَقيت	لَقيت	أنتَ
بِتلاقي	بِتلاقي	لَقيتي	لَقيتي	أنتِ
بيلاقي	بيلاقي	لَقى	لَقى	هو
بِتلاقي	بِتلاقي	لَقِت	لَقِت	هي
بِنلاقي	بِنلاقي	لَقينا	لَقينا	نحن احنا
بِتلاقوا	بِتلاقوا	لَقيتوا	لَقيتوا	أنتو
بيلاقوا	بيلاقوا	لَقوا	لَقوا	هنّ همّ

تـمـرين ١: الجذر والوزن (في الصف)

اكتبوا كل الافعال الجديدة في الوزن المناسب:

المصدر	المضارع	الماضي	الوزن
			I فَعَلَ ، يَفعل
			II فَعَّلَ ، يُفَعِّل ، التَّفعيل
			VIII اِفتَعَل ، يَفتَعِل ، الاِفتِـعال
			X اِستَفعَل ، يَستَفعِل ، الاِستِفعال

---

²This verb is actually a mixing of two different wazns (لَقى,يلقى -- لاقى، يلاقي), both of which exist, but common usage is الماضي of one wazn and المضارع of the other.

تمـريـن ٢: المفردات الجديدة (في البيت) 🎧

اكتبوا كلمة من الكلمات الجديدة في كل جملة:

Pay close attention to the prepositions; they will help you find the right word.

١. أحب قراءة الجرائد و .... العربية كثيراً. واليوم قرأت في جريدة "الأيام" اليمنية .... ممتازة عن البرنامج الاقتصادي الجديد للحكومة اليمنية.

٢. هذه صورة صديقتي ساندي ووالدتها وأختها

.... واحد من

في شارع "برودواي" في نيو يورك.

٣. ....، وبعد سنة ونصف من مقابلات العمل، .... ابن عمّي سعيد .... ممتازة وبمرتّب ممتاز في وزارة الاقتصاد.

٤. كنت سعيدة جداً بتجربتي في الحياة في فرنسا ولم أشعر بـ .... عندما عشت هناك.

٥. .... كثير من الشباب العرب من مصر وسوريا وفلسطين في السفر الى السعودية والإمارات لأن .... العمل هناك كثيرة.

٦. في رأيك، هل هذا الفيلم .... للأولاد في عمر الـ ١٢ سنة؟

٧. كانت والدتي – الله يرحمها – دائماً .... ـني على الدراسة.

٨. قررت المدرسة أن .... ٣ طلاب لأنّهم كانوا يتغيّبون عن صفوفهم كثيراً ولأنهم .... في كل امتحاناتهم. قررت المدرسة ألا تقبلهم في السنة القادمة.

٩. كانت لها علاقات عاطفية كثيرة ولكنّها أخيراً تَزَوَّجَت و ....

١٠. ما زلنا نتذكر "مارتن لوثر كينغ الابن" عندما قال "عندي .... "!

١١. هذه البنت ـــــــــــــــ في ماذا ستفعل بعد أن ـــــــــــــــ من الدراسة في الجامعة.

١٢. أخذت المديرة اجازتها السنوية ولا أظنّ أنها سـ ـــــــــــــــ الى المكتب قبل أسبوعين.

🎧 **تـمـريـن ٣: الأفعال الجديدة (في البيت)** 🎧

اكتبوا الأفعال الجديدة في هذه الجمل.

You will use the same verbs more than once.

١. أحياناً أشعر أنّي لن ـــــــــــــــ من واجباتي !! أمس ـــــــــــــــ منها في الساعة الثانية بعد نصف الليل!

٢. يا شباب، هل ـــــــــــــــ أنّ الطقس سيكون أحسن غداً؟

٣. ـــــــــــــــ وظيفة جديدة للصيف القادم، الحمد لله! وأنت يا كريم، هل ـــــــــــــــ وظيفة للصيف؟

٤. يا سامية، هل ـــــــــــــــ الكتب التي كنت بحاجة اليها؟

٥. هم ـــــــــــــــ أنّ حياتهم صعبة ولكني لا ـــــــــــــــ أنها صعبة إلى هذه الدرجة!

٦. كانت مرتّباتنا قليلة و ـــــــــــــــ قليلة إلى الآن!

٧. ـــــــــــــــ نسكن في نفس بيتنا القديم قرب المستشفى الحكوميّ.

تـمـريـن ٤: المفردات في جمل (في البيت) 🎧
استمعوا إلى جمل المفردات واكتبوا الجمل من "أخيراً" الى "الغربة".

تـمـريـن ٥: اسألوا زملاءكم (في الصف)

You have learned some synonyms in the new vocabulary. Perhaps because of its long history and wide geographical use, Arabic has many synonyms that you will need to learn to communicate with different speakers and in formal and informal situations. To ensure that you are activating new words (and not using an old word that might be a synonym), in this chapter we begin to italicize the words for which you should use new vocabulary. Focus on using the new words as you ask your classmates these questions. Get as many relevant details as you can, but work quickly so that you can interact with several different partners.

Which of your classmates:

1. Had *a job* they would like to *return* to next summer? What is it? How is the salary?

2. Has a sibling, cousin, or friend whose family is *encouraging him* or *her* to marry and *settle* down? What do they tell these people?

3. Knows someone who has *failed* (في) a class? What would they do if they failed a class? Would they retake it?

4. Knows someone who feels *like a stranger* in this country? What should they do? Where can they find help?

5. Has some tough decisions *ahead of her* or him this year? What are they?

6. *Thinks that firing* an employee who misses work a lot is *appropriate*? How would they fire them?

7. Knows where you can *find* good articles and *journals* about the Middle East?

8. *Thinks that* job opportunities will be plentiful when they *finish* their studies? Why or why not?

القصة بالعامية

تمرين ٦: "ليش قررت ابقى بأمريكا؟" / "أخبارنا ممتازة" /

"ليه قررت اعيش في أمريكا؟" **(في البيت)** 🎧

استمعوا الى محمد واكتبوا فقرة لكل سؤال:	استمعوا الى حسن واكتبوا فقرة لكل سؤال:
Give as many details as you can.	Give as many details as you can.
١. ليه محمد قرر يعيش في أمريكا؟	١. ليش قرر حسن يبقى بأميركا؟
٢. كان عايز يعمل ايه بعد ما خد الدكتوراه؟	٢. شو كان بده يعمل بعد ما أخد الدكتوراه؟
٣. كان بيعمل ايه في جامعة القاهرة؟ كان مبسوط هناك ولّا لأ؟ ليه؟	٣. شو كان بيعمل بجامعة دمشق؟ كان مبسوط هونيك ولّا لأ؟ ليش؟؟
٤. تفتكروا محمد كان مبسوط أكتر في مصر ولّا في أمريكا؟ ليه؟	٤. بتظنوا إنُّه (إنّو) حسن مبسوط أكتر بالشام أو بأميركا؟ ليش؟
٥. اسمعوا محمد بيتكلم عن الماضي وكان بيعمل ايه في جامعة القاهرة:	٥. اسمعوا حسن يحكي عن شو كان بيعمل بجامعة دمشق:
Write the verbs. How does he express the past here and why?	Write the verbs. How does he express the past here and why?
	٦. شاهدوا الفيديو "أخبارنا ممتازة": مين بيحكي ومع مين؟ شو هي الأخبار وليش هي ممتازة؟

🎧 **تمرين ٧: المفردات في جمل (في البيت)** 🎧

استمعوا إلى جمل المفردات واكتبوا الجمل من "فرصة" الى "وظيفة".

القواعد ١

Sentence Complements أَنَّ وإنَّ

The word "that" in English has three completely different uses: (1) To point to something ("**that** chair"), (2) to identify or specify a noun ("the long report **that** you wrote"), and (3) to introduce a sentence containing reported information or opinion ("I read **that** she died"). Note that the first two uses refer to nouns, while the third use involves a sentence that complements a verb (e.g., "to say that," "to read that," "to think that," "to remember that"). These three different functions are fulfilled by different words in Arabic. We will focus on the third function here, linking verbs to sentence complements.

In English verbs used to report information and opinions can take sentence complements with the conjunction "that," such as:

Mike thinks *that history is interesting.*
Susan says *that she's not coming.*
Mary knows *that she wants to go to law school.*
I read that *the economy is doing better.*

This conjunction is frequently omitted in spoken English, however. While the sentences above might occur more often in writing and formal contexts, they are typically heard in the following form:

Mike thinks *history is interesting.*
Susan says *she's not coming.*
Mary knows *she wants to go to law school.*
I read *the economy is doing better.*

In Arabic, however, the equivalent of "that" is not usually omitted, and in formal Arabic, it cannot be omitted. The Arabic equivalents to verbs such as "to think that," "to know that," "to read that," "to say that," must be linked to a sentence complement with the Arabic equivalent to "that," أَنَّ[3].

In formal Arabic, sentence complements must be introduced with أَنَّ. In addition to ظنَّ, the following verbs you know can also take أَنَّ. Memorize these verb phrases as units so that you remember to use أَنَّ when forming complex sentences:

يعرف أَنَّ : أعرف أَنَّ الحصول على الدكتوراه سيأخذ ٥ سنوات.

قرأ أَنَّ : قرأتُ في الجريدة أَنَّه مات، الله يرحمه.

شعر بأَنَّ : يشعر بأَنَّ والده لا يشجعه على دراسة المسرح.

فهم أَنَّ : فهمت أَنَّ العودة الى بلدها تعني انقطاع العلاقة.

---

[3] Do not confuse this particle with the particle أنْ, which links a main verb to a dependent verb. The difference between أَنَّ and أنْ in Arabic parallels the English distinction between "that" and "to" in sentences like "I thought that he was better" and "I refused to visit him." Just as they are not interchangeable in English (we do not say, for example, "I thought to he be better" or "I refused that I visit him"), they mean different things in Arabic as well.

تذكّر أنَّ :	تذكرتُ أنَّهم لن يكونوا في البيت اليوم.
يعني أنَّ :	الطقس مثلج، وهذا يعني أنَّنا سنتأخر.
علم أنَّ :	علمت المديرة أنَّكِ ما انتهيت من كتابة المقالة.
أظنّ أنَّ :	أظنّ أنَّهم استقرّوا في حياتهم.

In formal Arabic, the verb قال / يقول *to say* requires إنَّ:

| قال إنَّ : | تقول الجرائد إنَّ الطقس سيبقى بارداً لِعدّة أيام. |

In formal Arabic أنَّ behaves like another conjunction you have learned, لأنَّ, in that it must be followed by a noun or attached pronoun heading a جملة اسمية —in fact لأنَّ consists of لِ + أنَّ, so you already know the pronoun suffixes.

أنِّي ...	*that I*
أنَّكَ -كِ ...	*that you*
أنَّهُ ...	*that he/it*
أنَّها ...	*that she / it*
أنَّنا ...	*that we*
أنَّكم ...	*that you*
أنَّهم ...	*that they*

In spoken Arabic the conjunction إنّه (also spelled إنّو) or إنّ is used, often as a fixed word, and pronouns do not have to be attached:

قال إنّه بيحب وظيفته وما بده يلاقي وظيفة جديدة.

بحس إنّه أنا ما رح اخلّص هالشغل قبل الموعد ورح افشل!

عرفتوا إنّه رفيقنا هِشام رح يتجوز ويستقرّ أخيراً؟!

قال إنّه بيحب شغله ومش عايز يلاقي شغل جديد.

دايماً باحس إني مش حاخلّص الشغل قبل المعاد وحافشل!

عرفتوا إنَّ زميلنا هاشم حيتجوز ويستقرّ أخيراً؟!

Finally, remember that in print, أنَّ will usually not carry shadda and will resemble أنْ. However, these two particles are used and pronounced differently, and you must learn which verbs take أنْ and which verbs take أنَّ. It is important to pay attention to what **follows** أنْ: Remember that أنْ must be followed by a جملة فعلية headed by المضارع المنصوب, while أنَّ must be followed by a جملة اسمية. It is also a good idea to memorize أنْ or أنَّ as a unit with verbs that take one or the other, as you do with prepositions. This list contains the verbs you have learned so far that take either أنْ or أنَّ:

أنَّ + جملة اسمية *that*	أنْ + جملة فعلية *to*
ظنّ أنَّ	أراد أنْ
عرف أنَّ	استطاع أنْ
قرأ أنَّ	رغب في أنْ
علم بأنَّ / علم أنَّ	رفض أنْ
شعر بأنَّ / شعر أنَّ	يحب أنْ
تذكّر أنَّ	قرر أنْ
كتب أنَّ	شجّع .. على أنْ
فهم أنَّ	يمكن أنْ
(هذا) يعني أنَّ	

تمرين ٨: أنّ (في البيت)

What information or opinions would you like to report?

١. الجو ممطر وهذا يعني أنّ ....
• ....

٢. ظنَّت امّي أنّ ....
• ....

٣. أشعر بأنّ ....
• ....

٤. هل تعرفين أنّ ....
• ....

٥ – قرأت في الجريدة أنّ ....

• ....

٦ – الاستاذ يقول إنّ ....

• ....

٧ – أنتم لا تعلمون أنّ ....

• ....

٨ – كلنا نفهم أنّ ....

• ....

٩ – لا أحد يعرف أنّ ....

• ....

١٠ – اليوم في الصباح تذكرت أنّ ....

• ....

تـمـريـن ٩: ما الخبر؟ عرفت أنّ . . . (في الصف)

Reporting news or information, be it official or gossip, involves using verbs with أنّ. Think of and write down a piece of news or gossip that you read, found out about yourself, or heard from someone else. Use the verbs قرأ أنّ, عرف أنّ, قال إنّ, ظنّ أنّ. When you are finished, turn your paper over and whisper your piece of news to الجار/الجارة on your right. Then pass on what the person on your left just told you. Take turns hearing and reporting the news until time is called. Then, tell your classmates the last thing you heard. How far is it from the original?

القصة بالفصحى

تـمرين ١٠: لماذا قررت البقاء هنا؟ (في البيت وفي الصف) 🎧

Watch القصة بالفصحى and answer the questions below. The dictation exercise can be completed in the book or online.

1. At home: Imagine that tomorrow you will host a webinar for new immigrants from Arab countries to the US. You have asked محمد أبو العلا to be a guest on the show to talk about his experiences as an immigrant. To prepare, listen to محمد tell his story بالفصحى. It is appropriate for this to be a formal discussion, so listen for language models you can use while interviewing or being interviewed.

2. In class: In groups of three, play the roles of host, Mohammad, and Malak. As the host, ask your guests specific questions about their experiences. As Mohammad or Malak, tell your story from your character's perspective but feel free to add creative details.

3. استمعوا إلى محمد واكتبوا ما يقول: As you listen and write, pay attention to sentence patterns. Whenever you hear و you should be thinking about what two or more things are being linked. Often, this link involves a repeated grammatical form, such as a pair of مصادر or فعل مضارع, etc. What new word do you hear for جاء إلى؟ Listen also for a new connector, إذ (this is not the same as إذا *if*), that Mohammad uses twice. What does it seem to mean?

لماذا (١) .... (٢) .... (٣) في أمريكا؟ ....

حضرت إلى (٤) .... (٥) .... خمس عشرة

(٦) .... (٧)، .... (٨) .... في

(٩) .... من دراستي و(١٠) .... إلى مصر، إذ

(١١) .... (١٢) .... (١٣) .... في جامعة

القاهرة، و(١٤) .... كذلك (١٥) .... بعض

(١٦) .... في (١٧) .... (١٨) .... " "، ؛

ولكن بعد (١٩) .... (٢٠) .... الدكتوراه،

(٢١) .... (٢٢) .... (٢٣) ....

(٢٤) .... أمامي هنا (٢٥) .... ، و(٢٦) ....

(٢٧) .... (٢٨) .... (٢٩). و .... ملك على

(٣٠) .... (٣١) .... ، لأنها كانت (٣٢) .... هنا،

ولكني لم (٣٣) .... (٣٤) .... (٣٥) ....،

و (٣٦) .... أستطع أيضاً (٣٧) ....،

إذ (٣٨) .... الجامعة، و(٣٩) .... (٤٠) ....

يعني (٤١) .... الحمد لله، (٤٢) .... (٤٣) ....

مترجماً في الامم (٤٤) .... ، و(٤٥) .... حياتنا

(٤٦) .... ، ولكني (٤٧) .... (٤٨) .... أشعر بـ

(٤٩) .... هنا.

القواعد ٢

نفي الماضي: لم + المضارع المجزوم 🎧

You know how to negate الماضي with ما, as in: ما شربت قهوة اليوم. This pattern is shared among all varieties of Arabic. However, while it is the normal way to negate the past tense in spoken Arabic, it is not generally used in modern written formal Arabic. Rather, the particle لَم is used with المضارع to give the meaning of the negated past[4]:

she did not work	=	لم تَعمَلْ = ما عَمِلت
he did not find	=	لم يَجِدْ = ما وَجَدَ

In case of this negation construction, المُضارع takes a form called المُضارع المَجزوم, which is the third and final type of المُضارع. In particular, note that the verb forms for the persons هم, أنتم, and أنتِ omit the final ن. The final سُكون on the other person appears only in fully vocalized texts. Learn to recognize these endings when you see or hear them, but be aware that it is the particle لم that signals the negation of the past. The following chart shows the endings of المضارع المجزوم on the verb يفعل:

لم + المُضارع المَجزوم

لم نَفعَلْ	لم أفعَلْ
لم تَفعَلوا	لم تَفعَلْ لم تَفعَلي
لم يَفعَلوا	لم يَفعَلْ لم تَفعَلْ

When you are writing formal compositions, practice using لم instead of ما to negate past tense verbs.

---

[4] In classical Arabic both structures are used and there seems to be a slight difference in verbal aspect between the two. In modern Arabic, though, the difference in the usage is primarily the degree of formality.

تمـرين ١١: المضارع المجزوم (في البيت)

A. The events described in these sentences did not actually take place. Rewrite the sentences and use لم + المضارع المجزوم to indicate this:

مثال: سافرتُ إلى لبنان. ←——— لم أسافرْ إلى لبنان.

١. زاروا الجبال العالية والبحر الجميل وشعروا براحة كبيرة.

٢. أخذتْ أمي استراحة قصيرة.

٣. استمتعتَ بالجلسة مع الدكتور.

٤. اِلتحق أبناء عمي بالجيش.

٥. نزلتم معاً في نفس الغرفة في الفندق.

٦. قرأوا المقالة الجديدة في مجلّة «الأهرام الاقتصادي».

٧. حصلتِ على وظيفة مناسبة.

٨. شاهدتُ مباراة كرة السلة.

٩. سافر الرئيس العراقي إلى سوريا لمقابلة الرئيس.

١٠. رجعنا من الجولة تعبانين.

B. Choose five of the above sentences to write out an expanded version of them by making up a reason why the action did not take place:

مثال:

سافرتُ إلى لبنان. ←——— لم أسافرْ إلى لبنان بسبب المشاكل السياسية.

المضارع المرفوع والمنصوب والمجزوم

Review the particles that govern the three المضارع endings. Remember that the **default form** of المضارع is المرفوع. In other cases, the following rules apply:

المضارع المجزوم follows these particles:	المضارع المنصوب follows these particles:	المضارع المرفوع follows these particles:
لَمْ	أنْ	سَـ / سَوفَ
	ألّا (أنْ + لا)	لا
	لِـ	
	لَنْ	

تمـريـن ١٢: المضارع المرفوع والمنصوب والمجزوم (في البيت) 🎧

Complete these sentences by writing the verb in parentheses in the correct form with the appropriate المرفوع, المنصوب or المجزوم endings:

١. قال سليم إنه لن _____ بالاستقرار إلّا بعد أنْ _____

على وظيفة. (شعر، حصل)

٢. قرّروا ألّا _____ على شركة طيران الشرق الأوسط. (سافر)

٣. اختي لا _____ في الزواج الآن لأنّها صغيرة. (رغب، ما زال)

٤. أخرج من البيت عادةً في الثامنة صباحاً و _____ في الرابعة بعد الظهر. (عاد)

٥. أقاربي لا _____ أنّ الشركة فصلتني من العمل. (عرف)

٦. كانت مشغولة جداً ولذلك لم _____ موعدها مع الدكتور. (تذكّر)

٧. لماذا لم _____ يا وفاء؟ ظننت أنّك جوعانة ! (أكل)

٨. متى سـ _____ لزيارتنا؟ (جاء + أنتم)

٩. لماذا _____ أنْ _____ مع عائلتكِ؟ (رفض، سكن)

١٠. سـ _____ إلى النادي بعد الانتهاء من المذاكرة إن شاء الله. (ذهب + أنا)

١١. لم _____ بخبر وفاة عمّتهم إلّا بعد ٣ أسابيع. (علم)

١٢. قالت هِند إنها لن _____ اجازتها السنوية في باريس هذه السنة. (قضي)

١٣. لن _____ أنْ _____ معكم طويلاً اليوم. (استطاع، جلس)

١٤. قرروا أنْ _____ أمام المركز و _____ الجولة من هناك.

(تجمّع، بدأ)

مراجعة النفي

Negation is one aspect of Arabic grammar in which there are notable differences between the formal and informal registers, mostly in the particles used. Formal Arabic uses the specialized negation particles you have learned, whereas in spoken Arabic, ما is more commonly used. You have also heard مش used in colloquial Arabic for ليس . Review the negation particles in formal Arabic:

المصري	الشامي	Negates	Particle
ما .. ش	ما	الفعل المضارع	لا + المضارع المرفوع
ما .. ش	ما	الفعل الماضي	ما + الماضي
مش حَـ	ما رح/حَـ	المستقبل	لن + المضارع المنصوب
ما .. ش	ما	الماضي	لم + المضارع المجزوم
مش	مو	Existential sentences[5]	ليس + جملة اسمية

تمريـن ١٣: النفي (في البيت أو في الصف)

You feel like saying "No!" to everything today. Answer these أسئلة accordingly, using as many different negation forms as you can. In writing, be formal and write in all the منصوب, مرفوع , and مجزوم endings on the verbs. In speaking, use the variety you are learning.

١. هل عرفت أنّ صديقك يعيش في الكويت الآن؟

٢. في رأيك، هل الفشل أصعب شيء في الحياة؟

٣. هل قرّرت أنْ تخرج مع زملائك بالليل؟

٤. هل تحب/ين أنْ تسافر/ي معنا لنشاهد البحر والجبال؟

٥. هل قرأت أنّ شركة "دل" ستفصل ٥٠٠ موظف؟

٦. هل تذكّرت أنّ الموعد مع الدكتور غداً؟

٧. هل ستأخذ/ين إجازة في الأسبوع القادم؟

٨. هل هناك علاقة بينك وبينها؟

٩. هل تريد/ين أن تعمل/ـي معنا على الواجب؟

١٠. هل يمكنك أنْ تجيء/تجيئي معنا الى الفندق لنقابل الأستاذ؟

١١. هل ستقضي/ن العطلة مع عائلتك؟

---

[5] In addition to existential sentences, ليس also negates other kinds of جمل اسمية and can be conjugated for person. We will introduce this use of ليس in *Al-Kitaab Part 2*.

القراءة

تمرين ١٤: "أرغب في الحصول على منحة دراسية" (في الصف)

1. First read: Be sure to read both pages of the text. Using good reading strategies, skim through the text that follows. What kind of text is it and how can you tell? What kinds of information can you expect to find upon closer reading?

2. Second read: Who are these letters from? What kinds of generalizations can you make?

3. What is the most popular destination? لماذا في رأيك؟

4. Reading strategies: You can see that there is not much overt punctuation in these letters. Use the Arabic punctuation—the connectors such as و and ف — to help you separate the prose into sentences to focus on. Get as much as you can out of the text and discuss بالعربية: If you could give one منحة to someone in this group, who would you choose and why?

أرغب في الحصول على منحة دراسية

الدولة : فلسطين

عنوان الموضوع : فلسطين - رام الله

انا شاب فلسطيني ارغب بالحصول على منحة للماجستير مع العلم اني حاصل على شهادة بكالوريوس Computer Science بتقدير جيد . ارجو من حضرتكم الكريمة مساعدتي بأي وسيلة كانت مع الشكر الجزيل لكم ولجهودكم .

الدولة : فلسطين

عنوان الموضوع : القدس

هذه رسالة اوجهها الى الرابطة الليبية لحقوق الانسان . انا شابة فلسطينية اريد منكم مساعدتي في الحصول على منحة دراسية في كندا مع العلم انني لم انتهي بعد من دراستي اي انني لم اتخرج بعد وسوف اتخرج بإذن الله هذه السنة في شهر ٥ او ٤ وسأخضع لامتحانات شهادة الوزارة والثانوية العامة في شهر ٦ وسأنتهي في بداية الشهر ٧ او في منتصفه . وارجو منكم مساعدتي في الحصول على منحة للدراسة خارج البلد وفي كندا بالتحديد لرغبتي الشديدة في ذلك مع فائق الاحترام والشكر .

الدولة : فلسطين

عنوان الموضوع : القدس

انا شاب فلسطيني من اسرة متوسطة الحال وحلمي ان احصل على منحة لدراسة الهندسة المعمارية في بلد من اوروبا بالأخص الدول الناطقة بالانجليزية لانني جيد ما الى حد مع العلم انني السنة القادمة انهي دراستي الثانوية واني بدأت التحضير للجامعة فارجو ان تساعدوني في الحصول على منحة وشكراً .

الدولة : اليمن

الإيميل: NSRI17@HOTMAIL.COM   التليفون : ٠٠٩٦٧٧٣٣٧٢٠٩٩٧

عنوان الموضوع : اليمن

انا طالب يمني حاصل على شهادة ثانوية بمعدل ٨٥,٣٧ ارغب في الحصول على منحة لدراسة ادارة الأعمال في اي جامعة معتمدة في العالم وياريت تكون في كندا او امريكا او في اي دولة متقدمة . وانا اناشد ذوي الأختصاص في هذا الشأن واملي فيهم كبير حيث انني عندي الهمة للدراسة والعزيمة والإصرار وحيث ان فرص المنح الدراسية في اليمن قليلة خصوصا لسكان الريف .

١

الدولة : الجزائر

الإيميل: FLYBACK-WC@HOTMAIL.FR   التليفون : ٠٦٦٣٤٦٧٥١٣

عنوان الموضوع : الجزائر

السلام عليكم ورحمة الله وبركاته.انا شاب جزائري وطالب جامعي فرع لغة انجليزية اتوجه الى الرابطة الليبية لحقوق الانسان ان تساعدني في تحقيق حلمي المتمثل في الحصول على منحة دراسية لدراسة اللغة الانجليزية في كندا...بالتوفيق لجميع الاخوة الطموحين.

الدولة : فلسطين

عنوان الموضوع : فلسطين\الخليل\ايطا

السـلام عليكم ورحمة الله وبركاته يعني انا قرأت كل المشاكل والهموم وبصراحة تأكدت انه المثل اللي بيقول اللي بيشـوف هموم غيره بتهون عليه همومه، والله يعينكوا ويصبركوا ويعطيكوا اللي ببالكو . انا مشـكلتي انه انا ما جبت معدل منيح بالتوجيهي ٧٥ جيد يعني ناجح مع انه انا باسـتطاعتي اجيب في الثمانين ، بس وفاة امي الله يرحمها عملت فيَّ شغلات . منيح اللي نجحت ، وبعدين لما كنت بدي ادرس بالجامعة سـبحان الله والله ما كان معنا نشتري خبز أكل للدار فاضطريت اشتغل واساعد أبوي انا واخي اللي ترك المدرسة وهو بالتوجيهي مع انه كل معدلاته بالـ ٩٠ . بس هيك الدنيا بدها ، والواحد دايما يحكي الحمد لله . واتمنى انه تساعدونا بمنحة دراسية لانه والله نفسي ادرس بالجامعة وامنية حياتي وحلم عمري اني أفوت الجامعة وشكراً .

الدولة : فلسطين\ الخليل

الإيميل: amort_alzaman@hotmail.com

التليفون : ٠٥٩٩٤٧٢٢٠٢

عنوان الموضوع : محافظة الخليل الحاووز الاول

أنا طالبة انهيت دراستي الثانوية العامة السنة وارغب بشدة الحصول ع منحة دراسية لانهاء دراستي والتخرج بتفوق من الجامعة لانه بجد الحالة الاقتصادية سيئة جدا وانا متفوقة بدراستي واحب الدراسة جدا واريد ان ادرس مختبرات طبية بكل تمني ورجاء. ارجو منكم مساعدتي ومساعدة طلاب فلسطين بالحصول على منح دراسية وتكملة دراسـتنا بنجاح لتحقيق شيء ما بحياتنا وارجو الرد علينا واعطاءنا فرص .

الاستماع: مع العائلة والأصدقاء

تمريـن ١٥: "أنا جدة خالد" (في البيت) 🎧

Watch the video "أنا جدة خالد"

استمعوا واكتبوا:

١. من يتكلم؟ ماذا نعرف عن حياتها؟ ماذا فهمت عن قصة زواجها؟

٢. ما رأيها في بقاء محمد في أمريكا؟

٣. ما رأيها في ملك، زوجة محمد؟ لماذا؟

٤. ماذا تريد لِخالد؟

5. After you have understood the content of the text, go back and listen again to the grammar. Listen, in particular, to the grammatical endings on the nouns. You will hear endings such as وفاته *his death*, in which the formal grammatical ending affects the pronunciation of the suffix ـه. What else do you notice?

الكتابة

تمريـن ١٦: نشاط كتابة (في البيت)

A university in an Arab country has announced a new program for foreign students to come and study Arabic language and culture there. Write a letter of application to the program, using these formulaic opening and closing phrases:

حضرة الأستاذ الدكتور

It is appropriate to address the letter to (opening)

تَحِيّة طَيِّبة وبعد، فـ . . .

Warm greetings (formulaic opening for letters)

وتفضّلوا بقبول شكري واحترامي،

Please accept my thanks and respect, (closing)

الحوار

اللغة والثقافة

The preposition مع can also indicate possession, as in the following expressions:

مَعِك مصاري   مَعاك فلوس
you have money

مَعِك حق!   مَعاك حق!
You are right! (literally, right is with you)

تمرين ١٧: "انت بس ارجع" / "انت بس ارجع"   (في البيت) 🎧

استمعوا الى طارق وعماد واكتبوا فقرة لكل سؤال:	استمعوا الى الحوار بالشامي واكتبوا فقرة لكل سؤال:
١. فين طارق وفين عماد؟ بيتكلموا عن ايه؟	١. وين غسان ووين عماد؟ عن شو عم يحكوا؟
٢. مين عنده مشكلة؟ ايه هي؟	٢. مين عنده مشكلة؟ شو هي؟
٣. صاحبه رأيه ايه في مشكلته؟ لازم يعمل ايه؟	٣. شو رأي رفيقه بمشكلته؟ شو لازم يعمل؟
٤. ايه رأيك في الموضوع؟ لازم يعمل ايه؟	٤. شو رأيك بالموضوع؟ شو لازم يعمل؟

تمـارين المراجعة

تمـرين ١٨: أوزان الفعل   (في البيت) 🎧

This exercise is available online only.

تمرين ١٩: كم؟ (في البيت)

اكتبوا الرقم مع الشكل المناسب لكل كلمة.

١. عمري الآن _____ وعندما أتخرج إن شاء الله سيكون عمري

_____ (سنة)

٢. لي _____ و _____ و

_____ و _____ (أخ، أخت، عمّ، خال)

٣. في عطلة الصيف سأذهب لزيارة عائلتي وسأبقى هناك _____.

(أسبوع)

٤. زوجتي مشغولة جداً بعملها في المستشفى ولا تنام أكثر من

_____ يومياً. (ساعة)

٥. عائلتي ما زالت تسكن في نفس البيت منذ _____. (سنة)

٦. في صفنا _____ و _____ و

_____ و _____. (طالبة،

طالب، كرسي، باب، طاولة)

٧. فيلمي المفضل هو _____

_____ وشاهدته _____. (مرة)

٨. أكبر صف درست فيه في الجامعة كان فيه _____. (طالب)

٩. في هذه المدينة _____. (جامعة)

تمـرين ٢٠: القراءة الجهرية (في البيت أو في الصف) 🎧

Read the following passage, first silently for comprehension, then aloud to practice pronunciation. When you are ready, record the passage and submit it to your teacher either online or as instructed by your teacher.

اسمي ماهر عاصي النوري، من عائلة النوري، وهي عائلة شامية قديمة وعريقة. ونحن تُجّار منذ مئات السنوات ونعمل في سوق الحَميدِيّة. والدي عاصي كان يتاجر بالقُطن المصري والهندي طوال حياته، وأنا قضيت سنوات كثيرة من عمري أعمل معه ، وعندما أصبح عندي أولاد بدأت آخذهم معي الى السوق عندما كانوا صغاراً ليساعدوا جدهم ويساعدوني ويتعلّموا التجارة ، والحمد لله أن ابني الثاني أسامة يحب هذا العمل ويرغب في أن يكون تاجراً مثل جده. أحب التجارة، وأفهمها جيداً، ولكن يوم التاجر طويل جداً وليس عنده عطل أو إجازات، ولذلك ، عندما علمت بفَتح وظيفة في وزارة الاقتصاد قررت أن آخذها. كنت أقضي أيامي كلها في السوق، ولكن بعد أن وجدت الوظيفة أصبح عندي وقت أكثر للعائلة. مع الأسف، تُوُفِّيَت زوجتي أم طارق بعد ذلك بأربع سنوات وأصبح الأولاد بلا أم . . . . هذه إرادة اللّه، والإنسان ليس أمامه إلا القبول بما يريده اللّه.

Grammar Reference Charts

Grammar Index فهرست القواعد

English–Arabic Glossary قاموس إنكليزي – عربي

Arabic–English Glossary قاموس عربي– إنكليزي

Grammar Reference Charts

بالفُصحى: Pronouns

ضمائر النصب Object of Verb	ضمائر الملكية Possessive / With Preposition	الضمائر المنفصلة Independent / Subject
يَعرِفــني	كِتابــي	أنا
يَعرِفــكَ	كِتابــكَ	أَنْتَ
يَعرِفــكِ	كِتابــكِ	أَنْتِ
يَعرِفــهُ	كِتابــهُ	هُوَ
يَعرِفــها	كِتابــها	هِيَ
يَعرِفــنا	كِتابــنا	نَحْنُ
يَعرِفــكُم	كِتابــكُم	أَنْتُم
يَعرِفــهُم	كِتابــهُم	هُمْ

بالشامي:

ضمائر النصب Object of Verb	ضمائر الملكية Possessive / With Preposition	الضمائر المنفصلة Independent / Subject
بيَعرِفــني	كتابــي	أنا
بيَعرْفــَك	كتابــَك	إنت
بيَعرْفــِك	كتابــِك	إنتِ (انتي)
بيَعرْفــهُ *	كتابــهُ - (كتابــو)	هُوَّ
بيَعرِفــ(ـهـ)ـا *	كتابــ(ـهـ)ـا *	هِيِّ
بيَعرِفــنا	كتابــنا	نِحْنا
بيَعرِفــكُن	كتابــكُن	إنتو
بيَعرِفــ(ـهـ)ُن *	كتابــ(ـهـ)ُن *	هِنّ

* The هـ is silent in these pronouns.

بالمصري:

ضمائر النصب Object of Verb	ضمائر الملكية Possessive / With Preposition	الضمائر المنفصلة Independent / Subject
بِيعرَفـني	كِتابـي	أنا
بِيعرَفـَك	كِتابـَك	إنتَ
بِيعرَفـِك	كِتابـِك	إنتِ (انتي)
بِيعرَفـُه *	كِتابـُه *	هُوَ
بِيعرَفـها	كِتابـها	هِيَ
بِيعرَفـنا	كِتابـنا	إحنا
بِيعرَفـكو	كِتابـكو	إنتُو
بِيعرَفـهُم	كِتابـهُم	هُمَّ

* The ه is silent in these pronouns.

تصريف الفعل: Verb Conjugation

المضارع المجزوم	المضارع المنصوب	المضارع المرفوع	الماضي	الضمير
أفْعَل	أفْعَل	أفْعَل	فَعَلْتُ	انا
تَفْعَل	تَفْعَل	تَفْعَل	فَعَلْتَ	أنتَ
تَفْعَلي	تَفْعَلي	تَفْعَليـنَ	فَعَلْتِ	أنتِ
يَفْعَل	يَفْعَل	يَفْعَل	فَعَل	هو
تَفْعَل	تَفْعَل	تَفْعَل	فَعَلَتْ	هي
نَفْعَل	نَفْعَل	نَفْعَل	فَعَلْنا	نحن
تَفْعَلوا	تَفْعَلوا	تَفْعَلونَ	فَعَلْتُم	أنتم
يَفْعَلوا	يَفْعَلوا	يَفْعَلونَ	فَعَلوا	هم

Grammar Endings on الفعل المضارع

المضارع المجزوم	المضارع المنصوب	المضارع المرفوع
Verbs following:	Verbs following:	Main verb in sentence Verbs following:
- لَمْ	- أَنْ - لَنْ - لِـ	سَـ / سَوفَ

Negation Particles and Their Usage

المصري	الشامي	Negates	Particle
ما .. ش	ما	الفعل المضارع	لا + المضارع المرفوع
ما .. ش	ما	الفعل الماضي	ما + الماضي
مش حَـ	ما رح/حَـ	المستقبل	لن + المضارع المنصوب
ما .. ش	ما	الماضي	لم + المضارع المجزوم
مش	مو	Sentences with no verb	ليس + جملة اسمية

Verbal Patterns أوزان الفعل

المصدر	المضارع	الماضي	الوزن
(varies)	يَفعُل يَحصُل يَفعَل يَذهَب يَفعِل يَنزِل يَفعِل يَعمِل	فَعَلَ حَصَلَ فَعَلَ ذَهَب فَعَلَ نَزَلَ فَعِلَ عَمِلَ	I
التَّفعيل التَّدخين	يُفَعِّل يُدَخِّن	فَعَّل دَخَّنَ	II
المُفاعَلة المُشاهَدة	يُفاعِل يُشاهِد	فاعَلَ شاهَدَ	III
الإفعال الإمْكان	يُفعِل يُمْكِن	أفعَلَ أمْكَنَ	IV
التَّفَعُّل التَّذَكُّر	يَتَفَعَّل يَتَذَكَّر	تَفَعَّل تَذَكَّر	V
التَّفاعُل التَّبادُل	يَتَفاعَل يَتَبادَل	تفاعَلَ تَبادَل	VI
الانْفِعال الانْقِطاع	يَنْفَعِل يَنْقَطِع	انْفَعَلَ انْقَطَعَ	VII
الافْتِعال الالْتِحاق	يَفْتَعِل يَلْتَحِق	افْتَعَلَ الْتَحَقَ	VIII
الاسْتِفْعال الاسْتِمْتاع	يَستَفْعِل يَستَمْتِع	اسْتَفْعَلَ اسْتَمْتَعَ	X

Grammar Index

فهرست القواعد

English Terms

Arabic Terms

قاموس إنجليزي – عربي

English – Arabic Glossary

English

Arabic

The term **AB** refers to **Alif Baa**, third edition.
The numbers refer to the lesson in which the term appears

English	Arabic
(to be) able 9	اِسْتَطاعَ ، يَسْتَطيع ، الاسْتِطاعَة قِدِر ، يِقِدِر قِدِر ، يِقْدَر
about (to talk ___) 7	عَنْ
about whom? 8	عَمَّن ؟ (عَنْ + مَن؟)
about what? 7	عَمَّ ؟ (عَن+ماذا؟)
(to be) absent from, miss (e.g.: __ school) 12	تَغَيَّبَ عن، يَتَغَيَّب ، التَّغَيُّب غاب (غِبت) ، يغيب غاب (غِبت) ، يِغيب
acceptable, passing 8	مَقْبول
accident 7	حادِث ج. حَوادِث حادْثة
(on) account of, because of 5	بِسَبَب + اسم
(making the mutual) acquaintance (of), getting to know (one other) 7	تَعارُف
(to become) acquainted with, get to know, meet 11	تَعَرَّف على ، يَتَعَرَّف على ، التَّعَرُّف على تْعَرَّف على ، يِتعَرَّف على اِتعَرَّف على، يِتعَرَّف على
activity 1	نَشاط ج. نَشاطات / أنْشِطة
actually 3	في الحَقيقة بِالحَقيقة
(in) addition to 12	بِالإضافة إلى بِالإضافة لـ بالإضافة لـ
address 1	عُنْوان ج. عَناوين عِنوان
adjective 5	صِفة ج. صِفات
admissions (e,g,: office of __) 2	القُبول
after (followed by a verb) 8	بَعْدَ أنْ (+ فعل) بَعد ما بَعد ما
afternoon 9	بَعْدَ الظُّهْر بَعد الضُّهر بَعد الضُّهر
age 2	عُمْر ج. أعْمار
ago, since 6	مُنْذُ مِن مِن
airplane AB	طائِرة ج. طائِرات طَيّارة ج. طَيّارات طيّارة ج. طَيّارات
Algeria AB	الجَزائِر
all 4	كُلّ (+ الجمع) كِلّ (+ الجمع)
also 2	أيْضاً كَمان كَمان
also, likewise 13	كَذلِك كَمان كَمان
always 2	دائِماً دائماً دائماً
Amman (capital of Jordan) AB	عَمّان
among, between 11	بَيْنَ بين بين
among (quantity) of 11	مِن

English	Arabic
ancient *(for things, not for people)* ,old *AB*	قَديم/ة
angry, annoyed; upset *AB*	زَعْلان/ة ج. زَعلانين
anthropology *3*	عِلم الإنْسان
(I was) appointed *(passive)* *12*	عُيِّنْتْ اتْعَيَّنْتْ اِتْعَيِّنْتْ
appointment, *(fixed)* time *10*	مَوْعِد ج. مَواعيد مَعاد
appropriate, suitable *13*	مُناسِب/ة مُناسِب/ة
Arab, Arabic *AB*	عَرَبيّ/ة ج. عَرَب
area, region *1*	مِنْطَقَة ج. مَناطِق مَنطقة مَنطقة
are not, is not	لَيْسَ مو ، ما مِش
army *3*	جَيْش ج. جُيوش
around, roughly *9*	حَوالَيْ حَوالي حَوالي
article *(e.g.: newspaper ___)* *13*	مَقالة ج. مَقالات
as, like *8*	كَما + جملة فعلية مِتل ما زي ما
as far as __ is concerned *5*	بالنسبة لِ ___ بالنِّسبة إلـ ___
as for..., *9*	أمّا ... فَـ...
astonishing, strange *AB*	عَجيب/ة ج. عَجيبون ، عَجيبين
aunt *(maternal)* *2*	خالة ج. خالات
aunt *(paternal)* *3*	عَمّة ج. عَمّات
autumn, fall *5*	الخريف
(to) awaken, wake up *10*	صَحا (صَحَوْتُ) ، يَصحو ، الصَّحْو فاق (فِقت) ، يْفيق صِحي (صِحيت) ، يِصحى

English	Arabic
Baccalaureate *7*	الثّانَويّة العامّة
bachelor's degree *2*	بَكالورْيوس
Bahrain *AB*	البَحْرَيْن
basketball *6*	كُرة السَّلة
bathroom *AB*	حَمّام ج. حَمّامات
(to) be, is *4, 10*	كانْ ، يَكون ، الكَوْن كانْ ، يْكون كانْ ، بِيكون
beautiful, pretty *AB*	جَميل/ة ج. جَميلون ، جَميلين حِلو/ة ج. حِلوين حِلوة ج. حِلوين
because *6*	لِأَنَّ (+ جملة اسمية) لَأَنَّهُ (لَأَنّو) لإنّ عَشان ، عَلَشان
because, since *13*	إذ
because of, on account of *5*	بِسَبَب (+ اسم)
because of that, for that reason, so, thus *6*	لِذَلِك مِنْشان هيك عَشان كِدا
(to) become *10*	أَصْبَحَ ، يُصْبِح صار ، يْصير بَقى ، يِبقى
before, in front of *(spatial)* *13*	أمامَ قِدّام قُدّام

English	Arabic
before, prior to 4	قَبْلَ أَنْ (+ المضارع المنصوب) قَبْل ما + verb قَبْل ما + verb
(to) begin 9	بَدَأَ ، يَبْدَأ ، البَدء بَدا ، يِبدا بَدَأ ، يِبدَأ
behind, beyond 5	خَلف
belonging to, for, have 7	لِـ + اسم/ضمير
(the) best...5	أَحْسَن
between, among 11	بَيْنَ بين بين
big (also: important; old) AB	كَبيرة ج. كِبار كُبيرة ج. كُبار كِبيرة ج. كُبار
the biggest or oldest 7	أَكْبَر (+ اسم نكرة)
black (m) AB	أَسْوَد ج. سود إسْوِد
book AB	كِتاب ج. كُتُب كُتاب
boy, son (also: child) AB	وَلَد ج. أولاد ج. وُلاد ج. وِلاد
boyfriend AB	صاحِب
bread AB	خُبْز خِبز عيش
break, rest period 10	اِسْتِراحة ج. اِسْتِراحات
breakfast 9	الفُطور الفُطور الفِطار
(to) eat breakfast 9	فَطَرَ ، يَفْطُر، الفُطور فِطِر، يِفطَر فِطِر، يِفطَر
brother AB	أخ ج. إخْوَة ج. إخْوة ج. إخْوات
building AB	بِناية ج. بِنايات بِنايِة عِمارة، ج. عِمارات
bus AB	أوتوبيس ج. أوتوبيسات
business administration 6	إدارة الأَعْمال
busy with 2	مَشْغول/ة بـ ج. مَشْغولون ، مَشْغولين
but AB	لِكِن بَسّ بَسّ
by, with (use with things) AB	بِـ
caliph, successor (note: m.) 4	خَليفة ج. خُلَفاء
car AB	سَيّارة ج. سَيّارات عَرَبيّة ج. عربيّات
cat AB	قِطّة ج. قِطَط بِسّة ج. بِسَس قُطّة ج. قُطَط
center 2	مَرْكَز ج. مَراكِز
chair AB	كُرْسي ج. كَراسي ، كَراسٍ كِرْسي
chance, opportunity 13	فُرْصة ج. فُرَص
(to) cheer (on), encourage (to) 13	شَجَّعَ على ، يُشَجِّع شَجَّع على ، يُشَجِّع ، التَّشْجيع شَجَّع على ، يِشَجِّع
chess 9	الشَّطَرَنْج
chicken AB	دَجاج دْجاج فِراخ

C

English	Arabic
child; boy, son *AB*	ولد ج. أولاد ج. وْلاد ج. وِلاد
childhood *4*	الطُّفولة
China *1*	الصّين
cinema, the movies *AB*	السّينما
city *AB*	مَدينة ج. مُدُن
class, classroom *AB*; season, semester *(e.g.: spring ___) 5*	فصْل ج. فُصول صَفّ ج. صُفوف
classmate, colleague *(m.) 4*	زَميل ج. زُمَلاء ج. زَمايِل زِميل ج. زَمايِل/زُمَلا
classmate, colleague *(f.) 4*	زَميلة ج. زَميلات زِميلة ج. زَميلات
clock *(also: hour; o'clock) AB*	ساعة ج. ساعات
close to, near *AB*	قَريب/ة (من) ج. قَريبون ، قَريبين قُرَيِّب/ة ج. قُراب قُرَيِّب/ة (من) ج قُرَيِّبين
cloudy, overcast *5*	غائِم مْغَيِّم مِغَيِّم
club *(e.g.: sport __) 9*	نادي (نادٍ) ج. نَوادي (نوادٍ)
coffee *AB*	قَهْوة
cold *(e.g.: I feel ____) AB*	بَرْدان /ة ج. بَرْدانين
cold *(e.g.:____ weather) 5*	بارد/ة بَرْد بَرَد
colleague; classmate *(m.) 4*	زَميل ج. زُمَلاء ج. زَمايِل زِميل ج. زَمايِل ، زُمَلا
colleague; classmate *(f.) 4*	زَميلة ج. زَميلات زِميلة ج. زَميلات
college, school in a university *3*	كُلِّيّة ج. كُلِّيّات كِلِّيّة ج. كِلِّيّات
coming *(e.g., week, year) 10*	قادِم/ة ج. قادِمون ، قادِمين جايي/ة ج. جايين جايّ/ة ج. جايين
commerce, trade *6*	التِّجارة
company *6*	شَرِكة ج. شَرِكات شِرْكة ج. شِرْكات شِرْكة
comparative *12*	مُقارَن/ة
congratulations *3*	مَبروك
(response to) congratulations *3*	بارَك اللَّهُ فيك الله يبارِك فيك/ لَك الله يبارك فيك/فيكي
(to) consider, think that *13*	ظَنَّ أنّ ، (ظَنَنْتُ أنَّ) ، يَظُنّ ، الظَّنّ ظَنّ (ظَنّيت) ، يْظُنّ إنّه (إنّو) افتَكَر ، يِفتِكِر إنّ
(to) continue to, still *(lit: do not cease) 13*	ما زالَ ، لا يَزال + المضارع المرفوع / اسم بَعد (pronoun +) لِسّه
copybook, notebook *AB*	دَفْتَر ج. دَفاتِر
(to) correspond, exchange letters *8*	راسَلَ ، يُراسِل ، المُراسَلة راسَل ، يُراسِل راسِل ، يِراسِل
country *2*	بَلَد ج. بِلاد / بُلْدان
(of) course, naturally *12*	طَبْعاً
cousin *(f., maternal) 3*	بِنْت خال/ة ج. بَنات خال/ة

English	Arabic
cousin (f., paternal) 3	بِنْت عَمّ/ة ج. بَنات عَمّ/ة
cousin (m., maternal) 3	إِبْن خال/ة ج. أَبْناء خال/ة ج. وُلاد خال/ة
cousin (m., paternal) 3	إِبْن عَمّ/ة ج. أَبْناء عَمّ/ة ج. وُلاد عَـمّ/ة ج. وِلاد عَمّ/ة
crazy 7	مَجْنون/ة ج مَجانين
(over) crowdedness 5	الإِزْدِحام الزَّحمة الزَّحمة
culture 1	الثَّقافة
(to be) cut off 11	اِنْقَطَعَ ، يَنْقَطِع ، الاِنْقِطاع اِنْقَطَع ، يِنْقِطِع اِنْقَطَع / اِتْقَطَع ، يِنْقِطِع / يِتْقِطِع
dance, dancing 6	رَقَصَ ، يَرْقُص ، الرَّقْص رَقَص ، يُرْقُص رَقَص ، يِرْقُص
darling, dear (m.) AB	حَبيب ج. أَحِبّاء ج حَبايِب ج حَبايِب
darling, dear (f.) AB	حَبيبَة ج. حَبيبات
daughter, girl AB	بِنْت ج. بَنات
day 6	يَوْم ج. أَيّام يوم ج. إِيّام يوم ج. إِيّام
daytime 2	النَّهـار النَّهار
death 7, 12	مَوْت ، وَفاة
deceased 7	مَرْحوم/ة ج. مَرْحومون ، مَرْحومين
(to) decide 12	قَرَّرَ ، يُقَرِّر ، التَّقْرير قَرَّر ، يْقَرِّر قَرَّر ، يِقَرِّر
decision 12	قَرار ج. قَرارات
degree (e.g. university), diploma 12	شَهادَة ج. شَهادات
degree (e.g. of temperature) 5	دَرَجَة ج. دَرَجات
delicious (also: good-hearted) AB	طَيِّب/ة ج. طَيِّبون ، طَيِّبين ج. طَيِّبين
department 1	قِسْم ج. أَقْسام
to descend, to leave the house; 9	نَزَل مِن ، يَنْزِل ، النُّزول طِلع مِن ، يِطلَع نِزِل مِن ، يِنزِل
descent, origin 5	أَصْل ج. أُصول
of _____ descent 5	مِن أَصْل (+ nisba adjective)
(to have a) desire to, want to 13	رَغِبَ في ، يَرْغَب في ، الرَّغْبة في كان بِدُّه كان عايز
desserts, sweets 4	الحَلَوِيّات ، الحُلُو الحِلو الحَلَوِيّات
dictionary 8	قاموس ج. قواميس
(to) die 7	ماتَ ، يَموت ، المَوْت مات ، يْموت ، الموت مات ، يِموت ، الموت
difficult, hard AB	صَعْب/ة
dinner 9	العَشاء العَشا العَشا
diploma, degree 12	شَهادة ج. شَهادات
director 12	مُدير ج. مُدَراء ، مُديرون ، مُديرين

English	Arabic
(to) dismiss, fire (e.g.: from a job) 13	فَصَل ، يَفْصِل ، الفَصْل فَصَل ، يفصِل فَصَل ، يِفصِل
distant (from), far AB	بَعيد (عَنْ) ج. بَعيدون ، بعيدين بْعاد ج. بُعاد بعيد ج. بُعاد
(to) do 8	فَعَل ، يَفْعَل ، الفِعل عِمِل ، يَعمِل عَمَل ، يِعمِل
doctor (m.) AB	دُكتور ج. دَكاتِرة ج. دَكاتْرة
doctor (f.) AB	دُكتورة ج. دُكتورات
dog AB	كَلْب ج. كِلاب كَلِب ج. كُلاب
door AB	باب ج. أبْواب ج. بْواب
(to) draw 6	رَسَم ، يَرْسُم ، الرَّسْم رَسَم ، يِرسُم رَسَم ، يِرسِم
dream 13	حُلْم ج. أحْلام حِلِم حِلْم
drill AB	تَمْرين ج. تَمارين
(to) drink AB	شَرِبَ ، يَشْرَب ، الشُّرب شِرِب ، يِشْرَب شِرِب ، يِشْرَب
the dual 6	المُثَنَّى
during, throughout 8	طِوال طول طول
each, every 11	كُلّ + اسم مُفرد في إضافة كِلّ
east 2	الشَّرق
easy AB	سَهْل/ة
(to) eat 4	أكَلَ ، يأكُل ، الأكْل أكَل ، ياكُل أكَل ، ياكُل
economics 7	الاقْتِصاد
Egypt AB	مِصْر مَصْر مَصِر
Egyptian 1	مِصريّ/ة مَصري/ة مَصري/ة
eight AB	ثَمانية ثْمانة ثَمانْية
eighty 5	ثَمانون ، ثَمانين ثْمانين
elementary, primary 4	ابْتِدائيّ/ة
eleven 5	أحَدَ عَشَر إدَعش حِداشر
emotional, romantic 11	عاطِفيّ/ة ج. عاطِفيّون ، عاطِفيّين
employee (white collar; m.) 2	مُوَظَّف ج. مُوَظَّفون ، مُوَظَّفين مُوَظَّف ج. مُوَظَّفين
employee (white collar; f.) 2	مُوَظَّفة ج. مُوَظَّفات مُوَظَّفة ج. مُوَظَّفات
(to) encourage (to), cheer (on) 13	شَجَّع على ، يُشَجِّع ، التَّشجيع شَجَّع على ، يْشَجِّع شَجَّع على ، يِشَجِّع
(got) engaged to 11	خُطِبَت لِ انْخَطَبِت لَ انْخَطِبِت لِ
engineer 11	مُهَنْدِس/ة ج. مُهَندِسون ، مُهَندِسين
engineering 3	الهَنْدَسة
English 1	انْجليزي/ة (انكليزي/ة) ج. انْجليز (انْكليز)

English	Arabic
(to) enjoy 10	اِسْتَمْتَعَ بِـ ، يَسْتَمْتِع بِـ ، الاِسْتِمْتاع بِـ
(to) enter, join (e.g.: school or army) 8	الْتَحَقَ بِـ ، يَلْتَحِق بِـ ، الاِلْتِحاق بِـ
(to) enter 8	دَخَلَ ، يَدْخُل ، الدُّخول دَخَل ، بِدخُل دَخَل ، يُدخُل
evaluation (comprehensive), grade 8	تَقْدير
evening 2	المَساء المَسا المِسا
every, each 11	كُلّ + اسم مُفرد في إضافة كِلّ
every day 4	كُلّ يَوْم كِلّ يوم كُلّ يوم
examination, test AB	اِمْتِحان ج اِمْتِحانات
example 1	مِثال ج. أَمْثِلة
excellent 8	مُمْتاز/ة ج. مُمتازون ، مُمتازين
except 9	إلّا
(to) exchange 11	تَبادَلَ ، يَتَبادَل ، التَّبادُل تْبادَل ، بِتْبادُل اِتْبادِل ، بِتْبادِل
(to) exchange letters, correspond 8	راسَلَ ، يُراسِل ، المُراسلة راسَل ، يُراسِل راسِل ، يراسِل
expensive 11	الـ(غالي)/ة ، (غالٍ)
experience (life___) 11	تَجْرِبة ج. تَجارِب تَجرُبة ج. تَجارُب
eye 5	عَيْن ج. عُيون ، أَعْيُن عين ج. عُيون عين
(to) fail 13	الفَشَل ، فَشِلَ (في) ، يَفْشَل فَشِل (بـ) ، بِفْشَل فَشَل (في) ، بِفْشَل
fall, autumn 5	الخَريف
(to) fall behind, be late 10	تَأَخَّرَ ، يَتَأَخَّر، التَّأَخُّر تْأَخَّر ، بِتْأَخَّر اِتْأَخَّر ، بِتْأَخَّر
family (i.e. immediate ___) 2	أُسْرَة ج. أُسَر عيلة ج. عِيَل عيلة ج. عائلات
family (i.e. extended___) 3	عائِلة ج. عائِلات عيلة ج. عِيَل عيل
family member, relative 3	قريب ج. أَقارِب / أَقْرِباء ج. قَرايبين ج. قَرايِب
far, distant (from) AB	بَعيد/ة (عَنْ) ج. بَعيدون ، بعيدين بْعيد ج بُعاد بِعيد ج بُعاد
father (more formal address) 1	والِد ج. والِدون ، والِدين بابا بابا
favorite 9	مُفَضَّل/ة
(to) feel (i.e.: an emotion) 5	شَعَرَ بِـ ، يَشْعُر بِـ ، الشُّعور بِـ حَسّ بـ ، يْحِسّ حَسّ بـ ، يِحِسّ
feminine 1	مُؤَنَّث
feel better! AB	سَلامتك
fifty 5	خَمْسين ، خَمْسون
finally, at last 13	أخيراً
(to) find 13	وَجَدَ ، يَجِد ، الوُجود لَقى(لْقيت) ، يْلاقي لَقى (لَقيت) ، يِلاقي
I did not find 13	لم أجِدْ = ما وَجَدتُ ما لقيت ما لقيتش
(to) find out about, learn of 12	عَلِمَ بِـ ، يَعْلَم بِـ ، العِلْم بِـ عِرِف ، يَعرِف عِرِف ، يِعرَف

F

English	Arabic
fine, OK *(said of people or things) AB*	جَيِّد/ة ج. جَيِّدون ، جَيِّدين مْنيح/ة ج. مْناح كْوَيِّس/ة ج. كْوَيِّسين
(to) finish *13*	إنْتَهى مِنْ ، يَنْتَهي ، الانْتِهاء خَلَّص من ، يْخَلِّص خَلَص ، يِخْلَص ، يِنتهي
(to) fire, dismiss *(e.g.: from a job) 13*	فَصَل ، يِفْصِل ، الفَصْل فَصَل ، يِفصِل فَصَل ، يِفصِل
first *(m.) 4*	أوَّل ج. أُوَل، أوائِل أوَّل
first *(f.) 4*	أولى
fish *(collective) 4*	سَمَك
five *AB*	خَمْسة خَمْسة
flight, trip *10*	رحلة ج. رحلات
football, soccer *6*	كُرة القَدَم
for, to, in order to *6*	لِ + مصدر/مضارع منصوب مِنْشان عَشان ، عَلَشان
for, in relation to *5*	بالنِّسْبة لِ بالنِّسْبة إلـ__
for, belonging to; have *7*	لِ + اسم/ضمير
foreign, strange *AB*	غَريب/ة ج. غُرَباء
foreign, foreigner *13*	أَجْنَبيّ/ة ج. أجانِب
foreign affairs *7*	الخارْجيّة الخارْجيّة الخارْجيّة
for that reason *6*	لِذلِك مِنْشان هيك عَشان كِدا
forty *5*	أرْبَعون ، أرْبَعين
four *AB*	أرْبَعة أرْبَعة
fourth *4*	رابِع/ة
frankly, honestly *10*	بصَراحة
French, French person *2*	فَرَنْسيّ/ة ج. فَرَنْسيّون ، فَرَنْسيّين فَرَنساوي ج فَرَنساويّين
Friday *6*	الجُمْعة
friend *(m.)*, boyfriend *AB*	صاحِب ج. أصْحاب ج. صْحاب ج. أصْحاب
friend *(f.)* girlfriend *AB*	صاحْبة ج. صاحِبات رفيقة ج. رفيقات صاحْبة ج. صاحْبات
friend *(m.) 4*	صَديق ج. أصْدِقاء رْفيق ج. رِفقات صاحِب ج. أصْحاب
friend *(f.) 4*	صَديقة ج. صَديقات رْفيقة ج. رفيقات صاحْبة ج. صاحْبات
from *1*	مِنْ
(in) front of, before *(spatial) 13*	أمام قِدّام قُدّام
fruits *4*	فَواكِه
future *8*	المُسْتَقْبَل
(future marker) 7	سَ ، سوفَ رَح ، حَـ حَـ
G game, match *10*	مُباراة ج. مُبارَيات ماتش ج. ماتشات
(to) gather *(together) 11*	تَجَمَّع ، يَتَجَمَّع ، التَّجَمُّع تْجَمَّع ، يِتْجَمَّع اتْجَمَّع ، يِتْجَمَّع

English	Arabic
gathering, meeting *10*	جَلْسة ج. جَلْسات
(to) get, obtain *6, 8*	حَصَلَ على ، يَحْصُل على ، الحُصول على أخَذ ، ياخُذ خَد ، ياخُد
general, public *7*	عامّ /ة
(to) get to know, become acquainted with, meet *11*	تَعَرَّف على ، يَتَعَرَّف على ، التَعَرُّف على تْعَرَّف على ، بِتْعَرَّف على إتعَرَّف على ، بِتعَرَّف على
get well soon! *AB*	سَلامتك
get well soon *(reply)*! *AB*	الله يسَلّمك
getting to know *(one another)*, making the mutual acquaintance *(of)* *7*	تَعارُف
girl, daughter *AB*	بِنْت ج. بَنات
girlfriend, friend (f.) *AB*	صاحِبة ج. صاحِبات رْفيقة ج. رفيقات صاحْبة ج. صاحْبات
(to) go *6*	ذَهَبَ إلى ، يَذْهَب ، الذَّهاب راح ع ، يْروح راح ، يْروح
(to) go out, leave *(a place)* *9*	خَرَجَ ، يَخْرُج ، الخُروج طِلِع ، يِطلَع خَرَج ، يُخْرُج
God *AB*	الله
good *AB*	جَيِّد/ة ج. جَيِّدون ، جَيِّدين مْنيح/ة ج. مْناح كْوَيِّس/ة ج. كْوَيِّسين
good-hearted *(people; also: delicious)* *AB*	طَيِّب/ة ج. طَيِّبون، طَيِّبين
government *8*	حُكومة ج. - حُكومات
grade, evaluation *8*	تَقْدير ج. تَقْديرات
graduate fellow, teaching assistant *6*	مُعيد/ة ج. مُعيدون، مُعيدين
(to) graduate *6*	التَّخَرُّج ، تَخَرَّجَ من ، يَتَخَرَّج تْخَرَّج ، بِتْخَرَّج من اِتْخَرَّج من ، بِتْخَرَّج
grammar *1*	القَواعِد
grandfather *3*	جَدّ ج. جُدود ، أجْداد
grandmother *3*	جَدّة ج. جَدّات سِتّ ، تيتة سِتّ
great! *AB*	تَمام
green *(masc.)* *AB*	أخْضَر
half *9*	نِصْف نُصّ نُصّ
happy *AB*	سَعيد/ة ج. سُعَداء مَبْسوط/ة ج. مَبْسوطين مَبْسوط/ة ج. مَبْسوطين
hard, difficult *AB*	صَعْب/ة
have *(lit.: at)* *2*	عِنْد عَند عَند
have *(lit.: for, belonging to)* *2*	لِـ + اسم، ضمير إل
(to) have, take *(a meal)* *10*	تَناوَل ، يَتَناوَل ، التَّناوُل
have to, must *AB*	لازِم
he *AB*	هُوَ هُوّ هُوّ

H

English	Arabic
health *11*	صِحّة صَحّة صِحَّة
(to) help *(someone) (with)* 8	ساعَدَ في ، يُساعِد ، المُساعَدة ساعَد في ، يساعِد ، المُساعَدة ساعِد في ، يساعِد ، المُساعْدة
here *12*	هُنا هون هِنا
hers *AB*	ـها –
high *(m.)* 5	(الـ)عالي/ ة ، (عالٍ)
his *AB*	ـهُ –
history *2*	التّاريخ
hobby *6*	هِواية ج. هِوايات
homesickness, longing for one's native land, feeling a stranger in a strange place *13*	الغُرْبة
homework *AB*	واجِب ج. واجِبات وَظيفة ج. وَظايِف ج. واجْبات
(to do) homework, review lessons, study *8*	ذاكَرَ ، يُذاكِر ، المُذاكَرة دَرَس ، يِدْرُس ، الدِّراسة ذاكِر ، يِذاكِر، المُذاكَرة
honestly, frankly *10*	بِصَراحة
hospital *7*	مُسْتَشْفى ج مُسْتَشْفَيات مِسْتَشْفى ج مِسْتَشْفَيات
hot *(e.g.: I feel __) AB*	مْشَوِّب/ة ج. مْشَوِّبين حَرّان/ة ج. حَرّانين
hot *(e.g.: __ weather)* 5	حارّ شوب حَرّ
hotel *11*	فُنْدُق ج. فَنادِق
hour *(also: o'clock; watch; clock) AB*	ساعة ج. ساعات
house *AB*	بَيْت ج. بُيوت بيت ج. بْيوت بيت
how? *AB*	كَيْفَ؟ كيف؟ إزَّيّ؟
how are you? *AB*	كَيْفَ الحال؟ كيفك؟ إزَّيَّك؟
how many/much? *3*	كَم؟ كام؟
how much? *(price)* 7	بِكَم؟ بْقَدّيش؟ بِكام؟
humidity *5*	رُطوبة
hundred *5*	مِئة(مائة) ج. مِئات مِيّة ج. مِيّات مِيّة ج. مِيّات
hungry *AB*	جَوْعان/ة ج. جَوْعانون ، جَوْعانين جوعان/ة، جوعانين جَعان/ة ج. جَعانين
husband *3*	زَوْج ج. أزواج جوز ج. جْواز جوز ج. اِجواز
I *AB*	أنا
ice, snow *5*	ثَلْج تَلج تَلج
if *10*	إذا (+ الفعل الماضي) لَوْ (+ الفعل الماضي)
if *(hypothetical)* 10	لَو
ill, sick *AB*	مَريض/ة ج. مَرْضى

English	Arabic
important, powerful (also: big; old) AB	كَبير/ة ج. كِبار كُبيرة ج. كُبار كِبيرة ج. كُبار
in 1	في
in order to, to, for 6	لِ +مصدر/ مضارع منصوب مِنشان عَشان ، عَلَشان
individual (person) 4	فَرْد ج. أفْراد
(to) intend, mean 10	قَصَدَ ، يَقصِد ، القَصْد قَصَد ، يُقصُد قَصَد ، يُقصُد
international 8	دُوَليّ/ة ، دَوليّ/ة
interview 10	مُقابَلة ج. مُقابَلات
Iran AB	إيران
Iraq AB	العِراق
is, (to) be 4, 10	كانَ ، يَكون ، الكَوْن كانْ ، يْكون كانْ ، يْكون
is not, are not 7	لَيْسَ مو ، ما مِش
Israel AB	إسرائيل
Japan 1	اليابان **J**
job, position 6	وَظيفة ج. وَظائِف ج. وَظايِف ج. وَظايِف
(to) join, enter (e.g.: school or army) 8	الْتَحَقَ بِـ ، يَلْتَحِق بِـ ، الالْتِحاق بِـ
Jordan AB	الأُرْدُن
journal, magazine 13	مَجَلّة ج. مَجَلّات
juice AB	عَصير
kind, nice, pleasant AB	لَطيف/ة ج. لِطاف ، لُطَفاء ج. لُطَفا ج. لُطاف **K**
king 10	مَلِك ج. مُلوك ج. مُلوك
(to) know 3	عَرَفَ ، يَعْرِف ، المَعْرِفة عِرِف ، يَعرِف عِرِف ، يِعرَف
(to get to) know, become acquainted with, meet 11	تَعَرَّفَ على ، يَتَعَرَّف على ، التَعَرُّف على تْعَرَّف على ، يِتعَرَّف على اِتعَرَّف على ، يِتعَرَّف على
Kuwait AB	الكُوَيت
lady; Mrs. AB	سَيِّدة ج. سَيِّدات **L**
language 2	لُغَة ج. لُغات
last 12	آخِر
late 10	مُتَأَخِّر/ة ج. مُتَأَخِّرون ، مُتَأَخِّرين مِتأَخِّر/ة ج. مِتأَخِّرين مِتأَخِّر/ة ج. مِتأَخِّرين
(to be) late, fall behind 10	تَأَخَّرَ ، يَتَأَخَّر ، التَأَخُّر تْأَخَّر ، يِتأَخَّر اِتْأَخَّر ، يِتأَخَّر
law 3	الحُقوق
(to) learn (a language, a new word) 1	التَّعَلُّم ، تَعَلَّمَ ، يَتَعَلَّم تْعَلَّم ، يِتعَلَّم اِتْعَلَّم ، يِتعَلَّم
(to) learn, study 1	الدِّراسة ، دَرَسَ ، يَدْرُس دَرَس ، بِدْرُس دَرَس ، يِدْرِس

(to) learn of, find out about 12	عَلِمَ بِـ ، يَعْلَم بِـ ، العِلْم بِـ عِرِف بـ ، يَعْرِف بـ عِرِف بـ ، يِعرَف بـ
(to) leave (the house), (to) descend, 9	نَزَلَ مِن ، يَنْزِل ، النُّزول طِلِع من ، يِطلَع نِزِل من ، يِنزِل
Lebanon AB	لُبْنان
lecture 6	مُحاضَرة ج. مُحاضَرات مُحاضْرة ج. مُحاضْرات
less 9	إلا
lesson AB	دَرْس ج. دُروس ج. دْروس
letter 3	رِسالة ج. رَسائِل مَكتوب ج. مَكاتيب جَواب ج. جَوابات
library AB	مَكْتَبة ج. مَكْتَبات
Libya AB	ليبيا
life 6	الحَياة
like, similar to 8	مِثْل + اسم مِتِل زَيّ
like, as 8	كَما (+ فعل) مِتِل ما زَيّ ما
likewise, also 13	كَذٰلِك كَمان كْمان
(to) listen to 4	اِسْتَمَعَ إلى ، يَسْتَمِع إلى ، الاسْتِماع إلى سِمِع ، يِسمَع سِمِع ، يِسمَع
literature 1	أدَب ج. آداب
little, small AB	صَغير/ة ج. صِغار زْغير/ة ج. زْغار صُغَيَّر/ة ج. صُغَيَّرين
(a) little bit (adverb) AB	قَليلاً شْوَيّ شِوَيّة
(to) live, be alive 7	عاشَ ، يَعيش ، العَيْش/المَعيشة عاش ، يْعيش عاش ، يِعيش
(to) live, reside (e.g.:_ in Egypt) 1	السَّكَن ، سَكَنَ ، يَسْكُن ساكِن/ساكْنة ساكِن/ساكْنة
(to) live (i.e.: to reside or stay; e.g.: _ in a hotel) 10	الإقامة ، أقامَ ، يُقيم
loneliness 5	الوِحْدة
Lonely, only 2	وحيدة/ة ج. وحيدون ، وحيدين
long, tall AB	طَويل/ة ج. طِوال ج. طْوال ج. طُوال
longing for one's native land, feeling a stranger in a strange place, homesickness 13	الغُرْبة
(to) love AB	الحُبّ ، أحَبَّ ، يُحِبّ حَبّ ، يْحِبّ حَبّ ، يِحِبّ
lunch 9	الغَداء الغَدا الغَدا

madam AB	مَدام
magazine, journal 13	مَجَلّة ج. مَجَلّات
making the mutual acquaintance (of), getting to know (one another) 7	تعارُف
man AB	رَجُل ج. رِجال رِجّال ج. رْجال راجِل ج رِجّالة
many, much 5	كَثيراً كتير كِتير
market 11	سوق ج. أسواق
married (adjective) 3	مُتَزَوِّج/ة ج. مُتَزَوِّجون ، مُتَزَوِّجين مِتْجَوِّز/ة ج. مِتْجَوِّزين مِتْجَوِّز/ة ج. مِتْجَوِّزين

English	Arabic
masculine *1*	مُذَكَّر
master's degree *2*	الماجِسْتير
match, game *10*	مُباراة ج. مُبارَيات ماتْش ج. ماتْشات
Mauritania *AB*	موريتانيا
May God rest her soul *7*	رَحِمَها الله/ يَرحَمُها الله الله يِرحَمها الله يِرحَمها
(to) mean, intend *10*	قَصَدَ ، يَقصِد ، القَصْد قَصَد ، يُقصُد قَصَد ، يُقصُد
(it) means *13*	يَعْني
meat *4*	لَحْم ج. لحُوم
medicine *3*	الطِّب
(to) meet *10*	المُقابَلة ، قابَلَ ، يُقابِل قابَل ، يقابِل قابِل ، يقابِل
(to) memorize *4*	الحِفْظ ، حَفِظَ ، يَحْفَظ حِفِظ ، يِحفَظ حِفِظ ، يِحفَظ
Middle East *2*	الشَّرق الأوسَط
milk *AB*	حَليب / لَبَن حَليب لَبَن
ministry *7*	وِزارة ج. وِزارات
minute *9*	دَقيقة ج. دَقائِق دْقيقة ج دَقايِق دِقيقة ج دقايِق
Miss *AB*	آنِسة ج. آنِسات
(to) miss, be absent from *(e.g.: _ school) 12*	تَغَيَّب عَن ، يَتَغَيَّب ، التَّغَيُّب غاب (غِبت) ، يْغيب غاب (غِبت) ، يِغيب
Monday *6*	الإثْنَيْن التَّنين الاتْنين
money *2*	مال مَصاري فِلوس
mistake, wrong *AB*	غَلَط
more *10*	أكْثَر أكْثَر أكْتَر
morning *AB*	صَباح
Morocco *AB*	المَغْرِب
mosque *10*	جامِع ج. جَوامِع
most of *11*	مُعظَم (+ اسم جمع)
mother *1*	والِدة ج. والِدات والْدة ، ماما والْدة ، ماما
mother *8*	أُمّ ج. أُمَّهات إمّ ج. إمَات
mountain *11*	جَبَل ج. جِبال ج. جْبال
movie *AB*	فيلم ج. أفْلام
the movies, cinema *AB*	السّينَما
Mr., Sir *AB*	سَيِّد ج. سادة
Mrs., Lady *AB*	سَيِّدة ج. سَيِّدات

much, many *5*	كَثيراً كْتير كِتير
music *4*	الموسيقى
must, have to *AB*	لازِم
my *AB*	ـي
name, noun *AB*	اِسْم ج. أسْماء ج. أسامي ج. أسامي
nationality *1*	الجِنْسِيّة
naturally, of course *AB*	طَبْعاً
near, close to *AB*	قَريب/ة (من) ج. قَريبون ، قَريبين قُرَيِّب (من) ج. قُرَيِّبين قُراب
negation *8*	النَّفي
(negative past tense marker) *12*	لم (+ المضارع) = لم يُسافِر ما (+ الفعل الماضي) = ما سافَر ما (+ الفعل الماضي) ش = ما سافِرش
neighbor *AB*	جار ج. جيران
new *AB*	جَديد/ة ج. جُدُد جْديد/ة ج. جْداد جِديد/ة ج جُداد
news *AB*	خَبَر ج. أخْبار
newspaper *9*	جَريدَة ج. جَرائِد ج. جَرايِد ج. جَرايد
next, coming *12*	قادِم/ة ج. قادِمون ، قادِمين جايِي/ة ج. جايِين جايّ/ة ج. جايين
nice, kind, pleasant *AB*	لَطيف/ة ج. لِطاف ، لُطَفاء ج. لُطَفا ج لُطاف
Nice to have met you! *13*	فُرْصة سَعيدة!
Nice to meet you! *AB*	تَشَرَّفنا!
night *10*	لَيْلَة ج. لَيالي ، لَيالٍ ليلة ليلة
nine *AB*	تِسْعة
ninety *5*	تِسْعين ، تِسْعون
no *AB*	لا
no one, none *(of) 11*	لا أحَد (مِن) ما حَدا ما حَدِّش
noon *9*	الظُّهر الضُّهر
is not *AB*	لَيسَ مو ، ما مش
not to *13*	ألّا = (أنْ+لا)
notebook, copybook *AB*	دَفْتَر ج. دَفاتِر
nothing *AB*	لا شَيْء ولا شي ولا حاجة
noun, name *AB*	اِسْم ج. أسْماء ج. أسامي ج. أسامي
now *3*	الآن هَلَّق دِلْوَقتي
number *AB*	رَقْم ج. أرْقام نِمْرة ج. نِمَر نِمرة ج. نِمَر
number *9*	عَدَد ج. أعْداد

English	Arabic			
(to) obtain, get 6, 8	حَصَّل على ، يَحْصُل على ، الحُصول على	أخَد ، ياخُد	خَد ، ياخُد	**O**
o'clock (also: hour; watch; clock) 9	ساعة ج. ساعات			
of, among (quantity) 11	مِن			
office AB	مَكْتَب ج. مَكاتِب			
officer 3	ضابِط ج. ضُبّاط	ظابِط ج. ظُبّاط	ظابِط ج. ظُبّاط	
oil 4	زَيْت ج. زُيوت			
OK, fine	جَيِّد	مْنيح	كْوَيِّس	
old (also: big; important) AB	كْبير/ة ج. كْبار	كْبير/ة ج. كُبار	كِبير/ة ج. كُبار	
old, ancient (for things, not for people) AB	قَديم/ة			
the oldest or biggest 7	أكْبَر (+ اسم نكرة)			
Oman AB	عُمان			
on AB	عَلى			
once, (one) time 11	مَرّة ج. مَرّات			
one AB	واحِد			
one of (m.) 11	أحَد			
only 5	فَقَط	بَسّ	بَسّ	
only; lonely 2	وَحيد/ة ج. وَحيدون ، وحيدين			
opinion about 8	رَأْي ج. آراء في			
opportunity, chance 13	فُرْصة ج. فُرَص			
or 9	أوْ			
(in) order to, for 6	لِ + مصدر / مضارع منصوب	مِنْشان	عَشان ، عَلَشان	
origin, descent 5	أصْل ج. أُصول			
of _____ origin 5	مِن أصل + (nisba adjective)			
other (m.) 9	آخَر ج. آخَرون ، آخَرين	تاني	تاني	
other (f.) 9	أُخْرى ج. أُخْرَيات	تانية	تانية	
over crowdedness 5	الازْدِحام	الزَّحمة	الزَّحمة	
overcast, cloudy 5	غائِم	مْغَيِّم	مِغَيِّم	
(its) own, private; special 9	خاصّ/ة			
page AB	صَفْحة ج. صَفَحات	ج. صَفْحات	ج. صَفْحات	**P**
Palestine AB	فِلَسْطين			
Palestinian 1	فِلَسْطيني/ة ج. فِلَسْطينيّون ، فِلَسْطينيّين			
(piece of) paper AB	وَرَقة ج. أوْراق			

English	Arabic
paragraph *9*	فَقرة ج. فَقَرات ، فِقْرة ج. فِقْرات
(to) pass, spend *(time)* 12	قَضَى ، يَقْضِي ، القَضاء قَضَى ، يْقَضّي قَضى ، يِقَضّي
(to) pass, succeed *(e.g.: _ an exam)* 8	نَجَحَ في ، يَنْجَح في ، النّجاح في نْجِح بِـ ، يِنْجَح نَجَحْ في ، يِنجَح في
passing, acceptable *8*	مَقْبول
past *(tense)*, past *(week, month, etc.)* 8	الماضي/ة
pen *AB*	قَلَم ج. أقْلام
people *(note: sing. = human being)* 2	ناس (م. إنسان)
pharmacology *11*	الصَّيْدَلَة
pharmacy *11*	صَيْدَليّة ج. صَيْدَليّات
Ph.D. *2*	الدُّكتوراه
photography *6*	التَّصْوير
picture *3*	صورة ج. صُوَر ج. صِوَر
pita bread *AB*	خُبْز عربي خِبز عربي عيش شامي
(to) play *6*	لَعِبَ ، يَلْعَب ، اللَّعِب لِعِب ، يِلعَب ، اللِّعب لِعِب ، يِلعَب ، اللَّعِب
please *(addressing a male)* AB	مِنْ فَضْلَك
please *(addressing a female)* AB	مِنْ فَضْلِك
pleased to meet you! *AB*	تَشَرَّفْنا
plural *2*	الجَمع
political science *3*	العُلوم السِّياسيّة
position, job *6*	وَظيفة ج. وَظائِف ج. وَظايِف
possible *AB*	مُمْكِن
(it is) possible to *10*	يُمْكِن أنْ مُمْكِن ؛ قِدِر ، يِقدِر مُمكِن ؛ قِدِر ، يِقدَر
powerful, important *(also: big; old)* AB	كَبير ج. كِبار كْبير ج. كْبار كْبير ج. كْبار
(to) pray, do ritual prayers *10*	صَلَّى ، (صَلَّيْتُ) ، يُصَلّي ، الصَّلاة (صَلَّيت) ، يُصَلّي (صَلّيت) ، يِصَلّي
(ritual) prayer *10*	صَلاة ج. صَلَوات
predicate *2*	الخَبَر
preparatory *(school = junior high)* 7	إعْداديّ/ة
president, head *8*	رَئيس ج. رُؤَساء
pretty, beautiful *AB*	جَميل/ة ج. جَميلون ، جَميلين حِلو/ة ج. حِلوين حِلو/ة ج. حِلوين
primary, elementary *4*	إبْتِدائيّ/ة
prime minister *8*	رَئيس الوُزَراء
prior to, before *4*	قَبْلَ + اسم قَبل + اسم قَبل + اسم

English	Arabic
private, *(its)* own; special *9*	خاصّ/ة
problem *AB*	مُشْكِلة ج. مَشاكِل ، مُشْكِلات مِشْكْلة
professor *(m.)* *AB*	أُسْتاذ ج. أَساتِذة
professor *(f.)* *AB*	أُسْتاذة ج. أُسْتاذات
program *9*	بَرْنامَج ج. بَرامِج
pronoun *2*	ضَمير ج. ضَمائِر
prophet *3*	نَبِيّ ج. أَنْبِياء
psychology *3*	عِلْمْ النَّفس
public, general *7*	عامّ /ة
Qatar *AB*	قَطَر **Q**
(one) quarter *9*	رُبْع ج. أَرْباع رُباع
question *AB*	سُؤال ج. أَسْئِلة
quickly, in a hurry *10*	بِسُرْعة بْسُرْعة
the Quran *AB*	القُرآن
rain *5*	مَطَر ج. أَمْطار شِتي **R**
rainy, raining *5*	مُمْطِر ، ماطِر شِتي
(to) read *4*	قَرَأَ ، يَقْرَأُ ، القِراءة قَرا ، يِقْرا ، القْراية
ready *AB*	جاهِز/ة ج. جاهِزون ، جاهِزين ج. جاهْزين ج. جاهْزين
really?! *1*	صحيح؟!
really?! *1*	والله؟! والله؟!
really! truly! indeed! *2*	فِعْلاً
(to) receive, welcome *10*	الاِسْتِقْبال ، اِسْتَقْبَلَ ، يَسْتَقْبِل اِسْتَقْبِل ، يِسْتَقْبِل اِسْتقْبِل ، يِسْتقْبِل
(to) refuse *8*	الرَّفْض ، رَفَضَ ، يَرْفُضُ رَفَض ، يِرْفُض رَفَض ، يُرْفُض
region, area *1*	مِنْطِقة ج. مَناطِق مَنْطِقة مَنْطِقة
(in) relation to, for *5*	بِالنِّسْبة لِـ بالنسبة إلـ
relationship *(pl.: relations)* *11*	عَلاقة ج. عَلاقات (بَيْنَ)
relative, family member *3*	قَريب ج. أَقارِب ، أَقْرِباء ج. قَرايِبين ج. قَرايِب
religion *3*	دين ج. أَدْيان
(to) remember *4*	تَذَكَّرَ ، يَتَذَكَّر ، التَّذَكُّر تْذَكَّر ، يِتذَكَّر فاكِر /ة ج. فاكْرين
(to) reside, live *1*	السَّكَن ، سَكَنَ ، يَسْكُن ساكِن ساكِن/ساكْنة ساكِن/ساكْنة
(to) reside, stay *(e.g. in a house, hotel)* *10*	الإقامة ، أَقامَ ، يُقيم
rest period, break *10*	اِسْتِراحة ج. اِسْتِراحات
restaurant *4*	مَطْعَم ج. مَطاعِم

English	Arabic
(to) return 13	رَجَعَ ، يَرْجِع ، الرُّجوع رِجِع ع ، يِرْجَع رِجَع ، يِرْجَع
(to) return 9	عادَ ، يَعود ، العَودة رِجِع ع ، يِرْجَع رِجَع ، يِرْجَع
(to) review (lessons; i.e.: do home work, study) 8	ذاكَرَ ، يُذاكِر ، المُذاكَرة دَرَس ، يِدرُس ، الدِّراسة ذاكِر ، يِذاكِر ، المُذاكَرة
rice 4	أُرُزّ
romantic, emotional 11	عاطِفيّ/ة ج. عاطِفِيّون ، عاطِفِيّين
room AB	غُرْفة ج. غُرَف غِرْفة ، أوضة ج. أُوَض أوضة ج. إِوَض
root 8	جَذر ج. جُذور
roughly, around 9	حَوالَيْ حَوالي حَوالي
(to) run 6	جَرى ، يَجْري ، الجَري رَكَض ، يِرْكُض جِري ، يِجري
saddening, distressing 7	مُحْزِن/ة بيزَعِّل بيزَعِّل
salad 4	سَلَطة ج. سَلَطات
(the) same...1	نَفْس الـ...
Saturday 6	السَّبْت
Saudi Arabia AB	السَّعودية
(to) say 4	قالَ ، يَقول ، القَوْل قال ، يْقول قال ، يِقول
scholarship, grant 12	مِنْحة ج. مِنَح
school 4	مَدْرَسة ج. مَدارِس
school, college (in a university) 3	كُلِّيّة ج. كُلِّيّات كِلِّيّة ج. كِلِّيّات
science 3	عِلْم ج. عُلوم
sea 11	بَحْر ج. بِحار ، بُحور ج. بْحور
season (e.g.: spring ___ ; also:class) 5	فَصْل ج. فُصول
second (e.g.: the ___ lesson) 4	ثانٍ ، (الـ)ثاني/ة تاني / التّاني تاني / التّاني
secondary (school=high school) 7	ثانَويّ/ة ثانَوي ثانَوي
(to) see 13	رَأى ، يَرى ، الرُّؤْية شاف ، يْشوف شاف ، يِشوف
(to) see, watch AB	شاهَدَ ، يُشاهِد ، المُشاهَدة شاف ، يْشوف شاف ، يِشوف
semester 5	فَصْل دِراسيّ
sentence AB	جُمْلة ج. جُمَل
(to become) settled, to settle down 13	الاسْتِقْرار ، اِسْتَقَرَّ ، يَسْتَقِرّ اِسْتَقَرّ ، يِسْتَقِرّ اِسْتَقَرّ ، يِسْتَقِرّ
seven AB	سَبْعة
seventy 5	سَبْعين ، سَبْعون
several 11	عِدّة (+ اسم جمع نكرة) كَم + مفرد كام + مفرد
shame (on you; lit.: not legal) 12	حَرام

English	Arabic
she *AB*	هِيَ هِيّ هِيّ
short *AB*	قَصيرة ج. قِصار قُصَيِّرة ج قُصَيِّرين
shy *7*	خَجول/ة
shyness *11*	الخَجَل
sick, ill *AB*	مَريض/ة ج. مَرْضى
similar to, like *8*	مِثْل + اسم مِتِل زَيّ
since, because *13*	إذ
since, ago *6*	مُنْذُ مِن وَقت ما مِن ساعة ما
singular *2*	المُفْرَد
Sir, Mr. *AB*	سَيِّد ج. سادة
sister *AB*	أُخْت ج. أخوات ج. إخوات ج. إخوات
(to)sit *9*	جَلَسَ ، يَجْلِس ، الجُلوس قَعَد ، يُقعُد ، القَعدة قَعَد ، يُقعُد ، القُعاد
six *AB*	سِتّة
sixth *9*	سادِس/ة
sixty *5*	سِتّون ، سِتّين
(to)sleep, go to sleep *10*	نامَ (نِمْتُ) ، يَنام ، النَّوم نام (نِمْت) ، يْنام ، النّوم نام (نِمْت) ، بِنام ، النّوم
small, little *AB*	صَغيرة ج. صِغار زْغيرة ج. زْغار صُغَيِّرة ج. صُغَيِّرين
(to) smoke *9*	دَخَّنَ ، يُدَخِّن ، التَّدخين دَخَّن ، يْدَخِّن دَخَّن ، بِدَخِّن
snow, ice *5*	ثَلْج تَلَج تَلَج
so, thus...*5*	فَ ...
so, thus, because of that, for that reason *6*	لِذلِك مِنشان هيك عشان كدا
soccer, European football *6*	كُرة القَدَم
sociology *3*	عِلْم الاِجْتِماع
some of *9*	بَعْض + (اسم جمع في اضافة)
someone *11*	أَحَد حَدا حَدّ
something *AB*	شَيء ج. أشياء شي ج. إشيا حاجة ج. حاجات
something else? *AB*	شيء آخَر؟ شي تاني؟ حاجة تاني؟
sometimes *5*	أَحْياناً
son *3*	إِبْن ج. أَبْناء ج. وُلاد ج. وِلاد
son, boy *(also: child)* *AB*	وَلَد ج. أَوْلاد ج. وُلاد ج. ولاد
sorry! *AB*	آسِف/ة مَعلِشّ
soup *4*	شوربة
south *13*	جَنوب

English	Arabic
spacious, wide *AB*	واسِع/ة
(to) speak, talk *(about)* 4	تَكَلَّمَ عن ، يَتَكَلَّم ، الكَلام حَكى عن ، يِحكي ، الحَكي اِتْكَلَّم عن ، يِتكلَّم
special; *(its)* own, private 9	خاصّ/ة
specializing, specialist in 2	مُتَخَصِّص/ة في ج. مُتَخَصِّصون ، مُتَخَصِّصين مِتْخَصِّص/ة ج. مِتْخَصِّصين
(to) spend, pass *(time)* 12	قَضى ، يَقْضي ، القَضاء قَضى ، يْقَضّي قَضى ، يِقَضّي
sports 6	الرِّياضة
spring 5	الرَّبيع
state, province 2	وِلاية ج. وِلايات
*(nation-)*state 8	دَولة ج. دُوَل
(to) stay, reside 10	أقامَ ، يُقيم ، الإقامة
(to) stay up late 10	سَهِرَ ، يَسْهَر ، السَّهَر سِهِر ، يِسهَر سِهِر ، يِسهَر
still, continue to *(lit.: do not cease)* 13	ما زالَ، لا يَزال + المضارع المرفوع / اسم بَعد (+ pronoun) لِسّه
story *AB*	قِصّة ج. قِصَص
strange, foreign *AB*	غَريب/ة ج. غُرَباء
(feeling a) stranger in a strange place, longing for one's native land, homesickness 13	الغُرْبة
street *AB*	شارِع ج. شوارِع
student *(m.) AB*	طالِب ج. طُلّاب
student *(f.) AB*	طالِبة ج. طالِبات طالْبة ج. طالْبات
(to) study *(i.e.: review lessons, do homework)* 8	ذاكَرَ ، يُذاكِر ، المُذاكَرة دَرَس ، يدرُس ، الدِّراسة ذاكِر ، يِذاكِر ، المُذاكرة
(to) study, learn 1	الدِّراسة ، دَرَسَ ، يَدْرُس دَرَس ، يِدرُس دَرَس ، يِدرِس
study *(of)*, studies 3	دِراسة ج. دِراسات
subject, topic 9	مَوضوع ج. مَواضيع ، موضوعات
(to) succeed, pass 8	النَّجاح ، نَجَحَ في ، يَنْجَح نَجَح بـ ، يِنجَح نَجَح في ، يِنجَح
Sudan *AB*	السّودان
sugar *AB*	سُكَّر سِكَّر
sugar, medium *AB*	سُكَّر وَسَط سِكَّر وَسَط سُكَّر مظبوط
suitable, appropriate 13	مُناسِب/ة مْناسِب/ة
summer 5	الصَّيْف الصِّيف الصِّيف
sun 5	الشَّمْس
Sunday 6	الأحَد الحدّ الحدّ
sunny 5	مُشْمِس مِشْمِس شَمْس
sweets, desserts 4	حَلَوِيّات ، حُلْو حِلو

English	Arabic
swimming *6*	السِّباحة السَّباحة
Syria *AB*	سوريّا
table *AB*	طاوِلة ج. طاوِلات طاوْلة ج. طاوْلات طَرابيزة ج. طَرابيزات
(to) take *12*	أخَذَ ، يأخُذ ، الأخْذ أخَذ ، ياخُد خَد ، ياخُد
(to) take, have (a meal) *9*	تَناوَل ، يَتَناوَل ، التَّناوُل
tall, long *AB*	طَويل/ة ج. طِوال ج. طُوال ج. طُوال
tea *AB*	شاي
(to) teach *3*	التَّدريس ، دَرَّس ، يُدَرِّس عَلَّم ، يْعَلِّم دَرَّس ، يْدَرِّس
teaching assistant, graduate fellow *6*	مُعيد/ة ج. مُعيدون ، معيدين
telephone *AB*	تِليفون ج. تِليفونات ، هاتِف ج. هواتِف
telephone number *AB*	رَقم تِليفون نِمرة تِليفون نِمرة تِليفون
temperature *5*	دَرَجة الحَرارة
ten *AB*	عَشَرة
test, examination *AB*	اِمْتِحان ج. اِمْتِحانات
thank you *AB*	شُكْراً
thanks to *8*	بِفَضْل (+ اسم)
that *(after a verb; e.g.: to think__) 13*	أنَّ
that *(demonstrative pronoun) (m.) 6*	ذٰلِك (مؤنَّث : تِلْك)
that *(demonstrative pronoun) (f.) 6*	تِلْك (مُذَكَّر: ذٰلِك)
that's all, only *AB*	فَقَط بَسّ بَسّ
theater *13*	مَسْرَح ج. مَسارِح
then, *9* بعد ذلك	ثُمَّ بَعدين بَعدين
there *12*	هُناك هونيك هناك
there is/are *7*	هُناك فيه فيه
there is/are not *AB*	لَيسَ هُناك ما فيه ما فيش
they *2*	هُم هِنّي هُمّ
(to) think (about doing something) *13*	فَكَّر ، يُفَكِّر (أنْ + المُضارع المنصوب) فَكَّر ، يْفَكِّر + المضارع (بِـ no) فَكَّر ، يِفَكَّر + المضارع (بِـ no)
(to) think that, consider *13*	ظَنَّ أنَّ ، (ظَنَنْتُ أنَّ) ، يَظُنّ ، الظَّنّ ظَنّ (ظَنّيت) ، يْظُنّ إنّه (إنّو) اِفْتِكَر ، يِفتِكِر إنّ
third *(e.g.: the ___ lesson) 9*	ثالِث تالِت تالِت
(one) third *9*	ثُلْث تِلِت تِلت
thirsty *AB*	عَطْشان/ة ج. عَطْشانين

thirty *5*	ثَلاثون ، ثَلاثين تلاتين تلاتين
this *(m.) AB*	هٰـذا هادا ، هَيدا دا
this *(f.) AB*	هٰـذِه هادي ، هَيدي دي
three *AB*	ثَلاثَة تْلاتة تَلاتة
throughout, during *8*	طِوالَ طول طول
Thursday *6*	الخَميس
thus, so... *5*	فَـ...
thus, so, because of that, for that reason *6*	لِذٰلِكَ مِنْشان هيك عَشان كدا
thus, so *7*	هٰـكَذا هيك كِدا
time *(e.g.: I have___) 9*	وَقْت ج. أوْقات
(one) time, once *11*	مَرّة ج. مَرّات
tired *AB*	تَعْبان/ة ج. تَعْبانون ، تَعْبانين
to, in order to, for *6*	لِ + مصدر / مضارع مِنْشان عَشان ، عَلَشان
to, toward *AB*	إلى عَ ، لَ لـ
today *2*	اليَوْم اليوم النهاردا
together *(e.g.: with one another) 11*	مَعاً مَع بَعض مَع بَعض
together *(e.g.: altogether, all of them) 12*	جَميعاً مع بَعض ، كِلّنا سَوا مع بَعض
tomorrow *2*	غَداً بُكرة بُكرة
tonight *10*	اللَّيْلَة
topic, subject *9*	مَوضوع ج. مَواضيع ، موضوعات
tour *11*	جَولة ج. جَولات
tourism *11*	السِّياحة
toward, to *AB*	إلى عَ ، لَ لـ
trade, commerce *6*	التِّجارة
translation *(from...to) 2*	التَّرْجَمَة (مِن .. إلى)
translator *2*	مُتَرْجِم/ة ج. مُتَرْجِمون ، مُتَرْجِمين
(to) travel *(to) 4*	السَّفَر ، سافَرَ إلى ، يُسافِر يْسافِر عَ يِسافِر
tree *AB*	شَجَرة ج. شَجرات ، شَجَر
truly, indeed, really *2*	فِعْلاً
Tuesday *6*	الثُّلاثاء التَّلاتا التَّلات
Tunisia or Tunis *AB*	تونس
Turkey *AB*	تُرْكيا
twenty *5*	عِشْرون ، عِشْرين

English	Arabic
two *AB*	اِثْنان ، اِثْنَيْن تْنين اِتْنين
uncle *(maternal)* 2	خال ج. أخْوال
uncle *(paternal)* 3	عَمّ ج. أعْمام ج. عْـمام
(to) understand 10	فَهِمَ ، يَفْهَم ، الفَهْم فِهِم ، يِفْهَم فِهِم ، يِفْهَم
United Arab Emirates *AB*	الإمارات العَرَبِيّة المُتَّحِدة
United Nations 1	الأُمَم المُتَّحِدة
United States of America 1	الوِلايات المُتَّحِدة الأمْريكيّة
university *AB*	جامِعة ج. جامِعات جامْعة ج. جامْعات جامْعة ج. جامْعات
upset; annoyed, angry *AB*	زَعْلان/ة ج. زَعْلانين زَعْلان/ة زَعْلانين زَعْلان/ة ج. زَعْلانين
usually 10	عادةً غالِباً
vacation, leave *(of absence)* 12	إجازة ج. إجازات أجازة ج. أجازات
vacation, holiday 12	عُطْلة ج. عُطْلات عُطْلة ج. عُطَل أجازة ج. أجازات
vegetables 4	خُضار
veil *AB*	حِجاب
verb 4	فِعل ج أفعال
very 5	جِدّاً كِتير قَوي
(to) visit 12	زارَ ، يَزور ، الزِّيارة زار ، يْزور زار ، يِزور
(to) wake up, awaken 10	صَحا (صَحَوْتُ) ، يَصْحو ، الصَّحْو فاق (فِقت) ، يُفيق صِحي (صِحيت) ، يِصحى
(to) wake *(someone)* up 9	أيْقَظَ ، يوقِظ ، الإيْقاظ فَيَّق ، يْفَيِّق صَحّى (صَحّيت) ، يِصَحّي
(to) want to 8	أرادَ أنْ ، يُريد ، الإرادة كان بِدُّه كان عايِز
(to) want to, have a desire to 13	رَغِبَ في ، يَرْغَب في ، الرَّغْبة كان بِدُّه كان عايِز
watch *(also clock, hour)* *AB*	ساعة ج. ساعات
(to) watch, see *AB*	شاهَدَ ، يُشاهِد ، المُشاهَدة شاف ، يْشوف شاف ، يِشوف
water *AB*	ماء مَيّ مَيّة
we 2	نَحْنُ نِحْنا إحْنا
weak 8	ضَعيف/ة ج. ضُعَفاء ضَعيف/ة ج. ضُعاف ضَعيف/ة ج. ضُعاف
weather 5	الجَوّ ، الطَّقْس الطَّقس الجَوّ
Wednesday 6	الأرْبِعاء الأرْبِعا الأرْبَع
week 6	أُسْبوع ج. أسابيع إسْبوع
welcome *(formal)* *AB*	مَرْحَباً (بـ)
welcome *AB*	أهْلاً وسَهْلاً
(you're) welcome *AB*	عَفْواً

well (adverb) 5	جَيِّداً مْنيح كْوَيِّس
what? (in questions using verbs) 1	ماذا ؟ + فعل شو؟ + فعل فعل+ إيه؟
what? (in questions without verbs) AB	ما؟ شو؟ إيه؟
whatever 13	ما + فعل
what's wrong? AB	ما بِكَ/بِكِ ؟ شو بِكِ/بَك؟ ما لَك/ما لِك؟
when? 6	مَتَى؟ إِمتى؟ إمتى؟
when (not a question) 11	عِنْدَما (+ جملة فعلية) لَمّا لَمّا
where (not a question; also, "in which") 2	حَيْثُ
where? AB	أَيْنَ؟ وين؟ فين؟
which...? 1	أَيّ ...؟
white (masc.) AB	أَبْيَض ج. بيض
who?, whom; whoever 1	مَن؟ مين؟ مين؟
why? 6	لِماذا؟ ليش؟ ليه؟
wide, spacious AB	واسِع/ة
wife 3	زَوْجَة ج. زَوْجات مَرة مراة
wife 7	حَرَم
window AB	شِبّاك ج. شَبابيك شِبّاك شْبّاك
winter 5	الشِّتاء الشِّتوِيّة الشَّتا
with (people) AB	مَعَ
with, by (things) AB	بـ
without 13	بدون
(a) woman (note: def. form is also collective) AB	إمْرَأة (المَرْأة) ج. نِساء مَرة ج. نِسوان سِت ج. سِتّات
word AB	كَلِمَة ج. كَلِمات كِلْمة ج. كِلِمات كِلْمة ج. كِلِمات
(to) work 1	عَمِلَ ، يَعْمَل ، العَمَل اشْتَغَل ، يِشْتِغِل ، الشِّغِل اِشْتَغَل ، يِشتَغِل ، الشُّغْل
work (n) 2	الـشُّغْل ، العَمَل الشِّغِل الشُّغْل
worker 13	عامِل ج. عُمّال
(the) world 9	العالَم
(to) write 4	كَتَب ، يَكْتُب ، الكِتابة كَتَب ، يِكْتِب كَتَب ، يِكتِب
wrong, mistake AB	غَلَط
Y year 1	سَنة ج. سَنَوات ، سنين سِنة
(two) years 6	سَنَتان ، سَنَتين سِنْتين سَنَتَيْن

English	Arabic
Yemen *AB*	اليَمَن
yes *AB*	نَعَم إيه أيوه
yesterday *4*	أمْس امبارِح اِمْبارِح
you (m.) *AB*	أنْتَ إنْتِ اِنْتَ
you (f.) *AB*	أنْتِ إنْتي اِنْتي
you (pl.) *2*	أنْتُم إنتو
you (polite form, f.) *AB*	حَضْرَتُك حَضْرْتِك حَضِرْتِك
you (polite form, m.) *AB*	حَضْرَتُك حَضْرْتَك حَضِرْتَك
young; small, little *AB*	صَغيرة ج. صِغار زْغيرة ج. زْغار صُغَيَّرة ج. صُغَيَّرين

قاموس عربي – إنجليزي
Arabic – English Glossary

English

The term AB refers to Alif Baa, *third edition.*
The numbers refer to the lesson in which the term appears

Arabic

English	Arabic
see ب – ن	اِبن
one of *(m.)* 11	أَحَد
no one, none *(of)* 11	لا أَحَّد (مِن) ما حَدا ما حَدِّش
Sunday 6	الأَحَد الحَدّ الحَدّ
eleven 8	أَحَدَ عَشَر إدَعْش حِداشر
to take 12	أَخَذَ ، يأخُذ ، الأَخْذ أَخَد ، ياخُد خَد ، ياخُد
to be late, fall behind 8	تأَخَّرَ ، يَتأَخَّر ، التأَخُّر تأَخَّر ، بِتأَخَّر اِتأَخَّر ، بِتأَخَّر
finally, at last 13	أخيراً
other *(m.)* 9	آخَر ج. آخَرون ، آخَرين تاني تاني
other *(f.)* 9	أُخرى ج. أُخرَيات تانية تانية
last 12	آخِر
late 10	مُتأَخِّر ج. مُتأَخِّرون، مُتأَخِّرين مِتأَخِّر ج. مِتأَخِّرين مِتأَخِّر ج. مِتأَخِّرين
brother AB	أخ ج. إخْوَة ج. إخْوِة ج. إخْوات
sister AB	أُخْت ج. أخوات
literature 1	أدَب ج. آداب
because, since 13	إذ
if 10	إذا (+ الفعل الماضي) لَوْ (+ الفعل الماضي)
history 2	التّاريخ
Jordan AB	الأُردن
rice 6	أُرْز
professor *(m)* AB	أُسْتاذ ج. أَساتِذة
professor *(f)* AB	أُستاذة ج. أُستاذات
family *(i.e. immediate ____)* 2	أُسْرَة ج. أُسَر عيلة ج. عِيَل
Israel AB	إسْرائيل
sorry! *(adj)* AB	آسِف/ة مَعلِشّ
descent, origin 5	أصْل ج. أصول
of __ descent, origin 5	مِنْ أصْل...
to eat 4	أكَلَ ، يأكُل ، الأكْل أكَل ، ياكُل أكَل ، ياكُل
see أنْ	ألّا
less, except 9	إلّا

English	Arabic
God *(sometimes used alone as expression of delight)* AB	اللّه
really?! *1*	والله؟! والله؟!
Thanks be to God *AB*	الحَمْدُ لِلّه
May God have mercy on her *(=Rest her soul)* 7	رَحِمَها الله/ يَرحَمُها الله الله يِرحَمها الله يِرحَمها
In the name of God *(said when beginning something)* AB	بِسْمِ اللّه
God willing *AB*	إنْ شاءَ اللّه
There is no God but God *(said when hearing bad news)* AB	لا إلهَ إلا اللّه
Whatever God intends *(said when praising someone)* AB	ما شاءَ اللّه
to, toward *AB*	إلى عَ، لَ لـ
mother *8*	أُمّ ج. أُمّهات إمّ ج. إمّات
United Nations *1*	الأُمَم المُتَّحِدة
in front of, before *(spatial)* 13	أمامَ قُدّام قُدّام
as for... *9*	أمّا ... فَـ ...
United Arab Emirates *AB*	الإمارات العَرَبِيّة المُتَّحِدة
yesterday *9*	أمسِ امْبارِح امْبارِح
to *(marks nonfinite verb)*	أنْ (+ المضارع المنصوب)
not to *13*	ألا (=أنْ + لا)
that *(introduces sentence complement)* 13	أنّ
I *AB*	أنا
you *(m.)* AB	أنْتَ إنْتَ اِنْتَ
you *(f.)* AB	أنْتِ إنْتِ اِنْتي
you *(pl.)* 2	أنْتُم اِنْتو اِنْتو
feminine *1*	المُؤَنَّث
English *1*	إنْجليزي (إنكليزي) ج. إنْجليز (إنكليز)
Miss *AB*	آنِسة ج. آنِسات
people *(note: sing. = human being)* 2	ناس (م. إنسان)
welcome *AB*	أهْلاً وسَهْلاً
or *9*	أوْ
bus *AB*	أوتوبيس ج. أوتوبيسات
Europe	أوروبا
first *(m.)* 4	أوّل ج. أُوَل/أوائل أوّل
first *(f.)* 4	أولى

now *3*	الآنَ هَلَّق دِلْوَقتي
which...? *1*	أيِّ...؟
any	أيّ / أيَّة
Iran *AB*	إيران
also *2*	أيْضاً كَمان گَمان
where? *AB*	أيْنَ؟ وين؟ فين؟
with, by *(things) AB*	بِـ
sea *11*	بَحْر ج. بِحار ، بُحار ج. بْحور
Bahrain *AB*	البَحْرَيْن
to begin *9*	بَدَأَ ، يَبْدَأُ ، البَدْء بَدا ، يِبْدا بَدَأ ، يِبْدأ
primary, elementary *4*	اِبْتِدائي/ة
subject of a nominal sentence *2*	المُبْتَدَأ
to exchange *11*	تَبادَلَ ، يَتَبادَل ، التَّبادُل تْبادَل ، يِتْبادُل اِتْبادَل ، يِتْبادِل
see د – و – ن	بِدون
cold *(e.g.: I have a __)*	بَرْد
cold *(e.g.: __weather) 5*	بارِد/ة بَرِد بَرِد
cold *(e.g: I feel ___) AB*	بَرْدان/ة ج. بَرْدانين
congratulations *3*	مَبْروك
(response to) congratulations *3*	بارَكَ اللّهُ فيك الله يِبارِك فيك/ فيكي الله يِبارك فيك/ لَك
program *9*	بَرْنامَج ج. بَرامِج
game, match *10*	مُباراة ج. مُباريات ماتش ج. ماتشات
after *8*	بَعْدَ أنْ (+ فعل) بَعد ما بَعد ما
afternoon *9*	بَعْدَ الظُّهْر بَعد الضُّهر بَعد الضُّهر
far, distant *(from) AB*	بَعيد/ة (عَنْ) ج. بَعيدون ، بَعيدين بْعيد ج بْعاد بِعيد ج بُعاد
some of *9*	بَعْض (+ اسم جمع في اضافة)
bachelor's degree *2*	بكالوريوس
country *2*	بَلَد ج. بِلاد / بُلْدان
son *3*	اِبْن ج. أبْناء ج. وُلاد ج. وِلاد
cousin *(m., maternal) 3*	اِبْن خال/ة ج. أبْناء خال/ة ج. وُلاد خال/ة ج. وِلاد خال/ة
cousin *(m., paternal) 3*	اِبْن عَمّ/ة ج. أبْناء عَمّ/ة ج. وُلاد عَمّ/ة ج. وِلاد عَمّ/ة
daughter, girl *AB*	بِنْت ج. بَنات
cousin *(f., maternal) 3*	بنت خال/ة ج بَنات خال/ة

English	Arabic
cousin (f., paternal) 3	بِنْت عَمّ/ة ج. بَنات عَمّ/ة
building AB	بِناية ج. بِنايات بِنايةِ عِمارة ج. عِمارات
door AB	باب ج. أبْواب ج. بْواب
house AB	بَيْت ج. بُيوت بيت ج. بْيوت بيت
white (m.) AB	أبْيَض ج. بيض
between, among 11	بَيْنَ بين بين

ت

English	Arabic
commerce, trade 6	التِّجارة
translation (from...to) 2	تَرْجَمَة (مِن .. إلى)
translator 2	مُتَرْجِم/ة ج. مُتَرْجِمون ، مُتَرْجِمين مْتَرْجِم ج. مْتَرجمين
Turkey AB	تُرْكِيّا
nine AB	تِسْعَة
ninety 5	تِسْعين ، تِسْعون
tired AB	تَعْبان ، تَعْبانين ج. تَعْبانون
that (demonstrative pronoun) (f.) 6	تِلْكَ
great! AB	تَمام
Tunisia or the city of Tunis AB	تونِس

ث

English	Arabic
culture 1	الثَّقافة
one third 9	ثُلْث تِلْت تِلت
three AB	ثَلاثَة تْلاتة
third 9	ثالِث تالِت
thirty 5	ثَلاثون ، ثَلاثين تلاتين تْلاتين
Tuesday 6	الثُّلاثاء التّلاتا التّلات
snow, ice 5	ثَلْج تَلج تْلج
then 9	ثُمَّ بَعدين بَعدين
eight AB	ثَمانية ثْمانة تْمانية
eighty 5	ثَمانون ، ثَمانين ثْمانين تْمانين
two AB	إثْنان ، إثْنَيْن تْنين اِتْنين
Monday 6	الإثْنَيْن التَّنين الاتْنين
second 4	ثانٍ ، الثّاني/ة تاني /التاني تاني /التاني
secondary 7	ثانَوِيّ/ة ثانَوي ثانَوي
Baccalaureate 7	الثّانَوِيّة العامّة
the dual 6	المُثَنّى

English	Arabic
mountain 11	جَبَل ج. جِبال ، ج. جُبال
grandfather 3	جَدّ ج. جُدود ، أَجْداد ج. جُدود
grandmother 3	جَدّة ج. جَدّات ستّ ، تيتة جدّة/ستّ
very 5	جِدّاً كْتير قَوي
new AB	جَديد ج. جُدُد جْديد ج. جُداد جِديد ج جُداد
root 6	جَذر ج. جُذور
experience (life___) 11	تَجْرِبة ج. تَجارِب تَجْرُبة ج. تَجارُب
newspaper 9	جَريدَة ج. جَرائِد ج. جَرايِد ج. جَرايد
to run; go running 6	جَرى ، يَجْري ، الجَري رَكَض ، يِرْكُض جِري ، يِجري
Algeria AB	الجَزائِر
jussive mood (verbs) 13	المَجْزوم
magazine, journal 13	مَجَلّة ج. مَجَلّات
to sit 9	جَلَس ، يَجْلِس ، الجُلوس قَعَد ، يُقعُد ، القَعدة قَعَد ، يُقعُد ، القُعاد
gathering, gather 10	جَلْسة ج. جَلْسات
(to) gather (together) 11	التَّجَمُّع ، تَجَمَّعَ ، يَتَجَمَّع تْجَمَّع ، يِتْجَمَّع اِتْجَمَّع ، يِتْجَمَّع
plural 2	الجَمع
Friday 6	الجُمْعة
together (i.e.: altogether, all of them) 12	جَميعاً مع بَعض، كِلّنا سَوا مع بَعَض
university AB	جامِعة ج. جامِعات جامْعة ج. جامْعات جامْعة ج. جامْعات
sentence AB	جُمْلة ج. جُمَل
beautiful AB	جَميل/ة ج. جَميلون ، جَميلين حِلو/ة ج. حِلوين حِلو/ةً ج. حِلوين
crazy 7	مَجنون/ة ج مَجانين
south 13	جَنوب
foreign, foreigner 13	أَجْنَبِيّ ج. أَجانِب
nationality 1	الجِنسيّة
ready AB	جاهِز/ة ج. جاهِزون ، جاهِزين ج. جاهْزين ج. جاهْزين
weather 5	الجَوّ ، الطَّقس
good AB	جَيِّد/ة ج. جَيِّدون ، جَيِّدين مْنيح/ة ج. مْناح كْوَيِّس/ة ج. كْوَيِّسين
well (adverb) 5	جَيِّداً مْنيح كْوَيِّس
neighbor AB	جار ج. جيران
vacation, leave (of absence) 12	إجازة ج. إجازات أجازة ج. أجازات
tour 11	جَولة ج. جَولات

English	Arabic
hungry *AB*	جَوْعان ج. جَوْعانون ، جَوْعانين جوعان ، جوعانين جَعان ج. جَعانين
to come *10*	جاءَ (إلى) ، يَجيء ، المَجيء إجاع (إجيت) ، بِجي جا (جيت) لـ ، يِجي
army *3*	جَيْش ج. جُيوش

ح

English	Arabic
to love *AB*	الحُبّ ، أَحَبّ ، يُحِبّ حَبّ ، يْحِبّ حَبّ ، يِحِبّ
darling, dear *(m.) AB*	حَبيب ج. أَحِبّاء ج حَبايِب ج حَبايِب
darling, dear *(f.) AB*	حَبيبة ج. حَبيبات
veil *AB*	حِجاب
accident *7*	حادِث ج. حَوادِث حادْثة
conversation *1*	مُحادَثة
hot *(e.g.: __ weather) 5*	حارّ شوب حَرّ
hot *(e.g.: I feel __) AB*	حَرّان/ة ج. حَرّانين
wife *7*	حَرَم
shame *(on you; lit.: not legal) 12*	حَرام
saddening, distressing *7*	مُحْزِن/ة بيزَعِّل بيزَعِّل
the best... *5*	أَحْسَن ...
to get, obtain *6, 8*	حَصَلَ على ، يَحْصُل ، الحُصول أَخَد ، ياخُد خَد ، ياخُد
you *(formal, f.) AB*	حَضْرَتُكِ حَضْرْتِك حَضْرِتك
you *(formal, m.) AB*	حَضْرَتُكَ حَضْرْتَك حَضْرِتَك
lecture *6*	مُحاضَرة ج. مُحاضَرات مُحاضَرة ج. مُحاضَرات
to memorize *4*	حَفِظَ ، يَحْفَظ ، الحِفْظ حِفِظ ، بِحفَظ حِفِظ ، بِحفَظ
law *3*	الحُقوق
actually *3*	في الحَقيقة بالحَقيقة في الحَقيقة
government *8*	حُكومة ج. حُكومات
milk *AB*	حَليب / لَبَن حَليب لَبَن
dream *13*	حُلْم ج. أَحْلام حِلِم حِلِم
sweets, desserts *4*	الحَلَوِيّات ، الحُلْو الحِلو الحَلَوِيّات
bathroom *AB*	حَمّام ج. حَمّامات
roughly, around *9*	حَوالَيْ حَوالي
life *6*	الحَياة
where *(not a question; also, "in which") 2*	حَيْثُ
sometimes *5*	أَحْياناً

خ

English	Arabic
news *AB*	خَبَر ج. أَخْبار

English	Arabic
predicate of a nominal sentence *2*	الخَبَر
bread *AB*	خُبْز خِبز عيش
pita bread *AB*	خُبْز عربي خِبز عربي عيش شامي
shyness, abashment *11*	الخَجَل
to go out *9*	خَرَجَ ، يَخرُج ، الخُروج طِلع، يطلَع خَرَج، يُخرُج
to graduate *6*	التَّخَرُّج ، تَخَرَّج (من) ، يَتَخَرَّج تْخَرَّج (من) ، يِتْخَرَّج اِتْخَرَّج (من) ، يِتْخَرَّج
foreign affairs *7*	الخارِجِيّة الخارْجِيّة الخارْجِيّة
fall, autumn *5*	الخَريف
special; *(its)* own, private *9*	خاصّ/ة
specializing, specialist in *2*	مُتَخَصِّص/ة في ج. مُتَخَصِّصون ، مُتَخَصِّصين مِتَخَصِّص/ة ج. مِتَخَصِّصين
green (m.) *AB*	أخْضَر (مؤنث: خضراء)
vegetables *4*	خُضار
she got engaged to *11*	خُطِبَتْ لِ اِنخَطَبِت لَ اِتخَطَبِت لِ
behind, beyond *5*	خَلْف
caliph, successor *(note: m)* *4*	خَليفة ج. خُلَفاء
five *AB*	خَمْسة خَمْسِة
fifty *8*	خَمْسين ، خَمْسون
Thursday *6*	الخَميس
uncle *(maternal)* *2*	خال ج. أخْوال
aunt *(maternal)* *2*	خالة ج. خالات
well, fine *(said of people)* *AB*	بِخَيْر مْنيح كْوَيِّس
chicken *(collective)* *AB*	دَجاج دْجاج فْراخ
to enter *8*	دَخَلَ ، يَدْخُل ، الدُّخول دَخَل ، يِدخُل دَخَل ، يُدخُل
to smoke *9*	دَخَّنَ ، يُدَخِّن ، التَّدْخين دَخَّن ، يْدَخِّن دَخَّن ، بِدَخِّن
degree *(e.g.: of temperature)* *5*	دَرَجة ج. دَرَجات
temperature *5*	دَرَجة الحَرارة
to study *1*	الدِّراسة ، دَرَسَ ، يَدرُس دَرَس ، يِدرُس دَرَس ، بِدرِس
to teach *3*	التَّدْريس ، دَرَّسَ ، يُدَرِّس عَلَّم ، يْعَلِّم دَرَّس ، بِدَرِّس
lesson *AB*	دَرْس ج. دُروس ج. دْروس
study *(of)*, studies *3*	دِراسة ج. دِراسات
school *4*	مَدْرَسة ج. مَدارِس
copybook, notebook *AB*	دَفْتَر ج. دَفاتِر

د

	English	Arabic
	minute 9	دَقيقة ج دقايق دْقيقة ج دَقائِق دَقيقة ج. دَقائِق
	doctor (m.) AB	ج. دَكاتْرة ج. دَكاتْرة دُكتور ج. دَكاتِرة
	doctor (f.) AB	دُكتورة ج. دُكتورات
	Ph.D. 2	الدُّكتوراه
	business administration 6	إدارة الأعْمال
	director 12	مُدير ج. مُديرون ، مُديرين ، مُدَراء
	(nation-) state 8	دَولة ج. دُوَل
	international 8	دُوَليّ/ة ، دَوليّ
	always 2	دائِماً دائِماً دائِماً
	without 13	بِدون
	religion 3	دين ج. أدْيان
ذ	that (demonstrative pronoun) (m.) 6	ذلِك (مؤنث: تِلْك)
	also, likewise 13	كَذلِك كَمان كَمان
	so, thus 6	لِذلِك مِنْشان هيك عَشان كدا
	to study (i.e.: review lessons, do homework) 8	ذاكَرَ ، يُذاكِر ، المُذاكَرة دَرَس ، يِدرُس ذاكِر ، بِذاكِر ، المُذاكْرة
	to remember 4	تَذَكَّرَ ، يَتَذَكَّر ، التَّذَكُّر تْذَكَّر ، بِتذَكَّر فاكِر /ة ج. فاكْرين
	masculine 1	المُذَكَّر
	to go 6	ذَهَبَ ، يَذْهَب ، الذَّهاب راح ع ، يْروح راح ، يِروح
ر	president 8	رَئيس ج. رُؤَساء
	to see 13	رَأى ، يَرى ، الرُّؤْية شاف ، يْشوف شاف ، بِشوف
	opinion 8	رَأْي ج. آراء
	one quarter 9	رُبْع ج. أرْباع
	spring (season) 5	الرَّبيع
	four AB	أرْبَعة أرْبَعة
	forty 5	أرْبَعين ، أرْبَعون
	Wednesday 6	الأرْبِعاء الأربَعا الأرْبَع
	fourth 4	رابِع/ة
	to return 13	رَجَعَ ، يَرْجِع ، الرُّجوع رِجِع ع ، يِرجَع رِجِع ، يِرجَع
	man AB	رَجُل ج. رِجال رِجّال ج. رِجال راجِل ج رِجّالة
	welcome (formal) AB	مَرحَباً (بِ)
	trip, flight 10	رِحْلة ج. رحلات
	deceased 7	مَرْحوم/ة ج. مَرْحومون ، مَرْحومين

English	Arabic
to correspond, exchange letters 8	راسَلَ ، يُراسِل ، المُراسَلة راسَل ، يُراسِل راسِل ، يِراسِل
letter 3	رِسالة ج. رَسائِل مَكتوب ج. مَكاتيب جَواب ج. جَوابات
to draw 6	رَسَمَ ، يَرْسُم ، الرَّسْم رَسَم ، يِرْسُم رَسَم ، يِرْسُم
humidity 5	رُطوبة
to want to, have a desire to 13	الرَّغْبة ، رَغِبَ في ، يَرْغَب كان بِدُّه كان عايِز
to refuse 8	الرَّفْض ، رَفَضَ ، يَرْفُض رَفَض ، يِرفُض رَفَض ، يُرفُض
dance, dancing 6	الرَّقْص ، رَقَصَ ، يَرْقُص رَقَص ، يُرقُص رَقَص ، يِرقُص
number AB	رَقْم ج. أرْقام نِمرة ج. نِمَر نِمرة ج. نِمَر
center 2	مَرْكَز ج. مَراكِز
break, rest period 10	اِسْتِراحة ج. اِسْتِراحات
to want to 8	الإرادة ، أراد أنْ ، يُريد كان بِدُّه كان عايِز
sports 6	الرِّياضة
(over) crowdedness 5	الاِزْدِحام الزَّحمِة الزَّحمة
upset; annoyed, angry AB	زَعْلان ج. زَعلانين
classmate; colleague (m.) 4	زَميل ج. زُمَلاء ج. زَمايِل زِميل ج. زَمايِل /زُمَلا
classmate; colleague (f.) 4	زَميلة ج. زَميلات زِميلة ج. زِميلات
husband 3	زَوْج ج. أزواج جوز ج. جْواز جوز ج. اِجواز
wife 3	زَوْجَة ج. زَوْجات مَرة مِراة
married (adjective) 3	مُتَزَوِّج/ة ج. مُتَزَوِّجون ، مُتَزَوِّج/ة مِتْجَوِّز/ة ج. مِتْجَوِّزين مِتْجَوِّز/ ة ج. مِتْجَوِّزين
to visit 12	زارَ ، يَزور ، الزِّيارة زار ، يْزور زار ، يِزور
still, continue to (lit.: do not cease) 13	ما زالَ ، لا يَزال + المُضارِع المَرفوع/اسم بَعد (+ pronoun) لِسّه

English	Arabic
(future marker) 7	سَـ/ سَوْفَ رَح، حَـ حَـ
question AB	سُؤال ج. أسْئِلة
because of, on account of 5	بِسَبَب + اسم في إضافة
Saturday 6	السَّبْت
swimming 6	السِّباحة السِّباحة
seven AB	سَبْعة
seventy 5	سَبْعين ، سَبْعون
week 6	أسْبوع ج. أسابيع إسْبوع
six AB	سِتّة
sixty 5	سِتّين ، سِتّون
mosque 10	مَسْجِد ج. مَساجِد

English	Arabic
theater 13	مَسْرَح ج. مَسارِح
quickly 10	بِسُرعة بِسْرعة
to help 8	ساعَد في ، يُساعِد ، المُساعَدة ساعَد في ، يْساعِد ، المُساعِدِة ساعِد في ، يِساعِد ، المُساعْدة
happy AB	سَعيد ج. سُعَداء مَبسوط ج. مَبسوطين مَبسوط ج. مَبسوطين
Saudi Arabia AB	السَّعوديّة
to travel 4	السَّفَر ، سافَرَ (إلى) ، يُسافِر يْسافِر (عَ) يِسافِر
sugar AB	سُكَّر سِكَّر
sugar, medium AB	سُكَّر وَسَط سِكَّر وَسَط سُكَّر مَظبوط
to live, reside 1	السَّكَن ، سَكَنَ ، يَسْكُن ساكِن/ساكْنة ساكِن/ساكْنة
salad 4	سَلَطة ج. سَلَطات
Get well soon! I hope you feel better! AB	سَلامتَك
get well soon (reply)! AB	الله يِسَلِّمك
name, noun AB	إسْم ج. أَسْماء ج. أسامي ج. أسامي
to listen to 4	إسْتَمَع إلى ، يَسْتَمِع ، الاسْتِماع سِمِع ، يِسمَع سِمِع ، يِسمَع
fish (collective) 4	سَمَك
year 1	سنة ج. سنَوات ، سِنين سنة
(two) years 6	سَنتَين سِنْتين سَنَتَين
to stay up late 10	السَّهَر ، سَهِرَ ، يَسْهَر سِهِر ، يِسهَر سِهِر ، يِسهَر
easy AB	سَهل
black (m.) AB	أسْود ج. سود إسْوِد
Sudan AB	السّودان
Syria AB	سوريّا
hour; o'clock; clock AB	ساعة ج. ساعات
market 11	سوق ج. أسواق
tourism 11	السِّياحة
Mr.; Sir AB	سَيِّد ج. سادة
Lady; Mrs. AB	سَيِّدة ج. سَيِّدات
car AB	سَيّارة ج. سَيّارات عَرَبيّة
cinema, the movies AB	السِّينما

 ش

English	Arabic
tea AB	شاي
window AB	شُبّاك ج. شَبابيك شِبّاك شِبّاك
winter 5	الشِّتاء الشّتْويّة الشّتا

English	Arabic
tree *AB*	شَجَرة ج. شَجرات ، شَجَر
to encourage (to), cheer (on) *13*	شَجَّع (على) ، يُشَجِّع ، التَّشجيع شَجَّع (على) ، يْشَجِّع ، بِشَجِّع
to drink *AB*	شَرِبَ ، يَشْرَب ، الشُّرب شِرِب ، بِشْرَب شِرِب ، بِشْرَب
soup *4*	شوربة
street *AB*	شارِع ج. شَوارِع
Nice to meet you! *AB*	تَشَرَّفنا!
east *2*	الشَّرق
Middle East *2*	الشَّرق الأوسَط
company *6*	شَرِكة ج. شَرِكات شِرِكة ج. شِركات شِرْكة
chess *9*	الشَّطرنج
to feel *(i.e.: an emotion) 5*	شَعَرَ بِـ ، يَشْعُر ، الشُّعور حَسّ بـ ، يْحِسّ حَسّ بـ ، يْحِسّ
work *2*	الشُّغْل ، العَمَل الشُّغل الشُّغل
busy with *2*	مَشْغول بِـ، مَشْغولون ، مشغولين
hospital *7*	مُسْتَشفى ج مُسْتَشْفَيات
thank you *AB*	شُكْراً
problem *AB*	مُشْكِلة ج. مَشاكِل ، مُشْكِلات مِشْكُلة
sun *5*	شَمْس
sunny *5*	مُشْمِس مِشمِس شَمس
to watch *AB*	شاهَدَ ، يُشاهِد ، المُشاهَدة شاف ، يْشوف شاف ، بِشوف
degree, diploma *12*	شَهادة ج. شَهادات
thing, something *AB*	شَيء ج. أشياء شي ج. إشيا حاجة ج. حاجات
nothing *AB*	لا شَيْء ولا شي ولا حَاجة
something else? *AB*	شَيء آخَر؟ شي تاني؟ حَاجة تاني؟
to become *10*	أَصْبَحَ ، يُصْبِح صار ، يْصير بَقى ، بِيقى
morning *AB*	صَباح
really?! *1*	صَحيح
friend *(m.)*, boyfriend *AB*	صاحِب ج. أصْحاب ج. صُحاب
friend *(f.)*, girlfriend *AB*	صاحِبة ج. صاحِبات صاحْبة ج. صاحِبات صاحْبة ج. صاحْبات
to wake up *10*	صَحا ، يَصحو ، الصَّحو فاق (فِقت) ، يفيق صِحي (صِحيت) ، بِصحى
friend *(m.) 4*	صَديق ج. أصْدِقاء رفيق ج. رِفقات صاحِب ج. أصحاب
friend *(f.) 4*	صَديقة ج. صَديقات رُفيقة ج. رُفيقات صاحْبة ج. صاحْبات

ص

English	Arabic
honestly, frankly 10	بِصَراحة
hard, difficult AB	صَعْب
small, little; young AB	صَغير/ة ج. صِغار زْغير ج. زْغار صُغَيَّر ج. صُغَيَّرين
class, classroom AB	صَفّ ج. صُفوف ج. صُفوف فَصْل ج. فُصول
see under وصف	صِفة
page AB	صَفْحَة ج. صَفَحات ج. صَفْحات
(to) pray, do ritual prayers 10	صَلى ، (صَلّيتُ) ، يُصَلّي ، الصَّلاة (صَلّيت) يُصَلّي (صَلّيت) ، يِصَلّي
prayer 10	صَلاة ج. صَلَوات
picture 3	صورة ج. صُوَر ج. صِوَر
photography 6	التَّصْوير
pharmacology 11	الصِّيْدَلة
pharmacy 11	صَيْدَليّة ج. صَيْدَليّات
summer 5	الصَّيْف الصِّيف الصِّيف
China 1	الصّين
ض officer 3	ضابِط ج. ضُبّاط ظابِط ج. ظُبّاط ظابِط ج. ظُبّاط
present/incomplete tense	المُضارِع
weak 8	ضَعيف ج. ضُعاف ، ضُعَفاء ضُعيف ج. ضُعاف ضِعيف ج. ضُعاف
pronoun 2	ضَمير ج. ضَمائر
iDaafa, possessive construction	الإضافة
in addition to 12	بِالإضافة إلى بالإضافة لـ بالإضافة لـ
ط medicine 3	الطِّبّ
of course, naturally AB	طَبْعاً
restaurant 4	مَطْعَم ج. مَطاعِم
childhood 4	الطُّفولة
weather 5	الطَّقْس الجَوّ
student (m.) AB	طالِب ج. طُلّاب
student (f.) AB	طالِبة ج. طالِبات طالْبة ج. طالْبات
to be able to 9	اِسْتَطاع ، يَسْتَطيع ، الاِسْتِطاعة قِدِر ، يِقْدِر قِدِر ، يِقْدَر
during, throughout 8	طِوالَ طول طول
long, tall AB	طَويل ج. طِوال ج. طُوال ج. طُوال
table AB	طاوِلة ج. طاوِلات طاوْلة ج. طاوْلات طَربيزة ج. طَرابيزات
delicious (food); good-hearted (people) AB	طَيِّب/ة ج. طَيِّبون ، طَيِّبين

English	Arabic
airplane *AB*	طائِرة ج. طائِرات طَيّارة ج. طَيّارات طيّارة ج. طيّارات
to think that, consider *13*	ظَنَّ أَنَّ ، (ظَنَنْتُ أَنَّ) ، يَظُنّ ، الظَنّ ظَنّ (ظَنّيت) ، يْظُنّ انّه (إنّو) اِفتَكَر ، يِفتِكِر إنّ
noon *9*	الظُّهر الضُّهر
afternoon *9*	بَعدَ الظُّهر بَعد الضُّهر بَعد الضُّهر
astonishing, strange *AB*	عَجيب/ة ج. عَجيبون ، عَجيبين
several *11*	عِدّة + جمع indefinite كَم + مفرد كَم + مفرد
number *9*	عَدَد ج. أعْداد
preparatory (___ school = junior high) *7*	إعْداديّ/ة
Arab, Arabic (m.) *AB*	عَرَبيّ/ة ج. عَرَب
to know *3*	عَرَف ، يَعرِف ، المَعرِفة عِرِف ، يَعرِف عِرِف ، يِعرَف
to get to know, meet *11*	تَعَرَّف على ، يَتَعَرَّف ، التَعَرُّف تْعَرَّف على ، يِتعَرَّف اِتعَرَّف على ، يِتعَرَّف
getting to know one other *1*	تَعارُف
Iraq *AB*	العِراق
ten *AB*	عَشَرة
twenty *5*	عِشْرين ، عِشْرون
dinner *9*	العَشاء العَشا العَشا
juice *AB*	عَصير
thirsty *AB*	عَطشان/ة ج. عَطشانين
emotional, romantic *11*	عاطِفيّ/ة
vacation *12*	عُطَل ، عُطلة ج. عُطَل عُطلة ج. عُطَلات أجازة ج. أجازات
most of *11*	مُعْظَم
you're welcome *AB*	عَفواً
relationship (pl.: relations) *11*	عَلاقة ج. عَلاقات
to learn of, find out about *12*	عَلِمَ بِ، يَعلَم ، العِلم عِرِف بـ ، يَعرِف عِرِف ، يِعرَف
to learn (e.g.:_ a language, a new word) *1*	تَعَلَّم ، يَتَعَلَّم ، التَعَلُّم تْعَلَّم ، يِتْعَلَّم اِتعَلَّم ، يِتعَلَّم
science *3*	عِلم ج. عُلوم
anthropology *3*	عِلْم الإنْسان
sociology *3*	عِلْم الاِجْتِماع
psychology *3*	عِلْم النَفْس
political science *3*	العُلوم السِياسيّة
the world *9*	العالَم
on, on top of *AB*	عَلى

high 5	(الـ)عالي/ ة ، (عالٍ)
uncle (paternal) 3	عَمّ ج. أعْمام ج. عْـمــام
aunt (paternal) 3	عَمَّة ج. عَمّات
general, public 7	عامّ
age 2	عُمْر ج. أعمار
to work 1	عَمِلَ ، يَعْمَل ، العَمَل اِشْتَغَل ، يِشْتِغِل ، الشِّغِل اِشْتَغَل ، يِشْتَغِل ، الشُّغُل
worker 13	عامِل ج. عُمّال
Oman AB	عُمان
Amman (capital of Jordan) AB	عَمّان
on, about 7	عَنْ
on, about what...? 7	عَمّ (عَنْ ماذا)...؟
about whom...? 8	عَمَّن (عَنْ+مَن)...؟
have (lit.: at; see عندي 7)	عِنْد عَنْد عَنْد
I have (lit.: at me) AB	عِنْدي عَنْدي عَنْدي
when (not a question; e.g.:___ I was young) 11	عِنْدَما + فعل لَمّا لَمّا
address 1	عُنْوان ج. عَناوين عِنوان
it means 13	يَعني
meaning 8	مَعْنى
to return 9	عادَ ، يَعود ، العَوْدة رجع ع ، يِرجَع رِجَع ، يِرجَع
usually 10	عادةً غالِباً عادةً
graduate fellow, teaching assistant 6	مُعيد/ة ج. مُعيدون ، معيدين
(extended) family 3	عائِلَة ج. عائِلات عيلة ج. عِيَل عيلة ج. عائلات
to live, be alive 7	عاشَ ، يَعيش ، العَيْش/المَعيشة عاش ، يْعيش عاش ، بِعيش
I was appointed (passive) 12	عُيِّنْتُ اتْعَيَّنْتْ اتْعَيَّنْتْ
eye 5	عَيْن ج. عُيون/أعْيُن عين ج. عْيون عين
tomorrow 2	غَداً بُكرة بُكرة
lunch 9	الغَداء الغَدا الغَدا
longing for one's native land, feeling a stranger in a strange place 13	الغُرْبَة
strange, foreign AB	غَريب/ة ج. غُرَباء
Morocco AB	المَغْرِب
room AB	غُرْفَة ج. غُرَف غِرفة ، أوضة غرفة ، أوضة ج. أوَض أوضة ج. إوَض

غ

English	Arabic
wrong, mistake *AB*	غَلَط
expensive *11*	ال(غالي)/ة ، (غالٍ)
to be absent from, miss *(e.g.:__ school)* *12*	تَغَيَّبَ عَن ، يَتَغَيَّب ، التَّغَيُّب غاب (غِبت) ، يْغيب غاب (غِبت) ، بِغيب
cloudy, overcast *5*	غائِم مِغَيِّم مْغَيِّم
thus, so *5*	فَـ...
individual *(person)* *4*	فَرْد ج. أفْراد
singular *2*	المُفرد
opportunity *13*	فُرْصة ج. فُرَص
Nice to have met you! *13*	فُرْصة سَعيدة!
French, French person *2*	فَرَنْسِيّ ج. فَرَنْسِيّون ، فَرَنْسِيّين فَرَنساوي ج فَرَنساوِيّين
to fail *13*	فَشِلَ (في) ، يَفْشَل ، الفَشَل فِشِل (ب) ، بِفْشَل فَشَل (في) ، يِفْشَل
to dismiss, fire *(e.g.: from a job)* *13*	فَصَلَ ، يَفْصِل ، الفَصْل فَصَل ، بِفصِل فَصَل ، بِفصِل
class, classroom; also season *(e.g.:spring_)* *5*	فَصْل ج. فُصول
semester *5*	فَصْل دِراسيّ
come in! please! *(e.g., have a seat)* *AB*	تَفَضَّل! / تَفَضَّلي! تْفَضَّل! / تْفَضَّلي! اِتْفَضَّل! اِتْفَضَّلي!
thanks to *8*	بِفَضْل+ اسم
please *(addressing a male)* *AB*	مِنْ فَضْلَك
please *(addressing a female)* *AB*	مِنْ فَضْلِك
favorite *9*	المُفَضَّل
to eat breakfast *9*	فَطَّرَ ، يَفْطُر ، الفُطور فِطِر ، يِفطَر ، الفطور فِطِر ، يِفطَر ، الفِطار
breakfast *9*	الفُطور الفطور الفِطار
to do *8*	فَعَلَ ، يَفْعَل ، الفِعل
verb *5*	فِعل ج. أفعال
really!, indeed *2*	فِعْلاً
paragraph *9*	فقرة ، فِقرة ج. فَقَرات
only *5*	فَقَط بَسّ بَسّ
(to) think *(about doing something)* *13*	فَكَّرَ في ، يُفَكِّر ، التَّفكير (أنْ + المضارع المنصوب) فَكَّر ، يْفَكِّر + المضارع (بـ no) فَكَّر ، يِفَكِّر + المضارع (بـ no)
fruits *4*	فَواكِه
money *7*	مال فِلوس مَصاري
Palestine *AB*	فِلِسْطين
Palestinian *1*	فِلِسْطيني/ة ج. فِلِسْطينِيّون ، فِلِسْطينِيِّين

ف

hotel *11*	فُنْدق ج. فَنادِق
to understand *10*	فَهِمَ ، يَفْهَم ، الفَهْم فِهِم ، يِفَهَم فِهِم ، يِفهَم
in *1*	في
movie *AB*	فيلمْ ج. أفلام
(to) meet *10*	قابَلَ ، يُقابِل ، المُقابَلة قابَل ، يْقابِل قابِل ، يقابِل
(to) receive, welcome *10*	اِسْتَقْبَلَ ، يَسْتَقْبَل ، الاِسْتِقْبال اِسْتَقْبَل ، يِسْتَقْبِل اِسْتَقْبِل ، يِسْتَقْبِل
before *4*	قَبْل + اسم قبل + اسم، قبل ما + verb قبل + اسم، قبل ما + verb
admissions *2*	القُبول
interview *10*	مُقابَلة ج. مُقابلات
acceptable, passing *8*	مَقْبول
future *8*	المُسْتَقْبَل
(comprehensive) evaluation, grade *8*	تَقْدير
old, ancient *(for things, not for people) AB*	قديم
coming, next *12*	قادِم/ة ج. قادِمون ، قادِمين جايي/ة ج. جايين جايّ/ة ج. جايين
to decide *12*	قَرَّرَ ، يُقَرِّر ، التَّقْرير قَرَّر ، يْقَرِّر قَرَّر ، يقَرِّر
to stabilize, become settled *13*	اِسْتَقَرَّ ، يَسْتَقِرّ ، الاِسْتِقْرار اِسْتَقَرّ ، يِسْتَقِرّ اِسْتَقِرّ ، يِسْتَقِرّ
decision *12*	قَرار ج. قَرارات
to read *4*	قَرَأَ ، يَقْرَأ ، القِراءة قَرا ، يِقْرا ، القِراية قَرا ، يِقرا ، القِراية
the Quran *AB*	القُرآن
close *AB*	قَريب/ة (من) ج. قَريون ، قَريبين قُراب ج. قُرَيِّب/ة ج. قُرَيِّبين
family relative *3*	قَريب/ة ج. أقارِب / أقْرِباء قَرايبين قَرايِب
comparative *12*	المُقارَن
department *1*	قِسْم ج. أقْسام
story *AB*	قِصّة ج. قِصَص
to mean, intend *10*	قَصَدَ ، يَقصِد ، القَصد قَصَد ، يُقصُد قَصَد ، يُقصُد
economics, economy *7*	الاِقْتِصاد
short *AB*	قَصير ج. قِصار قُصَيّر ج قُصَيِّرين
to spend, pass *(time) 12*	قَضى ، يَقْضي ، القَضاء قَضّى ، يْقَضّي قَضى ، يِقْضي
cat *AB*	قِطّة ج. قِطَط بِسّة ج. بِسَس قُطّة ج. قُطَط
Qatar *AB*	قَطَر
to be cut off *11*	اِنْقَطَعَ ، يَنْقَطِع ، الاِنْقِطاع اِنْقَطَع ، يِنْقِطِع ؛ اِنْقَطَع ، يِتْقِطِع
grammar *1*	القَواعِد

English	Arabic
a little *(adverb)* AB	قَليلاً شُوَيّ شِوَيّة
pen AB	قَلَم ج. أقلام
dictionary 8	قاموس ج. قَواميس
coffee AB	قَهْوة
say 4	قالَ ، يَقول ، القَوْل قال ، يْقول قال ، يِقول
article *(e.g.: newspaper _)* 13	مَقالة ج. مَقالات
to reside, stay 10	الإقامة ، أقامَ ، يُقيم
also, likewise 13	كَذلِكَ كَمان كَمان
like, as 8	كَما + فعل مِتِل ما زَيّ ما
important, powerful; big; old AB	كَبير ج. كِبار كَبير ج. كُبار كِبير ج. كُبار
the biggest or oldest 7	أكْبَر (+ اسم نكرة)
to write 4	كَتَبَ ، يَكْتُب ، الكِتابة كَتَب ، يِكْتُب كَتَب ، بِكْتِب
book AB	كِتاب ج. كُتُب كُتاب
office AB	مَكْتَب ج. مَكاتِب
library AB	مَكْتَبة ج. مَكْتَبات
much, many 5	كَثيراً كْتير كِتير
more 10	أكْثَر أكْتَر أكتر
basketball 6	كُرة السَّلّة
soccer, European football 6	كُرة القَدَم
chair AB	كُرْسي ج. كَراسي ، كْراسِ كِرْسي
all 4	كُلّ+ الجمع كِلّ
each, every 11	كُل+ المفرد
college, school *(in a university)* 3	كُلِّية ج. كُلِّيّات كِلِّية ج. كِلِّيات
dog AB	كَلْب ج. كِلاب كِلِب ج. كُلاب
to speak 4	تَكَلَّمَ (عن) ، يَتَكَلَّم ، الكَلام حَكى عن ، يِحكي ، الحَكي إتْكَلَّم (عن) ، يِتكلَّم
word AB	كَلِمَة ج. كَلِمات كِلمة ج. كِلمات كِلْمَة ج. كِلمات
how many / much? 3	كَمْ؟ كام ؟
how much? *(price)* 7	بِكَم؟ بْقَدّيش؟ بِكام؟
as 8	كَما (+ فعل) مِتِل ما زَيّ ما
to be 4, 10	كانَ ، يَكون ، الكَوْن كانْ ، يْكون كانْ ، بِكون
Kuwait AB	الكُوَيْت
fine, good, OK AB	كْوَيِّس/ة ج. كْوَيِّسين

how? *1*	كَيْف؟ كِيف؟ إزَّيّ؟	
How are you? *1*	كَيْف الحال؟ كَيْفك؟ إزَّيَك؟	
in order to *6*	لِـ + مصدر/مضارع مِنْشان عَشان ، عَلَشان	**ل**
because *6*	لِأنَّ (+ جملة اسمية) لِأنَّه لِإنّ ، عَشان ، عَلَشان	
why? *6*	لِماذا؟ ليش؟ ليه؟	
for, belonging to *7*	لِـ + اسم/ضمير إلـ	
no *AB*	لا	
milk *AB*	لَبَن/ حَليب حَليب لَبن	
Lebanon *AB*	لُبْنان	
to enter, join I *(e.g.: school or army)* *8*	اِلْتَحَقَ بِـ ، يَلْتَحِق ، الاِلْتِحاق	
meat *4*	لَحْم ج. لُحوم	
must, have to *AB*	لازِم	
nice, kind, pleasant *AB*	لَطيف ج. لِطاف ، لُطَفاء ج. لُطَفا ج لُطاف	
to play *6*	لَعِبَ ، يَلْعَب ، اللَّعِب لِعِب ، يِلْعَب ، اللَّعِب لِعِب ، يِلعَب ، اللَّعِب	
language *2*	لُغة ج. لُغات	
but *AB*	لـٰكِن بَسّ بَسَ	
past negation particle *12*	لم (+ المضارع) = لم يُسافِر ما (+ الفعل الماضي) = ما سافَر	
	ما (+ الفعل الماضي) ش = ما سافِرْش	
future negation particle *12*	لَنْ + المضارع المنصوب	
if *(hypothetical)* *10*	لَوْ	
Libya *AB*	ليبيا	
is not, are not *7*	لَيْسَ مو ، ما مِش	
night *10*	لَيْلَة ج. ليالي ، لَيالٍ ليلة ليلة	
tonight *10*	الليلة	
what? *(in questions without verbs)* *AB*	ما؟ شو؟ إيه؟	**م**
past negation particle	ما + الماضي ما (+ الفعل الماضي) ـش	
what's wrong? *AB*	ما بِكَ/بِكِ ؟ شو بِكَ/بَكِ؟ ما لَك/ما لكِ؟	
what? *(in questions using verbs)* *1*	ماذا ؟ + فعل شو؟ + فعل فعل+ إيه؟	
why? *6*	لِماذا؟ ليش؟ ليه؟	
still, continue to *(lit.: do not cease)* *13*	ما زالَ ، لا يَزال + المضارع المرفوع / اسم بَعد (+ pronoun) لِسّه	
master's degree *2*	الماجِسْتير	
hundred *5*	مِئَة (مائة) ج. مِئات مِيَّة ج. مِيَّات مِيَّة ج. مِيَّات	

English	Arabic
to enjoy *10*	اِسْتَمْتَعَ بِـ ، يَسْتَمْتِع ، الاسْتِمْتاع اِسْتَمْتَع بِـ ، يِسْتَمْتِع اِسْتَمْتَع بِـ ، يِسْتَمِتع
when? *6*	مَتى؟ إمْتى؟ إمتى؟
like, similar to *8*	مِثْل + اسم مِتِل زَيّ
example *1*	مِثال ج. أَمْثِلة
test, examination *AB*	اِمْتِحان ج. اِمْتِحانات
madam *AB*	مَدام
city *AB*	مَدينة ج. مُدُن مِدينة
once, (one) time *11*	مَرَّة ج. مَرّات
woman *AB*	اِمْرَأَة ج. نِساء مَرة ج. نِسوان سِت ج. سِتّات
sick *AB*	مَريض ج. مَرْضى
drill *AB*	تَمْرين ج. تَمارين
evening *2*	المَساء المَسا
Egypt *AB*	مِصْر مَصِر مَصْر
Egyptian *1*	مِصْرِيّ مَصري مَصري
the past tense *8*	الماضي
rain *5*	مَطَر ج. أَمْطار شِتي
rainy, raining *5*	مُمْطِر ، ماطِر شِتي مَطَر
with (people) *AB*	مَع
together (i.e.: with one another) *11*	مَعاً مَع بَعْض مَع بَعض
never mind! Don't worry about it! *AB*	مَعليش مَعلِهْش/ مَعليش
it is possible to (impersonal, does not conjugate) *10*	يُمْكِن أَنْ مُمْكِن، قِدِر مُمْكِن، قِدِر، يِقْدَر قِدِر، يِقْدَر
possible *AB*	مُمْكِن
king *10*	مَلِك ج. مُلوك
who?, whom; whoever *1*	مَنْ؟ مين؟ مين؟
from *AB*	مِن
scholarship, grant *12*	مِنْحَة ج. مِنَح
since, ago *6, 10*	مُنْذُ مِن، مِن وَقْت ما مِن، من ساعة ما
to die *7*	ماتَ ، يَموت ، المَوْت مات ، يْموت ، الموت مات ، يْموت ، الموت
Mauritania *AB*	موريتانيا
music *4*	الموسيقى
water *AB*	ماء مَيّ مَيّة
excellent *8*	مُمْتاز/ة ج. مُمْتازون ، مُمْتازين

English	Arabic
ن	
prophet *3*	نَبِيّ ج. أنْبِياء
to succeed, pass *8*	نَجَحَ في ، يَنْجَح ، النَّجاح نِجِح في ، يِنجَح نَجَحْ في ، يِنجَح
we *2*	نَحْنُ نِحنا إحنا
club (e.g.: sports _) *9*	نادي (نادٍ) ج. نَوادي (نَوادٍ)
to descend, to leave the house; to stay in a hotel *9*	نَزَلَ ، يَنْزِل ، النُّزول طِلِع ، يِطلَع من نِزِل ، يِنزِل
the nisba adjective *7*	النِّسْبة
as far as ___ is concerned *5*	بِالنِّسْبة لِـ بالنسبة إلى
appropriate, suitable *13*	مُناسِب مُناسِب
women *AB*	نِساء (م. اِمْرَأة ، المَرْأة) نِسوان (م. مَرة) سِتّات (م. سِتّ)
activity *1*	نَشاط ج. نَشاطات ، أنْشِطة
half *9*	نِصْف نُصّ نُصّ
area, region *1*	مِنْطَقة ج. مَناطِق مَنْطِقة مَنْطِقة
yes *AB*	نَعَم إيه أيوه
the same... *1*	نَفْس الـ
negation *8*	النَّفْي
daytime *2*	النَّهار النَّهار
to finish *13*	اِنْتَهى مِن ، يَنْتَهي ، الاِنتِهاء خَلَّص من ، يِخَلِّص خَلَص من ، يِخلَص ، يِنتهي
to take, have (a meal) *9*	تَناوَل ، يَتَناوَل ، التَّناوُل
to sleep, go to sleep *10*	نامَ (نِمْتُ) ، يَنام ، النَّوم نام (نِمْت) ، يْنام ، النَّوم نام (نِمْت) ، يِنام ، النَّوم
ه	
this (m.) *AB*	هٰذا هادا ، هَيدا دا
this (f.) *AB*	هٰذِه هادي ، هَيدي دي
thus, so, in this way, that way *7*	هٰكَذا هيك كِدا
telephone *AB*	هاتِف ، تليفون
interrogative (yes/no?) particle *AB*	هَل؟
they *2*	هُم هِنّي هُمّ
here *12*	هُنا هون هِنا
there; there is/are *7, 12*	هُناك هونيك فيه هناك فيه
engineering *3*	الهَنْدَسة
engineer *11*	مُهَنْدِس/ة ج. مُهَندِسون ، مُهَندِسين
he *AB*	هُوَ هُوْ هُوّ
hobby *6*	هِواية ج. هِوايّات
she *AB*	هِيَ هِيْ هِيّ

English	Arabic
homework AB	واجِب ج. واجِبات وَظيفة ج. وَظايِف ج. واجْبات **و**
to find 13	وَجَدَ ، يَجِد ، الوُجود لَقى(لْقيت) ، يْلاقي لَقى (لَقيت) ، يِلاقي
one AB	واحِد
someone 11	أَحَد حَدا حَدّ
loneliness 5	الوِحْدة
only; lonely 2	وَحيد/ة ج. وَحيدون ، وحيدين
piece of paper AB	وَرَقة ج. أُوراق
ministry 7	وِزارة ج. وِزارات
prime minister 8	رَئيس الوُزَراء
pattern 8	وَزن ج. أوزان
wide, spacious AB	واسِع
adjective 5	صِفة ج. صِفات
subject, topic 9	مَوضوع ج. مَواضيع ، موضوعات
work, position 13	وَظيفة ج. وَظائِف ج. وَظايِف ج. وَظائِف
employee (white collar; m.) 2	مُوَظَّف ج. مُوَظَّفون ، مُوَظَّفين مْوَظَّف ج. مْوَظّفين
employee (white collar; f.) 2	مُوَظَّفة ج. مُوَظَّفات مْوَظّفة ج. مْوَظّفات
appointment 10	مَوْعِد ج. مَواعيد مَعاد
death 12	وَفاة
time (general) 10	وَقْت ج. أوْقات
son, boy, child AB	وَلَد ج. أولاد ج. وُلاد ج. ولاد
father 1	والِد ، ج. والِدون ، والِدين
mother 1	والِدة ج. والِدات والْدِة ، ماما والْدة ، ماما
state, province 2	وِلاية ج. وِلايات
United States of America 1	الوِلايات المُتَّحِدة الأمريكِّية
Japan AB	اليابان **ي**
to wake (someone) up 9	أَيْقَظَ ، يوقِظ ، الإيقاظ فَيَّق ، يْفَيِّق صَحّى (صَحّيت) ، يِصَحّي
Yemen AB	اليَمَن
day 6	يَوْم ج. أَيّام يوم ج. إيّام يوم
today 2	اليَوْم اليوم النهاردا

Credits

Illustrations throughout the book were created by Lucinda Levine, Chevy Chase, MD.

Lesson 6
Drill 13 text comes from BBC Arabic website (http://news.bbc.co.uk/hi/arabic/talking_point/newsid_4380000/4380375.stm) and is used with permission. Original photos were recreated by the illustrator, Lucinda Levine.

Lesson 7
Drill 14: Text of this obituary is reprinted from Al-Ahram newspaper in Cairo, Egypt, 12/27/2008, reprinted by permission (http://weekly.ahram.org.eg/).

Lesson 8
Drill 17: Article on the cabinet ministers reprinted from Alrai newspaper, Amman, Jordan (www.alrai.com).

Lesson 9
Drill 16: Video of woman going about her day includes music by Shinji Inagi and Chad Jensen, all used by permission, and was filmed by Scott Zuniga.

Lesson 10
Drill 14: The text about King Fuad comes from Karim Thabet, His Majesty the King of Egypt and Europe, Dar Al-Hilal, Cairo (1931).The text about Khomeini is from the website http://www.imamcenter.net/flash_content/material/imam/define/program.htm.

Lesson 11
Drill 14: Website reprinted by permission of Elite Tour (http://www.elitesyria.com/). Map created by Christopher Robinson, Laurel, MD.

Lesson 12
Drill 15: Website reprinted by permission of American University of Cairo (www.masrawy.com/News/Egypt/Politics/2009/july/19/american_university.aspx).

Lesson 13
Drill 14: Excerpts from this website are used by permission of www.aloathan.com.